Why Do You Need this New Edition?

The environment and definition of small group and team communication is changing now more than ever. From the rise of Computer-Mediated Communication to an ever-increasing cultural and geographic diversity among team members, the real-world of small group and team communication is constantly evolving. *Small Group and Team Communication* helps put the concepts into their proper context in today's world. What follows are just some of the new features you will find only in the fifth edition:

- Updated practical examples show how team decision-making processes and concepts apply to real-world events and people.
- Ethics coverage makes connections to all aspects of group communication and decision-making.
- Updated coverage of Computer-Mediated Communication (CMC) demonstrates the impact it has on verbal and nonverbal communication, group decision-making, and virtual team leadership.
- Increased coverage of cultural diversity's impact on group communication and the growing need for cultural sensitivity.
- New media examples of group communication from Facebook and Second Life.

PEARSON

Small Group and Team Communication

FIFTH EDITION

Thomas E. Harris

University of Alabama

John C. Sherblom

University of Maine

Allyn & Bacon

Boston   Columbus   Indianapolis   New York   San Francisco   Upper Saddle River
Amsterdam   Cape Town   Dubai   London   Madrid   Milan   Munich   Paris   Montreal   Toronto
Delhi   Mexico City   Sao Paulo   Sydney   Hong Kong   Seoul   Singapore   Taipei   Tokyo

Acquisitions Editor: Jeanne Zalesky
Assistant Editor: Megan Lentz
Marketing Manager: Blair Tuckman
Production Manager: Kathy Sleys
Editorial Production and Composition Service: Sudip Sinha/Aptara®, Inc.
Creative Director: Jayne Conte
Cover Designer: Bruce Kenselaar
Manager, Rights and Permissions: Zina Arabia
Manager, Visual Research: Beth Brenzel
Manager, Cover Visual Research & Permissions: Karen Sanatar
Image Permission Coordinator: Craig A. Jones
Printer/Binder/Cover Printer: R.R. Donnelley & Sons, Inc.

Credits appear on Page 281, which constitutes an extension of the copyright page.

Library of Congress Cataloging-in-Publication Data

Harris, Thomas E.
Small group and team communication/Thomas E. Harris, John C. Sherblom.—5th ed.
   p. cm.
   ISBN-13: 978-0-205-69298-9
   ISBN-10: 0-205-69298-2
   1. Teams in the workplace.   2. Communication in organizations.   3. Small groups.   I. Sherblom, John, 1949–II. Title.
   HD66.H3746 2010
   658.4'036—dc22

                                                         2009037704

10 9 8   DOH   15 14

Allyn & Bacon
is an imprint of

PEARSON

www.pearsonhighered.com

ISBN-10:   0-205-69298-2
ISBN-13: 978-0-205-69298-9

Contents

5   Diversity in Groups: The Strength of Different Perspectives   72

6   Verbal and Nonverbal Communication   89

9 Decision Making and Problem Solving   141

10 Creativity in the Small Group Process   161

Preface

pieces updated by numerous recent studies published in the major topic areas. Boxed and organizational examples appear throughout the text to illustrate each topic, such as the use of self-directed work teams at Whole Foods, General Electric, Delta Airlines and Harley Davidson and in NASCAR and Formula One racing. Classroom applications also provide each chapter with an interactive approach to learning the topic.

The text is designed to be consistent in approach with current efforts to achieve active learning in which each chapter's information is presented using the PowerPoint slides and the lecture outlines provided and then worked with interactively through exercises and discussion. The Instructor's Manual presents lecture outlines and exercises for each chapter, which are accompanied by the approximate time, materials, forms, and other materials needed to use them in class. A series of shorter exercises and one or two longer ones are available for each chapter.

In an increasingly diverse, yet tightly networked world, effective small group communication is essential. We interact with each other through the Internet in many new ways—via e-mail, instant messaging (IMs), Facebook, YouTube, Twitter, and Second Life. How we engage in our small group communication in each medium matters.

Small Group and Team Communication explores the many ways in which we are interconnected and the communication strategies we can use at work and in our social groups. Using a systems perspective as our basic orientation, we describe small groups as complex open systems reliant upon communication to achieve success. Whether it is in the creation of Wikipedia, Google, YouTube, or Formula One racing, effective small group communication and teamwork are important. To be effective we have to consider our group roles, norms, cohesion, process, and phases of development; but that is not enough. We also need to examine our personal verbal and nonverbal communication and listening styles. To succeed as a member of a team, we need to consider the limits of our personal experience and perspective, recognize the creative strength of diverse perspectives in decision making and problem solving, develop our conflict-management skills, and strengthen our leadership skills. The challenge of small group communication in the 21st century—for each group member to engage in participatory leadership in a culturally diverse and geographically disperse team—requires personal development of skills and abilities. To be successful necessitates an understanding of group process, participation style, ethical group behavior, and the influences of the medium—such as in the medium of computer-mediated communication.

New To This Edition

Small Group and Team Communication, Fifth Edition is grounded in a systems perspective, informed by up-to-date small group research literature, illustrated with contemporary examples from current business and public group practices, and supported with revised *Instructor's Manual* containing exercises demonstrating key concepts. The systems perspective focuses on the communication relationships between and among group members and describes the multiple contextual influences—such as computer mediated, ethical, gender, power, race, and task—on these relationships. The research literature includes classic pieces updated by numerous recent studies published in the major topic areas. Business and organizational examples appear throughout the text to illustrate each topic, such as the use of self-directed work teams at Whole Foods, General Electric, Delta Airlines, and Harley-Davidson and in NASCAR and Formula One racing. Classroom exercises also provide each chapter with an interactive approach to learning the topic.

The text is designed to be used in an interactive classroom environment conducive to learning in which each chapter's information is presented using the PowerPoint slides and the lecture outlines provided and then worked with interactively through exercises and discussion. The *Instructor's Manual* presents lecture outlines and exercises for each chapter, which are accompanied by the approximate time, instructions, forms, and other materials needed to use them in class. A series of shorter exercises and one or two longer ones are available for each chapter.

Chapter Overview

Chapter 1 begins with the creation of Wikipedia, YouTube, and Google to introduce the power of working together. Disney, Honda, Marriott, Merck, Nordstrom, Proctor & Gamble, Sony, and Wal-Mart all use small groups at work, as do more than 70% of all U.S. companies. Chapter 1 describes the importance of small group communication and introduces the central concepts of symbolic behavior, shared meaning, interpersonal attraction, attitude similarity, need complementarity, need for affiliation, and commitment to the group goals and activities.

Chapter 2 opens with the complexity of modern systems and relates the concepts of complex systems to small group roles, relationships, and realities. The chapter applies the open systems theory concepts of wholeness, synergy, openness, transformation, interdependence, feedback, entropy, and equifinality and the complex systems theory concepts of quantum change, double-loop learning, sensitivity to initial conditions, strange attractors, phase space, bifurcation points, irreversibility to small group communication. This chapter's tables and discussion demonstrate the complexity of small group and team communication; the effects on group roles, rules, responses, relationships, and realities; and the need for an understanding of these potential influences for a group to be successful.

Chapter 3 introduces the concepts of group norms, roles, cohesion, and groupthink. It begins with a humorous example of a norms violation in the Tour de France bicycle race and then provides serious examples of poor group decisions, such as the Bridgestone ATX tire blow-outs and the University of Wisconsin's photo doctoring for the appearance of diversity. The ethical issues and effective group decision-making processes are discussed.

Chapter 4 develops the concepts of group phases. For simplicity sake, the forming, storming, norming, performing phase terminology is used consistently throughout this chapter, but building on this terminology the chapter develops concepts of linear, cyclic, and nonsequential phases as well. The importance and communication characteristics of each phase are described, and an example of the use of teams at the Mayo Clinic is included.

Chapter 5 focuses on the importance of diversity to successful group work. Diversity is defined, described, and examined from multiple perspectives. Both the importance of diverse perspectives to good decision making and the challenges that it represents to group communication are presented. The chapter concludes with a discussion of the challenges and benefits of using geographically dispersed, computer-mediated virtual teams in organizations, supported with an example of Boeing's use of a multinational team in its work on the International Space Station.

Chapter 6 opens with a joke to illustrate the verbal and nonverbal aspects of communication. What makes something funny? What gives meaning to communication and to its interpretation? A discussion of ambiguity, the concept of meanings being situated in people rather than in words, the importance of connotative verbal meanings, and the effects of nonverbal communication are explained.

Chapter 7 highlights listening and feedback with Abbott and Costello's "Who's on First?" routine, followed by underscoring the importance of listening with the example of a near midair jet collision. Listening styles are culturally influenced but changeable, and listening is an important leadership skill to develop. The keys to active listening are presented, and the chapter ends with a discussion of providing and receiving feedback.

Chapter 8 describes the evolution of ongoing groups into teams. It begins with the example of a "Dream Team," identifies the qualities of team characteristics, and describes the types of teams most often used in organizations. Effective team-management styles, parallel teams, and self-managing work teams allow a fuller understanding of team structure and diversity.

Chapter 9 develops the important stages in the process of decision making and problem solving through the easy-to-remember DECIDE model: Define the goal, Examine the constraints, Consider the alternatives, Initiate a decision, Develop an action plan, and Evaluate the results. Examples are used to illustrate the steps in decisions leading to the *Challenger* disaster, Coca-Cola's blunder with "New Coke," and Tylenol's successful response to the cyanide scare. Taleb's description of the "Black Swan" phenomenon exemplifies decisions leading to the current U.S. and world economic condition. Finally, characteristics of computer-mediated decision-making groups are explored.

Chapter 10 investigates creativity and underscores its importance in small group discussion, decision making, and problem solving. It discusses the barriers and presents a number of facilitators for creative group process. Examples throughout the chapter demonstrate creativity in the invention of the stethoscope, placement of a lime into a Corona, introduction of the car phone, and development of Pringles potato chips.

Chapter 11 introduces a set of group decision-making techniques: brainstorming, focus groups, the nominal group technique, Delphi technique, synectics, buzz sessions, idea writing, and listening teams; problem-solving tools of flowcharts, fishbone diagrams, and Pareto's principle; performance-evaluation techniques of RISK and performance evaluation and review (PERT); business examples of Total Quality Management and Six Sigma; and small group presentation formats of forum, panel, colloquium, and symposium presentations. An example of the successful Six Sigma project at Dow Chemical shows the importance of decision-making techniques.

Chapter 12 defines conflict, recognizes its place in small group discussion, and describes ways to make it both manageable and productive to the group decision-making process. The ethics of productive conflict management are presented, as are the need for effective leadership and mutual respect, and a commitment to a creative group process.

Chapter 13 explains leadership in small groups as beginning with vision, credibility, and competence; utilizing Lee Iacocca's "9 C's" (curiosity, creative, communicate, character, courage, conviction, charisma, competent, common sense); providing a survey of federal employees who would prefer a better boss to more money and benefits; and challenging us with a discussion of research that investigates differences in the evaluation of leaders based on their race or gender. Finally, expectations of leaders in technologically mediated groups are discussed.

Chapter 14 focuses attention on the evaluation phase of the group process—describes the necessity of evaluation and the different methods and guidelines of obtaining it and provides sample evaluation forms.

Chapter 15 describes the small group communication process occurring in a computer-mediated communication (CMC) environment. It discusses the uses, benefits, and challenges of the CMC medium for small group communication and describes criteria for selecting a medium for a communication task, finding a language demand–technology fit, and matching media richness to the communication function. The chapter makes suggestions for effective communication use of technology in face-to-face group meetings, through text-based computer-mediated communication, and in newer CMC environments such as the immersive virtual world of Second Life.

Each chapter highlights an important aspect of small group communication. Each examines that aspect in depth and integrates it into the larger discussion of small group communication purpose, process, task, and accomplishment, utilizing theory, research, and practice.

Special Features

Ethics, Diversity, Computer-Mediated Communication, and Real-World Examples

The importance and influence of ethics, diversity, and computer-mediated communication (CMC) on effective small group discussion processes, decision making, and problem solving are highlighted throughout the book.

Ethical coverage is applied and discussed in examples throughout the text as tied to multiple aspects of small group communication. Extended discussions of ethics occur in relation to group discussion behavior (Chapter 1), diverse groups (Chapter 5), professional groups (Chapter 8), decision making and problem-solving processes (Chapter 9), productive conflict management (Chapter 12), and the evaluation of group behaviors and decisions (Chapter 14).

Diversity is the focus of Chapter 5 and is integrated into topics throughout the book. For example, Chapter 3 describes how diverse perspectives help mediate the tension between group cohesion and groupthink; Chapter 4 describes the effect on the phases of group process; Chapter 6 describes the differences in verbal and nonverbal communication interpretations and expectations; Chapter 7 describes culturally diverse listening styles; and Chapter 13 describes the effects of diversity on perceptions and evaluations of group leaders.

The influences and effects of small group computer-mediated communication (CMC) are discussed in Chapter 15. In addition, the influence of the CMC medium on verbal and nonverbal cues is described in Chapter 6, on group decision making in Chapter 9 and on virtual leadership in Chapter 13.

Chapter 8 relates small group communication to the business world by describing the importance and use of organizational work teams. This real-world approach occurs throughout the text, with business examples provided in Chapters 1, 3, 4, 5, 9, 10, and 11 and is supported by shorter examples in each chapter. This approach is designed to take the application of the concepts presented in the book beyond the classroom through the multiple examples detailing everyday group and team activities.

Supplemental Instructor Materials: Instructor's Manual/Test Bank, MyTest Test Bank, and PowerPoint Slides

The *Instructor's Manual/Test Bank, MyTest Test Bank,* and *PowerPoint Slides* are available to instructors at www.pearsonhighered.com/irc. The instructor's manual contains complete lecture outlines and a variety of exercises and test questions for each chapter. The chapter outlines are coordinated and intended to be used with the PowerPoint slides. The outlines provide comparable section headings and additional information explaining the key points listed on the slides, making the slides easy to use and the lecture outlines easy to follow. Evaluation forms and other course materials are also provided in the instructor's manual. All can be downloaded, edited, printed, copied, and used with students to make the classroom lively and interactive.

Chapter exercises, available in the *Instructor's Manual* include four to six interactive classroom exercises for each chapter with instructions, answers, and approximate times listed as needed. Instructors can select and use those exercises they believe most useful for their students and course objectives. All of the exercises have been tested with college and university students to verify their usefulness. They are designed to foster high levels of participation, creating an ongoing group and team communication environment. For example, Chapter 1 exercises include Icebreaker: What interests other class members?; The value of groups: Increasing information and insights; Learning about effective groups and teams: Are you lonely? Hold a meeting!; Horse trading: A test of individual versus group decision making; and Inventing the light bulb. Chapter 2 uses the zoo story which provides an actual example of systems thinking, along with two ethics exercises and two team activities. Chapter 3 provides a role-play exercise that explores values, norms, and cohesion as participants decide who gets the new computer that an office work group has been allocated and then discuss the values and perspectives upon which that decision is made (seniority, most technical work, most deserving person, having the oldest computer). A group identity exercise for Chapter 4 has a group develop a name, logo, and slogan designed to work together to define a coherent group goal, vision, and image.

Examples of longer exercises appear in the Chapter 6 "To Catch a Spy" exercise, in which participants make judgments about each other based on their verbal and nonverbal communication and then have the opportunity to reflect on the accuracy (and inaccuracy) of their predictions. In Chapter 7, a "non-debate" exercise has participants choose a side of an important issue, develop their argument, and then listen carefully to, and paraphrase, the other side of that issue. Other chapters provide similar exercises.

Small group and team communication is a body of knowledge and set of skills that are most easily learned through student involvement. With 50 to 60 different exercises available, an instructor will be able to customize the use of this book to his or her own approach. In several experiments with different types of class structures, all of the exercises have been used with great success. However, if the instructor wishes to lecture and/or facilitate more discussion, time may be a consideration.

The *Instructor's Manual* provides a format for the instructor to teach the course based on individual chapters or to adopt a semester-long team approach where class members learn to work together over a lengthy period of time to produce a viable solution to a campus, local, or other real-world problem. Guidelines for a semester-long team approach are provided.

The *Test Bank* contains over 470 questions blending multiple choice, fill-in-the-blank, and essay, organized by chapter. The MyTest online test-generating software includes all the questions found in the *Test Bank* section of the *Instructor's Manual/Test Bank*. It is available at www.pearsonmytest.com (access code required).

PowerPoint slides are designed to go along with the lecture outlines for each chapter. These slides include examples of the tables and figures that appear in the book and provide additional examples and supplemental slides to make the lectures lively, creative, fun, and involving. The *MyCommunicationKit for Small Group and Team Communication* is a book-specific, dynamic, interactive study tool for students. Offerings are organized by chapter and include practice exams (with page references), relevant media and video cases, learning objectives, and weblinks. Available at www.mycommunicationkit.com, see your local Pearson representative for details. **mycommunicationkit**

Acknowledgments

We would like to recognize and thank the people who helped us with this book and made its publication possible. We thank our spouses, Shelia Harris and Liz Sherblom, who have provided social-emotional support and helped with suggestions throughout our decision-making processes. We also thank the reviewers: Stephen D. Cooper, Marshall University; Danette Ifert Johnson, Ithaca College; Andrew Lovato, Santa Fe Community College; Daryl W. Wiesman, Clemson University; and Alan Yabui, Bellevue Community College for their helpful comments that lead us to add material and streamline other areas to make this edition an even more accessible and better read than the last. And we thank our Pearson, Allyn & Bacon editorial and production team for their work helping us to clarify and refine the concepts and the writing while keeping the book on production schedule. Our goal has been to write a book that reviews the best research and makes it accessible by applying its concepts to small group communication in everyday life and the workplace. We hope that you find the book stimulating, its concepts interesting, and the examples of their application enjoyable.

CHAPTER

1

Small Groups: Power, Definition, Attraction

CHAPTER OUTLINE

CHAPTER OBJECTIVES

- Introduce the types of groups.
- Describe the power of groups.
- Examine the reasons for joining groups.
- Explain the basis for interpersonal attraction.
- Outline the characteristics and coordination of small groups.
- Explain group synergy.
- Describe characteristics of the small group communication process.
- Demonstrate the role of small groups in organizations.

KEY TERMS

Attitude similarity
Communication
Coordinating mechanisms
Decision-making groups
Educational or learning groups
Ethics
Interactivity
Interdependence
Interpersonal attraction
Meetings

Need complementarity
Pattern
Physical proximity
Primary group
Problem-solving groups
Process
Shared meaning
Simultaneously sending and
    receiving
Small group

Small group communication
Social and casual groups
Substance
Symbolic behavior
Synergy
Teams
Therapeutic group
Transactional process
Work groups

Show up on time. Know your lines. Respect your fellow actor, your director, and yourself. . . . When your friends are up for a part, encourage them. When you're in a play, give the other actors the stage when it's theirs; when it's your turn take the stage with gusto—and then give it back to them. . . . Be yourself: be all the yous you are, but don't let them crowd out the smart one.

(Alan Alda, *Things I overheard while talking to myself,* 2007)

The names Ward Cunningham and Richard Stallman do not mean much to most of us, but if you look them up in Wikipedia you will discover that they are credited with developing the concepts for a wiki technology and for a free online encyclopedia to which groups of people can contribute reference materials. If you Google *Google* you will discover that it was developed by Larry Page and Sergey Brin. YouTube was co-founded by Chad Hurley, Steve Chen, and Jawed Karim. Few great ventures are started by a single individual alone. More often they are created by people working together. A troupe of actors, a network of friends, a social group, a church congregation, a community, a village, professional colleagues, family relatives, acquaintances in a social networking site, and active blog participants all form groups. Individuals join most of these groups, except for the families into which they are born, as actors who work together to accomplish a specific task. Group members take on roles and work together, much like stage actors, to collectively produce a show, a product, an event, a company, or a social phenomenon. Hence, Alan Alda's pithy comments apply as well to working in groups as they do to going on stage. Show up on time, be prepared, respect yourself and others, participate fully, take turns, and be all that you can be in the group. Group work can be exciting, ego enhancing, and creative. It can also be boring, demeaning, and frustrating. The key to successful, satisfying group participation is effective communication. This book is about developing effective communication strategies that help make group work more satisfying and successful—strategies that help groups produce work that is fun, useful, and sometimes even exceptional in its results.

Groups and teams are used in every aspect of human activity. Later in the book, we will make a distinction and use a more restricted definition of the word *team* to describe a type of ongoing, experienced, cohesive group, but for now we can think of groups and teams as synonymous. The information in this book applies equally well to both.

Work groups and teams have become a cornerstone in the operation and success of many of today's organizations. Frank Williams, who is the head of one of the most successful Formula One race teams of all times, says, "Teamwork is an essential ingredient on and off the race track" ("The team," 1998, p. 24). In 1986, a near fatal car accident left Williams confined to a wheelchair. Not letting that accident stop him, however, he developed a racing team that has outperformed the other 11 international teams that compete in the approximately 16 Formula One races held globally each year. He credits his team's success to his first team priority: an "emphasis on communication" with every team member. At Suburban Hospital in Bethesda, Maryland, teams are credited "with reducing errors, shortening the amount of time patients spend in its 12-bed ICU (intensive care unit) and improving communication between families and medical staff" (Appleby & Davis, 2001, p. B1). Appleby and Davis suggested "one reason that teamwork is so vital in modern medicine is the speed at which advances are being made" (p. B2). Teams keep the members up-to-date. "In high-pressure workplaces, such as nuclear plants, aircraft cockpits, or the military, teamwork is essential to survival" (Appleby & Davis, 2001, p. B2). Minretek Systems uses the collective insights of its employees working in teams to undertake its scientific research into the investigation of counterterrorism, criminal justice, and the environment (Pomeroy, 2004). Motorola, Ritz-Carlton Hotels, Boeing, Federal Express, and Texas Instruments all see teams as critical to their organizational success.

Types of Small Groups

Small groups are everywhere and are of many types. Family, work, school, and leisure activities all often involve small groups. In each context we work with others to come to common understandings and to make decisions that affect each of us to some degree. Each type of small group can be characterized by the kind of communication that takes place within it.

Our immediate family is, for most of us, a significant small group affiliation and may be referred to as a *primary group* or a basic social unit to which we belong. This type of small group tends to be the most informal, and we ordinarily remain members in it over a long period of time. *Social and casual groups* extend our primary-group relationships. Sports teams, discussion groups, school or church groups, and other special-interest or activity groups may all provide extended social primary-group relationships. Our membership in these groups may be solely for companionship, or we may use these affiliations to help us understand and deal with important issues in our lives or to develop professional, personal, or social roles and skills.

Educational or learning groups are concerned primarily with discovering and developing new ideas and ways of thinking. These may include educational courses, seminars, or enlightenment groups. An extension of this type of group is the *therapeutic group,* in which members come together to learn about themselves and their relationships with others. The communication in this type of group is characterized by discussion and analysis of a particular issue, but it may not be organized in such a way or vested with authority to solve problems directly. Support, therapy, and consciousness-raising groups, whose main task is the development and maintenance of group process and relationships, are not the main focus of this text.

Decision-making and *problem-solving groups,* on the other hand, are convened for the express purpose of making a decision, solving a problem, or dealing with specific issues. A board of directors may meet to determine company goals and policies or to deal with the latest budgetary dilemma. Committees are problem-solving groups that are assigned a task, usually by some other person or group. They may be formed either as standing committees that exist for an extended period of time or as ad hoc committees—those intended to accomplish a specific task rapidly and to be disbanded when the task is completed. Social and political organizations often have various committees, ranging from personnel and membership to program and executive.

A work group may be seen as a type of problem-solving group. Work groups have evolved in the last 20 years within business organizations and occur at all organizational levels, from McDonald's crews to high-level executive retreats where organizational policy and direction are determined. The immediate office group or production team is an ongoing part of most jobs, and the effectiveness of these groups can influence an individual's productivity level and happiness within the organization. Continuous improvement teams and self-managing work groups are two specialized examples of work groups. Their goals are to increase the quality and performance effectiveness of their groups.

In addition to problem-solving groups, conference groups are formed with representatives from several different groups. In many cases, their meetings provide vital information-sharing and coordinating opportunities. Made possible through the use of computers and teleconferencing equipment, these groups provide people in disparate locations the ability to communicate and solve problems of mutual concern. Further, the informal liaisons provided by the availability of electronic media for communication add another layer to these mediated communication groups. Many in the business and professional world use e-mail and other Internet services regularly and are members of various online groups. The particular communication strategies used in small groups depends to some degree on the context of the interaction and the goals the group wants to accomplish. Electronic communication poses different issues for small group communication than does face-to-face communication. Different face-to-face situations and contexts place different types of demands on the communication interactions. These contexts and influences on small group communication will be explored.

The Power of Groups

Disney, Honda, Marriott, Merck, Motorola, Nordstrom, Procter & Gamble, Sony, and Wal-Mart all began with a small group of motivated and gifted individuals meeting on a regular basis. These and many more great companies can trace their beginnings to small group decision-making processes. Not all of their first attempts succeeded, but they believed in the importance of group effort and ultimately developed highly successful companies based on the effective work of small groups (Collins & Porras, 2002).

Surowiecki (2004) argues that a collective intelligence that he calls "the wisdom of crowds" exists in groups of people in the ability "to act collectively to make decisions or solve problems. . . . Groups benefit from members talking to and learning from each other . . . [and can] come up with good solutions to a wide array of problems" (p. 7). He examined three types of problems that small groups are particularly good at solving—problems that have solutions that can be found in the world, problems that require group members to coordinate their activities with one another, and problems that require self-interested, distrustful people to cooperate in order to contribute to the public good: "Under the right circumstances, groups are remarkably intelligent, and are often smarter than the smartest people in them" (p. xiii). As a result, more companies are shifting away from traditional hierarchy management to "team-based management, in which everyone has input into how the business is run" (Parker, 2005, p. 1D). Corporations are increasing their reliance on team management (Crown, 2007). "Recent estimates conclude that group-based work methods exist in nearly 70% of U.S. firms" (Lowry, Roberts, Romano, & Cheney, 2006, p. 632). "The importance of team building is well established, and its high use is expected to continue in the coming years" (Cummings & Worley, 2005, p. 230). Learning to be an effective team member is important.

Defining Small Group Communication

Communication represents symbolic behavior that occurs as a *transactional process* among people, in which all the parties are continually and *simultaneously sending and receiving* information to develop a sense of shared meaning. A *small group* is a collection of at least 3 and usually fewer than 20 individuals who are interdependent, influence one another over some period of time, share a common goal or purpose, assume specialized roles, have a sense of mutual belonging, maintain norms and standards for group membership, and engage in interactive communication. This network of individuals works together in a group that exists within a network of interacting groups, as illustrated in Figure 1.1. The network of groups may form a corporation, a civic organization, or a social movement. *Small group communication* is the transactional process of using symbolic behavior to achieve a shared meaning among group members over a period of time to accomplish this purpose and task. There are three key concepts in this definition: transactional process, symbolic behavior, and shared meaning.

Transactional Group Process

Communication is more than the mere exchange of messages and transfer of information from one person to another. Early models of communication focused on senders putting their messages into words and gestures and sending them through channels to

FIGURE 1.1   A Group Represents a Network of Individuals Participating Within a Network of Groups

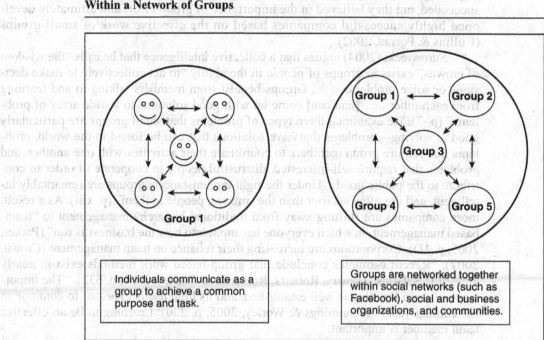

Individuals communicate as a group to achieve a common purpose and task.

Groups are networked together within social networks (such as Facebook), social and business organizations, and communities.

Small groups are often best conceived of as networks of individuals who interact with each other and focus their time and attention on a common purpose, goal, and task. The group's purpose and power may be participated in differentially by group members or shared in an egalitarian way, but the group members interact with each other for the accomplishment of this purpose and task.

receivers. The conscientious sender tried to make the message as clear as possible so that the receiver could take the information and act as expected. When that did not occur, it was considered to be a failed communication.

This one-way, linear flow of messages has been criticized for neglecting the receiver's influence. This criticism led to the development of interactional models of communication. Feedback was added, and the importance of reciprocal message exchanges between the sender and receiver was recognized. Although this represented an important improvement, these models still envisioned communication as a sophisticated ping-pong match in which the sender served and the receiver was expected to return the serve. The receiver's failure to return the serve as expected represented a communication breakdown. Neither of these approaches adequately describes communication failures or helps to facilitate better communication. A certain appeal exists in the simplistic notion that human communication breaks down along straightforward lines. However, this concept tends to ignore the interactive dynamic of the communication process itself. In small group communication, all group members are both senders and receivers who simultaneously send and receive verbal and nonverbal messages. One cannot *not* communicate (Watzlawick, Beavin, & Jackson, 1967). Although our communication may not be what we intended, we nevertheless communicate something. Remaining silent during an important meeting is as much a communication as speaking. Standing someone up for an appointment or a date is a message, whether we intend it that way or not.

It is interesting to note how we adapt our own behaviors and speech patterns to accommodate others in a group. An intriguing test of this concept is to sit in a small group and when another person is speaking, make eye contact with that person and scratch your nose. Notice what that person does. We are frequently unaware of the extent to which we modify our behaviors or what we are saying in response to the behaviors and reactions of other group members. This adaptation is often not conscious, but it has an important effect on the group process.

Once we accept the impossibility of not communicating, we can begin to understand why the actions we take, and to which we attribute little or no importance, may have an effect in a small group out of proportion to what we intended. How often we attend group meetings; whether we arrive early, on time, or late; where we sit; how often and when we speak; our tone of voice; and our other nonverbal behaviors—all communicate something. They affect our role in the group process and the group dynamic as much as the content of what we say.

Symbolic Behavior

An important defining characteristic of being human is our capacity to use and respond to a system of significant symbols (Miller, 2006). The meanings of both verbal and nonverbal communication exist in the symbolic significance we attribute to the words and nonverbal behavior. The meanings exist in us as individuals, not in the words or behaviors themselves. Later in this book, we develop a discussion of small group verbal and nonverbal communication, but consider for a moment how different people respond to the nation's flag, to obscene words, to public displays of affection, or to their school colors. Our reactions to symbols are based on the importance we as individuals and as social groups attach to them. The use and abuse of symbols is an inherently human activity (Wood, 2000). Small groups participate in this activity through their transactional group processes to create their shared meaning.

Shared Meaning

Because we each assign somewhat different symbolic significance to verbal and nonverbal expressions, arriving at a common or "shared" set of meanings can be difficult. Our individual meanings are shaped by our internal states as much as by our shared group environment. If I am in the mood to listen to music and someone tells me to buy CDs, I am likely to think in terms of music CDs rather than the certificates of deposit (CDs) that person may have meant. The development of some sense of *shared meaning* is, however, essential to small group communication, and an ideal for small group meetings is to end with everyone arriving at a more-or-less shared understanding of the meaning of the ongoing communication. This is difficult to achieve in actual fact because we are each deeply influenced by our own set of experiences and assumptions. Nonetheless, it is important for a group to strive toward this ideal.

TABLE 1.1   Group Ethos

Pluralistic	Pluralistic group members need not be uniformly like-minded. Their involvement in this group revolves around a particular interest.
Social Movement	A core sense of identity transcends the interest in the group. Members identify with the group and its cause.
Administrative–Technical	Efficiency, expertise, and roles replace personality in group participation.
Hybrid	An intermix of ethos, difficult to tell where one ends and another begins because identity and interest are not always neatly separated.

For more information, see Patrick (2006).

Patrick (2006) identified different types of ethos that small groups take on as pluralistic, social movement, administrative–technical, or hybrid in style. Pluralistic groups have members who join for a particular reason or interest. In social movement groups, members identify heavily with the group's cause or purpose and therefore with the group work. Administrative–technical groups focus on task efficiency and personal expertise. Hybrid groups represent some combination or mixture of the other three types. Descriptions of these types are presented in Table 1.1. Knowing the type of group ethos will enhance our understanding the group's communication patterns, meaning structures, and underlying value system.

Why We Join Groups

Working in groups can be gratifying, and it can be frustrating. As social beings, we seek opportunities to join with others who share our interests or who help us meet our needs. Groups can help us define, clarify, and understand important issues through discussion and the sharing of multiple perspectives. Groups can also help us develop our leadership skills and facilitate our understanding of particular topics. By working with and explaining issues to others, we clarify our understanding of a given topic, strengthen our ability to organize our thoughts, develop our ability to think through problems, and learn to better articulate our thoughts to others. We join groups for many reasons. Four of the most common are: (1) interpersonal attraction; (2) a need for affiliation, meaning, or identity; (3) a commitment to group goals and activities; and (4) assignment to the group by someone else (see Figure 1.2).

Interpersonal Attraction

The three major influences on *interpersonal attraction* are physical proximity, attitude similarity, and need complementarity (Miller, 1990).

Physical proximity refers to the closeness and amount of interaction possible with other group members in the same physical location. When we all work for the same organization, go to the same university, or live in the same community and see each other on a regular basis, it becomes easier to establish close interpersonal relationships and

FIGURE 1.2 Why We Join Groups

Interpersonal Attraction

Physical Proximity
Attitude Similarity
Need Complementarity

Personal Need for Affiliation

Why We Join Groups

Commitment to Group
Goals and Activities

Assignment by
Someone Else

---

develop our friendships. While long-distance relationships are possible, the distance it-self usually places a stressor on the relationship, making it more difficult to grow or maintain (McShane & Von Glinow, 2003). However, proximity alone does not mean that we will want to interact with a particular person. That desire for interaction depends on at least two other characteristics: attitude similarity and need complementarity.

Attitude similarity is one of the reasons we find some people more appealing to talk to than others. When people have economic, political, and social views that are similar to our own, we are more likely to enjoy interacting with them (Cohen, Fink, Gadon, & Willits, 2001). We do not have to agree with every attitude or opinion some-one holds, but we do usually need to feel some basic attitude similarities, particularly in areas that are likely to be relevant to interaction and arise in our discussions. How-ever, studies show that having a pleasant, congenial conversation with someone with whom we disagree can ease our initial feelings that we simply "do not get along" with that person because of his or her views on a subject (Miller, 1990). Alternately, getting into a heated disagreement with someone because of differing attitudes or opinions can put a strain on even the best relationship.

Need complementarity suggests that we are drawn to other individuals because of a psychological fit. Although we do not always fully agree with a person's attitude or perspective, we share complementary needs. For example, if I like taking charge, am well organized, and am willing to do more than my fair share of the work, I may work well with people who are looking for a leader. Similarly, they may find me an at-tractive member of their group and allow me to take on that role. Likewise, we are drawn to people we admire or from whom we believe we can learn something. We may also find some group members more directly useful than others for accomplishing the group's goals. To the degree that each member brings a different set of needed skills to the group a need complementarity is being fulfilled within the group.

Thus, interpersonal attraction, as defined by proximity, attitude similarity, and need complementarity, is one of the reasons we join, become active in, and remain in groups. Group affiliations are typically not limited to our attraction to the good looks or popularity of other members but extend to an affiliation with those who share similar views or who, while being quite different from us, complement our abilities and help fulfill a personal or group need.

Personal Need for Affiliation

Groucho Marx is credited with saying, "I would not want to be a member of any club that would accept me as a member." Most of us, however, need some amount of social contact and frequently find this need met through the relationships we develop in groups. Being a member of student government, a motorcycle riding club, a model train society, a sorority or fraternity, an intramural volleyball team, or a skydiving club adds a dimension to our personal identities. Belonging to groups helps us develop and refine our interests, enhances the way we spend our time, and cultivates the type of activities we enjoy.

In addition to participation in social groups, many individuals find their work satisfying in part because it provides an affiliation and identity with a work group. Most of us spend more time working than we do pursuing any other activity. It makes sense that we identify a part of ourselves with that work and enjoy participating in that group activity. Organizations spend a great deal of time and energy trying to align our individual identities with group goals and objectives (Harris & Nelson, 2008; Schein, 1997). Groups, whether social or work related, offer affiliation, meaning, and identity to our lives.

Commitment to Group Goals and Activities

Groups have reasons, purposes, and goals for existing that draw us to them. These can range from saving the world, to changing the grading system, to finding a new method for marketing a product. The old expression that "politics makes strange bedfellows" highlights the notion that people with very different personalities and purposes, and from different backgrounds, may share a common goal and often find themselves members of the same group. You might, for example, work out three times a week at a gym and find that you are more motivated to maintain a regular workout schedule because you work out with a group. The three or four people you join during these workouts might have little in common with you outside the gym, but you become a tight-knit group with feelings of interconnectivity within the gym context. If the gym's management tried to close the facility during the hours that your group normally works out, you would probably band together to achieve the mutually important goal of maintaining an open facility during those hours. This is the nature of groups. They often form around common purposes even when the individual members' backgrounds and life experiences may be very different.

Assignment by Someone Else

We do not always have the option of deciding which groups we will join, however. In almost any organization, there are necessary—sometimes arbitrary—assignments to groups. Frequently we find ourselves in groups that are important to us but that we do not necessarily identify with or that we did not select for ourselves. We were assigned to these groups by someone else. Even so, participation in these groups can be surprising, fulfilling, and fun.

Characteristics and Coordinating Mechanisms of Small Groups

Three principal characteristics define small groups. These characteristics are interdependence–interactivity, the number of interactions, and synergy. In addition to these three characteristics, Salas, Sims, and Burke (2005) identified a set of coordinating mechanisms of small groups that are of interest in defining the roles and activities group members must take on.

Interdependence and Interactivity

Meeting and talking with one another is not enough to constitute a small group. If people are primarily interested in individual accomplishments, have little or nothing vested in the activities of one another, or are frequently absent from meetings, we do not consider this collection of people a small group. We would prefer to call them a collection of people or a gathering. We restrict the term small group to contexts in which the members are interdependent and interactive to the point that each person is affected by the group process.

This interdependent group might be a pickup basketball team or the board of directors of a large corporation. A family sitting around the dinner table discussing family matters, reviewing the day's activities, and resolving important family issues also constitutes a small group because of their communication interaction and their emotional, financial, and caring interdependencies. On the other hand, a disengaged set of family members sitting together in silence in front of the television set cannot really be called an interdependent group. An accidental or momentary meeting of friends at a local restaurant might qualify as a small group if they experience an interdependence, a common goal, or a shared sense of purpose and engage in interactive communication roles. Strangers chatting casually during a one-time meeting in a restaurant would not.

Small group communication can take place in casual, informal settings, as well as in more formal business, community, social, sports, and school settings. Many important decisions are made by groups of friends, business associates, or public officials talking informally over a cup of coffee about their shared issues and concerns. The key to defining small group communication is not the setting or the context but the *interdependence* and *interactivity* of the group and the subsequent quality of their communication.

TABLE 1.2   Exponential Number of Interactions

People and Interactions

Number of people in a group	2	3	4	5	6	7	8
Number of possible interactions	2	9	28	75	186	441	1,016

Exponential Number of Interactions

A second characteristic of small groups is the dynamic resulting from the number of potential interactions among the members. As we add members to our small group, we multiply the number of potential interactions. This increase alters the possibilities for communication among group members. As shown in Table 1.2, the potential number of comments and alternative viewpoints increases exponentially as each new person is added to the group. This can be seen simultaneously as one of the major benefits and one of the major drawbacks to small group communication.

Each of the interactions requires attention, and as the number of interactions grows, a group needs an increased sensitivity to and understanding of background issues. Increased numbers of interactions create a more complex decision-making process as the number and diversity of relationships within the group must be taken into account. The increased numbers of interactions become difficult to manage when there are too many participants. Outcomes, however, also have an opportunity of becoming more sophisticated as a greater diversity of perspectives must be taken into account and addressed, but, "Too large groups usually backfire" (Yang, 2006, p. 122). Jeff Bezos, founder and CEO of Amazon.com, has a two-pizza rule—if a group cannot be fed by two pizzas, it is too large. In any case, the size of a group is an important influence.

Synergy

Synergy comes from the Greek word *sunergos,* which means "working together." Synergy results when two or more people work together, share their ideas with open minds and mutual respect, and manage conflict in ways that empower all members. "Several individuals working together and building on each other's strengths can potentially generate more and better solutions than if these people worked alone" (McShane & Von Glinow, 2000, p. 312). The major advantage of working in a group is that the group as a whole is greater than the sum of its parts. The group process itself creates an outcome that is different and often superior to what any of the individual group members would have generated on their own. Synergy occurs when one person's ideas stimulates another's thoughts during the discussion, causing a third person to think of something totally new. This new idea might be refined by the first person or by a fourth person, incorporated within a new idea by the second, and extended further by the third. As this group process continues, something emerges that is new, creative, and unique to the group and the interaction. In such an interactive thinking process, it becomes impossible and irrelevant to attribute the final solution or any set of ideas to a particular individual. The outcome is a new whole, no longer easily separable into its component parts.

The effectiveness of small groups lies in the dynamics of the decision-making process. Because members can bounce ideas off one another and the parts of many ideas can be recombined, coalescing to form new and different ideas, the result is frequently something entirely new and unexpected. This process of small group decision making is metaphorically analogous to the chemical reaction that produces water from hydrogen and oxygen. The water is an entirely new substance, having properties not easily explained by the characteristics of the hydrogen and oxygen molecules alone. This synergistic process is what makes small group decision making so potentially powerful. A review of 50 years of studies on cooperative decision making found that problem solving is more effective when done by groups rather than when done by individuals (Berko, 1996).

Coordinating Mechanisms

Salas and colleagues (2005) argued that a group or team must engage in a set of *coordinating mechanisms* to be effective. Group members must take on leadership functions to plan, coordinate, and organize their activities, assess their performance, motivate other members, and build a positive team atmosphere. Members must be able to develop common understandings, monitor performance, identify mistakes, provide feedback, anticipate needs, recognize responsibilities, work to achieve balanced workloads, be vigilant to changes in the environment, reallocate resources, and respond to changing conditions. Members must also believe in the team goal and processes of group interaction, develop a shared knowledge so they can anticipate each other's needs, and identify changes and adjust their strategies as needed. Group interaction is based on a mutual trust and shared belief that team members will perform their roles, admit mistakes, exchange messages, accept feedback, and look out for the interests of their teammates (see Table 1.3).

Characteristics of Small Group Communication

Each of us, as group members, brings our own definition, interpretation, personal history, and judgment concerning the appropriateness of any particular group activity. This perspective, in and of itself, creates an ongoing, continuous modification of that activity. Therefore, while a small group is communicating, it is nearly impossible to freeze-frame a given moment. That moment is defined by the continuity of all that has gone before, during, and even after that moment. The group process represents a complex communication transaction occurring between and influenced by each of the participants and their perceptions of those sequences of events. Group members, individually and collectively, provide a continual defining and redefining of the group: the member relationships; topics open for discussion; and group norms, rules, and roles. If, for instance, a group member suddenly gets angry at a particular point being made, that anger may trigger a group response. That one person's reaction may redefine the group discussion, even if only temporarily. This sense of a wholeness in a group's communication can also be seen in the experience of something that strikes the

TABLE 1.3   Coordinating Mechanisms of Teamwork

Coordinating Mechanism	Activities
Team Leadership	Coordinate, plan, organize activities; develop team knowledge; assess team performance; build positive team atmosphere; motivate team members
Mutual Performance Monitoring	Negotiate common understandings, identify mistakes, monitor team performance, provide feedback to facilitate correction
Backup Procedures	Anticipate team members' needs through accurate knowledge of responsibilities; recognize potential workload distribution problems; shift workload among members to achieve balance
Adaptability	Adjust strategies based on feedback information; identify cues that change has occurred; provide reallocation of resources; alter action in response to changing conditions; remain vigilant to changes in environment
Team Orientation	Take others' behavior into account during group interaction; believe in importance of team goal; consider alternative solutions provided by teammates
Shared Mental Models	Develop a shared knowledge of the relationships among the task team members will engage in and how the team members will interact; anticipate each other's needs; identify changes in team or task and adjust strategies
Mutual Trust	Express a shared belief that team members will perform their roles and protect the interests of their teammates; show a willingness to admit mistakes and accept feedback
Closed Loop Communication	Exchange messages and follow-up; acknowledging a message has been received and clarifying its meaning as intended

For more information, see Salas and colleagues (2005).

group as hysterically funny. Relating the humor of that incident to someone who was not present at that moment in the group often becomes impossible. "You really had to be there" to appreciate the humor within the process and context of the group.

Complex Transactions

Complex group transactions involve three elements: substance, pattern, and process. The *substance* consists of the content of the group interaction—the issues around which the group is formed and about which it communicates. The *pattern* represents the relationships and interactions among the group members. The *process* is the ongoing symbolically interpreted interface between the substance and the pattern. It is the catalyst that gives "life" to the group meetings.

If I say, "Let's meet at 7:30 on the Mall," the statement has a literal content meaning but also contains a relational, interactive element—an assumption of a pattern in our relationship. It assumes that it is appropriate for me to suggest the time and place of the meeting and that those to whom I am speaking are expected to show up. The way each of us interprets and reacts to this statement represents our relational interaction. If a group member shows up for the meeting at 7:35, is he late? Has he violated a group "timeliness norm"? Has he kept everyone waiting? Is he being rude or simply applying appropriate group expectations of what it means to be "on time?" Likewise, if I tell a joke in the middle of a serious group discussion, am I fulfilling an important group communication function of "lightening things up," engaging in inappropriate behavior by "wasting everyone's time," or "acting out" against the wishes of the group? Whether I am late for the group meeting when I arrive 5 minutes after the stated starting time or am wasting the group's time when I tell a joke depends on the norms of the group. All small group communication happens simultaneously on several levels. It involves what is said (the substance), the relationships and interactions among the people involved (the pattern), and the ongoing symbolically interpreted action (the process) that mediates between those two and that unites them. Each group develops its own norms for appropriate group substance, pattern, and process. These norms become important in the group's decision making and problem solving.

Interactive Complexities

Small groups share many of the communication characteristics that make interpersonal and public communication effective. Because of the complexity of the interactions in small groups, however, some important differences in the communication process also need to be taken into account. Like effective dyads, which are two-person relationships, the members of small groups are mutually interdependent and, therefore, mutually responsible for the success or failure of the group's communication. Just as in dyadic communication, participants in small groups share responsibility for speaking, listening, and providing feedback and empathy, but in small groups these responsibilities are made more complex by the multiple sets of interactions.

Group interactions share some similarities and some contrasts with most types of public speaking. In both cases, the speaker is attempting to present a message to an audience. In public speaking, the audience is not usually expected to participate, other than to listen. The preparation and success of the presentation are placed largely on the speaker. If one member of the audience in a public-speaking situation does not show up, the speech itself is probably not greatly affected. In a small group, on the other hand, each member is an important part of the communication interaction. If one member does not show up or does not participate, the whole group is affected.

Whereas public speaking can be effective in very large groups, a small group numbering more than 15 to 20 members can usually no longer function effectively. The potential number of interactions produced by the increased number of people overwhelms the dynamic of the group process itself. Because small group communication functions through the interaction among a group of people with different points of view, it depends on the ability of the group to hear and incorporate that multiplicity of ideas. When the number of possible interactions becomes too large, that integration and merging of ideas becomes difficult or impossible.

In addition, small groups tend to have an ongoing interactive identity that may or may not be substantially altered by changes in membership. This differs from the total interdependence of a dyad and the relative independence of a public-speaking context. In a dyad, if one of the two members quits, the dyad no longer exists. In a public-speaking forum, the speech is set ahead of time, and the makeup of the audience, although important in terms of the acceptance or rejection of the message and the speaker, plays a substantially different role. For the small group, the loss or addition of a group member may not completely reduce or enhance the group's ability to discuss issues, function effectively, or make progress, but it will substantially affect the group's process.

Groups in Organizations

Groups and teams, used effectively, produce outstanding results. They can enhance creativity and expand the scope of alternative solutions. Most successful companies and large corporations have been started by brainstorming in small groups, rather than by a single individual acting alone.

Small groups are the cornerstones of many aspects of organizational behavior, operating at all levels and playing major roles in the informal and formal interactions in organizations (Harris & Nelson, 2008). Organizations make use of committees, task forces, work groups, and a vast number of other types of groups and teams, ranging from electronic networks to interdisciplinary problem-solving groups.

Organizational Examples

The ability of teams to increase an organization's success is widely documented: "More companies are moving from traditional hierarchy management to team-based management, in which everyone has input into how the business is run" (Parker, 2005, p. 1D). Organizations use teams to increase innovation, enhance collaboration, increase effective communication, solve problems, and redefine traditional organizational structures.

The Whole Foods Company forms teams in every department (Parker, 2005). Each team operates as a separate enterprise with one team leader: "If the team comes in under its budget, the money left over is divided among the members" (Parker, 2005, p. 5D). At first glance, it might appear that the team would be motivated to reduce spending. However, satisfying the customer is the first priority, so teams do not intentionally limit quality or service to increase the leftover money: "Whole Foods, whose stock price is up 25 percent this year, has seen steady growth in its earnings as a result of its team structure" (Parker, 2005, p. 5D).

Seagate Technology paid $9,000 per employee to attend a 1-week team-building retreat in New Zealand designed to develop a cohesive team culture (Max, 2006). Dubbed "Eco Seagate," the retreat included all levels of staff, since collaboration is a companywide need. The goal was to learn to depend on other team members for overall success, no matter what the problem is.

Finally, Nucor, the nation's largest steel producer and recycler, has teams that figure out supply-flow problems, quality issues, vacation schedules, and even disciplinary actions. No supervisor dictates their every move (Parker, 2005). Since the team can act immediately to resolve issues and is ultimately responsible for the results, team members take their responsibilities seriously.

Meetings

Millions of *meetings* take place in U.S. organizations every day. However, meetings are often ineffective, according to 70% of surveyed American executives (de Janasz, Dowd, & Schneider, 2002). Many individuals believe meetings are a waste of time (Basil, 2000). Perhaps more important, "unproductive meetings are a costly drain on businesses" (Armour, 2006, p. 3B).

In one survey, 89% of American executives pointed to a lack of organization and planning as the major reasons for ineffective meetings. (Basil, 2000). Figure 1.3 presents some guidelines for increasing meeting effectiveness.

Committees, conferences, and meetings have fostered many tongue-in-cheek comments, such as "A meeting brings together a group of the unfit, appointed by the unwilling, to do the unnecessary"; "A camel is a horse designed by a committee"; "A conference is a meeting of people who singly do nothing, and who collectively agree that nothing can be done"; and "A conference is a meeting to decide when the next meeting will be held." Yet, small group meetings have persisted in organizations, and as organizations move to flatten hierarchies and increase the use of self-managed work teams, the amount of time spent communicating in small group meetings is likely to increase. Effective small group communication has moved from an advantage to a necessity in organizational work today.

FIGURE 1.3   Guide to Meeting Effectiveness

Meetings are vital to the group and team process. The following suggestions summarize common problems or issues with meeting effectiveness. Specialized groups often have particular formats and expectations that might require deviations from this list.

➢ **Before the Meeting**

1. Have a clear purpose for the meeting.
2. Consider using and distributing an agenda.
3. Include the right people and the right number.
4. Pick an appropriate meeting time.
5. Choose a location easily accessible to participants.
6. Avoid too many or too few meetings.
7. Provide notice, often written, well before the meeting.
8. Ask members to come prepared.
9. Start on time.

➢ **During the Meeting**

1. Limit socializing and get down to business.
2. Establish an orderly process.
3. If there is an agenda, use it as a guide—be flexible on specifics.

4. Start with the most important topics unless the meeting has a formal format.
5. Keep to the agreed-upon length of time.
6. Make certain adequate information is available.
7. End on time.
8. Summarize the meeting.
9. Consider scheduling the next meeting.
10. Try not to waste time.
11. Make certain quiet members can also contribute.
12. Make certain the meeting is not dominated by a few.
13. Avoid compromises that produce poor solutions.

➢ **After the Meeting**

1. Record key issues, assignments, deadlines.
2. Follow-up on all decisions.
3. Decide if the meeting was a success or failure.

Quality Decision Making Through Group Diversity and Ethics

Diversity among the members of a group is important for the quality of the group's decisions. Although we are more likely to be emotionally comfortable with a homogenous group or team, a heterogeneous group improves performance in terms of decision quality by bringing to bear important differences in opinions, perspectives, and insights (Jackson, May, & Whitney, 1995). The more we function in diverse groups, the greater the likelihood we will learn to profit from these expanded perspectives. Organizations view hiring a diverse workforce as not only the ethical and effective thing to do but as a way of getting a competitive advantage in terms of problem solving and attracting additional employees (Mehta, 2000). Diversity on a team is seen as fundamental to the team and to the organizational success (Ilgen Hollenbeck, Johnson, & Jundt, 2005; McGregor, 2006; Surowiecki, 2004).

The Ethics Resource Center (2000) defined *ethics* as "the standards of conduct that guide decisions and actions based on duties derived from our core values." To be applied to group work, ethics must be interpreted within the situational context of the decisions that the group must make. Unfortunately, this situational context can sometimes lead groups to make potentially unethical decisions (Robertson, Crittenden, Brady, & Hoffman, 2002). We offer a set of ethical guidelines to help provide direction for group work (see Figure 1.4). By adapting ethical approaches to group work, we can achieve greater success.

FIGURE 1.4   Ethical Behavior

Underlying all group and team success is a commitment by members to ethical behavior: "Ethics concerns the rights and responsibilities, privileges and obligations of our conduct within and between" group or team relationships (Anderson & Englehardt, 2001, p. 7). They are our standards of moral conduct or judgments about whether our actions, values, or decisions are right or wrong. Ethics focuses on what we actually do when we are part of a group. The following guidelines are not intended to cover all possible situations, but they will lead to greater group and individual effectiveness.

✓ Allow others' choices rather than forcing them.

✓ Follow through with group-related obligations.

✓ Be sensitive to individual group members' needs.

✓ Maintain confidentiality.

✓ Be honest, keep promises, and fulfill commitments.

✓ Practice fairness in work assignment and in dealing with and treating others.

✓ Strive for full participation by all members.

✓ Demonstrate concern for the group or team.

✓ Have tolerance for other members' ideas, strengths, and weaknesses.

✓ Focus on success for all group members, not just ourselves.

✓ Seek the greatest good for the group members.

Summary

As members of human society, it is almost impossible not to belong to or participate in small groups. Yet, not all such groups are equally satisfying, effective, and successful. Communication in small groups functions to allow group members to pool their individual knowledge and skills and to collectively formulate effective strategies for completing tasks.

Successful small group communication depends on the willingness and ability of each member to share in the responsibility for that interaction and communication. Ultimately, the success or failure of any communication interaction depends on the individuals involved and their ability to balance the dynamic of unique interaction patterns.

Small groups may be formal or informal, ranging from family and social groups to organizational work groups or boards of directors. Small groups are dynamic systems and, as such, must be viewed as interactive communicative networks. They gain their viability through the effective interaction between the substance (content), the pattern (relationships), and the process (action). This communicative network is responsible for the benefits of synergy for which small groups are uniquely suited.

Groups formed for reasons other than primary relationships—family and social companionship groups—frequently have at their core some type of problem-solving agenda. Most formal groups have specific reasons for existing, ranging from analyzing problems to resolving issues. Groups develop their particular personalities based on the nature of the issues around which they are convened, as well as on the characteristics of the group members and the environment in which the group is formed.

Communication forms the basis for small group interactions and is a determining factor in the outcomes of the group process. Effective small group communication strategies can help assure favorable outcomes, with members feeling empowered by having participated in creative problem solving. Poor communication strategies frequently predispose a group to unfavorable outcomes and a dissatisfied membership.

Gaining competence in small group communication is a lot like engaging in a physical exercise program. To gain strength and body tone, we have to work out using exercises and techniques designed for the particular muscle groups we want to work on. The better we understand the process and functions and the more regularly we exercise according to these principles, the greater the strength and body tone we are able to gain. Just working out in whatever way we feel like whenever the mood strikes does not generally produce desirable results. We need instruction in an overall exercise plan and discipline in carrying it out to measure our progress and achieve our goals.

For small group communication, this analogy translates into the importance of gaining an understanding of the theories and perspectives of how small group communication works, becoming familiar with a repertoire of communication strategies shown to be effective in small groups, and knowing when those strategies can be most usefully applied. When a small group succeeds in its endeavors, a theoretical base helps us understand how that success was achieved and helps us model future interactions accordingly. When the group's communication is less successful, a theory can help us understand where and how problems occurred and how to handle them better in future small group communication interactions. In addition, regular practice using small group communication strategies can help us develop skills and make better use of these strategies. Most of all, remember to keep a sense of humor, as illustrated in Figure 1.5.

FIGURE 1.5   Are You Lonely? Hold a Meeting!

Are You Lonely?
Work on Your Own?
Hate Making Decisions?

HOLD A MEETING

You can...

- SEE people
- DRAW flowcharts
- FEEL important
- IMPRESS your colleagues
- EAT donuts

All on
COMPANY TIME!!!

MEETINGS

...the practical alternative to work.

DISCUSSION QUESTIONS

1. What are the basic characteristics of a small group? How is a small group different from a group of friends gathering after a ball game or several members of an office getting together for lunch?

2. List three to five groups to which you have belonged in the past few years. Did you join because of

   A. Interpersonal attraction? Was it primarily physical proximity, attitude similarity, or need complementarity?
   B. A need for affiliation?
   C. A commitment to group goals and activities?
   D. Assignment by someone else?

   Which group(s) did you enjoy the most? Which group(s) did you find most gratifying in terms of accomplishing goals? Which group(s) were least satisfying? Least successful?

3. Provide an example of the (a) transactional, (b) symbolic, and (c) shared meaning aspects of small group communication. How do these examples help you understand the communication process in small groups?

4. Discuss what is meant by the statement that the "whole of the group is greater than the sum of its parts." Provide an example of this phenomenon from your own small group experiences.

5. There are numerous types of small groups, including primary, social, educational, therapeutic, problem-solving, work, conference, and computer-mediated communication groups. Have you participated in any such groups? Which ones? Which ones are you most familiar with? How do they differ from the ones you are least familiar with? When looking at the different types of groups, can you identify specific areas of interest to focus your study of small groups? What are they?

6. From your work experience, can you identify a small group success story? Do you have an example of when a small group was not successful on the job? What were the primary differences between the two groups?

REFERENCES

Alda, A. (2007). *Things I overheard while talking to myself.* New York: Random House.

Anderson, J. A., & Englehardt, E. E. (2001). *The organizational self and ethical conduct.* New York: Harcourt.

Appleby, J., & Davis, R. (2001, March 1). Teamwork used to be a money saver, now it's a lifesaver. *USA Today*, pp. 1B–2B.

Armour, S. (2006, July 6). Some companies aim to tame meetings. *USA Today*, p. 3B.

Basil, F. (2000, March 13). Advance planning is key to successful meetings. *Indianapolis Business Journal*, p. 21.

Berko, R. (1996, January). Education matters. *Spectra*, p. 8.

Cohen, A. R., Fink, S. L., Gadon, H., & Willits, R. D. (2001). *Effective behavior in organizations: Cases, concepts, and student experiences* (7th ed.). Boston: McGraw-Hill.

Collins, J. C., & Porras, J. I. (2002). *Built to last: Successful habits of visionary companies.* New York: Harper/Business Essentials.

Crown, D. F. (2007). Effects of structurally competitive multilevel goals for an independent task. *Small Group Research, 36*(2), 265–288.

Cummings, T. G., & Worley, C. G. (2005). *Organizational development and change* (8th ed.). Florence, KY: Thomson South-Western.

de Janasz, S. C., Dowd, K. O., & Schneider, B. Z. (2002). *Interpersonal skills in organizations.* Boston: McGraw-Hill.

Ethics Resource Center. (2002). *2002 national business ethics report summary.* Retrieved October 9, 2002, from http://ethics.org/200survey.html

Harris, T. E. & Nelson, M. D. (2008). *Applied organizational communication: Theory and practice in a global environment.* New York: Lawrence Erlbaum Associates.

Illgen, D. R., Hollenbeck, J. R., Johnson, M., & Jundt, D. (2005). Teams in organizations: From input-process-output models to IMOI models. *Annual Review of Psychology, 56,* 517–543.

Jackson, S. E., May, K. E., & Whitney, K. (1995). Understanding the dynamics of diversity in decision-making teams. In R. A. Guzzo, E. Salas, & Associates (Eds.), *Team effectiveness and decision making in organizations* (pp. 204–261). San Francisco: Jossey-Bass.

Lowry, P. B., Roberts, T. L., Romano, N. C., & Cheney, P. D. (2006). The impact of group size and social presence on small-group communication. *Small Group Research, 37*(6), 631–661.

Max, S. (2006, April 3). Seagate's morale-athon. *Business Week,* pp. 110–112.

McGregor, J. (2006, April 24). The world's most innovative companies. *Business Week,* pp. 63–74.

McShane, S., & Von Glinow, M. A. (2000). *Organizational behavior.* Boston: Irwin McGraw-Hill.

McShane, S. L., & Von Glinow, M. A. (2003). *Organizational behavior: Emerging realities for the workplace revolution* (2nd ed.). Boston: McGraw-Hill.

Mehta, S. N. (2000, July 10). What minority employees really want. *Fortune,* pp. 181–186.

Miller, K. (2006). *Organizational communication: Approaches and processes* (4th ed.). Belmont, CA: Wadsworth.

Parker, V. L. (2005, July 24). "Team-based" management gaining popularity. *Tuscaloosa News,* pp. 1D, 5D.

Patrick, B. A. (2006). Group ethos and the communication of social action. *Small Group Research, 37*(5), 425–458.

Pomeroy, A. (2004, July). Great places, inspired employees. *HR Magazine,* pp. 46–54.

Robertson, C. J., Crittenden, W. F., Brady, M. K., & Hoffman, J. J. (2002). Situational ethics across borders. *Journal of Business Ethics, 38,* 327–338.

Salas, E., Sims, D. E., & Burke, C. S. (2005). Is there a "big five" in teamwork? *Small Group Research, 36*(5), 555–599.

Schein, E. H. (1997). *Organizational culture and leadership* (2nd ed.). San Francisco: Jossey-Bass.

Surowiecki, J. (2004). *The wisdom of crowds.* New York: Doubleday.

The team as superstar. (1998). *Outlook, 1,* pp. 24–27.

Watzlawick, P., Beavin, J., & Jackson, D. (1967). *Pragmatics of human communication.* New York: W. W. Norton.

Wood, J. T. (2000). *Relational communication: Continuity and change in personal relationships* (2nd ed.). Belmont, CA: Wadsworth.

Yang, J. L. (2006, June 12). The power of number 4.6. *Fortune,* p. 122.

CHAPTER

2

Small Group Communication: A System of Interaction

CHAPTER OUTLINE

Understanding Small Group Success

Communication in Small Groups

A Systems Approach to Small Group Communication

   Systems Theory

   Open Systems

   Complex Systems

Summary

Discussion Questions

References

CHAPTER OBJECTIVES

- Understand groups as systems of interaction.
- Distinguish the four types of problem-solving groups.
- Provide a systems theory for small group communication.
- Explain a systems perspective on small group communication.
- Define the importance of system properties, including wholeness, synergy, openness, transformation, interdependence, feedback, entropy, equifinality, and environment.
- Describe complex systems and the processes of second-order change and double-loop learning.
- Apply the complex system concepts of initial conditions, strange attractors, phase space, bifurcation points, and irreversibility.

KEY TERMS

Bifurcation points

Complex systems

Double-loop learning

Entropy

Environment

Equifinality

Feedback

First-order change

Initial conditions

Input	Phase space	Synergy
Interdependence	Quantum change	Systems approach
Irreversibility	Second-order change	Systems theory
Openness	Single-loop learning	Transformation
Output	Strange attractors	Wholeness

But the twenty-first century world of complex systems is no place for . . . disabling and dispiriting images. We are confronted daily by events and outcomes that shock us and for which we have no answers. The complexity of modern systems cannot be understood by our old ways of separating problems, or scapegoating individuals, or rearranging the boxes on an org chart. In a complex system, it is impossible to find simple causes that explain our problems or to know whom to blame.

(Wheatley, 2007, p. 76)

"When people get together in groups there is a pull to communicate" (Pincus & Guastello, 2005, p. 637). The communication among group members regulates the process of the group, and a group coordination emerges. Patterns of speaking, listening, turn taking, silence, and participation develop in the group. Group behaviors, processes, and decisions take on qualities that cannot be attributed wholly to any particular group member. They may have a history and be a consequence of something agreed upon in the past, or they may be affected by multiple group influences.

Understanding Small Group Success

Understanding something about these influences and observing their effects on a group's process and outcome can be helpful. To illustrate these influences, problem-solving groups can be divided along two dimensions into four types (see Figure 2.1). The first dimension differentiates groups that successfully solve a problem from those that do not. The second dimension distinguishes those groups that understand why they were successful or unsuccessful in solving the problem from those that do not understand how they arrived at that outcome. If groups that have been successful understand why they were successful, they can repeat that success in the future. If groups that have failed understand why they have failed, they may understand better what strategies will help them be successful in the future and improve their probability of success in subsequent problem-solving endeavors. Groups that understand the reasons behind their successes and failures are able to consciously employ strategies that will facilitate future success and reduce the likelihood of future failure.

To be effective, groups must engage in a variety of practices ranging from establishing a clear set of commonly held group goals to developing norms for interpersonal communication. Six people getting together does not guarantee an effective group. Nor is effectiveness guaranteed by simply imitating a strategy used by an effective group, such as choosing a leader or following an agenda. Only by understanding

FIGURE 2.1   Successful and Unsuccessful Problem-Solving Groups

Unsuccessful ←————————————→ Successful

	Unsuccessful	Successful

Group Understands	**Group 1: Unsuccessful, but understands why.**
	Likely to be able to:
	   Learn from the failure.
	   Not make the same mistake again.
	   Apply knowledge and achieve success next time.
		Group 2: Successful, and understands why.
		Likely to be able to:
		   Repeat success again next time.
		   Achieve additional knowledge with each success.

Doesn't Understand	**Group 3: Unsuccessful and does not understand why.** Likely to be unsuccessful next time.	**Group 4: Successful, but does not understand why.** Lucky this time, but "clueless." Likely to be unsuccessful next time.

their decision-making, problem-solving group process as a whole can six people transform themselves into an effective small group.

Individuals who have a long history of working together successfully often have some common intuitive understanding of their communication expectations. However, even individuals who know each other well often find that the group process is more challenging than they anticipated. With an understanding of why groups are successful, people who are dedicated can form a group and achieve a successful group outcome not just once but repeatedly. Without that understanding they can only hope for the best each time they meet. A perspective and awareness of the complex influences on communication in small groups can help group members achieve that success.

Although it is theoretically possible to calculate the "personality" of a group by analyzing all the possible relationships and interactions between each and every group member, it is often not practical to do so. A perspective that looks at a group as a whole is more practical. A transactional model of communication in which "the properties of the group are irreducible to the properties of its individual members" (Laszlo, 1996, p. 26) suggests a systems orientation that underscores the dynamic, complex, ongoing process and nature of small groups as influenced by past, present, and future events, interactions, situations, and contexts. Treating small groups as systems of interaction with characteristics unique to the group provides an appreciation of the group's complexity and allows us to better examine and understand small group communication.

Communication in Small Groups

From a systems perspective, six basic elements of human communication underlie the study of small group communication. First, *communication is the recognition of some behavior that is meaningful to one or more participants in the group*. Because communication is tied to meaning, we are interested in meaning-centered activities. Systems thinking helps us conceptualize the ways in which small group communication is affected by changes in any number of verbal and nonverbal activities (such as language use, tone of voice, seating arrangement, styles of dress, and timeliness).

Second, *meaning is based in the symbolic interpretation of another's communication.* Because we cannot be inside someone else's head to understand his or her intended meaning, we depend on our own interpretations of the use of symbols, such as words, gestures, and other acts that can stand for something else. When someone says, "I'm hungry," we understand the meaning. Although we do not experience his or her hunger directly, we can equate the statement with our own feeling of hunger. Because our responses to others' communications are based on our own experiences, our communication difficulties are often based on different interpretations of the same symbolic words or gestures. My hunger may not be as immediate as yours. The temperature of the room may not feel as cold to me. My experiential background or slower cognitive processing may mean that it takes me longer to arrive at a similar understanding of a problem that appears obvious to you.

Third, *communication is contextual.* Numerous aspects of the system can influence how we understand and interpret the communication process. The same comment made in a different circumstance or by a different person may be interpreted quite differently.

Fourth, *communication allows us to apply meaning to the world.* We understand and interpret our world of experiences through the dynamic process of communication and the abstract meaning we give the symbols. The small groups in which we participate depend on those symbolic meanings and use them to accomplish the group's work.

Fifth, *our cognitive abilities are open systems* that continually respond to and learn from the different encounters we face in our daily lives. An open system, which we discuss in greater detail shortly, connects and responds to the activities occurring around it. Our earliest experiences with other people and the symbolic meanings we learn from them provide us with the initial conditions that form the basis for our subsequent learning experiences. As self-conscious beings, we "meta-communicate"— that is, we reflect on our communication and communicate with ourselves and others about our communication. This faculty allows us to think about what has occurred, is occurring, and even what is likely to occur. For example, we ask ourselves, "Was I successful?" "Was I right?" "Could I have said it differently?" "Am I making sense at this point in the conversation?" "What is my effect on the process?" "Have I made a positive contribution?"

Sixth, *we are simultaneously senders and receivers of communication.* Although we can isolate an individual in a small group as the sender or initiator of a message, the messenger and the message are not readily separated from the context of the group dynamics. For example, how the message is received and interpreted may be greatly divergent from the intent with which it was sent. Skillful speakers modify *how* they send a message depending on *who* will be receiving it. Message dynamics include both verbal and nonverbal elements and are continuous.

Small groups can be thought of as open, complex, dynamically changing systems of communication, and learning the vocabulary of a systems perspective can help a group member more clearly observe, analyze, and articulate what is occurring in the group. In this chapter, we look at the characteristics of open systems and complex systems and examine the communication functions of open, complex, small group systems that facilitate dynamic group processes.

A Systems Approach to Small Group Communication

A system is, by definition, a collection of interrelated parts or elements that function together to make a whole that is of a magnitude and order totally different from that of any of the individual parts. It is a set of elements bound together in interdependent relationships. The integrity of the whole depends on the mutual interaction among its parts.

Systems Theory

Systems are responsive and interactive, within themselves and within their environments—which are themselves systems. They are, therefore, multitiered, with each system part of a larger one. For example, the human body is made up of organ systems, which in turn are composed of cellular systems. Human beings are also part of social systems and ecological systems. Each system affects the ones with which it interacts, taking in, transforming, and putting out energies. When they work in harmony, each survives and thrives.

Systems theory provides an overall explanation for the complexity of small groups (Harris & Nelson, 2008; Tubbs, 2001), allowing us to highlight the less obvious, but important, elements of the communication interaction within small groups. Groups are made up of individuals possessing different motives, personalities, and skills. In Chapter 1, we noted the remarkable increase in interactions possible when we move from two people (two interactions) to eight people (1,016 interactions). Add roles, norms, and the myriad of other communication variables discussed throughout this text, and the group process is, indeed, complex. Accepting complexity as a fact of group life frees us from being surprised when the time of day, current personal crises, or diverse communication assumptions sidetrack even the most dedicated group. The systems perspective demands that we consider a large number of variables.

Systems theory is a way of perceiving and thinking, rather than a specific "how to do it" theory. As such, it has been difficult to test in an experimentally rigorous way (Eisenberg & Goodall, 2001). Learning specific steps to make our small groups work successfully is frequently more appealing than being asked to examine the big picture, but nothing is ever as simple as it first appears, and a *systems approach* provides us with a broad understanding from which to develop the specifics applicable to any particular group.

Open Systems

Systems theory is essentially a way of thinking about the complexity of interactions between and within living systems. In the 1960s, scholars began reporting their views regarding living systems in an effort to create a general systems theory—one that would explain the basic characteristics of living organisms (Miller, 1978; Thomas, 1975). This exciting period opened the door to a new type of thinking about how the parts of a system interrelate to create the whole. Again, the human body provides a useful example. While we humans pride ourselves on our ability to think and self-reflect, the brain would be useless without the other organs that provide life support. Most of us have probably experienced the difficulty of thinking straight when we are distracted by the pain or disability we experience when we sprain an ankle, twist a knee, or jam a finger in a drawer. The parts of the body are intimately interconnected. In small groups, the parts are the members—their needs and backgrounds, the subject about which they are meeting, and numerous other influences and interactions—all of which are interconnected. The straightforward biological analogy that "the leg bone is connected to the thigh bone" is, however, far easier to analyze and understand than even the simplest small group interaction. The role of communication, especially as symbolic behavior between people in the form of language or nonverbal behavior, is complex (Thomas, 1975) and is the glue that holds effective small groups and teams together.

To begin applying systems thinking to the group process, we need to first understand that we are dealing with systems of behavior between participants who are interrelated and interacting. Therefore, when we look at groups, we are examining a complex set of relationships between interdependent parts (Harris & Nelson, 2008). To demonstrate an application of a systems perspective to understanding small groups, we examine the concepts of wholeness, synergy, openness, transformation, interdependence, feedback, entropy, and equifinality. Table 2.1 lists these characteristics.

Wholeness and Synergy. Most of us are familiar with the concept that the whole is greater than the sum of its parts. *Wholeness,* in small groups, means that the results of people working with each other, as a team, are different from the results of those same people working in isolation. The result of this dynamic interaction is often referred to

TABLE 2.1   Characteristics of Open and Complex Systems

Characteristics of Open Systems	Characteristics of Complex Systems
Wholeness and Synergy	Second-order or quantum change
Openness	Double-loop learning
Transformation	Sensitivity to initial conditions
Interdependence	Strange attractors
Feedback	Phase space
Entropy	Bifurcation points
Equifinality	Irreversibility
Environment	

Teamwork and synergy.
(Photo courtesy of Corbis Digital Stock.)

as *synergy*. This synergy is created through the mixing and incorporating of each other's thoughts and messages. Through this mixing, the dynamic of the group interaction produces a larger, more creative solution, and it is this synergy that makes small groups so effective in solving problems. When we brainstorm in small groups, the outcome is usually greater than a simple adding up of the individual ideas. It leads to the creation of new ideas stimulated by the group's interaction itself. One member suggests an idea to which a second member responds. A third member combines the two ideas in a way that builds and adds onto them and stimulates the first member to have an additional thought that expands on those ideas. The process continues and produces a result that is not directly attributable to the ideas of any one of the participants but is, rather, the result of their interaction.

Openness.   All living organisms must be open to their environment. They must take in those energies or substances they need for their survival, use them up, and get rid of what they cannot use. They must self-regulate. "*Openness* refers to the energy import activities of the system, which it needs to 'stay in the same place,' that is to maintain its own dynamic steady-state" (Laszlo, 1996, p. 32). For example, as a living system, the human body must take in air, food, and water or it will close down and eventually die. To assure an effective small group process, we must maintain openness to the environment—to the context of energy and ideas in which the group operates.

In addition to being open and receptive to their environments, small groups need to examine the input for relevance and integrity. Just as the human body filters what it needs for its well-being from its inputs of food, water, and air and discards what is useless or harmful, so small groups must filter the input they receive to function effectively in their environments.

Transformation.   Groups represent an ongoing system of interaction, in which information and energy are taken in, processed (or filtered), and expressed in new forms (transformed). In other words, input undergoes a *transformation* into output through various interactive processes. For example, if we are working on redesigning an automobile in response to poor sales of our existing cars, we would do well to listen to the consumers who are telling us what they want. However, we also need to filter what the consumers say they want against what they are actually buying—in terms of style, price, or gas mileage. After receiving and filtering the input, we then work it into our new car design—we transform it. Without that openness to the environment and processing (transforming) of the input, we could end up designing a car that either perpetuates old, failed ideas or meets consumers' ideas of what they think they want but is too expensive to buy and run or too unusual in appearance and is not what they actually choose to buy. Thus, openness to input—information—is required, but the information needs to be filtered and transformed.

A group meeting to decide how best to develop the new automobile designs suggested by consumers would start by looking at data (*input*)—the characteristics of the existing cars, how these characteristics differ from what consumers say they want, how much it would cost to make the changes, what price increase consumers will absorb, and which changes are most important. With each round of discussion, new input is required. It is examined, discussed, and disputed (transformed), and then solutions are proposed or new questions are raised (*output*). The more complex the problem, the more iterations of input–transformation–output the group goes through in its process. This process is possible because groups are open or permeable to some degree and because the synergy of the group process permits the processing and transformation of ideas.

Interdependence.   Basic to the synergy of small groups is the *interdependence* of its members. To the extent that members depend on one another and share in responsibility for the group process, the group gains the benefit of the shared ideas and interactions. When members are *in*dependent, for example, rather than *inter*dependent, the group reverts to a simple collection of individuals. In basketball, five independent players cannot win many ball games. Even a single outstanding player cannot win without the support and mutual cooperation of other team members. The star player depends on others to pass the ball, work it down the court, and set up the shots. In addition, one inspired and talented player working interdependently with teammates can inspire those less gifted to play better than they might on their own. Although many of us have felt the frustration of trying to work with team or group members who did not carry their load, most often there is some mutual benefit to remaining involved and connected with the other members, and it can outweigh the negative aspects of depending on non-supportive group members. When difficulties do arise, it is time to look to communication strategies to help the group or team reach its common goal. Taking advantage of interdependence requires learning how to work with the other members. For example, when the records of 23 National Basketball Association teams from 1980 to 1994 were compared, the teams with the most "shared experience"—playing time together or low turnover—had the best win/loss records (Koretz, 2002).

Feedback. Giving and receiving *feedback* is an important consideration in small group communication. A group must pay attention both to the feedback that it receives from its larger environment in the form of its initial charge and directions and to the response to its presentations. It must also recognize the processes, style, content, and effect of the feedback that it provides its members. Positive feedback encourages creativity among group members and suggests an appreciation for diversity in thinking, perspectives, and opinions. Negative feedback encourages a reduction in deviation and can fulfill a corrective function to help keep the group on task, but it can also reduce creativity. If a group wants to consider new and different ideas, it needs positive feedback that encourages deviations from the expected ways of thinking and of doing things. If the goal is to maintain the status quo, negative feedback lets us know when we have strayed too far from it.

If I use *Robert's Rules of Order* (Robert, 1990) to maintain strict control over a small group discussion, I may be engaging in negative feedback. When I call the question or rule someone out of order, I have decided that he or she has violated the expected direction of the discussion or has veered off course. This kind of strict adherence to rules is likely to stifle creativity. In most organizations, pushing for changes that actually create improvement in product or performance requires positive feedback, in order to move people away from their habitual practices. After all, if the "old" ways were working, there would be no problems to address. Consideration of alternative points of view is a recognition of the role of positive feedback in helping to make the best decisions. The constructive use of feedback also helps prevent entropy.

Entropy. Living systems tend toward *entropy*—that is: disorganization, stagnation, and chaos. Without the energizing effect of new input, systems tend to lose focus and organization. They tend to stagnate. By increasing inputs of energy and information, groups can prevent entropy, but too much energy or information overload can cause chaos and disorganization. Openness and the filtering of inputs help keep the energy balance in a satisfactory state. Groups monitor and control their internal dynamics through the use of feedback. Pincus, Fox, Perez, Turner, and McGeehan (2008) examined entropy in small group conversational turn-taking dynamics. They found a drop in the complexity of turn-taking patterns and creativity in groups experiencing unresolved conflict.

When a group senses that it is overstimulated and is veering too far from its intended purpose, it can use negative feedback to keep itself from heading toward self-destruction. If everyone is talking at once and no one is listening, very little can be accomplished, and someone needs to insist on some degree of order. On the other hand, an overdependence on control or too many limits on new ideas through negative feedback lead to stagnation and entropy. When we as members of groups balance these competing forces, our groups can begin to move forward successfully, with an appreciation of equifinality.

Equifinality.   There is more than one way to skin a cat, suggests an old expression. *Equifinality* refers to the fact that living systems can take different routes to the same destination. There does not have to be a specific formula for how every group operates to achieve success. If you are interested in maintaining your physical health, you can watch your diet, do aerobics, lift weights, play sports, or combine any of these or other activities. So, too, can different groups achieve successful results by taking advantage of the unique combination of characteristics and strengths of their particular group.

Environment.   As we noted earlier, small groups are systems within systems. These larger systems form the *environment* within which they operate. Sometimes the processes that keep individual small groups functioning work against the larger good of the system on which it depends. The federal government is a system with many smaller systems subsumed within it. Frequently, one subsystem, open and responding to the needs of its immediate environment, works in direct opposition to another, to the detriment of the whole. For example, from 1988 to 1992, the Department of the Interior spent $66 million subsidizing the cost of irrigating farmlands to produce corn, barley, rice, and cotton. During the same period, the Department of Agriculture paid the same farmers $379 million to limit surplus crop production (Barr, 1993). Until these two departments broaden their perspectives to include the whole of the larger agricultural processes in which they both participate, they will perpetuate waste and ineffectiveness and, ultimately, we can assume, will exhaust the financial resources on which the health and maintenance of each of the agricultural subsystems depends. Therefore, to the extent possible, small groups or teams, as systems within systems, must understand and accommodate the totality of their environments.

Because diversity is a vitally important issue, we have devoted an entire chapter to enhance our understanding of it (see Chapter 5). However, two examples regarding diversity provide useful insights into the systems–subsystems connection (Gardenswartz & Rowe, 1993). When people are asked the benefits and challenges of living and working in a multicultural environment, they often mention differences in eating habits and conceptions of time.

At a lunch at a management meeting, the entrée is quiche lorraine made with ham. Two managers never touch their plates. Why? There could be several reasons, but a likely one would be religious prohibitions against certain foods. Kosher food laws adhered to by some Jews prohibit the eating of pork and shellfish. Devout Muslims also refuse pork and alcoholic beverages. Hindu religious beliefs prohibit the eating of meat of any kind. In addition, many individuals choose to eat a vegetarian diet. These subsystems prevail in spite of the possible clash with other subsystems because of the depth of individuals' beliefs.

Likewise, time consciousness on the part of Americans often clashes with the *mañana* attitude in Mexico and the *Inshallah* of the Arab world. While time is money in the United States, time is considered more elastic and relevant in terms of *mañana,* or sometime in the future, and of *Inshallah,* which may mean whenever it comes to pass. For some Americans, accepting that both views are legitimate perspectives often proves difficult and, ironically, time-consuming.

The massive increases in intranet and Internet connections have expanded the small group's universe. Not only is there a great deal more information available, but opportunities to connect digitally rather than in face-to-face group meetings have increased, allowing individuals from around the globe to participate in real-time decisions (Hof, 2005). Information, albeit not always accurate, is widely available. As of 2005, "53 million Americans have contributed material to the Net, from product reviews to eBay ratings, according the Pew Internet & American Life Project" (Hof, 2005, p. 81). The implications of these trends are discussed throughout this textbook.

Complex Systems

In addition to being open systems, small groups are also self-organizing *complex systems*. Small group communication processes are disorderly, discontinuous, chaotic, and transformational. Pincus and colleagues (2008) suggested that when people begin a process of information exchange, as they do in small groups, a global order emerges through their group interaction. Small groups evolve by managing their flows of information and becoming more or less flexible and complex in their discussion, depending on the conditions within the group and their environment. Being aware of these characteristics of complex systems and their interplay can help group participants to appreciate more fully the communication processes that occur and to make effective use of them in their group's interaction. Through their communication, small groups are capable of what has been called second-order or quantum change and of double-loop learning (Gemmill & Wynkoop, 1991) and participate in systems that show a sensitivity to initial conditions, the presence of strange attractors, phase space, bifurcation points, and irreversibility (Fuhriman & Burlingame, 1994).

Second-Order or Quantum Change.   Openness and change are essential small group communication processes. Groups transform themselves simply by their acts of communicating, learning, making decisions, solving problems, and even just being together. This transformation may be of two types. The first type, known as *first-order change,* involves a change in the content or topic of the group discussion. This type of change may involve moving from one issue to another or moving from one phase of problem solving or decision making to the next. These changes are relatively straightforward, are often explicitly undertaken, and do not require a change in the group members themselves or in the way they interact.

The second type of change, *second-order* or *quantum change,* describes a change in the group context or dynamic. It entails a change in the quality of the group interaction itself. If, for example, a group has developed a norm of polite, rational, and non-hostile discussion and at some point in that discussion a member of the group becomes angry, claims the group is ignoring the real problems by not addressing the underlying issues, and storms out of the meeting, the group is faced with responding to that outburst. The group may choose to treat it as an anomaly and ignore it, assuming, implicitly or explicitly, that the outburst is unique to that member or circumstance. The group may attribute it to a personality trait, to a temporary response to a stressful life situation, or to a "power play" enacted to control the group discussion around a particular issue. As coping techniques, none of these responses involves a transformational change for the group. If, however, the group uses the outburst as an opportunity to reflect on its group process and to establish new patterns of interaction, then the group itself has undergone a transformation. When the transformation is positive and constructive, this second-order change may result in new levels of trust, sincerity, and openness among group members, as an extension of their expanded ways of communicating with each other. On the other hand, the resultant second-order change may disrupt the ongoing work of the group. If the outburst triggers hidden hostilities in other members, it may irreparably harm the group process, causing the group to lose cohesion. Effective groups are those that can recognize these points of choice and change and understand the potential inherent in them for positive transformation.

Double-Loop Learning.   *Single-loop learning* is learning the particular procedures for doing something. *Double-loop learning,* on the other hand, is understanding the principles that underlie those procedures in ways that allow us to extrapolate, combine, and creatively invent new processes and procedures. It combines intuitive, "commonsense" understanding with the more solidly grounded information-based knowledge. The following analogy distinguishes between the single-loop learning of a cook and the double-loop learning of a chef. A cook is a person who can competently follow a recipe or learn the procedure for preparing a certain type of food. A good cook is one who follows a good recipe carefully and, therefore, prepares good-tasting food. A chef, however, understands the ingredients and processes described in the recipe and can read multiple recipes for the same dish and then extrapolate from the best of each recipe to create a new and unique dish similar to but not exactly like any of those recipes. While a cook depends on having the precise ingredients on hand to make a specific recipe, a chef is able to make a delicious dish with what she or he has on hand. The chef does more than memorize the quantities of individual ingredients or learn the specific procedures for preparation. A chef understands a set of general principles for preparing the dish and, based on the knowledge of these principles, can improvise and create a new dish.

Double-loop learning permits individuals and groups to apply general principles, without being tied to an exact replication of earlier successes. It depends on understanding the overriding concepts behind the procedures. Double-loop learning is important to small group communication processes, because these processes are dynamic and never happen exactly the same way twice. There is no one recipe for successful group communication. To be effective, members of small groups and teams have to learn the concepts and principles behind the processes and then, like a chef, reinvent the particulars of the process in each new group context.

Sensitivity to Initial Conditions.   In complex, chaotic systems, such as small groups, tiny variations in *initial conditions* can produce very large effects in subsequent events; and the same (or apparently same) influence can have substantially different consequences at different times in the process or in slightly different sets of circumstances. The impact of this observation on small group dynamics can be substantial, and it suggests at least two consequences. One is that first impressions are important. A second is that the same behavior may be perceived differently, depending on the context and the group's perceptions of the person doing the behaving. Although all of the consequences of first impressions may not become apparent for some time, even in "zero history" or newly formed groups, reputations, appearance, and personal style often precede us and provide information that may influence the group process in some unexpected way. First impressions create a baseline on which subsequent interactions are built. In addition, we have all probably felt the appropriateness or inappropriateness of a particular behavior in a given situation. Whereas one person may get away with a crude comment in a meeting and even be thought funny, another may be considered rude or embarrassing. However, depending on other factors, if either of these people had chosen a different time to make the comment, their receptions might have been different. Individual characteristics and interpersonal relationships within groups, as well as timing and circumstances, affect who can say what when.

First impressions interact with group relationships and expectations to establish patterns of response. For example, if I am 15 minutes late for the first group meeting, my being even 2 minutes late for the second one may cause other group members to comment on my "always being late." On the other hand, if I have always been on time for meetings and am then late for two meetings in a row later in the group process, my tardiness might go unmentioned or receive a different reaction from the group. Similarly, if I have contributed substantially to the group process, my late arrival for a meeting might receive little negative attention, whereas if I have been perceived as a nonproductive or obstructive group member, even a small infraction of the group norm might bring a harsh censure from other members.

Strange Attractors.   Group process evolves and takes on complex patterns. These patterns of communication and behavior are more or less constructive, are often not created or caused by any one individual or other particular influence, and, while non-repeating in an exact way, take on a recognizable form as the group is drawn into certain communication styles, topics, metaphors, turn-taking patterns, and energy levels. The complex of influences that underlie these patterns are called *strange attractors,* because even though their influence is often readily apparent, the cause of these influences frequently remains unidentified or unknown. The importance of this concept to small group communication is that it locates these attractors in the group and its processes, rather than in individual styles, personality conflicts, or other sources of individual influence. By locating the influences in the group process itself, this concept recognizes both the complexity of interaction patterns and the responsibility of the group and its participants to observe, reflect on, and take responsibility for the effectiveness of that process. We, the group members, are the system. While none of us individually, or even collectively, can control that system of communication, we do influence its patterns.

In other words, seemingly benign activities can create important influences on how the group functions and succeeds. When these attractors are assigned meaning by the group, they influence its patterns and processes (Wheatley, 1998).

Phase Space.   Systems change in time as they take in and transform information and meaning. *Phase space* describes a system's movements through time, particularly as it is affected by its sensitivity to initial conditions and strange attractors. In small groups, the communication itself changes as the group moves through different phases. Four relatively large, descriptive phases common in group development, growth, and change are the cycles of introduction (forming), conflict (storming), emergence (norming), and production (performing). The nature of these phases is described in greater detail in Chapter 4 and is mentioned here only as an example of the application of the concept of phase space to small groups. Phase space conceptualizes these descriptive phases as cycles that are recursive and dynamic. They are iterative because they repeatedly stretch and fold one into another (rather than building on each other in a straightforward linear relationship). Yet they are dynamic in their changing, spiraling, and growth. They spiral and build on each other, rather than return to their original starting places. Authentic group discussion and conflict require that a group has formed and members have gotten to know each other. Out of the knowledge of their different perspectives, conflict often emerges and can lead to a greater understanding on which the group can predicate its productive decision-making and problem-solving processes. Within that production phase, however, the additional greater understanding may stimulate additional conflict and even the formation of subgroup coalitions. These coalitions may themselves take different shapes as conflicts are resolved and new conflicts arise. Yet the group never truly returns to earlier phases but builds on them in ways that make these later phases qualitatively different in their interaction.

Bifurcation Points.   All moments or points in a group's process are not the same. Nor is the process one of stable, linear, and constant growth. Thresholds, or points of decision, are reached and crossed at times when the group is ready. *Bifurcation points* identify these decision points. At times, I have sat with a group of peers listening to a discussion, made a suggestion, and found my suggestion ignored, while the group went on discussing the issues. Fifteen or twenty minutes later, another group member suggested essentially the same idea and the group rallied around that as *the* answer, thanking and congratulating that member on the insight. When this occurs, I sometimes feel ignored, undervalued, and perhaps inarticulate in my ability to express ideas clearly, but often the group response has little to do with any of these factors; it has to do with my timing. The group had not reached the decision threshold at the time I made the suggestion and, therefore, could not hear and act on it. At other times, I have found myself not yet ready to make a decision when the group appeared to be at that threshold. I then have to decide how important that decision is to me. If it appears less important to me than to the others, I quietly let the group continue; but if it has particular significance for me, I may ask for a fuller explanation or further discussion, so that we can all move through the decision point together as a group.

Group communication and decision making happen at bifurcation points in time. To make effective contributions to the group, I have to be sensitive to where the group is in its process and communicate at a time in that process and in a way that helps the group move through the decision threshold. If I am early, the group may not be ready, but if the group is ahead of me, I may need to ask for help to catch up. Effective group process results when bifurcation points are negotiated and handled in ways that empower all group members to be involved in the decision making.

Irreversibility.   Group communication processes often appear to be cyclical, but as we noted earlier in discussing phase space and bifurcation points, they happen in time. Once something is said—whether in anger, frustration, enthusiasm, or excitement—it cannot be taken back and will have some impact on the participants and later group discussion. What is said may contribute to the effectiveness or the deterioration of the group process. Our groups may be able to move beyond it, incorporating it into our process and adding to our transformational growth, but we cannot truly start over. Each new beginning will be influenced by the past communication. Group communication happens within time and has, in that sense, the quality of *irreversibility*.

Example of Interactivity

Pincus and Guastello (2005) observed complex system patterns in five highly interactive qualities of small group communication: the group responses, rules, roles, relationships, and realities. They mapped the emergent processes of group conflict, closeness, and control onto these underlying patterns of interaction. Their analysis shows that group conflict generates reciprocal tensions within the relationships of the group in ways that stimulate both group coherence and change in the group's rules, roles, relationships, and realities. Interpersonal control, associated with leadership in the group, influences the group relational coherence. A change in leadership, for example, may stimulate an adaptation in group processes and can produce conflict and lead to a redefinition or the rules, roles, relationships, and realities of the group. Closeness plays a role in the group's ability to adapt, openly address and resolve its conflicts, and develop its decision-making processes (Pincus & Guastello, 2005). Their analysis provides an example of the complex sets of tensions and dynamics that exist in the communication processes of groups. These dynamics are presented in Table 2.2.

TABLE 2.2   Complex Systems Qualities Underlying Group Communication Processes

Quality	Definition
Responses	Verbal turn-taking patterns; who speaks to whom, when, and in what order
Rules	Often unstated guidelines for discussion of what may and may not be said and by whom
Roles	Personal boundaries; expectations for ways of interacting
Relationships	Role-interaction patterns among multiple group members
Realities	Schema guiding perceptual processes and judgments of group members: about each other, the group, its tasks, processes, and relationships

For more information, see Pincus and Guastello (2005).

This discussion of complex systems might seem, well, *complex,* but there are numerous examples of the influences of complex systems. One example is our first year of higher education with all the second-order changes (e.g., study habits, managing time), double-loop learning (making new friends, gaining skills), sensitivity to initial conditions (e.g., first week on campus), strange attractors (e.g., choosing a major), phase space (e.g., joining groups/organizations), bifurcation points (e.g., class discussion, group leadership), and irreversibility (e.g., choosing the college).

Summary

Systems thinking underscores the dynamic nature of groups. While there are limitations to systems thinking, as there are to any theoretical perspective, the basic elements of open systems (wholeness, synergy, openness, transformation, interdependence, feedback, entropy, equifinality, and environment) and of complex systems (second-order change, double-loop learning, sensitivity to initial conditions, strange attractors, phase space, bifurcation points, and irreversibility) all explain important characteristics of the small group communication process.

Underlying the application of a systems perspective to small group communication are five principles: (1) Communication is the study of meaningful behavior; (2) it is based on symbolic interpretation; (3) it is contextual; (4) it occurs in a complex open system; and (5) it involves multiple, embedded layers of simultaneous verbal and nonverbal elements of human communication. Small groups build on these basic communication principles, adding group and cultural norms and the roles group members play.

Small groups are both open and complex systems. We need to overlay our understanding of the open systems in which small groups operate with the concepts of sensitivity to initial conditions, the presence of strange attractors, phase space, bifurcation points, and irreversibility. In this way, we can appreciate the transformative roles of second-order change and double-loop learning in developing effective small group interactions.

DISCUSSION QUESTIONS

1. What are the advantages to having a small group effectiveness theory to guide you in your small group activities?

2. If groups are conceived of as living systems based on interdependence and interrelationships, what happens to a small group when parts of the system do not function well? Provide two examples from your own small group experiences that show the importance of understanding interdependence and interrelationships.

3. Explain the concept of transformation. Has this happened to your small group class since meeting the first day? Describe this process. Apply this concept to one of the classroom group exercises or to an example from small groups outside the classroom.

4. Explain how entropy and equifinality affect small group processes.

5. Describe an example of second-order change created in a small group in which you have participated. How does it differ from first-order change? Did double-loop learning occur? Explain.

6. Everyone has been advised to dress well for a job interview. How does this relate to first impressions? Why are first impressions important to a small group? Can you find examples other than dress or your first words that show the importance of first impressions?

7. Groups can take on peculiar characteristics. Describe how strange attractors, phase space, bifurcation points, and irreversibility affect the characteristics of a group. Find a small group experience for one of these characteristics. Can you or your group identify a small group experience that includes all four of these characteristics? Explain.

REFERENCES

Barr, S. (1993, January 25). $300 billion lost in waste, fraud, U.S. report claims. *Los Angeles Times,* p. B17.

Eisenberg, E. M., & Goodall, H. L., Jr. (2001). *Organizational communication: Balancing creativity and constraint.* New York: St. Martin's Press.

Fuhriman, A., & Burlingame, G. M. (1994). Measuring small group process. *Small Group Research, 25*(4), 502–519.

Gardenswartz, L., & Rowe, A. (1993). *Managing diversity: A complete desk reference and planning guide.* Chicago: Irwin.

Gemmill, G., & Wynkoop, C. (1991). The psychodynamics of small group transformation. *Small Group Research, 22*(1), 4–23.

Harris, T. E. & Nelson, M. D. (2008). *Applied organizational communication: Theory and practice in a global environment.* New York: Lawrence Erlbaum Associates.

Hof, R. (2005, June 20). The power of us: Mass collaboration on the Internet is shaking up business. *Business Week,* pp. 74–82.

Koretz, G. (2002, March 1). Chalk it up to teamwork. *Business Week,* p. 22.

Laszlo, E. (1996). *The systems view of the world: A holistic vision for our time.* Cresskill, NJ: Hampton.

Miller, J. G. (1978). *Living systems.* New York: McGraw-Hill.

Pincus, D., Fox, K. M., Perez, K. A., Turner, J. S., & McGeehan, A. R. (2008). Nonlinear dynamics of individual and interpersonal conflict in an experimental group. *Small Group Research, 39*(2), 150–177.

Pincus, D., & Guastello, S. J. (2005). Nonlinear dynamics and interpersonal correlates of verbal turn-taking patterns in a group therapy session. *Small Group Research, 36*(6), 635–677.

Robert, H. M. (1990). *Robert's rules of order* (Rev. ed.). Glenview, IL: Scott, Foresman.

Thomas, L. (1975). *The lives of a cell.* New York: Penguin.

Tubbs, S. L. (2001). *A systems approach to small group interaction* (7th ed.). Boston: McGraw-Hill.

Wheatley, M. J. (1998). Chaos and the strange attractor of meaning. In G. R. Hickman (Ed.), *Leading organizations: Perspectives for a new era* (pp. 158–176). Thousand Oaks, CA: Sage.

Wheatley, M. J. (2007). *Finding our way.* San Francisco, CA: Berrett-Koehler.

CHAPTER

3

Norms, Roles, Cohesion, and Groupthink

CHAPTER OUTLINE

Norms
   The Reason for Norms
   Types of Norms
   Norms and Diversity
   Violating Norms

Roles
   Types of Roles
   The Function of Roles

Cohesion
   Influences on Cohesion
   Consequences of Group Cohesion

Groupthink

Summary

Discussion Questions

References

CHAPTER OBJECTIVES

- Describe the importance and impact of group norms.
- Clarify the different types of group norms.
- Illustrate the concept of group roles.
- Outline the different types of roles.
- Discuss the functions of norms and roles.
- Describe group cohesion and groupthink.

KEY TERMS

Assigned roles	Explicit norm	Peripheral norm
Cohesion	Group norms	Role
Crucial norm	Groupthink	Social–emotional roles
Emergent roles	Implicit norm	Task roles

The Tour de France racers were riding together in a peloton from Bordeaux to Biarritz when, "with little warning, but as sometimes happens during long stages, somebody called for a bathroom break." Riders from the race's ten different teams hopped off their bikes to relieve themselves. Those who did not stop slowed down. Instead of extending this customary courtesy, French rider Dante Coccolo started to sprint while the others were taking their breaks, attempting to put a time gap between himself and the group. With luck and speed, he could even win this stage of the race; but his attempt backfired. He had breached peloton etiquette: "He had a habit of attacking on bathroom breaks," says Paul Sherwen, a Tour racer who was in the peloton that day. "He thought it was quite amusing. It's not illegal, but if 20 or 30 guys stop for a break and you go off on an attack, you're going to make 20 or 30 enemies. . . . When it was Coccolo's turn for his own bathroom break and he put his bike down on the grass, . . . a couple of guys slowed down and grabbed the bike. They wheeled it down the road for a kilometer or two and tossed it into a ditch. Everyone in the peloton was very happy about it." When Coccolo emerged from the woods, his bike was gone. He had to stand by the side of the road for five minutes until his team manager showed up in a sponsor car, put him on the hood, and drove him to retrieve his hijacked bike. Coccolo finished next to last that year, and he never rode in the Tour again.

(Hochman, 2006, p. 148)

Norms

Every group has a certain set of assumptions about how people are expected to behave. The standards vary with each group and within each group according to the different position or role each group member plays. The group leader and the newcomer, for example, are expected to behave differently. A newcomer may be expected to listen quietly and attentively rather than talk a great deal at the first meeting, while a leader is expected not only to talk but to have prepared an agenda for the meeting and to act to keep the group on task.

The Reason for Norms

Group norms define the nature of the group and the relationships among the group members by expressing the collective values of the membership and by identifying the place of group members within that value system. In every group, certain actions are approved of and others are frowned on. Knowing the norms means having a map, or a traveler's guide, for navigating the territory of group behavior and processes.

Group norms establish the accepted rules of behavior. They are the standards that regulate group members' behaviors (Hoigaard, Safvenbom, & Tonnessen, 2006). These standards represent the agreed-upon shared values, procedures, and beliefs that guide group members in their communication and group behaviors. In many cases, norms are prescribed by an organization's culture or by the prevailing understanding about how groups operate in a given situation. Norms define the nature of the group by telling us what we can and cannot do. The evolution of norms is inherent to the group development process.

Group norms are not imposed by some authority figure with power. They develop, emerge, and are accepted by group members as the common way of operating in the group. They may include the norms of the prevailing culture within which the group exists, as well as rules specific to the group itself. The etiquette we use when we go on a job interview is usually different from that we use to interact with our close friends. Most students and professors address each other more formally than they do their family members. These are the norms that we recognize and accept as part of the communication expectations within a specific cultural context and type of relationship. These cultural context expectations influence our small group communication patterns as well.

Norms influence our behaviors during the group process. They reduce ambiguity, help us to feel part of the group, and develop our overall sense of "groupness." We learn how to speak, who can participate at what time, who is deferred to on what subject matters, what can be talked about, the types of language and nonverbal communication we can use, and the numerous other standards governing our behavior. As operating procedures, norms have an important effect on how the group functions. A club, for example, might require those members arriving late for their 6:30 a.m. breakfast meeting to pay $1 for each minute they are late. This rule underscores the group norm of starting the meeting on time with everyone present. The payment of the late fee is voluntary and contributed by the member to stay within the accepted group norm.

Types of Norms

Norms can be crucial or peripheral to the group's task, and they may be stated explicitly or be implicit in the group's understanding. A *crucial norm* has a primary effect on how well the group performs its tasks. In some cases, this can be as simple as an expectation for regular, on-time attendance at meetings. In other cases, this can relate to how each member will contribute to accomplishing the task. Violation of a crucial norm usually brings some type of censure from the group. A *peripheral norm* outlines behaviors that should be engaged in or avoided but these are rarely essential to the effective functioning of the group. Violation of a peripheral norm—such as poor social etiquette, occasional bad manners, or mildly inappropriate behavior—makes us uncomfortable but may or may not be sanctioned by the group.

Norms can also be explicitly stated or implicitly understood within the group. An *explicit norm* is outlined in either written or oral form as a policy or group-sanctioned procedure. Attendance requirements, dress standards, task requirements, and important deadlines are, for example, often clearly stated. An *implicit norm* is an unstated preference of the group. Being courteous, bringing snacks, or doing a good job are often not clearly identified in the group's written guidelines or formal operating procedures but are understood as expectations of group members.

There are two key ways of identifying group norms. First, norms exist in the activities and behaviors that occur regularly. Group norms can be recognized in the communication interaction patterns of who talks to whom, what they talk about, whether there is an order or pattern to the sequence of who talks, which members stay after the meeting to chat, how seating is determined, and how the meeting is brought to order and closed. Second, a norm can be recognized when it is violated and the group reacts. What happens when someone brings up a taboo subject or interrupts someone else? A sudden group silence or negative response to a particular action indicates a violated group norm.

Norms and Diversity

The importance of understanding and being aware of norms is underscored when we examine the rapidly changing makeup of society, including dramatic changes in demographics, and in multicultural backgrounds and interests. The diversity of the United States workforce is growing rapidly. By the year 2050, "about half of all Americans will belong to what are now considered minority groups," according to the U.S. Department of Labor's 1999 report (Associated Press, 1999, p. 5B). In almost every aspect of life, we have increasing opportunities to work with diverse groups of individuals. Chapter 5 discusses the importance of diversity. The discussion here focuses on norms. As society changes, so do group and team norms.

In organizations, the predominant management culture of the past is being replaced with more diverse structures of organizing and more diverse voices of concern. Increasing diversity in the age, ethnic origin, cultural background, and personal characteristics of the population make an explicit discussion and understanding of group norms important. Group norms can no longer be taken for granted as preexisting and understood, but must be negotiated and accepted by all group members for a group to be effective in its communication and tasks. A survey of the Fortune 1000 companies reports that "91% of the respondents say their diversity initiatives help their organization to keep a competitive advantage" (Survey says, 2001, p. 8). "Corporations are urged to attend to diversity issues [in order] . . . to 'stay in business (and) thrive in the modern global environment'" (Nicotera, Clinkscales, Walker, 2003, p. 19).

To be effective in our communication we need to be aware of the effect of these changing norms. Otherwise, increasing diversity can create conflict in team-based work. Differences in age, background, ethnicity, religion, gender, education, work experience, and expectations can lead us to view the acts of others as deviant behavior. Today's organizations are "awash with the conflicting voices and views of the most age- and value-diverse workforce this county has known since our great-great-grandparents abandoned field and farm for factory and office" (Zemke, Raines, & Filipczak, 2000, p. 10). Even when focusing only on the values and expectations of the different generations currently at work, researchers draw critical distinctions among veterans (born between 1922–1943; 52 million people), baby boomers (born between 1943–1960; 73.2 million people), Generation Xers (born between 1960–1980; 70.1 million people), and Generation Nexters (born between 1980–2000; 69.7 million people) that affect how they view each other, work together in groups, and value their jobs (Zemke et al., 2000).

Violating Norms

We are likely to abide by group norms if we understand what they are, identify with the group's goals, plan to belong to the group for a long period of time, feel a high level of cohesiveness in the group, or decide that we are of lesser power or status than other group members. Conversely, if it is a one-time social gathering, we do not care about the group or its goals, or we believe we have more authority, power, or position than other group members, we might not feel as compelled to abide by the norms.

When group norms are violated, the group will usually impose some type of social sanction or punishment. This may be a light punishment that then increases in intensity if the norm is violated a second or third time. A first violation may mean that I am simply avoided or ignored for a while during the group process. For example, if I am 10 minutes late for a meeting, the group may not say anything the first time but also may not include me in the discussion for a while. If I am late a second time, when I arrive, group members may become more outspoken and express their irritation more directly through comments about my tardiness, or they may begin to joke about my attendance. If I am late a third time, they may express anger about my habitual lateness and remind me that it interferes with the group's ability to accomplish its task. In each case, the group is asking me to conform to the norm. The sanction imposed will also be contingent on the perception of my other contributions to the group and accomplishment of its task. If I am perceived as having contributed a great deal to the group and the achievement of its goals, my lateness to a meeting may be perceived as trivial and a sanction as unnecessary or inappropriate. If I am perceived as not having contributed my share to the group work overall, then my lateness to the meeting may become a focal point for the group's expression of anger toward my overall lack of contribution.

Few norms are carved in stone, however. Norms are socially constructed by the group and change as we move from group to group. Behavior that is severely sanctioned in one group may pass apparently unnoticed in another. It is important to remember, however, that groups take their norms seriously, and violating a norm can bring significant sanctions.

Group norms are not created or enforced by any one member and may change over time. Ultimately, they are maintained by the group as a whole. Although individuals may represent the group on occasion in making a norm explicit, it is the force of the group's sanction that makes a norm. Increasingly diverse groups can make norms difficult to maintain without scrutiny and challenge. Diversity brings new insights and reinterpretations of traditional group norms, and groups need to be continuously monitoring their norms to make sure they are inclusive of the diverse group members (DeNisi & Griffin, 2005).

Roles

Norms and roles are related but different from each other. Norms are expectations of behavior patterns for the group as a whole. Roles identify the particular way we, as individuals, are expected to act in a group. Hare (1994) stated that a *role* is associated with the position and status of a member in a group and implies the rights and duties of that member toward one or more other group members. Although this definition applies primarily to the formal group roles that members perform consciously, expectations are also associated with informal group roles. These expectations may become apparent only during the course of interaction in a group and thus may be less clear. They are, however, expectations just the same.

Just as norms direct the behavior of the group, roles apply to a particular individual's behavior: "Roles are 'packages' of norms that apply to particular group members" (Johns, 1988, p. 246). For example, we might expect someone to take notes at our meetings and distribute them to every member. The group norm of note taking suggests a specific role for a member, even if the member taking notes changes with each meeting.

Types of Roles

Scholars have divided roles into two general categories: (a) those that take into consideration the importance of the group's task and (b) those roles necessary for the social and emotional needs of the group (Ketrow, 1991). *Task roles* relate to getting the job done. *Social–emotional roles* relate to the group's climate and working relationships. Both types of roles are essential for a group to be effective. Task role specialists help move the group toward its goal attainment and help the group adapt to changes in needs and accomplishments along the way. Social–emotional role specialists assist the group with its social maintenance functions and develop ways of expressing and dealing with the emotional dimensions of discussion. In addition to these group roles, individuals also sometimes take on self-centered behaviors that focus on an individual's needs and may be detrimental to the overall group process. Table 3.1 describes these roles and behaviors.

The usefulness of role descriptions is in showing the many ways a participant can influence a small group's process. Effective group members frequently take on a variety of roles simultaneously.

In addition, groups can present difficult situations with multiple role expectations for members, so that what is expected of us in a group is not always clear (Hare, 1994). Sometimes group roles appear to collide and conflict, or may be confused by ambiguous or incompatible sets of expectations. You might be asked, for example, to be a group leader when, because of other obligations to the group, you do not have the time and energy needed to undertake the job. You might then experience role conflict (Griffin, 2005). At another time, you may not be certain what role to play or you may experience multiple and contradictory role demands from the group, leading to a sense of role ambiguity (Griffin, 2005). You experience role conflict when you are expected to act in a manner different from what you perceive to be your desired or designated group role, and role ambiguity when the role you are expected to play is unclear. An example of role conflict is being put in charge of a group when you do not want to or cannot take on the responsibility. Everyone in the group says you are a natural-born leader. You want no part of this role but accept it because of group pressure. An example of role ambiguity occurs when a group wants your input and leadership but does

TABLE 3.1   Group Roles

Group Task Roles	Group Maintenance Roles	Self-Centered Behaviors
Initiating: Proposing new ideas; proposing goals, plans of action, or activities; orienting; prodding the group to greater activity; defining the position of the group in relation to an external structure or goal; offering suggestions and approaches.	**Encouraging:** Praising; expressing warmth, support, and appreciation; recognizing the value of others' contributions; indicating positive feeling toward group members; reinforcing group unity and cohesiveness.	**Blocking:** Preventing progress toward group goals by constantly raising objections, repeatedly bringing up the same topic or issue after the group has considered and rejected it; preventing the group from reaching consensus; refusing to go along, accept, or support a group decision.
Elaborating: Clarifying ideas or suggestions; expanding ideas or suggestions; developing a previously expressed idea; providing examples, illustrations, and explanations.	**Supporting:** Agreeing or expressing support for another's belief or proposal; following the lead of another member; accepting another's suggestions and contributions.	**Being Aggressive:** Criticizing; threatening other group members; being a "noble fighter" preventing collaboration.
Coordinating: Integrating; putting together parts of various ideas; organizing the group's work; promoting teamwork and cooperation.	**Harmonizing:** Helping to relieve tension; mediating differences; reducing secondary tension by reconciling disagreement; suggesting a compromise or a new acceptable alternative; working to reconcile angry members.	**Withdrawing:** Remaining indifferent; refusing to contribute; avoiding important differences; refusing to cope with conflicts; refusing to take a stand; covering up feelings; giving no response to comments.
Summarizing: Pulling work and ideas together; orienting the group; reviewing previous statements; reminding the group of items previously mentioned or discussed.	**Gatekeeping:** Keeping communication channels open; helping "quiet" members get the floor and be heard; suggesting turn taking or a speaking order; asking someone to offer a different opinion.	**Dominating:** Interrupting; refusing to accept others' conclusions as being as valid as one's own; forcing a leadership role.
Recording: Keeping track of the group's work; keeping group records, preparing reports and minutes; serving as group secretary or historian.	**Process Observing:** Making comments on how the group is working, how the members are coordinating and working together.	**Status or Recognition Seeking:** Stage hogging, boasting, and calling attention to one's expertise or experience when not necessary to credibility or relevant to group's task; game playing to elicit sympathy; switching subject to area of personal expertise.
Evaluating: Critiquing ideas or suggestions; expressing judgments on the merits of information or ideas; proposing or applying criteria for evaluating information.	**Setting Standards:** Helping to set goals and standards for the group; assisting in setting norms or making norms explicit; suggesting rules of behavior for members; challenging unproductive ways of behaving; giving a negative response when another violates a rule or norm.	
Giving or Seeking Information: Presenting data; offering facts and information, evidence, or personal experience relevant to the group's task; asking others for facts and information, evidence, or relevant personal experience; asking questions about information provided by others; requesting evaluations; asking if the group is reaching consensus.		

TABLE 3.1   *(continued)*

Group Task Roles	Group Maintenance Roles	Self-Centered Behaviors
Opinion Giving: Stating beliefs, values, interpretations, judgments; drawing conclusions from facts and information.	**Tension Relieving:** Using humor or joking or otherwise relieving tension; helping new members feel at ease; reducing status differences; encouraging informality; stressing common interests and experiences within the group; developing group narratives, themes, and fantasies to build a common spirit and bond or to test a tentative value or norm.	**Special-Interest Pleading:** Demanding group time and resources for special-interest pleading; constantly advocating for one's subgroup or special interest; not allowing group influence over one's perceived self-interests.
Clarifying: Interpreting issues; making ambiguous statements more clear; asking for examples or further clarification.		
Consensus Testing: Asking if an apparent group decision is acceptable to all; suggesting that an agreement may have been reached and asking for verification of that agreement.		
Proposing Procedure: Suggesting an agenda of issues or a decision-making method; proposing a procedure to follow.		

not provide any guidelines for what is needed and, in practice, appears to neither want or accept your input or leadership. Role conflict and role ambiguity can be difficult problems for individuals and groups to deal with and may require either role analysis to determine what is expected of a particular role or role negotiation to ensure a common understanding of the role among all group members.

The Function of Roles

In addition to these issues, Bales (1950) identified four functional characteristics of roles that can create problems for groups. Certain roles can create privileged positions that allow (a) greater access to resources, (b) more direction of and control over other persons, (c) increased status—a sense of importance and prestige within the group, and (d) a greater sense of involvement in and identification with the group. Negotiating resources, direction, status, and involvement can at times be difficult for a group to manage and can create tensions among group members.

Because a small group is a collection of individuals bound together with some common purpose, the members each have an interest in playing their respective roles to achieve that purpose. In general, group members work to foster favorable impressions of themselves; to organize their multiple relationships with other group members; to develop a common understanding shared among group members of the group's goals, ambitions, preferred style of meeting, communicating, and accomplishing tasks;

and to express their feelings and thoughts while not exposing their personal vulnerabilities to too great an extent. Along these lines, Bochner (1984) developed a typology of five communication role functions that apply to communication in small groups: "(1) to foster favorable impressions; (2) to organize the relationship; (3) to construct and validate a conjoint worldview; (4) to express feelings and thoughts; and (5) to protect vulnerabilities" (p. 583). These functions are carried out both by the individual group members in their interactions with one another within the group and by the group as a whole in its interactions with the larger external world.

The roles we assume within a group to help it accomplish these goals are the consequences of several factors. Roles can be determined, assigned, or emergent. Some roles are determined by external factors. For example, in our families, the roles of mother, father, sister, brother, daughter, son, or cousin are determined by the nature of the relationships. While each of us may act out our roles with some creativity and deviation from an established social norm, certain behaviors and expectations are fairly standard (for example, taking care of children). Formal or *assigned roles* exist in most small groups and include note taking, scheduling, or chairing. *Emergent roles* are worked out among the members of the group. These roles are negotiated as the group activity proceeds and result from the interaction of the group members. For example, someone might be assigned the role of chairperson only to find out that a colleague has the expertise and experience to deal with a particular issue. For a while, that person will emerge as the group leader even though another person was explicitly assigned that role.

As systems thinking would predict, each group will develop a different set of roles for its participants. In one group, we might be the leader, in another the devil's advocate. At other times, we might be a newcomer or decide to be a silent observer. We accept these roles through the process of role assumption—trying to act in accordance with the expected behaviors anticipated by the group and with the norms associated with that role. Although the particular role may seem simple when it is described, the actual acceptance and acting out of the role can prove to be difficult.

Cohesion

"Group *cohesion* refers to the degree to which an individual member of a group feels an attraction to the group" (Schwarz & Schwarz, 2007). It "is the extent to which members are loyal and committed to the group" (Griffin, 2005, p. 629), creating a "force that binds group members together" (Keyton & Springston, 1990, p. 234). Although the group task and structure tend to be set, cohesion is a result of how well group members interact. Groups are not doomed to failure if the members do not get along, but cohesive groups fulfill important needs for the group members, increasing their willingness to contribute to the group. There is a relationship between group cohesion and decision quality, task performance, and satisfaction (Schwarz & Schwarz, 2007). Cohesive groups are more effective, more satisfied, and tend to make better decisions.

The degree of positive feeling felt in cohesive groups affects member participation and helps keep members motivated and willing to contribute extra time and effort to the group and to completion of its tasks (Schwarz & Schwarz, 2007). In more cohesive

Teams pursue common purposes based on forces that bind them together.

groups, members converse freely, are more interested in the achievements of the group, attend and actively participate in group functions, are interested in the activities of other members, willingly assist each other in achieving the group's tasks, and identify with the group in their use of language, speaking of "we" and referring to non-group members as "they" (Griffin, 2005).

Influences on Cohesion

There are a number of influences on the development of group cohesion. The size of the group, the background similarity of group members, the members' satisfaction with the task in which they are engaged and contentment with the social aspects of the group, and the success of prior group performance all contribute to a greater sense of group cohesion. Larger groups, for example, may find it more difficult to develop social and task cohesiveness among members than smaller groups do.

Hoigaard and colleagues (2006) reported a relationship among group norms, cohesion, and social loafing. They demonstrated that cohesive groups whose members have positive perceptions of the group's productivity and social support norms have reduced perceptions of social loafing among the group members. Social loafing describes a reduction in motivation and effort made by some members in a group. This reduction in the effort made by a few can ultimately reduce the group's overall performance. Social loafing can become endemic to the entire group process. When some members are perceived as "going along for the ride" without investing themselves heavily or contributing fully to the group's work, other members may reduce their effort to avoid the "sucker" role of doing an unfair portion of the group work. If this occurs, the group productivity norm may become one of expecting less of its members and producing less overall as a group. Group norms are moderators in this cohesion–performance relationship. Groups with high member cohesion and high group performance norms are typically the most effective and best performing groups (Hoigaard et al., 2006).

Cohesion develops in groups through communication among group members and with an increased pressure for conformity to group norms. Explicitly clarifying group goals, identifying member roles, and encouraging member involvement in the decision-making process—all contribute to greater group cohesion. Other influences, such as soliciting full member involvement in the decision-making process, involving members in clarifying group goals and member roles, and recognizing members' contributions, serve to develop group cohesion and reduce social loafing, as well. Finally, successfully accomplishing tasks, being productive, and being recognized as a successful group also strengthen and encourage group cohesion.

In addition, Mason (2006) indicated that there are a number of group influences that lead toward a convergence in group member perceptions, attitudes, and behavior. The shared work experience of being a group member; the self-selecting attraction–selection–attrition cycle through which people continue to participate in groups in which they have the most in common and drop out of groups with which they have less in common; the social pressure of the group itself toward greater uniformity in perceptions, attitudes, and beliefs; the individual's social identity of being a member of the group and hence thinking like a group member; and the emotional-contagion process through which human beings engage in behavioral mimicry and catch emotions from each other all guide individual group members toward greater homogeneity in attitudes, beliefs, and perceptions within the group.

Consequences of Group Cohesion

Cohesion produces many positive benefits for the group, such as good feelings about the group and membership in it, fulfillment of certain personal needs, the opportunity for personal expression, and feelings of personal success and productivity. Group cohesiveness enhances the group's decision-making process, the quality of the decisions made, and the overall productivity of the group. So, cohesion is an important factor for any group process. In general, group cohesion and performance are positively related (Griffin, 2005; Hoigaard et al., 2006). However, too much group cohesion can impair the decision-making process and even encourage groupthink (Mullen, Anthony, Salas, & Driskell, 1994).

Groupthink

Bridgestone Tire and Ford Motor Company made the news in 2000 for a series of decisions having tragic results. The Bridgestone/Firestone ATX and Wilderness tires mounted on the Ford Explorer were blamed for more than 270 deaths and 800 serious accidents ("Bridgestone and Ford," 2005). Evidence indicated that Bridgestone/Firestone had been aware of the problem since 1996 yet continued to supply the tires. Ford also appeared to have been aware of the problem but chose to discount its significance—perhaps because the Explorer was the best-selling Ford vehicle and accounted for one-fourth of Ford's sales (Healey & Nathan, 2000). In response to mounting pressure, however, 6.5 million tires were recalled in August 2000. Ford offered replacements through any tire dealership, and the inevitable lawsuits against Ford and Firestone began (Thomas, 2006). As early as 1996, a group of personal-injury lawyers and one of the nation's top traffic safety consultants had identified a pattern of failures in the Firestone ATX tires on Ford Explorers (Bradsher, 2001). However, they also had decided not to tell the National Highway Traffic Safety Administration (NHTSA) because they were "leery" of how NHTSA would handle the information. Dr. Ricardo Martinez, who administered the agency from 1994 to 1999, said this behavior appalled him. He pointed out that withholding the information meant the lawyers appeared to be putting their own possible benefits from winning personal injury cases and getting financial rewards above the needs of the public, which "would clearly be unethical" (Bradsher, 2001, p. 1A).

In 2000, the University of Wisconsin–Madison inserted the photo of an African American male into a crowd of white football fans for its fall admissions brochure (Wyatt, 2000). The digitally altered cover was intended to convey an appearance of a diverse student body even though as of the fall 1999 semester, fewer than 10% of the school's more than 41,000 students were non-White, and only 2.15% were Black. The digitally enhanced picture on the front of that brochure created a storm of negative publicity and a moment of national embarrassment for the university. Unable to "find an authentic picture of diversity," the university had made a decision that ultimately required reprinting all 106,000 copies of the brochure at a cost of $63,000, just to remove the picture (Wyatt, 2000, p. 5A).

In a 1996 advertisement, Ford Motor Company removed the faces of Pakistani, Indian, and Black employees and superimposed white faces in a photo (Parker-Pope, 1996). The photo was printed in newspapers worldwide. The employees whose faces had been changed reacted with shock. Ford, although embarrassed, argued that the alterations reflected the ethnic makeup of Poland, which is almost exclusively white, and that the photo was intended for that country only. The pressures to appear diverse or to conform to a particular country's culture provide interesting examples of the power of groupthink. Publishing a digitally enhanced photo broadcasts a group's poorly conceived decision.

How do groups of intelligent, professional people make such ill-conceived decisions that produce such negative consequences for their company's public image? More than 35 years ago, Janis (1972; 1982) suggested that the answer is groupthink. *Groupthink* is defined by Janis as a strong concurrence-seeking tendency among group members that leads to a deterioration in their decision-making process. Janis identified five influences on groupthink: antecedent conditions, concurrence seeking, symptoms, decision-making defects, and poor decision outcomes. The antecedents to groupthink are high levels of group cohesiveness, a provocative situational context that creates a sense of urgency or high stress, group isolation from the thinking and ideas occurring outside of the group, and a lack of leader impartiality. Concurrence-seeking tendencies within the group persuade members to go along and openly agree with a perceived group position even if they privately disagree. This leads to the symptoms of groupthink expressed as a

FIGURE 3.1   Janis's Groupthink Framework

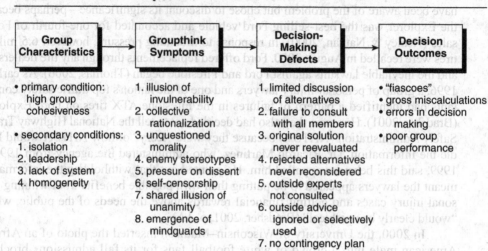

Group Characteristics	Groupthink Symptoms	Decision-Making Defects	Decision Outcomes

• primary condition: high group cohesiveness
 	
• secondary conditions:
  1. isolation
  2. leadership
  3. lack of system
  4. homogeneity
	1. illusion of invulnerability
	2. collective rationalization
	3. unquestioned morality
	4. enemy stereotypes
	5. pressure on dissent
	6. self-censorship
	7. shared illusion of unanimity
	8. emergence of mindguards
		1. limited discussion of alternatives
		2. failure to consult with all members
		3. original solution never reevaluated
		4. rejected alternatives never reconsidered
		5. outside experts not consulted
		6. outside advice ignored or selectively used
		7. no contingency plan
			• "fiascoes"
			• gross miscalculations
			• errors in decision making
			• poor group performance

pressure to conform, self-censorship, perception of out-group members, and an illusion of unanimity within the group. Decision-making defects include an incomplete assessment of alternatives, a failure to examine risks associated with the preferred choice, an inadequate search for information, a selective bias in processing the information, and a failure to consider alternative contingency plans. This generally leads to an inability to make high-quality decisions and to poor group decision-making outcomes. Henningsen, Henningsen, Eden, and Cruz (2006) suggested that groupthink really represents two processes that may occur concurrently among members of a group: Those group members who have a high-degree of confidence in a preferred group solution are emboldened as their preference is reinforced by the group discussion, while members who have more doubts about that solution experience increasing pressure to remain silent and comply.

Janis originally developed groupthink theory to explain the group processes leading up to: (a) the catastrophic Bay of Pigs decision by the United States to send Cuban expatriates on an invasion to overthrow the Cuban government, (b) President Kennedy's handling of the Cuban Missile Crisis, and (c) the U.S. march to war in Vietnam (see Figure 3.1). Other researchers have added analyses of such historic events as breaking into the Democratic headquarters at Watergate, the arms-for-hostages deal, the *Challenger* shuttle O-ring disaster, and the Hubble Telescope's flawed initial development as examples of poor decision making perpetuated by groupthink processes (Whyte, 1989). These historically significant decisions and events point to the key issue in groupthink. As group members, we too often unknowingly make achieving unanimity within the group or solving an immediate problem our goal rather than making the best decision.

Effective decision making depends on a full consideration of a variety of dissenting points of view. Group consensus is best achieved after a full and critical discussion of alternative views. When dissent is ignored, discussion is cut off, or consensus is arrived at too early, the quality of the group decision can suffer. Kroon,

TABLE 3.2   Janis's Groupthink Characteristics

Groupthink is evidenced when the following characteristics emerge during small group interactions:

1. Group members rush to a conclusion without considering all the alternatives.
2. Decisions are not carefully reexamined, even when there are indications of possible dangers.
3. Little time is spent discussing the reasons alternative courses of action were rejected.
4. The group limits itself to a small range of possible alternative courses of action.
5. Members create rationalizations to avoid dealing directly with warnings.
6. Group pressure is put on any individual who expresses doubts or questions the group's arguments or proposals.
7. Group members censure their own doubts.
8. Members believe everyone is in unanimous agreement without any testing of the premise.

Kreveld, and Rabbie (1992) suggest that more diverse, heterogeneously composed groups are less susceptible to groupthink. Greater diversity leads a group to critically evaluate ideas and arguments from multiple perspectives and makes it less likely to take on the groupthink characteristics identified in Table 3.2.

Summary

Norms, roles, cohesion, and the potential of groupthink all present challenges for effective small group discussion, decision making, and problem solving. A small group can improve its chances of being effective by including three elements in its discussions. First, the group should be conscious of the way it develops group norms and should explicitly review and discuss them, asking how effective they are for achieving group social–emotional and task needs. Second, group members should discuss the roles that they need to undertake. Before assigning roles, however, they should clarify the role expectations and when and how they need to be accomplished. Then, through group discussion and negotiation, they should match group members to appropriate, desirable, and compatible roles. Third, they should discuss group cohesion—how group members can maintain the social–emotional cohesiveness to work effectively together while still maintaining the critical differences in perspective necessary to withstand the threat of groupthink. Maintaining this balance can be difficult but is imperative for a group to maintain its long-term happiness, productivity, and effectiveness.

DISCUSSION QUESTIONS

1. Are there group norms at your educational institution? What are they? In the group of individuals you spend time with, are there group norms? What are they? In both cases, how did you identify these norms? How did you adapt to these norms?

2. What are the functions of norms in groups?

3. At this point in your small group and team communication course, what roles have you accepted and performed? Explain. Have you experienced any role conflict(s)? Explain.

4. Identify an emergent role.

REFERENCES

Associated Press. (1999, September 3). Demographics will challenge employers and government. *Tuscaloosa News*, p. 5B.

Bales, R. G. (1950). *Interaction process analysis: A method for the study of small groups*. Reading, MA: Addison-Wesley.

Bochner, A. (1984). The functions of human communication in interpersonal bonding. In C. Arnold & J. Bowers (Eds.), *Handbook of rhetorical and communication theory* (pp. 544–621). Boston: Allyn & Bacon.

Bradsher, K. (2001, June 24). Defects in SUV tires discovered, kept quiet by lawyers. *Tuscaloosa News*, pp. 1A, 8A.

Bridgestone and Ford settle dispute over defective tires. (2005, October 13). *New York Times*, p. C5.

DeNisi, A. S., & Griffin, R. W. (2005). *Human resource management* (2nd ed.). Boston: Houghton Mifflin.

Griffin, R. W. (2005). *Management*. Boston: Houghton Mifflin.

Hare, A. P. (1994). Types of roles in small groups. *Small Group Research, 25*(3), 433–448.

Healey, J. R., & Nathan, S. (2000, September 21). Further scrutiny puts Ford in the hot seat. *USA Today*, p. 1B.

Henningsen, D. D., Henningsen, M. L. M., Eden, J., & Cruz, M. G. (2006). Examining the symptoms of groupthink and retrospective sensemaking. *Small Group Research, 37*(1), 36–64.

Hochman, P. (2006, June 12). PACK mentality. *Fortune*, pp. 145–151.

Hoigaard, R., Safvenbom, R., & Tonnessen, F. E. (2006). The relationship between group cohesion, group norms, and perceived social loafing in soccer teams. *Small Group Research, 37*(3), 217–232.

Janis, I., (1972). *Victims of groupthink*. Boston: Houghton Mifflin.

Janis, I., (1982). *Groupthink* (2nd ed.). Boston: Houghton Mifflin.

Johns, G. (1988). *Organizational behavior: Understanding life at work* (2nd ed.). Glenview, IL: Scott Foresman.

Ketrow, S. M. (1991). Communication role specializations and perceptions of leadership. *Small Group Research, 22*(4), 492–514.

Keyton, J., & Springston, J. (1990). Redefining cohesiveness in groups. *Small Group Research, 21*(2), 234–254.

Kroon, M. B. R., Kreveld, D. van, & Rabbie, J. M. (1992). Group versus individual decision making: Effects of accountability and gender on groupthink. *Small Group Research, 23*(4), 427–458.

Mason, C. M. (2006). Exploring the process underlying within-group homogeneity. *Small Group Research, 37*(3), 233–270.

Mullen, B., Anthony, T., Salas, E., & Driskell, J. E. (1994). Group cohesiveness and quality of decision making. *Small Group Research, 25*(2), 189–204.

Nicotera, A. M., Clinkscales, M. J., Walker F. R. (2003). *Understanding organization through culture and structure*. Mahwah, NJ: Lawrence Erlbaum Associates.

Parker-Pope, T. (1996, February 2). Ford puts Blacks in whiteface, turns red. *Wall Street Journal*, p. B8.

Schwarz, A. & Schwarz, C. (2007). The role of latent beliefs and group cohesion in predicting group decision support systems success. *Small Group Research, 38*(1), 195–229.

Survey says diversity improves bottom lines and competition. (2001, July). *HR Focus*, p. 8.

Thomas, K. (2006, July 22). Firestone's manufacturers will notify owners of recalled tires. *Tuscaloosa News*, p. 5B.

Whyte, G. (1989). Groupthink reconsidered. *Academy of Management Review, 14*, 40–56.

Wyatt, S. (2000, September 23). Doctored photo highlights need to diversify. *Tuscaloosa News*, p. 5A.

Zemke, R., Raines, C., & Filipczak, B. (2000). *Generations at work: Managing the clash of veterans, boomers, Xers, and Nexters in your workplace*. New York: AMACOM.

CHAPTER 4

Phases of Group Development: Forming, Storming, Norming, and Performing

CHAPTER OUTLINE

Forming: Hello, Orientation, and Inclusion

Storming: Conflict in Groups

Norming: Emergence as a Group

Performing: Making Decisions and Solving Problems

Adjourning: Terminating, Saying "Good-Bye"

Usefulness of the Phase Model
   Modifications
   Organizational Teams

Overriding Influences
   Formal or Informal Group
   Task and Social Dynamics
   Primary and Secondary Tensions

Summary

Discussion Questions

References

CHAPTER OBJECTIVES

- Understand the four phases of group process.
- Explain the importance of the forming stage and its communication characteristics.
- Outline the factors occurring in the storming phase.
- Illustrate how the norming phase occurs.
- Discuss the performing phase.
- Show how the termination phase operates.
- Understand modifications to the phase model.
- Specify the kinds of communication occurring during each phase.
- Introduce the role of organizational teams.

KEY TERMS

Conflict
Emergence
Formal group
Forming
Informal group
Norming

Organizational teams
Performing
Phase model
Primary tension
Secondary tension
Social dynamics

Social loafing
Storming
Task dynamics
Termination

In 1974 I joined a men's group that formed after a weekend retreat in which we all participated. More than thirty years later, we are still meeting every Wednesday morning for seventy-five minutes before the workday begins. . . . These discussions are open, probing, and often profound. The key to their success is what we call "honest conversations," saying what you really believe without fear of judgment, criticism, or reprisal.

(George, 2007, p. 129)

Numerous models of group process development have been articulated over the years (see Table 4.1). Early developmental models tended to view group processes as linear paths. Recent models propose a cyclic, punctuated equilibrium process in which groups alternate between phases of action and inertia based on their awareness of time and deadlines, or as nonsequential phases with multiple paths to decision making that

TABLE 4.1   Models of Group Phase Development

Type of Group Model	Shown to Be Useful for Describing and Analyzing
Linear Models: path-dependent phase models	Decision-making, problem-solving group processes
	Developmental problem-solving group processes
	Ongoing task-oriented, self-analytic, work groups
	Management training groups
	Training new groups to identify and change aspects of group process
	Ongoing work group training to change group process and structure
Cyclic Models: path-dependent cyclical models	Therapy groups working through emotions
	Task-oriented groups dealing with drive-positive or -negative emotional reactions
	Cohesive groups dealing with issues of identification, self-awareness, groupthink
Nonsequential Models: non-path-dependent models	Work groups formed to concentrate on task-related, time-management strategies
	Multiple-function groups: particularly to develop mutual member support, productivity
	Ongoing decision-making groups; particularly to review decision-making processes

For more information, see Chang et al. (2006).

are contingent upon internal and external influences on the group (Chang, Duck, & Bordia, 2006). For our present purposes we draw on the insights of each of these multiple perspectives: linear, cyclic, and nonsequential. For clarity we will use only one naming convention to identify each of the phases but will work to describe the characteristics of the multiple processes within each of those phases.

Early group researchers, such as Tuckman (1965, 1977) and Fisher (1970), were among the first to identify group phases. Although not all groups follow them, or follow them in order, the phases describe common group experiences (Verdi & Wheelan, 1992; Wheelan & McKeage, 1993). Recognizing the phases can be important to facilitating group process because the communication of the group usually changes with the phase it is in. The way the group deals with these changes can affect how it deals with challenges and makes decisions.

Therefore, it would be misleading to suggest that the group process is always orderly or moves through these phases in a linear sequence, but a discussion of the phases provides a descriptive picture of what to expect, in a general way, of a group engaged in decision making and problem solving. If a group skips one of the phases, the resulting group decision-making process may be incomplete, or the phase may have to be revisited by the group at a later time.

In any case, there are some identifiable phases, and newly formed groups frequently go through them. These phases, following Tuckman (1965, 1977), have come to be known as forming, storming, norming, and performing. These stages are shown in Figure 4.1. *Forming* describes the initial orientation phase of getting to know other group members. *Storming* describes the conflict phase that often occurs once group members have gotten to know one another well enough and become comfortable enough to state their opinions openly and honestly. *Norming* describes the emergent process through which common group understanding, rules for discussion, focus on issues, and an orientation to task become established within the group. *Performing* describes the phase of task accomplishment, social reinforcement, and goal achievement. For many task-oriented groups, these phases are followed by a termination phase, once the task is accomplished.

FIGURE 4.1   The Four-Phase Model Plotted on an "S" Curve
This curve indicates that groups work through the phases, although not necessarily in the orderly pattern shown on this curve. At some point, the group will terminate or disband because their tasks have been completed. For teams, a point is reached at which some reforming is necessary to replace unnecessary steps, change ineffective procedures, or develop new goals.

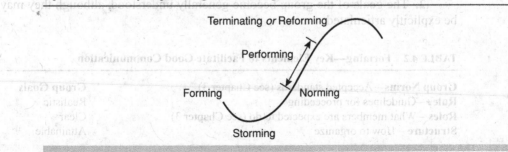

Forming: Hello, Orientation, and Inclusion

The first stage for any group is forming. During this period, we are deciding who we are as a group, what our purpose is, whether we want to be a member of the group, who the other group members are, and what our place or role will be in the group. This phase in group development focuses on issues of inclusion and attempts to identify the parameters of acceptable behavior within the group (Wheelan & McKeage, 1993). During this phase of a group's development, members are uncertain about the other members and how the actual group process will unfold and are often hesitant to contribute much (Wellings, Byham, & Wilson, 1991).

As a new group member, I observe you and you observe me. I would like to appear attractive, competent, pleasant, and bright. I am likely to smile, act pleasantly, and make small talk. Our communication is not likely to be overtly disagreeable, argumentative, confrontational, or overly revealing about our personal lives. I would like to know if you are friendly, intelligent, and agreeable or arrogant, mean, and hostile. You are likely to want to know the same about me. So, I will probably be polite, quiet, observant, and somewhat inquisitive.

This initial group meeting period holds some uneasiness, tension, and awkwardness that is normal and to be expected. We do not know one another well and have not as yet established our group operating procedures, norms, or roles. This sense of uneasiness and uncertainty is called *primary tension* and may be evidenced in the small talk, awkward silences, and search for friendly faces that often surround the initial conversations. When members introduce themselves and identify their reasons for being in the group, people gradually begin to relax. Humor can be used to release some of these tensions and feelings as well.

Once the primary tension is released, the group begins to devote itself to the task at hand, trying to define its purpose, establish some type of agenda, develop some working rules, and begin the group process. Important characteristics in this first phase are that most of the communication is tentative. As the group devotes itself to becoming oriented to its purpose, conflict is avoided, played down, or ignored, and group members usually ask more questions than make statements regarding their beliefs. The forming phase includes communication about the characteristics summarized in Table 4.2.

1. This phase contains a number of questions that can help group members develop a clear understanding of the task at hand.

2. The goals of the group become generally understood, although they may not be explicitly articulated.

TABLE 4.2   Forming—Key Elements to Facilitate Good Communication

Group Norms—Accepted standards (see Chapter 3)	**Group Goals**
Rules—Guidelines for proceeding	Realistic
Roles—What members are expected to do (see Chapter 3)	Clear
Structure—How to organize	Attainable

3. Some uncertainty regarding the group's task may be expressed. Articulating this uncertainty and the task at hand is important; otherwise, there may be only apparent or pseudo agreement, as members simply "go along to get along." A lack of a clear understanding and consensus on this task can create the basis for conflict later in the group process.

4. There may be some tentative role assignments. In particular, a leader is likely to emerge or be explicitly selected. Depending on the group, leadership may be seen as an important status symbol that can create difficulties during the storming phase, or it may be perceived as a simple formality or as necessary to the functioning of the group.

The key element to facilitate good communication in this phase is the establishment of group norms, rules, roles, and structure. Realistic, clear, and attainable group goals need to be established as well.

In general, this phase is marked for members by an initial uncertainty and often a hesitation to disclose personal information, creating a primary tension. Supportive group behaviors can help members build interpersonal trust and get better acquainted. Precautions should be taken to provide an open, safe environment for the giving and receiving of information and expression of feelings. Any issues of confidentiality must be understood so that group members can build interpersonal trust. It is important for members to explicitly assess their commitment to the group and the task, recognizing any ambivalence and coming to terms with any approach-avoidance feelings toward other group members, the task itself, and the time and energy commitments that will be required of them. The purpose of the group must be clearly and openly discussed so that members can match their individual expectations against the group's aim. Misconceptions concerning the purpose of the group and role confusion can create negative emotions that distort group functioning, leading to silent withdrawal by group members or expressive acting out of self-oriented roles by some members. These feelings may also affect attendance at meetings, timeliness in accomplishing tasks, and dropout rates of group members during the later phases of task accomplishment. During this first step in group formation, productivity and group accomplishments tend to be low since members are still exploring this new collective (Montebello, 1994, p. 35).

The group can maintain some flexibility in topic areas to be discussed to meet the needs of individuals in the group, but all topics should be put forward at this time. Once we get to know the members of a group, we may still experience anxiety about the group's overall purpose, process, and goals or about the other group members, their perspectives, and their intentions. These types of concerns, based on our understanding of the group and other group members, bring us to the second phase of group process—storming.

Storming: Conflict in Groups

The storming phase is the most complex phase in a group's process. *Conflict* frequently erupts over issues of power, authority, and competition within the group (Wheelan & McKeage, 1993). We have gotten to know each other well enough to work through our initial polite or "niceness" phase. Now we can be more honest and forthright in our opinions and positions. As this happens, we discover our areas of disagreement. Conflicts may occur over task issues as we begin presenting our ideas. Different views are expressed. Some are accepted; others are rejected. Members vie for control of the discussion. People take sides and break into different factions and coalitions. This is an important phase for the group, and rather than avoiding or glossing over conflict in this phase it should be seen as a way for a group to begin to define and deal with the difficult issues inherent in the task at hand.

Conflict occurs, in part, because group members are now comfortable enough with one another to present their real views and opinions. Do you argue more often with your friends or with strangers? With strangers, we tend to be more polite and "on our best behavior." With friends—the people we feel the most comfortable with, care about the most, spend the most time with, and who know us the best—we are likely to be more honest, forthright, and willing to state and argue our beliefs. Similarly, in small groups, as we get to know one another and each member's positions better, we are likely to become more honest and less tentative in stating our positions. This more open communication brings us into honest disagreements and conflict.

A number of theorists have suggested that this phase of group conflict is important to fostering subsequent group feelings of cohesion and cooperation, as well as leading to a more effective decision-making process (Verdi & Wheelan, 1992; Wheelan & McKeage, 1993). Yet, some groups become so concerned with these inevitable conflicts that they attempt to avoid them, and in avoiding them they avoid or suppress important aspects of the group's issues. This avoidance may create a *secondary tension* that stifles the development of long-term group cohesion and of effective group decision making and problem solving.

As the group continues to meet and the primary tension subsides, an interdependence based on sharing and association develops, resulting in a group identity and sense of cohesion. When we begin to feel part of the group we are responding to several positive developments (Cohen, Fink, Gadon, & Willits, 2001). These include a sense of purpose and clear goals, realistic expectations regarding members' abilities, frequency of interactions, effective leadership, and a climate that results in feelings of being valued and accepted.

There are other factors that threaten cohesion. As you might expect, a lack of purpose, unrealistic expectations, few interactions, poor leadership, and a poor climate weaken any group. In addition, unstable membership, group deviants who do not conform to group norms, cliques that are more committed to their own needs than those of the group as a whole, and individuals who simply do not show interest in making a commitment to helping the group succeed also threaten cohesion (Arrow & McGrath, 1993; Cohen et al., 2001).

There are also communication behaviors that create difficulties during the conflict stage (see Table 4.3). These include disruptive behaviors, interpersonal conflict, and weak interpersonal skills such as listening, providing feedback, and being supportive. Members do not always know how to give and receive feedback that is both supportive of other members and constructive in developing the group cohesion and task. Sometimes people think giving advice or solving another's problems is support. These techniques are often not advantageous in a group setting and can create disruptive patterns of talk and

TABLE 4.3   Storming—Communication Concerns

Disruptive behavior
Interpersonal conflict
Lack of interpersonal skills in listening
Inadequate feedback
Lack of support

behavior within the group. In addition, it is difficult for some people to talk openly about their opinions and feelings or to disagree openly with another member. An atmosphere of trust and acceptance must be felt within the group for this to occur. To create this support-ive climate, group members must practice empathetic listening and be able to communi-cate nonjudgmental acceptance and disagreement.

Despite group selection practices, a group may have a member who is not well suited to the particular group and is causing disruption. It is important to decide whether the disruptive behavior is an expression of either primary or secondary ten-sion that may subside as the group progresses or is indicative of a more long-lasting problem. The group must decide, because it cannot function well if the disruptive be-havior continues. Either the leader or the group as a whole must speak with the mem-ber in a sensitive way to explain the effect the disruptions are having on the group and offer a constructive way of contributing to the group discussion.

Occasionally, some members may experience periods of dissatisfaction with the group or with some of its members. They may perceive someone in the group as hav-ing a pessimistic attitude, or they may be uncomfortable with someone's communica-tion style. These issues and concerns need to be dealt with openly in the group.

In addition, members take risks and feel vulnerable when they open up to the group. So members may not easily express themselves, may feel inhibited, or may lack the necessary social skills, resulting either in silence or in acting out against others.

As group members, we need to feel that we are being heard and that no one mem-ber is dominating the discussion. Several techniques can be used to facilitate group member participation. For example, the "group round" allows members to specify at the beginning of a meeting how much time they will need during the meeting to share their ideas and information. Time is set aside and carefully monitored to make certain the members stay within their time allocation. At the end of the agreed-upon time, if more time seems appropriate, other members can volunteer some of their time. A sec-ond approach restricts overly dominate members and encourages the more silent mem-bers to participate. One variation (and groups can use their own creativity to implement this approach) is to place a limit on the number of times any member may speak before all members have spoken at least once. For example, the group may decide that no one may speak more than three times before everyone has spoken at least once. Other sug-gestions include deciding if cross-talk between members but not directed to the entire group will be allowed, if feedback on specific issues will take place only at the end of the meeting, or if a general discussion at the end regarding the effectiveness of the group process would be helpful. Any norms developed by the group for its sessions should reflect the group members' priorities. Finally, early meetings may be guided by a leader who is responsible for promoting discussion and interaction among members based on open communication and nonjudgmental, empathic listening.

Some members may feel threatened by others, and it may take time for them to develop a basic trust. The normal resistance to self-disclosure can make a leader's task more difficult in these early sessions. As the group becomes more cohesive, members can share more leadership responsibility and have more input into the content of the sessions. In a supportive group, vulnerability is sensed by the other members and efforts are made to help the individual feel accepted. It is important for group members to feel comfortable and to know how to respond supportively to disclosure and emotional expression. Members may need to be encouraged to take the time they need to contribute to the group discussion.

Besides performing managerial functions, setting limits, and monitoring rules and procedures, a facilitative group member must demonstrate kindness, warmth, openness, and sincerity, taking an active role in encouraging other members to express feelings and in modeling ways to share concerns in the group (Hamilton, 2005).

The secret to effective group process is to try to air, hear, and accept as many conflicts as possible during this phase for the group to recognize multiple perspectives and develop a better understanding of the full complexity of the issues to be faced. Interpersonal and group conflicts are inevitable and an important part of the group process. Working through these conflicts depends on several factors, including the group members' understanding and agreement, apparent satisfaction, and willingness to trust one another's goodwill and to communicate empathy for diverse perspectives.

These attitudes help group members resolve conflict in this phase. If the conflicts are not fully resolved, however, this phase may be revisited, perhaps even repeatedly, as the group moves to phase three. If we do not understand, feel satisfied, or trust, we have difficulty becoming a cohesive, emergent group capable of making a decision or solving a problem.

Norming: Emergence as a Group

At this point in a group's evolution, differences have been expressed and the storm of conflict is subsiding. Member relationships are becoming more open and trusting, and the group begins to feel more cohesive. Open negotiation of goals, roles, expectations, group structure, and the division of labor is undertaken. Even though members have developed their positions and come to some understanding of the positions of other members of the group, there is a tendency for groups to move back and forth between conflict and emerging cohesiveness. Disagreements are rarely fully and permanently resolved. The major issues may have been resolved, but there are countless issues to be worked through, as the group begins working toward defining problems and solutions. While the interaction remains tentative, cooperation is on the rise. During this norming phase, new issues raise primary tensions, and proposed solutions raise secondary tensions.

Ideally, groups should proceed through phase two (storming) before tackling phase three (norming), but two human characteristics tend to muddy the process. First, we like to solve problems even before we have fully defined them. So, during phase two, it is very tempting to propose our own personal solution before the group completes a thorough examination of different viewpoints and issues. Second, as the group proceeds through the emergence phase, group members may feel the need to revisit issues that were in conflict during phase two because some aspect of the analysis appears incomplete. In this case, individuals may feel that they have not represented their position adequately and wish to restate it to become more comfortable with the outcome. If the conflict experienced in phase two has not been well managed or fully resolved, the group will, sooner or later, return to phase-two issues.

A group is likely to hit periods of silence from time to time. This silence may be marked by tension, as one tries to think of what to say next, or a member may withdraw from the group if he or she feels pressured to speak up when not ready to do so. Silence can also be a time for introspection, looking inside oneself for answers or reflecting on what has just been shared. A group facilitator must judge what type of silence is occurring to help the group progress.

Norming describes the group's willingness to settle on specific rules for how discussions will take place and decisions will be made. It is an important phase in the group process and sets the stage for the group's performance.

Performing: Making Decisions and Solving Problems

Performing identifies the real work phase of the group. It is characterized by an increase in task orientation and by open exchange and feedback. The group's social tension usually decreases as a sense of relief occurs and the group begins moving toward some type of solution, examines that solution, and begins to assess the impact it will have on the problem.

A problem-solving process consisting of four or five distinct steps can help the group function more effectively during this phase. Each of these steps is distinct and calls for different communication behavior from the leader and group members working through the problem-solving process. Table 4.4 shows some of the dos and don'ts for group members in this problem-solving process.

Adjourning: Terminating, Saying "Good-Bye"

"Groups that have a distinct ending point experience a fifth phase" (Verdi & Wheelan, 1992, p. 357). This final phase in a group's process is *termination*. In the original forming, storming, norming, and performing model, this phase was called adjourning. Even ongoing groups may reach a termination point through membership attrition or changing group needs. Loss of individual group members can also create small points of termination within the group. Finally, many task groups complete their task, and stop meeting.

If the group has really become interdependent in its working together—members enjoy talking with one another and the regularity of meetings, value the forum for expression, are cohesive in their relationships, and enjoy the interactions as well as the tasks—then the termination phase can be an awkward and stressful time for group members (Keyton, 1993). Impending termination may

TABLE 4.4   Group Members' Responsibilities for Facilitating Problem Solving in the Performing Phase

Step 1: Defining the Problem

DOs:	DON'Ts:
Do provide the pertinent data that you possess.	Don't discuss solutions.
Do provide the background context for the problem.	Don't blame or assess fault regarding the problem.
Do explain how this problem relates to others.	Don't move on in the process until everyone is clear about the definition of the problem.
Do ask other group members for whatever facts and data they possess.	Don't supply a lot of irrelevant information.
Do make sure that everyone understands all the facts and data.	Don't act as though you have already decided on a solution and are involving other members of the team as merely a formality.
Do restate the definition of the problem to ensure that all members are aware of what you want.	

Step 2: Generating Possible Solutions

DOs:	DON'Ts:
Do encourage "off the wall" comments.	Don't allow editing, evaluating, or criticizing of ideas.
Do challenge the group to push for as many possible solutions as it can think of.	Don't settle on the first "good" idea that surfaces.
Do "prime the pump" with your own ideas, especially if the group is stuck.	Don't punish other members who criticize ideas—just remind them of the ground rules.
Do set a time limit.	Don't spend much time advocating your ideas.
Do invite everyone to participate, even if you have to ask some members explicitly.	Don't spend much time on any one person or one good idea.
Do ask open-ended questions to spark the team's thinking.	Don't go beyond the time limit set unless the team explicitly wants to.
Do write down all ideas generated.	Don't quit until the time limit is up.
Do assure the team that all ideas are welcome and that no idea is silly.	
Do piggyback off one another's ideas.	

Step 3: Evaluating Solutions

DOs:	DON'Ts:
Do review all the items on the list of possible solutions and eliminate those with no support.	Don't allow the team to judge one another as they judge the ideas.
Do keep any item on the list that anyone is willing to discuss.	Don't get bogged down discussing the pros and cons; assess value quickly.
Do focus on looking at the positive and negative aspects of each solution.	Don't quit until you have clear consensus.
Do anticipate the consequences of each solution.	
Do make sure that each member has ample opportunity to provide input.	
Do invite members to combine solutions.	
Do ensure consensus by getting everyone's input.	
Do frequently restate what you hear to clarify the meaning.	

TABLE 4.4 *(continued)*

Step 4: Creating an Action Plan

DOs:

Do generate alternatives for implementation before choosing an action plan.

Do make sure that specific tasks are assigned.

Do make sure that time frames are set.

Do empower members with the authority to complete their tasks.

Do arrange a method of following up to ensure completion of the tasks.

Do include yourself as a person responsible for a task.

Do restate each member's role to clarify and ensure commitment.

DON'Ts:

Don't state roles and tasks in general, unmeasurable terms.

Don't assume that brilliant solutions produce brilliant action plans; be creative in your planning.

Don't forget to follow up.

cause disruption to the group's processes and conflict among the group members (Verdi & Wheelan, 1992). Many people find it difficult to terminate relationships and would simply rather avoid saying good-bye. There may also be an unwillingness to deal with the emotions tied to ending the group. Keyton (1993) observed that the termination phase may be characterized by anxiety about separation and conclusion, a degree of sadness, and some self-reflective evaluation, as well as positive feelings toward the group and its project.

A group's termination may form a pivotal point in an individual's life and activities, and members of groups can benefit by reflecting on, coming to terms with, and talking about the termination of the group. People say good-bye in different ways, but a special event that marks the end of the group may help members experience a sense of closure.

Keyton (1993) argues that not acknowledging the termination of a group may mean, for many people, not having to admit the end of a good group experience or the presence of bad ones. Yet, she asserts that this is an important phase in the group process. How we terminate our group activities affects how we will interpret, in retrospect, what we have accomplished and experienced as a group and what we expect of future groups. Good-byes, and their sense of closure, feelings of task accomplishment, and positive relational expression, are an important aspect of small group process.

Usefulness of the Phase Model

The *phase model* is an approach to understanding group process that suggests the importance of waiting to solve a problem until all the issues surrounding it have been discussed. People in Western societies, and in the United States in particular, tend to be "can do" individuals (Beamer & Varner, 2001). When we are faced with a problem, we prefer making a decision and acting on it, rather than going through the time- and energy-consuming steps of analysis. In acting quickly, however, we tend to miss some critical issues in the process. The phase approach outlines what should be done and operates as a functional checklist for a group.

Modifications

Not all groups follow this phase model in a strictly linear process. Poole and Roth (1989) studied groups and found that they frequently go through periods of disorganization. This disorganization creates cycles in their process, meaning the group can repeat some of the phases several times. A group might, for example, simultaneously operate with one foot in phase two and one foot in phase three in an effort to move forward. This is acceptable and may even be effective for the group. Group process can be messy.

The types of communication that occur in a group also shift and change from one phase to the next. Verdi and Wheelan (1992) described seven categories of statements. In the forming phase, "dependency" statements are common. These seek direction, show an inclination to conform to the dominant mood of the group, and express a desire to follow the general direction of the suggestions made. In the storming phase, "counterdependency" statements that assert independence and reject other members' attempts at leadership and authority become more prominent. "Fight" statements that imply participation in struggle through argumentativeness, criticism, and aggression also become more common. These are followed in the norming phase with "flight" statements indicative of avoidance of confrontation and perhaps of task. The "counterpairing" statements of this phase, expressing an avoidance of intimacy and of cohesion and a desire to keep the discussion distant and intellectual, gradually give way to an *emergence* of "pairing" statements that express a warmth of friendship, support, greater intimacy, and a general positive regard for other group members. Finally, in the performing phase, "work" statements representing the purposeful accomplishment of goal-directed, task-oriented activities become more prevalent.

This phase-interaction model suggests that effective groups are attentive to the group process and to assessing (1) the nature of the task, (2) the standards for evaluating various decision options, (3) positive qualities of the various possible choices, and (4) negative qualities of various options (Hirokawa & Rost, 1992). In other words, effective groups pay attention to the decision-making process itself and, even when they modify or deviate from the phase model, they make certain that the task is clearly analyzed before deciding on a solution.

Organizational Teams

This phase model also identifies the major points in *organizational teams* and of the leadership roles necessary in those teams. In stage one, primary organizational team issues are those of inclusion and acceptance. At this point, the team members get to know one another and gather information regarding the job at hand. One major difference between a decision-making group outside an organization and an organizational team is the assignment of a leader. In an organization, a leader is normally assigned, and the leader's

Surgery teams require outstanding teamwork and common goals.

job is to provide structure and direction for the organizational team members. In other decision-making groups, a leader is more likely to emerge during the group process, and the group members will have more influence on determining the role of the leader.

In stage two, issues of control and influence arise. Team members discover who has the power and decide which individuals to listen to. This stage is similar to the storming and norming phases, and the leader's role is to offer support and guidance without directing or controlling the group.

Stage three deals with commitment and cohesion. The team performs the actual task, and the leader focuses on facilitating its performance, providing the team the freedom and resources to act.

Overriding Influences

Three major influences affect a small group's process of working through these phases: whether the group is a formal or informal one, the task and social dynamics, and how the primary and secondary tensions affect the group dynamics.

Formal or Informal Group

A *formal group* has been sanctioned or mandated by some organization. In other words, the system (that is, an organization, social body, university, club) decides it needs to establish an additional subsystem with some specific duties. A committee is formed, a team is chosen, or a task force is named that is governed by a particular set of rules or procedures. In formal groups, the social structure is relatively well established, norms and roles are explicit, and group members are aware of the relationships within the group. When you are assigned to a task force, the purpose, goals, and membership are determined by the larger organization (your university or employer), and the group is formal.

An *informal group,* such as several classmates deciding to go to a sporting event or work colleagues organizing a surprise party, emerges and forms itself because of the interests of the members. A formal group has specific rules and operating procedures; informal groups develop their own rules and procedures as the need arises. Their interacting process is frequently based on implicit or larger social rules. Informal groups often fulfill social needs, while formal groups are more oriented toward accomplishing a specific task or goal. Finally, an informal group can disband spontaneously, while formal groups have a more permanent status or defined period of existence.

Both formal and informal groups can be highly effective. For example, at the world renowned Mayo Clinic, groups and teams are an integral part of the patient care process: "Specialists don't just visit a patient; they swarm the patient with an integrated team, diagnosing a complex problem, proposing treatment—and often slotting the patient for surgery within 24 hours of diagnosis" (Roberts, 1999, p. 150). Starting as an informal arrangement, teamwork is now "built into the treatment of patients, and it's integrated into the clinic's fabric of governance" (Roberts, 1999, p. 150).

Task and Social Dynamics

Task and social dynamics are interdependent issues that continually interact in the group system. *Task dynamics* deal with a group's purpose, structure, rules, procedures, and individual task-oriented assignments. The goals and objectives of the group, or getting the job done, can be viewed as the overriding group purpose. From a systems perspective our major concern with task dynamics is that they affect the group's accomplishments or productivity. Table 4.5 shows some appropriate task questions about a group's purpose and objectives.

Social dynamics describe the ability of individuals to work together as a group. The synergy created by bringing together individuals who possess different backgrounds also means that there are significant issues regarding membership composition, group processes, norms, roles, status, and leadership. To be an effectively functioning system, the parts of the system must work well together. If group members do not have a desire to understand and deal with the task, the group will founder and probably fail, or a few dedicated individuals will have to do all the work. If group members do not have some compatibility or enjoy one another's company, the group's cohesiveness will also suffer, but incompatibility among group members can be overcome. Open, involving communication motivates members to invest themselves in the process and builds a group's cohesion.

TABLE 4.5   Appropriate Task Questions

1. Why are we here?
2. What is to be accomplished?
3. What information and background are needed?
4. Do the group members have the ability, knowledge, and skills to do the assigned job?
5. What are the components of the problem?
6. What purpose(s) and goal(s) are driving this group?
7. What rules, procedures, and operating methods should be used?
8. How predictable is the outcome, and is it clear?
9. By what criteria will we be judged?
10. Can it be done?

Primary and Secondary Tensions

When the expected, initial period of uneasiness, awkwardness, and uncertainty within the group that is indicative of primary tension lasts too long, it can negatively affect the normal development of a group's dynamics and process. The group's pattern of communication and interaction; its development of norms, roles, and operating procedures; and its members' concerns for inclusion, acceptance, interpersonal trust, and support may all be adversely affected. When a period of extended primary tension occurs, a group may find it difficult to arrive at a consensus in defining its purpose, establishing an agenda, developing working rules, and beginning its work. Likewise, an avoidance of secondary tension through the suppression of conflict may stifle the development of group cohesion and of effective group decision making and problem solving. Group cohesion depends on the consensual development of clear group goals, member cooperation and interdependence, and individuals feeling valued and accepted. Achieving these feelings of cooperation, interdependence, and acceptance requires that conflicts be dealt with thoughtfully and respectfully, but openly and honestly. Avoidance of conflict will, in the long term, impede the progress of the group. To be successful, groups must openly confront both primary and secondary tensions as issues to be worked through rather than as problems to be avoided.

Social Loafing—A Threat to Group and Team Success

We've all been there. A group is formed, and it soon becomes obvious that some members do not plan to contribute a great deal. They seem to be along for a free ride. This phenomenon is called *social loafing,* which is the tendency to exert less effort when working in a group than when working alone (Cohen et al., 2001). Some members might just be lazy or have other pressing commitments. Perhaps they do not care about the issues being discussed or believe they have little to contribute. The United States is one of the most individualistic nations in the world (Sweeney & McFarlin, 2002). This might

(continued)

explain our tendency to look out for number one or to avoid commitment to the needs of the group.

There are consequences, however. We resent free riders, and the group is denied potentially useful input, the productivity of the group might be lessened, and there can be an erosion of group cohesiveness.

What can be done to overcome social loafing? First, we can obtain a commitment from each group member to the purposes of the group. Second, we can make certain that the rewards for participating are greater than for not participating. Third, we can actively involve reticent members through verbal and nonverbal communication and active listening.

Summary

Groups proceed through specific phases during their development. The orientation, or forming, phase is how the group sets itself up. This "first impressions make lasting impressions" phase is significant. During conflict, or storming, we see the importance of diverse positions and work through issues. After sufficient discussion, we move to phase three, emergence, or norming. After this consensus phase, we begin the performing phase, during which we make a commitment to the outcome.

Small groups tend to have messy processes. The phase model helps us describe the essential issues raised by group processes. During these four phases, norms will be established and reinforced. Knowing what is expected from the group helps us succeed.

DISCUSSION QUESTIONS

1. What are the advantages of a phase model of group development? Are there any weaknesses? Can any of the phases be skipped? Can they be rearranged?

2. What important communication characteristics occur in the forming stage? Why are these important?

3. Does conflict have a role in developing group cohesion? What is it?

4. During the forming stage, what actions and behaviors should be encouraged to create an effective group?

5. From your own group experience, identify some examples of the norming phase in a group.

6. How would you define cohesion in a small group or team? Why is it important?

REFERENCES

Arrow, H., & McGrath, J. E. (1993). Membership matters. *Small Group Research, 24*(3), 334–361.

Beamer, L., & Varner, I. (2001). *Intercultural communication in a global workplace*. Boston: McGraw-Hill Irwin.

Chang, A., Duck, J., & Bordia, P. (2006). Understanding the multidimensionality of group development. *Small Group Research, 37*(4), 327–350.

Cohen, A. R., Fink, S. L., Gadon, H., & Willits, R. D. (2001). *Effective behavior in organizations: Cases, concepts, and student experiences* (7th ed.). New York: McGraw-Hill.

Fisher, B. A. (1970). Decision emergence: Phases in group decision-making. *Speech Monographs, 37,* 53–66.

George, B. (2007). *True north.* San Francisco: Jossey-Bass.

Hamilton, C. (2005). *Communicating for results: A guide for business and the professions* (7th ed.). Boston: Wadsworth Cengage Learning.

Hirokawa, R., & Rost, K. (1992). Effective group decision making in organizations. *Management Communication Quarterly, 5,* 267–288.

Keyton, J. (1993). Group termination: Completing the study of group development. *Small Group Research, 24*(1), 84–100.

Montebello, A. R. (1994). *Work teams that work.* Minneapolis: Best Sellers.

Poole, M. S., & Roth, J. (1989). Decision development in small groups V: Test of a contingency model. *Human Communication Research, 15,* 549–589.

Roberts, P. (1999, April). Total teamwork: The Mayo clinic. *Fast Company,* pp. 149–162.

Sweeney, P. D., & McFarlin, D. B. (2002). *Organizational behavior: Solutions for management.* Boston: McGraw-Hill Irwin.

Tuckman, B. W. (1965). Developmental sequences in small groups. *Psychological Bulletin, 63,* 384–399.

Tuckman, B. W. (1977). Stages in small group development revisited. *Group and Organizational Studies, 2,* 419–427.

Verdi, A. F., & Wheelan, S. A. (1992). Developmental patterns in same-sex and mixed-sex groups. *Small Group Research, 23*(3), 356–378.

Wellings, R. S., Byham, W. C., & Wilson, J. M. (1991). *Empowered teams: Creating self-directed work groups that improve quality, productivity, and participation.* San Francisco: Jossey-Bass.

Wheelan, S. A., & McKeage, R. L. (1993). Developmental patterns in small and large groups. *Small Group Research, 24*(1), 60–83.

CHAPTER 5

Diversity in Groups: The Strength of Different Perspectives

CHAPTER OUTLINE

Defining Diversity in Small Groups

Assumptions and Stereotypes

Communication Contexts
Language Use
Nonverbal Communication

Diversity in Small Groups and Teams
Group Commitment and Consensus
Strength in Diversity

Making Diverse Groups Work
Conflict Management

Hierarchies of Power
Pressures for Conformity

Computer-Mediated Virtual Teams

Ethical Behavior

Summary

Discussion Questions

References

CHAPTER OBJECTIVES

- Define diversity and its role in small groups.
- Better understand the effect of stereotypes.
- Discuss the concept of communication contexts.
- Explain the effect of language use on diversity.
- Elucidate the influence of nonverbal communication on diversity.
- Outline the effect of diversity on group commitment and consensus.
- Present the strength obtained through diversity.
- Suggest ways to help diverse groups work effectively.
- Discuss diversity in computer-mediated virtual teams.

KEY TERMS

Conflict management	High-context environment	Nonverbal communication
Diversity	Insider–outsider allegiances	Power
Ethical behavior	Language use	Pressure for conformity
Hierarchies of power	Low-context environment	Stereotypes

W e can regard strangers or individuals who are different with hostility, or we can treat them as potential friends and important group members. Those who are different may prove to be and to have something valuable to contribute to our group's discussion and to our experiences of community.

(Lustig & Koester, 2003, p. ii).

Defining Diversity in Small Groups

"The demographics of most task-oriented groups have changed dramatically during the past three decades, resulting in less member homogeneity and greater member diversity" (Shapcott, Caron, Burke, Bradshaw, & Estabrooks, 2006, p. 702). This means that the work groups we are expected to participate in are increasingly diversity. This trend is likely to continue throughout the 21st century (Valenti & Rockett, 2008). The globalization of business, advent of multinational mergers and acquisitions, and increase in the number of multinational corporations have worked together to produce greater cultural diversity in organizations (Crown, 2007). This increasing diversity within organizations has, in turn, modified the composition of organizational work groups and teams, making them more diverse in their membership. The diversity in membership can benefit group performance "by increasing the range of task-relevant resources the group collectively holds [in the] different types of knowledge, skills, and abilities germane to performing the task" (Larson, 2007, p. 414). Performance gains emerge from the synergy of this group interaction that allow the group to accomplish a task that none of the individuals could achieve working alone (Larson, 2007).

Diversity describes the reality of our national and world community that is made up of people having cultures, languages, and social customs different from our own. Even when people in the United States speak the same language (and this cannot always be assumed) and share the same overall cultural value system, they often still have a different relationship to that value system than we sometimes expect. This diversity in language, culture, background, and values affect our small group communication. If a small group consists of members from diverse backgrounds, their diversity influences the group discussion. If the group itself is not as diverse in its membership as the larger organization or community of which it is a part, then it may have difficulty adequately representing and responding to the multiple needs of that organization or community. Either way, diversity must be considered. It can have a positive effect on the decisions that are made by a small group, but it can also make that communication more difficult. Valenti and Rockett (2008) suggest that "diversity provides groups with a greater resource of experiences and viewpoints, leading to greater creativity and better problem-solving ability. . . . [however, diversity can also] impede effective communication [and] . . . reduce informal communication, group cohesiveness, and social integration" (p. 179). Diversity in a group can work against group homogeneity and the convergence in members' perceptions, attitudes, and behavior in a way that leads to groupthink (Mason, 2006). It can affect a group's task performance, its members social interactions, and the discussion dynamics of the group. Hence, diversity in member backgrounds is not adequate to a successful group; those members must also work together closely and interact cooperatively for the group performance to be enhanced.

Nicotera, Clinkscales, and Walker (2003) defined diversity as "operating among persons who draw upon varied sets of rules and resources (embedded in their primary socializations—ethnic, national, regional, etc.) to enact social practices in organizational settings to accomplish organizationally related goals and objectives" (p. 26). To capitalize on the contributions of all members of our social, political, organizational, and group environments, we must first come to understand diversity as precisely what the term means—difference. This concept of difference implies not a hierarchy of values but a conception of different perspectives on given issues based on different life experiences, as outlined in Table 5.1.

Diversity is often used in popular expression to refer to the "other"—people who look, speak, or behave differently from what we expect in those with whom we are familiar (Griffin, 2005). In an organizational context, diversity often refers to people other than White males of Western European descent, who have different socialization experiences, different access to the dominant economic structure, and possibly a first language other than English. Beyond gender, race, and ethnic heritage, diversity also relates to differences in social and economic class, access to education, physical attractiveness and ability, and sexual orientation. Thus, diversity means that we may not share a common set of experiences or assumptions in certain important ways with those with whom we work and communicate.

Shapcott and colleagues (2006) suggested categories of diversity that include biographical differences such as ethnicity, gender, and educational background, and differences in personality, ability levels, and leadership styles. They point out that diversity in task-related attributes such as experience, knowledge, ability, and skills

TABLE 5.1   Diversity and Differences—Some Categories

Gender   Race   Age   Religion

Ethnic Heritage   Geographic Location

Social and Economic Class   Access to Education   Physical Ability

Sexual Orientation   Different Communication Contexts

Family Status   Physical Attractiveness   First Language

can have as much of an effect on group discussions as more immediately recognizable differences of gender, race, and ethnicity. Strubler and York (2007) cautioned that skill variety of team members—i.e., the different types of knowledge, skill, and perspective that team members bring to the work—are important to organizational group task performance.

Peeters, Rutte, van Tuijl, and Reymen (2006) indicate that differences in group members' extraversion, agreeableness, conscientiousness, emotional stability, neuroticism, and openness to experience can also have a big effect on the group discussion. Extraversion describes the extent to which a person is outgoing, talkative, sociable, gregarious, assertive, and active. Agreeableness is the degree to which a person is cooperative and friendly. Conscientiousness depicts how self-disciplined, organized, careful, thorough, responsible, hardworking, and achievement oriented a person is. Emotional stability refers to how calm, poised, and secure a person is in the group situation. Neuroticism is associated with behavioral tendencies toward being anxious, depressed, angry, embarrassed, worried, and insecure. Openness to experience describes how imaginative, curious, and artistically sensitive a person is. Each of these factors informs a person's experience and affects his or her performance in the group. Collectively they influence the group members' individual perceptions, participation, and experience of the group's purpose, procedures, and achievements.

Communication based on shared meanings among group members, therefore, cannot be taken for granted but must be actively pursued (Beamer & Varner, 2001). However, diversity does not make our group communication easier. It is often simpler when we share cultural values, common experiences, and basic assumptions with those with whom we interact. A common culture provides us with a measure of predictability in our interactions with the people around us, defining the shared ground rules for our behavior and communication (Klyukanov, 2005). When we work in a group of people who have very different life experiences and sets of assumptions, difficulties often arise as we try to work together toward a common goal. In response to these difficulties, organizations have instituted diversity training programs for their employees. A college in Massachusetts even had to institute civility rules for its faculty to ensure that unpopular points of view we allowed to be voiced. Although deeper cultural values and beliefs may not change, changes in behavior can effectively be made in groups—indeed must be made, for us to live and work together and to maintain a civil society (Neher, 1997).

Assumptions and Stereotypes

To understand how we have come to have such different life experiences, we need to understand the internal matrix—the pattern—that culture creates in our lives. As human beings, our relationships within social groups begin at birth. We depend on one another for our physical and psychological well-being and for our survival throughout our lives. We learn our automatic and perceptual responses to our surroundings from those who nurture and care for us. We learn how to behave and what cues to look for in any number of complex interactions that will lead to our survival, as well as to our acceptance and continued nurture. Thus, our values and systems of defining and understanding the external world are inculcated in us from the very beginning of our lives, when we begin to develop our basic assumptions, *stereotypes,* and prejudices.

As an example of different perspectives, the late Maine senator Edmund Muskie was fond of telling a joke about a Maine farmer who met a Texas rancher. The Maine farmer was bragging about how large a potato farm he owned when the Texan responded, "You only have 150 acres! Why, in Texas I could get into my truck and drive a day and a half and still not reach the end of my land." To this the Maine farmer responded dryly, "Yes, I once had a truck like that myself." Aside from the humor, this joke illustrates how our basic underlying assumptions and perspectives on even physical realities such as size and distance are culturally defined.

Each cultural group learns and perpetuates the truths and myths that have helped prior generations of that group survive and adapt to their surroundings. Part of that cultural adaptation includes stereotyping. Stereotyping as a form of categorization is part of the human condition. Because of the myriad of stimuli constantly coming into our awareness, we need to learn to categorize those stimuli that indicate danger to our survival and then develop appropriate responses to them. Stereotypes help us make immediate and potentially critical decisions, saving us from having to sort through each individual circumstance and from overloading our mental circuits (Neuliep, 2000).

In the United States, many different cultural traditions coexist (Nasser, 2006). Within the changing context of our country and communities, even stereotypes that may or may not have been relevant to prior generations no longer serve the purposes of our larger social matrix (Reece & Brandt, 2005; Zemke, Raines, & Filipczak, 2000). Because stereotypes are slower to change than the context in which they are applied, they frequently result in harmful, if sometimes unintended, consequences.

When we know few people from a different, identifiable group, each individual member of that group with whom we come into contact too often becomes a "token," representing all the members of that group (Hall, 2002). To the extent that this person confirms our stereotype, then the stereotype, rather than the individual, is likely to become the focus of our response. If the person behaves in a way noticeably different from our stereotype, we may attribute that to the person's being an exception, rather than to the stereotype being inaccurate and inappropriate for gauging our responses to members of that group. Research has shown that once we get to know members of groups other than our own, we tend to see them as individuals, rather than as members of the groups to which we have assigned them through our stereotyping (Hall, 2002).

Thus, stereotypes can be damaging to all of us. They tend to perpetuate myths about groups of people and to disallow perception of the valuable differences and acceptance of the positive contributions each unique individual has to contribute. None of us fits the uni-dimensionality of a stereotype very well. Yet, we may find ourselves at times bound up in living within the confines of the stereotypes imposed on us, and these confines interfere with our personal development as complete, unique, and creative human beings. Learning to relate to one another in more appropriate ways is critical not only to working in diverse groups but also to our growth as individuals.

Within a group, stereotyping can deny us the benefits of multifaceted perspectives. For example, when U.S. workers were asked who is most likely to be treated unfairly at work, 21% responded African Americans, 18% responded Arab Americans, 13% responded Hispanics, 12% responded Muslims, and 8% responded women (Haralson & Lewis, 2002). The events of September 11, 2001, resulted in negative perceptions in the United States toward Arab, Middle Eastern, South Asian, and other groups that are seen as different, and perhaps dangerous (Armour, 2002). Regardless of the reasons, however, the loss of diverse perspectives in a group can reduce our productivity and the quality of our group's decisions. Diversity is a complex issue that requires active thought and consideration for small groups to function well.

Communication Contexts

Subcultures within the United States and around the world develop different sets of rules for communication. These rules define diverse, culturally based sets of perceptual screens for viewing and communicating our experience (Hall, 2002). Culture does not just define how we perceive something; it defines the way we perceive and comprehend reality and how we understand the world itself, through our culturally defined and learned symbol systems (Nicortera, Clinkscales & Walker, 2003). These symbol systems influence our individual cognition and mental activities, including thinking, remembering, learning, and using language. Our social cognitions, our awareness of other people and their feelings and ideas; our interactions with others; development of our social and interpersonal skills; and our willingness to coordinate our actions with others are all influenced by our culture. Our individual cognition, social cognition, interactive functioning, and how we coordinate our actions with others all derive from that learned symbolic culture. Therefore, people who are socialized in different cultures perceive differently.

In addition, as individuals, we operate quite separately from one another. We think, feel, and respond within the confines of our own skin and minds. We can never really know what another person is thinking or would like to communicate. To cross the barrier between our individual selves, we must encode and send our messages according to the rules of communication we have learned and incorporated from our cultural environment. In turn, we decode and interpret one another's messages according to these same learned and adapted rules of communication. In the process of encoding and decoding these messages, a great deal of interpretation and hence misunderstanding can, and frequently does, occur. This happens even between people who share cultural norms and assumptions. When people have different sets of cultural assumptions, the misunderstandings are likely to be greater.

The more that can be taken for granted in a communication interaction, the "higher" the shared communication context can be said to be. Communication in a *high-context environment* means that less of the meaning needs to be explicitly stated. Much is simply understood within the commonly defined situation itself (Lustig & Kocster, 2003). On the other hand, a group made up of people from diverse backgrounds, cultures, and understandings cannot assume that common understanding and must be considered to be communicating in a *low-context environment*. Meanings, therefore, need to be explicitly communicated.

A rather dramatic clash of communication cultures occurred in the skies over New Jersey in 1997, when a passenger airplane preparing to land at an airport inadvertently flew into what had just been designated as an off-limits military training airspace. Two military jets approached the civilian aircraft in a reconnaissance maneuver to ascertain the identity of the aircraft. The civilian plane, which was equipped with an onboard computer programmed to avoid midair collisions, automatically took sudden evasive action, with some injury to passengers. Each aircraft and traffic control system—the civilian and the military—was operating on its own set of assumptions and responded to the situation based on those assumptions. Neither was aware of the other's intentions. If this type of miscommunication can happen between different flying subcultures operating within carefully constructed air-traffic-control guidelines and rules—a relatively high-context environment—it can happen as easily between individuals from different subcultures attempting communication in a small group. For this reason, we need to establish explicitly defined and mutually agreed upon sets of communication guidelines, rules, and interaction patterns for our group communication.

Language Use

One of the most obvious communication codes in use in small groups is language. Language is the principal way we cross the barrier between our own interior world and that of others (Neuliep, 2000). Our culture provides us with certain assumptions about the appropriate use of language. Different cultures often make quite different assumptions not only about particular words and grammar (the language per se) but also about the ideas and purposes for which those words can and should be used.

For example, in the Japanese culture, words are assumed to be used for social purposes to ensure harmony among group members, rather than for argument or settling differences in points of view (Beamer & Varner, 2001). Other social systems based on direct experience or pictographic representation of oral speech may have less language for abstract problem solving than those social systems based on more indirect relationships with their environments (Becker, 1991; Hoijer, 1991; Shuter, 1991). In many African cultures, the word is preeminent. Imaginative and vivid language is important, as is a call-and-response mode of communicating, indicating a link between the speaker and the listener. Interruption of the speaker, therefore, is expected and appreciated, and those who speak well in this type of exchange are likely to become leaders (Weber, 1991).

Moreover, beyond overt differences in language, most cultures treat men and women differently and teach them different ways to use language and to communicate nonverbally (Stewart, Cooper, Stewart, & Friedley, 2003). Even within a common language, particular inflections, vocabularies, and grammatical usage become enmeshed with the associative meanings we assign based on their presumed use by a particular identifiable group. Aside from regional identification, this attribution frequently occurs along a hierarchical continuum, reflecting the values of the social context in which we are operating. In this way, language use can convey cultural differences that may lead others to judge a person based on assumptions about racial, ethnic, educational, or class background (Victor, 1992). Language use can also act as a code that promotes *insider–outsider allegiances* within and between groups of people. To really hear each other, therefore, we need to be willing to forgo listening for educational, racial, or class privileging codes of language use and to listen consciously for the content and the intent of the message being communicated.

Nonverbal Communication

Nonverbal communication complements the use of language and is made up of deeply ingrained response patterns. It is often subtle and multidimensional (Remland, 2000) and may take the form of body or facial gestures, tone of voice, turn taking, use of time, or habits of dress or hairstyle. It is important to understand that different cultures attach different standards of appropriateness to nonverbal expressions, particularly those that are more easily controlled (Gardenswartz & Rowe, 1993). Although facial expressions, for example, may express the same emotions across cultures, the appropriateness of expressing those emotions may vary depending on culture and the context of the communication event (Victor, 1992). Even something as commonplace as a smile has different meanings in different cultures and contexts (Barna, 1991).

In addition, different subcultures in the United States communicate their understanding of what is being said differently. Some research indicates that African Americans may give more subtle conversational feedback in certain contexts than their White American counterparts, causing some White American speakers to assume their African American listeners have not understood what was said (Victor, 1992). Verbal and nonverbal communication is discussed at length in Chapter 6, but it is important to understand that we each communicate and interpret the communication of others differently.

Interestingly, however, research undertaken to look for universally agreed-upon traits of effective group leaders found that particular personality traits, such as "a sense of humor, flexibility, patience, resourcefulness, and consideration for others" (Neher, 1997, p. 218), are commonly held to be important across most cultures. Therefore, it appears that beneath the surface of quite different communication styles runs an undercurrent of a common human orientation toward social interaction.

Diversity in Small Groups and Teams

Group Commitment and Consensus

Within our small groups, we depend on one another for the success and productivity of those endeavors we share. To the extent that we each hold a stake in the outcomes of the decisions we make in the groups in which we participate, we benefit from everyone's involvement. People are more committed and work harder in a group if they feel their input and contributions are valued (Neher, 1997). If some members feel excluded or disenfranchised from the group, we may lose the benefit of their unique contributions and their support (Schreiber, 1996).

Our diverse backgrounds and relationships lead to different experiences and expectations within groups and organizations, as well as within the culture at large. People of different genders, racial characteristics, and sexual orientation experience life, the workplace, and groups differently and are sensitive to different issues and concerns (Gemmill & Schaible, 1991; Schreiber, 1996). Their varied personal experiences produce multiple and diverse opinions that can enhance the decision-making process and can lead to higher-quality decisions (Jackson, May, & Whitney, 1995). In organizations, homogenous teams often gel more quickly than do diverse teams, since the members share a common background. However, given time, diverse teams typically outperform homogenous teams in decision making and in gaining the members' commitment to the team's goals (Hickman & Creighton-Zollar, 1998; Reece & Brandt, 2005).

Being insensitive to diverse perspectives can lead to negative feelings and even members' sabotage of the group's efforts. Such insensitivity to difference has resulted an increasing number of charges of sexism and racism, as well as complaints of sexual harassment and "gay bashing" in the United States since 1990 (Neher, 1997). What some of us may take as a joke or a humorous remark in a small group or team can make others feel uncomfortable, unwelcome, discounted, or insulted—even if that was not our intent.

In addition, when we ask for and pay attention to only those contributions we expect from a participant based on her or his membership in a recognizable stereotyped group, we miss out on the true value of that person's multiple perspectives. For example, if we expect a woman to act only as the group nurturer or the "social specialist" within the group, rather than as a contributor to the task-oriented goal at hand, we overlook the other valuable experience and expertise she brings to the group (Powell, 1988). If we look to a man only for solutions to the task problems and do not encourage him to discuss or engage in the relationship issues and assumptions, we are not getting the maximum potential contribution from his multiple types of expertise and experiences. Likewise, if we dismiss the contributions of someone who has difficulty articulating a train of thought, who is quiet and slow to contribute, who seems to us to ramble on incessantly without ever making a point, or who we assume is a member of the group only for political reasons, we diminish the potential contributions of that person to the group. Alternately, if we assume that certain people have power, authority, knowledge, solutions, and the right answers, we may feel intimidated and find it difficult to challenge their points of view, assumptions, and proposed solutions. This internal censuring of ourselves can reduce the quality of group discussion and potential for creative decisions. Group potential is maximized when all participants feel comfortable in making contributions during every step of the process. We cannot arrive at a true group consensus in our decisions if we have not heard equally from all of the perspectives and considered all points of view.

Strength in Diversity

Diversity in a small group is valuable because it adds vital perspectives and insights when solving difficult or complex problems. It adds perspectives to the group that otherwise would be absent, and it lessens some of the destructive tendencies of group decision making, such as groupthink. Fostering diversity can be more important than a particular group's intelligence: "Making a group more diverse almost automatically makes it better at problem solving. . . . [O]n the group level, intelligence alone is not enough, because intelligence alone cannot guarantee you different perspectives on a problem" (Surowiecki, 2004, p. 44).

The strength of diversity is in the creative problem solving that comes from including different perspectives—perspectives not formed by the same background and context. A homogeneous group with a shared set of assumptions is less likely to come up with an innovative solution to a difficult problem. A diverse group has the advantage of bringing a variety of points of view.

Organizations, for example, have found that diversity initiatives significantly improve their bottom line. A survey by the Society for Human Resource Management and *Fortune* magazine found that "91% of respondents say their diversity initiative helps their organization keep a competitive edge" ("Survey says," 2001, p. 8). General Electric Power Systems reported a 13% gain in productivity from cross-functional and multicultural teams versus homogeneous teams (Robinson & Dechant, 1997).

Groups are dynamic interactive systems, depending on the experience and abilities of their participants. The synergistic effect of group process is achieved through a combination of the contributions and influences of the members. The more diverse the members of the group, the greater the potential for varieties of interaction and, therefore, the greater the potential for arriving at new and creative solutions.

For small, diverse groups to achieve these optimal results, however, they need to begin with open-minded participants and the concept of equifinality—that is, that there are different ways to solve a problem or achieve the overall goals. When we start with an assumption that there is more than one right way to solve a problem and more

Mercedes-Benz U.S. International. MBUSI, the first U.S. enterprise by Daimler-Benz, AG (predecessor to DaimlerChrysler), makes the M-Class, R-Class, and GL-Class sport utility vehicles. Everyone is a team member, and MBUSI has a firmly stated policy of valuing diversity. The company is committed to promoting and supporting an inclusive environment free from discrimination against any person on the grounds of race, color, religion, national origin, disability, sex, marital status, sexual orientation, or citizenship. Their success as a diversity-centered team organization has been a direct factor on the plant's 10 years of production success, resulting in a $600-million expansion, a doubling of the plant's production capacity to 160,000 vehicles a year, and the doubling of the plant's workforce to 4,000 team members.

than one right answer, we open ourselves to hearing and understanding important differences in perspective among group members, rather than silencing those differences and members, intentionally or unintentionally. If everyone agreed on the best course of action, there would be no purpose in meeting. Likewise, if we already had the best answer to the problem, why convene the group? Diverse groups provide the opportunity to explore different perspectives on a problem and make possible innovative solutions that result from combining those perspectives. When group members bring different viewpoints and backgrounds to the decision-making process, "they achieve a competitive advantage against organizations that are either culturally homogenous or fail to successfully utilize their diversity" (Gardenswartz & Rowe, 1998, p. 52).

To the extent that our groups and the organizations within which they exist are themselves part of the larger environment of social and economic realities, optimum solutions are relative to that total environment. Appropriate answers emerge from the context of the larger environment in which the problem is located, from an open exchange of ideas among the group members, and from the interaction between the group and its larger environment. For that reason, obtaining the contributions and commitment of as many diverse and representative members as practical offers the best hope for an optimal solution to a problem at any particular time and place.

Making Diverse Groups Work

Research has shown that the more individual group members participate and understand one another, the more creative solutions they are likely to develop (Kirchmeyer, 1993). However, for the group process to work the way it is intended and for each member to feel involved and appreciated, ground rules need to be established and maintained. Different groups come up with different ways of approaching this issue, and, obviously, the more diverse the group in terms of attitudes and communication assumptions, the more difficult and time-consuming this transactional aspect of group process becomes. However, the more important the task, the more important it is that all members be heard and understood, and the more important it may be to spend the time needed to focus on the communication process itself (Witherspoon & Wohlert, 1996).

Conflict Management

Among the most important communication rules and expectations to be established in small groups are those surrounding *conflict management*. Within the U.S. cultural model, conflict is an inevitable part of group creativity and communication. Differences between members and open confrontation of those differences are frequently seen as positive indicators of the creative process in action (Neher, 1997). On the other hand, research shown that Asian cultures make different assumptions about the appropriateness of confrontation than the U.S. culture does. Whereas in the United States and many Western cultures, truth resides in logic and debate, in Asian cultures, it is to be found in the totality of the person, and maintaining harmony is the goal of communication (Hall, 2002). Within the United States, Native American children raised in a tradition that emphasizes harmony with nature and the importance of the group over the individual learn better in a noncompetitive and cooperative environment. Children from a Mexican background who are taught to believe in cooperation may think that sharing answers or homework is a sign of solidarity and generosity (Calloway-Thomas, Cooper, & Blake, 1999). For many North Americans students, individual success is valued, and sharing is seen as cheating. These diverse backgrounds, so critical to the successful analysis and resolution of issues, can create barriers if they are not recognized and accepted.

Regardless of the cultural orientation to conflict, however, working with it is almost never easy. Whether conflict has a positive effect depends in large measure on how it is handled. If it leads to simmering animosities and an individual's withdrawal from participation in the group process, it may lead to negative effects on the group and on the task at hand. When conflict is taken as a necessary and inevitable part of the creative process apart from personalities, however, it can be constructive (Neher, 1997) and lead to more balanced involvement by minority as well as nonminority members (Kirchmeyer, 1993). Conflict management is dealt with at length in Chapter 12, but it is important to consider it within the context of managing the communication process in groups of diverse people.

Hierarchies of Power

Power is another sometimes subtle but pervasive issue with which we must deal within the context of diversity. Each of us makes assumptions regarding where and with whom power lies in any context. There are *hierarchies of power* throughout our socialization processes that we have come to take for granted, sometimes without being aware of the way in which we situate ourselves along the continuum. Clearly, the overriding assumption of social, economic, and political power in the U.S. has long resided with upper-class and upper-middle-class White Europeans of wealth and privilege. Other members of society have implicitly been located along multiple hierarchies of power in relation to this group. It is important to note, however, that embedded within this larger social context are subcultural hierarchies with different assumptions of what constitutes power. As Nathan McCall (1994) noted in his book *Makes Me Wanna Holler,* the apex of power in the inner-city neighborhood in which he came of age rests with those young men who most flout the rules of the larger White society.

In the workplace, however, and in many of the public groups in which most college graduates participate, the power paradigm of the predominantly White social and economic system continues to prevail (Harris & Nelson, 2008). Within the United States, organizational behaviors and expectations have been defined within the context of that privileged upper-middle-class, middle-aged, able-bodied, White male experience (Eisenberg & Goodhall, 2004; Gentile, 1996). Within that paradigm, the experiences and voices of women, people of color, the geriatric, those with other than attractive able bodies, the poor, and the undereducated have often been subordinated to that privilege. It is not surprising that research indicates that these diverse people have very different employment experiences.

Our challenge for the 21st century is to revise the social norms that underlie the economic realities of our culture that have proven resistant to long-term change. Moving beyond the mistrust of people in positions of power in a group is hard work for those accustomed to being marginalized. It is equally difficult for those who have been implicitly empowered by the culture to hear what people with different experiences have to say and offer. A necessary step may be for the empowered to place themselves consciously at the margins of the group process, permitting members they may consider to have less expertise to take the reins of power in the group and to be heard. Difficult as this may be, and as challenging as our desire to efficiently accomplish the group task, it can provide an opportunity to listen and gain valuable insights into our colleagues' frames of reference, thereby expanding our understanding of the issues we share as a group (Harris & Nelson, 2008). Power is a shared responsibility. We each participate in its use and abuse. It is the responsibility of each of us, as members of the group, to play our part in assuring that all voices, including our own, are heard and fully considered.

Pressures for Conformity

In spite of our best intentions, there is frequently a *pressure for conformity* in groups in order to get the job done and to move on. Group process is hard work, and it is particularly difficult when members come from widely different sets of assumptions, not only about the task but about the process itself. Even between individuals who share the same cultural norms and expectations, different experiences may cause one or another to approach a given task from a different perspective than that of the apparent majority of group members. There is frequently discomfort or outright hostility toward those members who consistently raise seemingly irrelevant issues or who refuse to go along with what appears to be a majority opinion. On the other hand, it is often the "deviant" individual who brings up issues that may otherwise go unnoticed or unacknowledged, thereby moving the group toward creative thinking and problem solving.

Although there is much agreement about the need for diverse perspectives in the development of creative solutions, the actual application of this notion in groups of diverse people is frequently fraught with difficulty. The social stigmas we attach subconsciously to those we deem less experienced or less able in some perceivable way interfere with our seriously taking account of their contributions and may interfere with their comfort in offering their points of view (Schreiber, 1996). Conflicting opinions and diverse perspectives are more easily expressed and entertained in groups of social "equals" than they are in groups of people from diverse ethnic or class backgrounds. Moving beyond our stereotypes remains the challenge in making real diversity work in our small groups and organizations. Equality does not imply that people are the same; it recognizes their differences and values them equally (Weber, 1991). In fact, the value of difference is in the diverse experiences and points of view people bring to bear on the decision and problem at hand. Setting explicit guidelines for overcoming pressures for conformity is essential to effective work in diverse groups and teams.

Computer-Mediated Virtual Teams

Not only are organizational work groups increasingly diverse, but in multinational corporations they are increasingly geographically distributed around the globe as well. Distributed teamwork has become commonplace in organizations, with an estimated

41 million workers around the globe working in virtual teams (Connaughton & Shuffler, 2007). These multinational, multicultural, distributed teams present both opportunities and challenges for organizations. "Boeing, for instance, uses a distributed multinational team composed of individuals from the United States, Japan, Europe, and Canada to develop new hardware for the International Space Station" (Connaughton & Shuffler, 2007, p. 388). These teams allow organizations to better meet their consumers' needs and enhance their company profit margins. Maintaining effective distributed teams that meet the needs of the team members and the organization is, however, a challenge (Connaughton & Shuffler, 2007). Krebs, Hobman, and Bordia (2006) described trust as a primary concern for distributed teams having diverse membership. Demographic dissimilarity and differences in country of birth can decrease the level of trust among group members, reducing their feelings of confidence in each other's abilities, diminishing their relational openness, and challenging their substantive and mutually influential information exchange. Krebs and colleagues (2006) found that distributed teams who meet via computer-mediated communication (CMC) maintain higher levels of trust, confidence, and productivity than those teams that meet face-to-face. This is an interesting finding, suggesting that the communication medium interacts with other cultural aspects to facilitate more cooperative and productive work teams.

Ethical Behavior

A proactive approach to diversity requires a careful adherence to *ethical behaviors* that guide our judgments about "whether actions are right or wrong and outcomes are good or bad" (McShane & Von Glinow, 2000, p. 14). Table 5.2 identifies some behaviors and dimensions to pay attention to during participation in group and team activities.

TABLE 5.2   Ethical Behavior for Working in Diverse Groups

Negative, Unethical Behaviors:

1. *Theft:* Stealing others' ideas, stealing or wasting their time
2. *Relationship manipulation:* Coercion, using status and arm twisting
3. *Interpersonal deception:* Lying, misleading by words or deeds, making false promises
4. *Discrimination:* Racist or sexist comments, jokes, or decisions
5. *Security violations:* Ignoring group policies or procedures
6. *Loss of impulse control:* Losing one's temper, verbal or physical violence toward others
7. *Sexual harassment:* Using position or reward power to compel personal or sexual relationship
8. *Backstabbing:* Verbally attacking someone behind his or her back, without the person knowing
9. *Evasiveness:* Sidestepping responsibility, passing the buck, refusing accountability

Positive Ethical Behavior:

10. *Altruistic deviance:* Violating group norms or social rules for the good of the group

Source: Hollwitz & Pawlowski (1997).

Summary

Changes in U.S. demographics and workforce composition have made the examination of diversity of groups an important issue (Nasser, 2006). In the United States, Caucasians of Western European ancestry are now outnumbered by Americans from Asian, African, Arabic, Hispanic, Middle Eastern, and Eastern European ancestry (Nasser, 2006; Reece & Brandt, 2005). Legal and moral issues, in addition to the basic issue of employee availability, surround the importance of organizations' accommodating varying types of diversity, disabilities, and diverse family patterns (Harris & Nelson, 2008; McShane & Von Glinow, 2000).

The importance of recognizing, accepting, and effectively utilizing differences of ethnicity, cultural heritage, gender, age, physical challenge, and other circumstances has been widely recognized and utilized by leading organizations (Reece & Brandt, 2005). As the first decade of the new millennium comes to a close, most new entrants into the workforce will be women and people from cultural minorities.

Overcoming our complex and deeply ingrained biases and prejudices against people different from ourselves can prove a difficult stumbling block to our effective use of diverse perspectives in small group and organizational settings. Our first instinct is to assume that what we know and expect is right (Barna, 1991). Because we all experience the need to reduce the uncertainty of interaction with strangers, we form ideas of what to expect from them based on certain categories or stereotypes that our socialization process has deemed important. Based on this categorical information, we "know" how to behave with those strangers. Although this is natural, the categories are often inadequate. We need to expand our points of view to take into account what is natural for those with whom we interact, as well as for ourselves, and see each other as unique individuals with diverse experiences and abilities.

Research has shown that incorporating diverse perspectives helps groups make better and more creative decisions most of the time. As difficult as it may be when interactions within a small group are consciously monitored and directed toward the inclusion of all members, the resulting synergistic effect of the group process is superior to any that could be achieved by a homogeneous group of people who share the same biases and perspectives. As we participate in groups with people different from ourselves, we need to examine and take into account our own perceptual biases and filters and allow others to be heard from their own points of view.

Accommodating different points of view and different ground rules for communication is time-consuming and often difficult but is worth the effort, if the result is a superior decision or an improved working or living environment. As Madrid (1991, p. 118) said, "what keeps our society together is tolerance for cultural, religious, social, political, and even linguistic difference; what makes us a unique, dynamic, and extraordinary nation are the power and creativity of our diversity." Beyond tolerance, it is the willingness to seek out, listen to, and appreciate difference that will be our greatest asset as we participate in diverse small groups.

DISCUSSION QUESTIONS

1. Define diversity. Does your definition take into account the members of your small group class? Is it inclusive of your educational setting? Is it too broad to be immediately useful?

2. Does valuing diversity come easily? Why or why not? Can you make some suggestions to enhance your group's ability to value diversity?

3. Are you a member of a group that has been stereotyped? Does your experience reflect the concepts identified in this chapter? How? Are there differences? What are they?

4. What is a communication context? What role does communication context play in our understanding of others?

5. Language use and nonverbal communication can convey cultural differences. Provide examples from your background of both of these.

6. How is small group effectiveness diminished by not valuing diversity or by believing in stereotypes? Provide at least three conclusions.

7. Explain the concept "White men of privilege." Do you agree with the concept? To what extent, and why or why not?

8. How does the pressure for conformity work against the valuing of diversity?

REFERENCES

Armour, S. (2002, May 10). Reports of workplace bias still on rise since Sept. 11. *USA Today*, p. 1B.

Barna, L. M. (1991). Stumbling blocks in intercultural communication. In L. A. Samovar & R. E. Porter (Eds.), *Intercultural communication: A reader* (pp. 345–353). Belmont, CA: Wadsworth.

Beamer, L., & Varner, I. (2001). *Intercultural communication in the global workplace* (2nd ed.). Boston: McGraw-Hill Irwin.

Becker, C. B. (1991). Reasons for the lack of argumentation and debate in the Far East. In L. A.

Calloway-Thomas, C., Cooper, P. J., & Blake, C. (1999). *Intercultural communication: Roots and routes*. Boston: Allyn & Bacon.

Connaughton, S. L., & Shuffler, M. (2007). Multinational and multicultural distributed teams. *Small Group Research, 38*(3), 387–412.

Crown, D. F. (2007). The use of group and groupcentric individual goals for culturally heterogeneous and homogeneous task groups. *Small Group Research, 38*(4), 489–508.

Eisenberg, E. M., & Goodhall, H. L., Jr. (2004). *Organizational communication: Balancing creativity and constraint*. Boston: Bedford/St. Martin's.

Gardenswartz, L., & Rowe, A. (1993). *Managing diversity: The complete desk reference*. San Diego: Pheiffer.

Gardenswartz, L., & Rowe, A. (1998, July). Why diversity matters. *HR Focus*, pp. 51–53.

Gemmill, G., & Schaible, L. Z. (1991). The psychodynamics of female/male role differentiation within small groups. *Small Group Research, 22*(2), 220–239.

Gentile, M. (1996). *Managerial excellence through diversity*. Prospect Heights, IL: Waveland.

Griffin, R. W. (2005). *Management* (8th ed.). Boston: Houghton Mifflin.

Hall, N. J. (2002). *Among cultures: The challenge of communication*. Boston: Thomson.

Haralson, D., & Lewis, A. (2002, April 10). Unfair treatment in the workplace. *USA Today*, p. 1B.

Harris, T. E., & Nelson, M. D. (2008). *Applied organizational communication: Theory and practice in a global environment*. New York: Lawrence Erlbaum Associates.

Hickman, G. R., & Creighton-Zollar, S. (1998). Diverse self-directed work teams: Developing strategic initiatives for 21st century organizations. *Business Source Elite, 27*, 44–47.

Hoijer, H. (1991). The Sapir-Whorf hypothesis. In L. A. Samovar & R. E. Porter (Eds.), *Intercultural communication: A reader* (pp. 244–251). Belmont, CA: Wadsworth.

Hollwitz, J. C., & Pawlowski, D. R. (1997). The development of a structured ethical integrity interview for pre-employment screening. *Journal of Business Communication, 34*(2), 203–219.

Jackson, S. E., May, K. E., & Whitney, K. (1995). Understanding the dynamics of diversity in decision-making teams. In R. A. Guzzo, E. Salas, & Associates (Eds.), *Team effectiveness and decision making in organizations* (pp. 204–261). San Francisco: Jossey-Bass.

Kirchmeyer, C. (1993). Multicultural task groups: An account of the low contribution level of minorities. *Small Group Research, 24*(1), 127–148.

Klyukanov, I. E. (2005). *Principles of intercultural communication.* Boston: Pearson.

Krebs, S. A., Hobman, E. V., & Bordia, P. (2006). Virtual teams and group member dissimilarity. *Small Group Research, 37*(6), 721–741.

Larson, J. R. (2007). Deep diversity and strong synergy. *Small Group Research, 38*(3), 413–436.

Lustig, M. W., & Koester, J. (2003). *Intercultural competence: Interpersonal communication across cultures* (4th ed.). Boston: Allyn & Bacon.

Madrid, A. (1991). Diversity and its discontents. In L. A. Samovar & R. E. Porter (Eds.), *Intercultural communication: A reader* (pp. 115–119). Belmont, CA: Wadsworth.

Mason, C. M. (2006). Exploring the process underlying within-group homogeneity. *Small Group Research, 37*(3), 233–270.

McCall, N. (1994). *Makes me wanna holler.* New York: Vintage Books.

McShane, S. L., & Von Glinow, M. A. (2000). *Organizational behavior.* Boston: Irwin McGraw-Hill.

Nasser, E. H. (2006, July 15). A nation of 300 million. *USA Today,* pp. 1A, 6A.

Neher, W. W. (1997). *Organizational communication: Challenges of change, diversity, and continuity.* Boston: Allyn & Bacon.

Neuliep, J. W. (2000). *Intercultural communication: A contextual approach.* Boston: Houghton Mifflin.

Nicotera, A. M., Clinkscales, M. J., & Walker, F. R. (2003). *Understanding organization through culture and structure.* Mahwah, NJ: Lawrence Erlbaum Associates.

Peeters, M. A. G., Rutte, C. G., van Tuijl, H. F. J. M., & Reymen, I. M. M. J. (2006). The big five personality traits and individual satisfaction with the team. *Small Group Research, 37*(2), 187–211.

Powell, G. N. (1988). *Women & men in management.* Newbury Park, CA: Sage.

Reece, B. L., & Brandt, R. (2005). *Effective human relations: Personal and organizational applications* (9th ed.). Boston: Houghton Mifflin.

Remland, M. S. (2000). *Nonverbal communication in everyday life.* Boston: Houghton Mifflin.

Robinson, G., & Dechant, K. (1997, August). Building a business case for diversity. *Academy of Management Executive,* 21–27.

Schreiber, E. J. (1996). Muddles and huddles: Facilitating a multicultural workforce through team management theory. *Journal of Business Communication, 33*(4), 459–473.

Shapcott, K. M., Carron, A. V., Burke, S. M., Bradshaw, M. H., & Estabrooks, P. A. (2006). Member diversity and cohesion and performance in walking groups. *Small Group Research, 37*(6), 701–720.

Shuter, R. (1991). The Hmong of Laos: Orality, communication, and acculturation. In L. A. Samovar & R. E. Porter (Eds.), *Intercultural communication: A reader* (pp. 270–276). Belmont, CA: Wadsworth.

Stewart, L. P., Cooper, P. J., Stewart, A. D., & Friedley, S. A. (2003). *Communication and gender* (4th ed.). Boston: Allyn & Bacon.

Strubler, D. C., & York, K. M. (2007). An exploratory study of the team characteristics model using organizational teams. *Small Group Research, 38*(6), 670–695.

Surowiecki, J. (2004). *The wisdom of crowds.* New York: Doubleday.

Survey says diversity improves bottom lines and competition. (2001, July). *HR Focus,* p. 8.

Valenti, M. A. & Rockett, T. (2008). The effects of demographic differences on forming intragroup relationships. *Small Group Research, 39*(2), 179–202.

Victor, D. A. (1992). *International business communication.* New York: HarperCollins.

Weber, S. N. (1991). The need to be: The socio-cultural significance of Black language. In L. A. Samovar & R. E. Porter (Eds.), *Intercultural communication: A reader* (pp. 277–282). Belmont, CA: Wadsworth.

Witherspoon, P. D., & Wohlert, K. L. (1996). An approach to developing communication strategies for enhancing organizational diversity. *Journal of Business Communication, 33*(4), 375–399.

Zemke, R., Raines, C., & Filipczak, B. (2000). *Generations at work: Managing the clash of veterans, boomers, Xers, and Nexters in your workplace.* New York: AMACOM.

CHAPTER

6

Verbal and Nonverbal Communication

CHAPTER OUTLINE

Functions of Verbal Communication
   Task
   Process
   Narratives and Fantasies

Structures of Meaning in Verbal Communication
   Denotative and Connotative Meaning
   Semantics
   Group Talk
   Humor

Nonverbal Communication
   Principles of Nonverbal Communication
   Types of Nonverbal Communication
   Powerless Stereotypes

Verbal and Nonverbal Cues in Computer-Mediated Communication

Summary

Discussion Questions

References

CHAPTER OBJECTIVES

- Discuss the functions of verbal communication.
- Explain group fantasies, metaphors, and narratives.
- Identify the structures of meaning in verbal communication.
- Outline the types and functions of group talk.
- Explain the principles of nonverbal communication.
- Illustrate the types of nonverbal communication.

KEY TERMS

Body language
Chronemics
Connotative meaning

Consciousness-raising talk
Denotative meaning
Encounter talk

Ethnocentrism
Eye contact
Facial expressions

Fantasy
Group fantasies
Group talk
Homophily
Humor
Inferences
Judgments
Kinesics
Metaphor

Narrative
Nonverbal communication
Observations
Paralanguage
Process
Problem-solving talk
Proxemics
Role-assumption talk
Semantics

Sex-role stereotyping
Silence
Symbolic
Synchrony
Task
Verbal communication

There is a joke about a man who visited a retirement home and was being shown around by the manager. They came out onto a large porch, overlooking the lawns and gardens, upon which a number of the current residents were sitting. As they stood there, one of the residents suddenly called out "34," and the rest of the group broke into laughter. After a few minutes of silence, another resident said "27," and again they all laughed. At this point, the man turned to the manager and said, "What is going on? Why are they laughing? What is so funny?" The manager replied that these residents had been there together as a group for so long that they had learned each other's jokes and had decided to number the jokes so that whenever someone wanted to tell one, they could just call out the number and the rest of them would remember the joke and laugh. The man asked if he could try. The manager said "Sure" and the man called out "32"! The residents all looked puzzled but remained silent. When the man asked the manager why no one had laughed, the manager simply replied, "Well, some people just don't know how to tell jokes."

Small group communication is a combination of verbal and nonverbal communication. Small groups build expectations about what these verbal and nonverbal communication characteristics will be like. Jokes, like any other form of communication, are told both verbally and nonverbally within a context of those group expectations. What makes a joke funny is the combination of verbal and nonverbal components.

Nothing never happens within the context of small group communication. Something is always taking place. Whether anyone is speaking or not, we simply cannot *not* communicate. The act of not speaking itself communicates something to those around us. When a person finds meaning in an action or a statement, whether that meaning is accurate or misinterpreted, communication has taken place. In this chapter, we discuss the various aspects of verbal and nonverbal communication that generate that meaning. We consider the roles of denotative (dictionary) meaning and connotative (associative) meaning in verbal communication and discuss the symbolic meanings assigned to both verbal and nonverbal communication. We will begin with verbal communication and conclude with nonverbal communication. Although we consider them separately in this chapter, we recognize that they occur simultaneously and work together, complementing and contradicting each other.

Verbal and nonverbal communication work together in a group discussion.

Functions of Verbal Communication

In discussing the role of verbal communication in groups, we first examine three functions of verbal communication—group task, process, and narrative.

Task

Group *task* involves developing a cognitive meaning that focuses on the either/or choices of a group and creates an understanding of the group's purposes, goals, and interactive processes. *Verbal communication* draws attention to the group's purpose and the context for the group interaction.

Small groups are usually formed to achieve a specific but complex goal. To do this, they must order their activities into a sequence that can be followed. If we are asked to serve on a task force, two of the first questions we might ask are, "What are we trying to accomplish?" and "What are the steps involved in accomplishing it?" We will be interested in the time constraints, the available resources, and other pertinent information as well, but developing an order for our group tasks is of primary importance to accomplishing it. If our group has an agenda, keeps notes, takes minutes, or even just periodically reviews what we have accomplished, we are using verbal communication to order our task. This ordering helps us keep track of our progress and to judge whether we have been successful in achieving our goal. The importance of developing and following a series of smaller tasks to accomplish our overall goal sometimes can be seen best when we join a group that is not successful. The tendency of the group to move directly to devising a solution rather than planning and working through the group problem-solving phases we discussed in Chapter 4 often leads to an ineffective shortcut. Because time has not been put into establishing the group's purpose and process, the results may be incomplete and substandard, and the group may lack unity in endorsing the final product.

Process

Group *process* is how we say something. It is often as important as what we say (task). The group norms, roles, and process all influence how well the group functions. Interrupting another member before she or he is finished may be considered rude in one small group but acceptable in another. A participant who is unable to contribute to the discussion may resent the meeting and its outcome in one group and not care in another. Many excellent meeting plans have been derailed because the group process was not adequately attended to. Attention to the process allows us to gently and diplomatically address issues that can create difficulties if left unattended.

Because small groups involve the use of interpersonal influence, verbal strategies that heighten that influence while achieving the desired goal serve the well-being of both the individual and the group. Group members who use positive, supportive verbal communication usually feel more satisfied with the results of their interactions than those who don't (Newton & Burgoon, 1990).

One of the best ways to distinguish between task and process orientations is to examine the concept of leadership. At the task level, we consider someone a successful leader if the group goal is accomplished. At the process level, we look at how the leader accomplishes that goal and whether she or he is successful as a facilitator, coach, persuader, and group participant (DuBrin, 2000). In terms of process, we are concerned with how the person leads, not if he or she always wins.

Narratives and Fantasies

In determining the success or failure of a group's verbal communication, we often look at the group narrative. How we talk about our group tells us something about how we feel toward the group. This group *narrative* combines both reality and myth. For example, when a team leader tells group members that they were picked because they are "the best and the brightest," there may be some wishful thinking along with a partial truth. To the members of a group facing a particularly difficult task, however, this remark can also provide a motivational statement.

Alternately, a leader may compliment a group for running like a "well-oiled machine" or may exhort them to "take the high road" in their decision making. Use of this type of metaphor may take on significance as a defining concept for the group and may go on to be quoted or referred to with pride by group members. The use of *metaphor* "makes us conscious of some likeness, often a strikingly novel and surprising likeness, between two fundamentally different things or processes" (Clancy, 1989, p. 24). Implicit in the comparison is a vision of how we, as a group, can and should operate. However, using metaphors to compress complicated concepts into more readily understandable ones needs to be done with some caution. The descriptions of groups found in the boxed text provides alternative metaphors with column A identifying generally more attractive images of a group.

Descriptions of Groups

A	B
One big, happy family	Insane asylum
Athletic team	Snake pit
First class	Zoo
Explorers	Quicksand
Warriors	Boiling cauldron
Stage	Swamp

Groups may also develop fantasies and stories that perpetuate the group image and serve to either motivate or derail the group's process toward its goal. Being considered "the best and the brightest" may be a fantasy, but it can provide a strong group incentive toward achieving excellence and living up to the group's perceived reputation.

Fantasy is "the creative and imaginative shared interpretation of events that fulfills a group's psychological or rhetorical need to make sense of their [sic] experience and to anticipate their [sic] future" (Bormann & Bormann, 1992, p. 110). Fantasies indicate the willingness of the group members to see events in a new or unique manner that has developed through the group's interactions. *Group fantasies* can be either positive and enhancing or negative and destructive. When stories and fantasies are shared by the group, they help develop a group's identity. Delta Air Lines has used slogans like "The Delta family feeling" and "We love to fly and it shows." If the majority of Delta employees accept these slogans as fantasy themes that they can work by then the slogans function to unify their goals and purposes. Often, the creation of a story or dramatized narrative provides a clear illustration that increases identification and interaction among group members (Witherspoon, 1997). For example, sharing examples of your own successful and unsuccessful group experiences with other group members can offer guidelines for your current group undertaking.

The narrative process provides sense making and identifies shared values among group members. When we say the customer is always right, we are telling people who work for our organization that the customer is valued over other organizational issues and concerns. If our school claims to be the best in a particular aspect of higher education because it fosters creativity, the people who attend or work for the school know that creativity is a value. On the other hand, groups seen as dysfunctional or serving no worthwhile purpose will likely live down to that expectation as well.

Structures of Meaning in Verbal Communication

The functions of verbal communication could not be achieved if it were not for the meaning we associate with words. In discussing meaning in verbal communication, we examine denotative and connotative meaning, semantic and symbolic meaning, group talk, and the use of humor.

Denotative and Connotative Meaning

Denotative meaning is what the word literally means or represents. It is the dictionary meaning of the word. However, the 500 most used words in the English language have more than 14,000 dictionary definitions. To understand what is being said, therefore, we depend not only on the denotative meaning but also on the connotative meaning—the context and associations we hold for the word(s) being used.

Connotative meaning depends on the multiple subjective realities carried by group members. Words have fuller meanings than those provided by a dictionary. When we respond that an idea is a "winner," the word in that context may have little denotative meaning, but it does have a clear connotative meaning suggesting that the idea is excellent, full of potential, exciting, and promising. In verbal communication, the group, as well as the larger social context, determines the meanings we assign to words.

The same is true of the connotative meanings generated by the words we use to refer to people. Referring to someone as "handicapped" or "disabled" labels that person rather than simply describing a physical condition. For example, I have a friend who has multiple sclerosis and must use a wheelchair to get around, but she does not consider herself "disabled." Instead she focuses her attention, and expects others to focus their attention, on what she can do rather than on what she can't do. She can't walk, but she is active, mobile, and fully employed person who has a professional job earning more money than I do. She has read more of the classics than I have, and she attends musicals, plays, symphony concerts, and operas with more frequency. She is more technically competent on her computer, a better conversationalist, and has more friends with whom she communicates on a regular basis. There are many ways in which she is more able than I, even though I can walk. Referring to her as "disabled" focuses on her inability to walk and ignores these many other aspects. This type of restricted focus can become a particular problem in small group communication when we accept the connotative meanings of the words we use to describe other group members or to identify the types of individuals we are trying to serve with our group project, labeling them as "the elderly," "the homeless," "the underprivileged," or "the disabled," as if these single-focus labels represent denotative facts rather than connotative interpretations of the facts. Labeling someone a "yuppie" is more likely to lead to a negative image than saying "young professional." Renaming group managers as team leaders, facilitators, and coaches can make a positive difference by redefining their roles, functions, and acceptance by the group. Would you rather be an employee or a team member? Do you want a manager to tell you what to do, or a leader to help you develop your abilities and support your project achievement? Language use is powerful.

Our language defines the world we see, live in, and respond to. It brings certain observable facts to our attention, while muting or ignoring others. An interesting example of this is Ervin-Tripp's (1968) interviews with Japanese American war brides living in the United States after World War II. These interviews revealed that the women had substantially different outlooks on life when they spoke in Japanese than when they spoke in English. When they spoke in English, they were more self-assertive and expressed more independence, especially when talking about a woman's ability to work outside the home, than when they spoke in Japanese. Li, a speaker of Chinese who is fluent in both English and Japanese, suggests that the language and syntax of Japanese itself shapes a female's speech to be more tentative and less assertive, while English allows more assertive linguistic expression and facilitates the more assertive conceptualizations associated with it (1996, personal communication). According to Orber and Harris (2001, p. 52), "Language is a guide to social reality."

Semantics

The study of meaning construction in language is called *semantics*. Three principles underlie the role of semantics, and help us understand how verbal communication functions. First, meanings are in people, not in words. A word means something because those who developed and who continue to use the word have agreed, and continue to agree, that it should mean that. Lederer's (1996) interesting examples of newspaper headlines found in Table 6.1 illustrate some unintentionally ambiguous and humorous messages.

Second, language is *symbolic*—that is, words are used to represent something else. The words of language are not themselves that something. For example, a school's grading scale represents something. If we say we have a 2.5 grade point average, we are not indicating what we actually learned, earned, or achieved, but the number does function as a symbol of that learning for some people in some contexts. Likewise, language is symbolic and representative within a context, but it is not the same as our experiences, observations, and feelings.

Third, language conveys meanings about observations, inferences, and judgments. Observations are based on factual occurrences, can be verified, and deal with the past or present. Inferences are deductions based on facts or indicators. *Judgments* are opinions, beliefs, or thoughts based on interpretations of a given set of facts or indicators.

During the O. J. Simpson trial for the violent murder of his wife and her friend, for example, there were observations made that Simpson had a temper. His wife had called 911 and started to file a complaint, claiming that he was violent and threatening her. From that information, some individuals inferred that he might have killed her. Finally, in deciding that he was not guilty beyond a reasonable doubt, the jury offered a judgment based on its interpretation of the facts as presented. Individuals and groups must take care in identifying their level of abstraction along the scale from objectively verifiable *observations,* to inferential opinions, to judgmental conclusions. Note that the first level, observation, allows for true or false, correct or incorrect conclusions. The second level, inference, is less certain, since we are taking information provided us and interpreting it. The third level, judgment, involves assumptions about the truth

TABLE 6.1   Simple, Symbolic, Semantics: Meanings Are Ambiguous, Interpreted by People

U.S. Newspaper Headlines

"Prince Charles backs bicycles over cars as he opens world talks."
"Iowa man's soon-to-be-amputated hand could hold key to murder."
"Beaches all washed up."
"Shop sells soup to nuts."
"One-legged escapee still on run."
"Fire officials grilled over kerosene heaters."
"Legislators tax brains to cut deficit."
"Man minus ear waives hearing."
"Bar trying to help alcoholic lawyers."

Alleged Insurance Claim Statements

Coming home I drove into the wrong house and collided with a tree I don't have.
I thought my window was down, but found out it was up when I put my head through it.
In my attempt to kill a fly, I ran into a telephone pole.
I had been driving for 40 years when I fell asleep at the wheel and had an accident.
My car was legally parked as it backed into the other car.
The other car collided with mine without giving warning of its intentions.
An invisible car came out of nowhere, struck my car, and vanished.

Signs Observed Around the World

In a Tokyo hotel: It is forbidden to steal hotel towels. If you are not a person to do such a thing,
    please do not read this notice.
In a Bucharest hotel: The lift is being fixed for the next day. During that time we regret that you
    will be unbearable.
In a Paris hotel: Please leave your values at the front desk.
In a Moscow hotel: You are welcome to visit the cemetery where famous Russian and Soviet
    composers, artists, and writers are buried daily except Thursday.
In a Swiss restaurant: Our wines leave you nothing to hope for.

Source: Lederer, 1996

based on subjective responses to our interpretations. All three of these levels—observation, inference, and judgment—are involved in our small group decision-making
and problem-solving communication processes. It is useful to our small group communication to consider, and discuss as a group, which levels we are using and when.

Group Talk

Groups use different types of *group talk*. Effective groups first define their goals and
objectives using task-oriented language. However, as noted earlier, problem solving is
rarely accomplished by task orientation alone. Because it occurs in the context of a
group made up of individual members, each with different experiences, strengths,

weaknesses, and styles of interaction, process must be attended to. While a group works toward solving problems, in the process of using language that addresses the perceived issues, each member also plays a role in offering meanings above and beyond the task-oriented *problem-solving talk*. For example, we may talk about something in a manner that indicates we perceive our role differently than the simple language we are using. If I speak with authority and particular knowledge on a given subject, I may be placing myself in the role of an expert and am engaging in *role-assumption talk*. If I respond "Really?" or "I wouldn't have thought that to be true" to your comment, my use of different tones and facial expressions may change the expressed meaning of my words and may place me in the role of an adversary. Table 6.2 shows examples of some challenging statements that tend to reduce group discussion.

Often, when a task is overwhelming or a great deal of time is being spent going in circles, groups try to reestablish their primary motivations. It would not be unusual for an individual to move away from role talk to *consciousness-raising talk*, which is primarily motivational, in an effort to refocus the group or keep it on target. In addition, in any group, there is the social–emotional discussion, which allows the members to become more familiar with one another. When group members stop talking about the task and decide to discuss their own interpersonal needs and orientations, they engage in *encounter talk*. Group talk is, therefore, multifaceted and multifunctional. At any given time, group

TABLE 6.2   Examples of Challenging Statements

1. We tried that before.	24. I don't like the idea.
2. Our problem is different.	25. You're right, *but* . . .
3. It costs too much.	26. You're 2 years ahead of your time.
4. That's beyond our responsibility.	27. We're not ready for that.
5. That's not my job.	28. Has anyone else ever tried it?
6. We're all too busy to do that.	29. It isn't in the budget.
7. It's too radical a change.	30. Can't teach an old dog new tricks.
8. We don't have the time.	31. Good thought, but impractical.
9. We don't have enough help.	32. It's too much trouble to change.
10. What you are really saying is . . .	33. Let's give it more thought.
11. We've always done it this way.	34. It won't work here.
12. Our group is too small for that.	35. Put it in writing for us to consider.
13. That's not practical for us.	36. We'll be the laughing stock.
14. I don't see the connection.	37. Not *that* idea again.
15. Bring it up in 6 months.	38. Let's all sleep on it.
16. We've never done it before.	39. Where'd you dig that one up?
17. We should look into it further before we act.	40. We did all right without it.
18. It will run up our overhead.	41. It's impossible.
19. We don't have the authority.	42. It's never been tried before.
20. That's too ivory tower.	43. Let's shelve it for the time being.
21. Let's get back to reality.	44. Let's form a committee.
22. That's not our problem.	45. It can't be done.
23. Why change it? It's still working okay.	

members may use verbal communication to convey any of the four types of messages: problem-solving talk, role-assumption talk, consciousness-raising talk, or encounter talk.

Humor

Finally, an important area of communication that is frequently overlooked is that of *humor.* Humor is based on our ability to take advantage of inconsistencies and incongruences (Duncan & Feisal, 1989). Humor uses the power of verbal communication to share messages, relieve stress, support group fantasies, integrate ideas, support common values, convey messages and meaning to people, and help listener acceptance (Bolman & Deal, 2003). Studies of effective groups indicate the importance of humor (DuBrin, 2000).

The effectiveness of groups, such as committees, has been the brunt of many jokes as well. Arthur Goldberg, former associate justice of the U.S. Supreme Court, observed, "If Columbus had an advisory committee, he probably would still be at the dock." Milton Berle, the comedian, described a committee as "a group who keep minutes and waste hours." Although this is not a call for a house comedian or a "class clown," humor is a useful tool for keeping the group cohesive and on task.

Nonverbal Communication

Although verbal communication directs the task and process aspects of the group discussion, *nonverbal communication* forms the context in which we discuss them. Our lives are filled with highly symbolic nonverbal communication activities. For example, most college students go through the formal graduation ceremony, replete with caps and gowns, speeches, hugs, and handshakes, even when there is no requirement that they attend or participate in graduation. They could, instead, receive their diplomas through the mail. Why do they take part? The nonverbal behavior is meaningful to them and to those individuals who supported their undergraduate careers. The public ceremony holds significance as a symbol of their achievement.

By definition, all behaviors that are not consciously verbal and that are assigned meaning by one or both of the parties in a communication interaction are nonverbal communication. Researchers have estimated that between 65% (Birdwhistell, 1970) and 93% (Mehrabian, 1981) of a message's meaning is nonverbal. We judge the strength and validity of messages dealing with affiliation, positive regard, power, interest, dominance, credibility, status, attitudes, and competence primarily through nonverbal communication (Andersen, 1999). In a group discussion, whether an idea is accepted or valued and to what degree frequently has as much to do with the presenter and the manner of presentation as with the literal meaning of the words used to express it.

Principles of Nonverbal Communication

For purposes of our discussion of nonverbal communication, we assume the presence of the eight guiding principles for small group communication that are summarized in Table 6.3.

TABLE 6.3   Nonverbal Communication—Principles and Effect

1. Our nonverbal communication affects the quality of our relationships.
2. Our nonverbal communication is likely to be believed more than our verbal communication.
3. Both parties assign meaning, and sometimes different meanings, to nonverbal communication behaviors.
4. Nonverbal behaviors are guided by the context and power of relationships.
5. Cultural norms and expectations guide our interpretation.
6. The things we notice lead to interpretation and the assignment of meaning.
7. Research suggests that women and men differently decode nonverbal cues.
8. With some attention, we can improve our nonverbal actions—symbolic behaviors and interpretations.

First, the quality of the relationships among group members is established and perpetuated through nonverbal behavior. We provide a great deal of nonverbal communication to others that indicates how we feel about them. Sitting next to someone at a meeting usually indicates some liking or attraction. Getting up and moving when someone sits next to us provides a message that may be interpreted negatively. In addition, our nonverbal behavior gives off information that allows other group members to interpret our words as well as our actions.

Second, when what we do and what we say are inconsistent, the nonverbal communication is more likely to be believed (Harris & Nelson, 2008). A popular saying expresses this as "You can't talk your way out of something you behaved your way into." If what we do contradicts what we say, people usually believe what we do. It is not enough to say a group is important to us; we must participate in the group's activities to demonstrate that importance.

Third, nonverbal communication becomes meaningful when one or more parties assign meaning to it. The importance of this is demonstrated when someone in our group assigns meaning to our actions, even when we did not intend to communicate that meaning. Thus, nonverbal communication can be assigned meaning even if only one of the parties decides to pay attention to it.

Fourth, our interpretations of group members' behaviors are guided by the context and power relationships. Organizational background, setting (e.g., family versus sports team), occupational and group affiliations, size of the group, the role of the individual in the group, and numerous other issues operate as intervening variables in the interpretation process. For example, two men each weighing more than 250 pounds can slap each other on their rear ends if they are playing professional football but are not likely to engage in the same behavior in a business meeting. Doing the right thing at the right time in the right place summarizes the fourth principle. Table 6.4 shows some likely interpretations of behaviors based on the context and relationships of the people engaging in them.

Fifth, groups operate within the norms and expectations of the culture of which they are a part. The way we respond to time, age, gender, race, class, ethnicity, or any number of other variables varies with the sociocultural context. The dominant culture of the United States dictates many of the norms and mores of smaller groups within that culture. For example, a person in the United States whose social and economic

TABLE 6.4 Relational Statements

People We Like:	People We Do Not Like:
Are assertive	Are pushy
Are good on detail	Are picky
Work well under pressure	Can't stand the heat
Are confident	Are conceited
Are task oriented	Are impossible to work with, real hard-nosed
Are enthusiastic	Are emotional
Follow through	Don't know when to quit
Stand firm	Are bullheaded
Have sound judgment	Have strong prejudices
Are open, speak their minds	Are mouthy
Are quiet, shy	Are secretive

culture emphasizes clock-based time may notice someone's promptness or tardiness; a Latin American may be much less likely to see this as an important issue.

Sixth, the things we notice, our perceptions of nonverbal cues, lead to meaning. Under this principle, a relaxed posture, leaning forward, decreased distance, increased touching, and enhanced attention all provide positive messages in U.S. culture (Hackman & Johnson, 1991).

Seventh, women and men may differ in their sensitivity to and accuracy in decoding nonverbal cues. La France, Henningsen, Oates, and Shaw (2009) report that women and men differ in the meanings they attribute to both verbal and nonverbal cues, and to how they interpret those meanings.

The eighth principle, in line with the seventh, suggests that although we can learn to be better at interpreting other people's nonverbal cues, we will have greater success in using the principles of nonverbal communication if we concentrate on improving our own actions and interpretations (Hackman & Johnson, 1991).

These eight principles help us frame our understanding of the role of nonverbal communication, but it is important to note that nonverbal communication can be ambiguous and misleading. Because nonverbal communication is framed within personal and social contexts, it is always important to try to understand the larger personal context of the communicator and to look for patterns, as well as for verbal corroboration. The functions of nonverbal communication including repetition, complement, accentuation, substitution, contradiction, and regulation are explained in Table 6.5.

Types of Nonverbal Communication

People interpret our involvement in the small group process through our nonverbal communication. Coker and Burgoon (1987) found that

"the behaviors that most strongly discriminated high from low involvement were general kinesic/proxemic attentiveness, forward lean, relaxed laughter, coordinated speech, fewer

TABLE 6.5   Functions of Nonverbal Communication

Function	Explanation
Repetition	Reinforcing verbal messages with nonverbal behaviors. Examples: A supervisor moving his or her arms while giving instructions. Telling and showing someone how to do a job. Giving an OK signal, or a pat on the back, along with verbal praise. The verbal and nonverbal are the same and work together to carry the message.
Complement	Using nonverbal messages to supplement, expand, modify, or provide details to a verbal message. Examples: Looking confident while conducting a briefing enhances the quality of the presentation. Speaking softly while discussing delicate information. The nonverbal adds to and facilitates the verbal message.
Accentuation	Using nonverbal communication to provide emphasis. Examples: The loudness of a person's voice often conveys the true strength of the message. A secret can be forecast by a whisper. A wink or a furrowed brow can add to the impact of the verbal message. Distance can indicate seriousness. The nonverbal accentuates and increases the power or effectiveness of the verbal message.
Substitution	Using a nonverbal behavior in place of a verbal one. Examples: A head nod to indicate yes, a pat on the back, a "knowing glance," or a "thumbs-up" for success. A symbolic action is called an emblem.
Contradiction	Making the nonverbal and verbal messages incongruent. Examples: A colleague's facial expression or vocal inflection gives a message opposite to the verbal one. Sarcasm is one of the best examples, since the tone of voice provides a meaning that is quite different from the stated one. Making someone wait and then saying that he or she is important can be an example. Someone's asking you what is wrong because of your appearance and your saying, defensively, "nothing," is another example.
Regulation	Using nonverbal behaviors to initiate, continue, interrupt, or terminate interactions. Examples: Eye contact, gestures, nods, head motions, and numerous other behaviors indicate how the interaction should progress.

silences and latencies, and fewer object manipulations. Behaviors most predictive of magnitude of involvement change were facial animation, vocal warmth/interest, deeper pitch, less random movement, and more vocal attentiveness." (p. 463)

We focus on five aspects of nonverbal communication that are important in small group communication: facial expression, paralanguage, body language, proxemics, and chronemics.

Facial Expressions show a person's willingness to interact (Remland, 2000) and can make a person appear sociable and relaxed (Gass & Seiter, 2007). Restricting our facial expression suggests a lack of involvement and interest. Smiling is a positive communication behavior that indicates to others that we are honest, intelligent, and worth joining in some venture (Harris & Nelson, 2008). Mirroring the facial expressions of another person shows interest and can increase persuasiveness (Gass & Seiter, 2007).

Eye contact is also critical to effective small group and interpersonal communication, but it is full of complex meanings and context-based assumptions. Although other cultures make different assumptions, in the United States we generally interpret direct eye contact as an indication of sincerity, credibility, honesty, and power (Andersen, 1999; Gass & Seiter, 2007). Eye contact increases a person's persuasiveness (Gass & Seiter, 2007). In addition, we tend to look at people with greater power more often than at people we consider to have less power. On the other hand, showing deference to power is accomplished through diminished eye contact by subordinates. A speaker is perceived as more confident if she or he maintains eye contact (Andersen, 1999).

In small group communication, eye contact can be used to increase or decrease the amount of interaction in the group. Those group members who are looked at most frequently tend to feel more empowered and involved. They may be more likely to contribute to the group than those who are not looked at. Conversely, if we ourselves refuse to look at the other group members, we will be left out of the conversation.

When we have to convey bad news, we tend to decrease our eye contact. On the other hand, in a leaderless performance group, such as some bands or dance companies, eye contact may be the principal means of communication between group members to assure that everyone works together (Rose, 1994). To be an effective group member, therefore, we need to be aware of and use effective eye contact and other facial expressions. This means we need to be aware of different cultural, personal, and role-related expectations and interpretations surrounding eye contact.

Paralanguage is the meaning we perceive, along with the actual words used to deliver a message. It is how we say something. This is a broad category that includes dialects, accents, pitch, rate, vocal qualities, pauses, and silences. A pleasing voice, for example, will make people more likely to listen to us, and a modulated voice is seen as more attractive and as indicating a better education and higher socioeconomic position than is a dynamic voice (Andersen, 1999). Considerable research indicates that people who speak in a clear voice and at a faster rate are more persuasive (Gass & Seiter, 2007). Particular accents and dialects carry associations that enhance or undermine our power and credibility in a group. Responses to certain vocal cues vary according to communicator and context (Buller & Aune, 1988; Buller & Burgoon, 1986). On another level, however, our emotions are clarified through our pitch, tone, rate, and other vocal behaviors that add to the words.

Paralanguage can be used to regulate the small group discussion. Our tone of voice can let the other group members know if we are approving or uncertain of or disagreeing with their contributions, and often in a group, "it's not what you said that bothered me, but how you said it."

Silence also has a number of uses. It can be used to create interpersonal distance or as an emotional response to a situation. It can indicate agreement or dissension or be used as a way of opting out of conflict. Silence may be used in response to respect for authority or as a means of defying that same authority. Thus, silence itself sends a message (Burgoon, Buller, & Woodall, 1996).

Body Language, or *kinesics,* consists of the messages we deliver through our physical appearance and by our movements and gestures. Our physical appearance sends a positive or negative message, depending on the context and the individuals receiving the stimulus. We all have built-in biases based on past experience and acculturation. For example, in the United States, studies have shown that tall, slim men are perceived as more qualified than short, stout men (Andersen, 1999; Remland, 2000).

Body movement and gesture provide a number of cues to the success or failure of group interaction. When successful communication between equals is taking place, there is frequently a *synchrony* in the body movements between individuals: "Rhythm seems to be the fundamental glue by which cohesive discourse is maintained" (Erickson, 1987). Being in sync with other members of your group means you all "march to the same basic tune." Anderson (1999) noted that numerous studies show how higher-status individuals engage in greater movement and have more relaxed posture. As with most nonverbal communication, it is difficult to generalize to all situations. However, the cues we get from body movements give us the sense of whether someone else is "on the same wavelength," thereby encouraging us to be, or discouraging us from being, open, forthcoming, and developing a group spirit. When individuals do not open up, other group members tend to view those members as judgmental, uncooperative, and nonresponsive (Remland, 2000).

How we clothe ourselves and our general appearance have an effect. Appropriate clothing and grooming can enhance credibility and facilitate persuasion (Gass & Seiter, 2007). This is made explicit when we are told to dress for the occasion—"dress for success" or "dress to impress." The underlying issue is that if other group members do not think we appear to fit the group norms, they will not give us credibility. Without credibility we have little, if any, influence within the group. Sooner or later, we will lose interest in the group and will become ineffective.

The way we move also has an effect. If we sit squarely facing the group, we will most likely be perceived as open and forthcoming and as interested in the group discussion. If we sit with our arms crossed, looking away from the group, or are relaxing in our chair, the message we give is one of being uninterested. Other group members interpret our actions as indications that we do or do not want to be a part of the group. Table 6.6 summarizes critical nonverbal behaviors.

We are judged by our behavior, not just our words. If what we do does not fit with what we say, group members tend to believe what we do. Therefore, positive nonverbal behaviors, as outlined in Table 6.7, are vital to our success in a group.

Proxemics is the study of how we use space to communicate (Gass & Seiter, 2007). The ways we structure, use, and are affected by space, that is our proximity to one another, is an important aspect of our communication (Neuliep, 2000). Sitting or standing close to another person may indicate a perceived similarity and affiliation. It can be a persuasive tactic for gaining allies in a small group discussion. However,

TABLE 6.6   Critical Nonverbal Actions

Facial display	**Clothing and general appearance**
Facial expression	**Body language** (kinesics)
Eye contact	Movement
Paralanguage (how we say something)	Gestures
Silence	

TABLE 6.7   Positive Nonverbal Behaviors

1. Time	Don't keep people waiting.
	Give adequate time to others.
2. Setting	Avoid furniture as a barrier.
	Create pleasant surroundings.
3. Physical Proximity	Closeness reduces status differences.
	Closeness promotes warmth.
4. Gestures	Make frequent use of open-palm gestures.
5. Head Movements	Use head nods.
	Tilted head indicates suspicion.
6. Facial Expression	Smile frequently.
7. Eyes	Make frequent, direct eye contact.
8. Voice	Communicate warmth.
	Avoid sounding bored or uninterested.

invading another person's space may or may not be effective depending on how it is perceived. Hall (1963) identified the study of personal space—the invisible boundary individuals draw around themselves—as proxemics. The space within this boundary is larger or smaller depending on the circumstances and the relationships among the people in an interaction. More powerful people tend to have freer use of the space around them than do less powerful individuals.

Significant issues surround physical setting and seating arrangements in the communication patterns experienced in small group communication. Sommer (1969) identified several types of seating patterns, shown in Figure 6.1. Individuals sitting across a table from each other maximize their interpersonal distance, increase their potential for sending and receiving both verbal and nonverbal messages and thus perhaps conflicting messages, and increase the likelihood of becoming competitive. Sitting with a corner of the table between participants reduces interpersonal distance, focuses attention on the project and materials rather than on the individuals' nonverbal behaviors, and may help enhance the cooperativeness of the participants. Sitting side by side reduces the interpersonal distance still further and, unless that interpersonal distance is too intimate to feel comfortable, may also be a cooperative seating arrangement. Different seating positions have been described as power spots (Kordia, 1986). Dominant positions are at the ends of a rectangular table (Cooper, 1979) and on the corners (Kordia, 1986). The middle of the table sides are considered less powerful places to sit but may be good places from which to observe the group interaction without getting drawn into the discussion. Also, sitting on a side next to a powerful individual may represent a powerful coalition within the group setting.

Less interaction and discussion take place around a rectangular table where people are positioned in rows. Leaders, or group members, can use circular settings to encourage discussion (Hamilton, 2005). Why would this work? Participants can more easily interact with one another, ask questions, and be aware of nonverbal actions. Ease of interaction can increase or decrease the communication.

FIGURE 6.1   Seating Arrangements

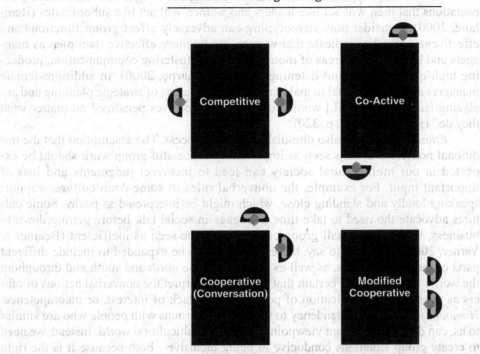

Although it is easy to make too much of seating patterns and lose sight of discussion patterns in groups, a creative group that is experiencing discussion difficulties may find that rearranging the seating influences that discussion.

Chronemics is the study of the use of time. Western cultures are particularly oriented toward clock-based time as an organizing principle in the work world (Dobkin & Pace, 2006). In western culture, time is money. Small groups organized in this context must be sensitive to the time-based expectations of many of their members and of the organizations within which they operate. Promptness is important but is also negotiable. The manipulation of time is an important dynamic in small group interactions. An individual who takes too much of a group's time may be poorly perceived and his or her contributions discounted. On the other hand, a person in an influential position may be granted more leeway in expectations for the use of time. As in all areas of nonverbal communication, to be effective, small group members must be sensitive to the time orientation of the group.

Powerless Stereotypes

Because we judge others based, in part, on their nonverbal actions, we can also be guilty of drawing invalid conclusions regarding them. Our culturally based expectations may make us prone to misjudge others, thereby reducing our group's effectiveness.

Sex-role stereotyping continues in many groups and organizations, fostering expectations that men will act like leaders and women will act like subordinates (Remland, 2000). Consider how stereotyping can adversely affect group functions and effectiveness. Studies indicate that women can be more effective than men as managers and leaders in the areas of motivating others, fostering communication, producing high-quality work, and listening to others (Sharpe, 2000). In addition, female managers are rated as equal to male managers in the areas of strategic planning and analyzing issues, "but, [still,] women often find themselves penalized no matter what they do" (Remland, 2000, p. 320).

Ethnocentrism can also diminish a group's success. The assumption that the traditional nonverbal actions seen as important to successful group work should be expected in our multicultural society can lead to incorrect judgments and loss of important input. For example, the nonverbal rules of some Arab cultures support speaking loudly and standing close, which might be interpreted as pushy. Some cultures advocate the need to take time to engage in social talk before getting down to business, which, in a small group context might be seen as inefficient (Beamer & Varner, 2001). Needless to say, these examples can be expanded to include different parts of the United States, as well as countries to the north and south and throughout the world. We must make certain that we do not interpret the nonverbal actions of others as necessarily an indication of powerlessness, lack of interest, or incompetence. *Homophily,* which is our tendency to want to be in groups with people who are similar to us, can deny us important viewpoints from our multicultural world. Instead, we need to create group situations conducive to being inclusive—both because it is the right thing to do and because it will enhance the group process.

Verbal and Nonverbal Cues in Computer-Mediated Communication

The computer-mediated communication (CMC) medium, with its reduced opportunity for nonverbal communication, creates a loss in social cues. This reduced accessibility to social cues can lead to less personal and more stereotyped impressions of other group members as represented by their gender, social class, race, ethnicity, or other categories and can facilitate the development of more biased and less effective communication relationships within the group (Hancock & Dunham, 2001; Lee, 2004; Walther, Loh, & Granka, 2005). Communicators need to be vigilant for this tendency. However, Walther and colleagues (2005) argue that the active communicator can adapt to the relative absence of nonverbal vocal, facial, and other physical cues in CMC by substituting explicit verbal cues for the unavailable nonverbal ones and by interpreting contextual and stylistic cues to gain information about other participants' characteristics, attitudes, and emotions. They indicate that communicators may require more time to develop the social–relational aspects of their communication; but given enough time and using somewhat different communication strategies, they are able to express and acquire the social–emotional communication information necessary to develop relationships and engage in effective group decision making. Current theories of

CMC, such as the social information processing, social identity of deindividuation effects, and hyperpersonal perspectives, acknowledge the influence of the medium on human impression management and interpersonal relationship development but conclude that active human communicators can (a) cope with the reduction in cues, (b) use alternative cues to process social information, (c) pay attention to their tendency to make biased impressions, and (d) consciously use the available social cues to overcome these tendencies (Postmes, Spears, & Lea, 1998; Tidwell & Walther, 2002; Walther, Loh, & Granka, 2005).

Summary

Once we gather a group of interested individuals to work on an issue, a significant influence on determining our success or failure will be the quality of the verbal and nonverbal communication. It is through these interactions that group and personal meanings are established.

Verbal communication allows group members to order the tasks, understand the process, and develop symbolic meaning through a group narrative. Traditionally, misunderstandings have been blamed on the way language was used to establish the group's "job." While the task is important, the power of language comes from its semantic and symbolic capacities. In addition, when groups use humor and engage in specific types of group talk, they often increase their chances for success.

Nonverbal communication includes all behaviors, other than verbal communication, that are assigned meaning by one or more of the participating parties. Among other things, it includes facial display, paralanguage, body language, proxemics, and chronemics. Effective group members understand the importance of both verbal and nonverbal communication.

DISCUSSION QUESTIONS

1. Distinguish among the task-ordering, process-orientation, and narrative functions of verbal communication. Why are these important to the small group and team communication process?

2. "We're number one!" is a popular characterization for a group, school, or organization. Identify three similar phrases used with groups you have been associated with. Are these metaphors or fantasies or both? Explain.

3. Identify for three other people five words you are certain will carry the same meaning—denote the same thing. Reexamine the list and see if you can provide some connotative meanings for the words. Share your list with several other people and see if your denotative words have the same meaning for the other group members.

4. Distinguish among problem-solving, role-assumption, consciousness-raising, and encounter talk. From your own experiences, provide an example of each.

5. Think of a joke about your college or university—or, perhaps, your college or university's chief rival. How does the telling of the joke, or humor in general, function in a group?

6. Return to the eight principles of nonverbal communication. Pick two principles, and provide new examples of how they operate in a group or team.

7. How can you use eye contact to increase your small group or team effectiveness?

8. What is synchrony? How does it function in small groups or teams?

9. Explain proxemics and chronemics. Are there universal rules for all cultures regarding these concepts? Explain.

REFERENCES

Andersen, P. A. (1999). *Nonverbal communication: Forms and functions*. Mountain View, CA: Mayfield.

Beamer, L., & Varner, I. (2001). *Intercultural communication in a global workplace*. Boston: McGraw-Hill Irwin.

Birdwhistell, R. L. (1970). *Kinesics and context: Essays on body motion communication*. Philadelphia: University of Pennsylvania Press.

Bolman, L. G., & Deal, T. E. (2003). *Reframing organizations: Artistry, choice, and leadership* (3rd ed.). San Francisco: Jossey-Bass.

Bormann, E. G., & Bormann, N. C. (1992). *Effective small group communication* (5th ed.). Edina, MN: Burgess.

Buller, D. B., & Aune, R. K. (1988). The effects of vocalics and nonverbal sensitivity on compliance: A speech accommodation theory explanation. *Human Communication Research, 14*(3), 301–332.

Buller, D. B., & Burgoon, J. K. (1986). The effects of vocalics and nonverbal sensitivity on compliance: A replication and extension. *Human Communication Research, 13*(1), 126–144.

Burgoon, J. K., Buller, D. B., & Woodall, W. G. (1996). *Nonverbal communication: The unspoken dialogue*. New York: McGraw-Hill.

Clancy, J. J. (1989). *The invisible powers: The language of business*. Lexington, MA: Lexington Books.

Coker, D. A., & Burgoon, J. K. (1987). The nature of conversational involvement and nonverbal encoding patterns. *Human Communication Research, 13*(4), 463–494.

Cooper, K. (1979). *Nonverbal communication for business success*. New York: AMACOM.

Dobkin, B. A., & Pace, R. C. (2006) *Communicating in a changing world: An introduction to theory and practice*. New York: McGraw-Hill.

DuBrin, A. J. (2000). *Applying psychology: Individual and organizational effectiveness* (5th ed.). Upper Saddle River, NJ: Prentice-Hall.

Duncan, W. J., & Feisal, J. P. (1989). No laughing matter: Patterns of humor in the workplace. *Organizational Dynamics, 17*(4), 18–30.

Erickson, F. (1987). The beat goes on. *Psychology Today*, pp. 21, 38.

Ervin-Tripp, S. M. (1968). An analysis of the interaction of language, topic, and listener. In J. A. Fishman (Ed.), *Reading in the sociology of language*. The Hague: Mouton.

Gass, R. H. & Seiter, J. S. (2007). *Persuasion: Social influence and compliance gaining* (3rd ed.). Boston: Allyn & Bacon.

Hackman, M. Z., & Johnson, C. E. (1991). *Leadership: A communication perspective*. Prospect Heights, IL: Waveland.

Hall, E. T. (1959). *The silent language*. Garden City, NY: Doubleday.

Hamilton, C. (2005). *Communicating for results: A guide for business and professionals*. Boston: Thomson Wadsworth.

Hancock, J. T., & Dunham, P. J. (2001) Impression formation in computer-mediated communication revisited. *Communication Research, 28,* 325–347.

Harris, T. E., & Nelson, M. D. (2008). *Applied organizational communication: Theory and practice in a global environment*. New York: Lawrence Erlbaum Associates.

Kordia, M. (1986). Symbols of power. In P. J. Frost, W. F. Mitchell, & W. R. Nord (Eds.), *Organizational reality: Reports from the firing line* (3rd ed.). Glenview, IL: Scott Foresman.

La France, B. H., Henningsen, D. D., Oates, A. & Shaw, C. M. (2009) Social-sexual interactions? Meta-analyses of sex differences in perceptions of flirtatiousness, seductiveness, and promiscuousness. *Communication Monographs, 76*(3), 263–285.

Lederer, R. (1996, July 27–28). Some headlines say far more than they mean to. *Patriot Ledger* (Quincy, MA), p. 36.

Lee, E. (2004). Effects of visual representation on social influence in computer-mediated communication. *Human Communication Research, 30,* 234–259.

Mehrabian, A. (1981). *Silent messages: Implicit communication of emotions and attitudes* (2nd ed.). Belmont, CA: Wadsworth.

Neuliep, J. W. (2000). *Intercultural communication: A contextual approach*. Boston: Houghton Mifflin.

Newton, D. A., & Burgoon, J. K. (1990). The use and consequences of verbal influence strategies during interpersonal disagreements. *Human Communication Research, 16,* 4, 477–518.

Orber, M. P., & Harris, T. M. (2001). *Interracial communication: Theory into practice.* Belmont, CA: Wadsworth Thomson Learning.

Postmes, T., Spears, R., & Lea, M. (1998). Breaching or building social boundaries: Side effects of computer-mediated communication. *Communication Research, 25*(6), 689–715.

Remland, M. S. (2000). *Nonverbal communication in everyday life.* Boston: Houghton Mifflin.

Rose, J. (1994). Communication challenges and role functions of performing groups. *Small Group Research, 25*(3), 411–432.

Sharpe, R. (2000, November 20). As leaders, women rule. *Business Week,* pp. 75–84.

Sommer, R. (1969). *Personal space: The behavioral basis of design.* Englewood Cliffs, NJ: Prentice-Hall.

Tidwell, L. C., & Walther, J. B. (2002). Computer-mediated communication effects on disclosure, impressions, and interpersonal evaluations: Getting to know one another a bit at a time. *Human Communication Research, 28,* 317–348.

Walther, J., Loh, T., & Granka, L. (2005). Let me count the ways: The interchange of verbal and nonverbal cues in computer-mediated and face-to-face affinity. *Journal of Language & Social Psychology, 24*(1), 36–65.

Witherspoon, P. D. (1997). *Communicating leadership: An organizational perspective.* Needham Heights, MA: Allyn & Bacon.

CHAPTER 7

Listening and Feedback: The Other Half of Communication

CHAPTER OUTLINE

CHAPTER OBJECTIVES

- Explain the importance of listening.
- Identify the role played by motivation in effective listening.
- Outline the four components of listening.
- Identify the barriers to effective listening.
- Define active listening.
- Clarify the barriers to active listening.
- Elucidate the four response methods of active listeners.
- Discuss the eight guidelines for feedback.
- Describe constructive feedback techniques.

KEY TERMS

Active listening

Arrogance

Constructive feedback

Disrespect

Distracting delivery

Evaluation

Expressing understanding

External noise

Faking attention

Feedback

Internal noise

Interpreting

Lack of interest

Listening styles

Long-term memory

Memory

Noise

Paraphrasing

Preprogrammed emotional responses

Receiving feedback

Questions

Selective attention

Sensing

Short-term memory

Thought speed

Who's on First?

Abbott: They give ball players nowadays very peculiar names.

Costello: Funny names?

Abbott: Nicknames. Pet names. Now, on the St. Louis team we have Who's on first, What's on second, I Don't Know is on third.

Costello: That's what I want to find out. I want you to tell me the names of the fellows on the St. Louis team.

Abbott: I'm telling you: Who's on first, What's on second, I Don't Know is on third.

Costello: You know the fellows' names?

Abbott: Yes.

Costello: Well, then, who's playin' first?

Abbott: Yes.

Costello: I mean the fellow's name on first base.

Abbott: Who.

Costello: The fellow playin' first base for St. Louis.

Abbott: Who.

Costello: The guy on first base.

Abbott: Who is on first.

Costello: Well, what are you askin' me for?

(from *The Naughty Nineties*, as quoted in Furmanek & Palumbo, 1991)

In any human communication process, effective listening is equally important as clear, articulate speaking. Sensitive, articulate expression of ideas is only one half of communication; careful, effective listening is the other half. Receiving the message being sent by the other person and accurately assigning meanings to that message are required for understanding and for any real communication. Abbott and Costello's "Who's on First?" routine can bring a smile to our faces, but ineffective communication and listening in real life is not often as funny.

In July of 2008, two jets, one landing and the other taking off, came within a half-mile of colliding at the John F. Kennedy International Airport. The FAA classifies this type of incident as a "proximity event," one in which aircraft fly too close to each other for aviation comfort. It was the second such event at the airport in less than a week. In this incident, a Boeing 757 and a Bombardier CRJ9 came within 600 feet of each other vertically and a half-mile horizontally. On the Saturday before, one passenger flight was landing at JFK when another was taking off and their flight paths crossed within 200 feet of each other vertically and a half-mile horizontally. The Boeing 757–Bombardier CRJ9 incident occurred when the Boeing 757 was handed off from the FAA's traffic control center in Westbury, NY, to the JFK control tower as the plane prepared to land. After the handoff, the pilot apparently didn't use the communication frequency the flight had been assigned to communicate with the JFK tower. Consequently, the JFK control tower did not establish contact with the flight until it was 1.5 miles from touching down on the runway. (cbsnews.com, retrieved July 11, 2008). That lack of communication almost led to a midair collision. There are times when communication—speaking, listening, and feedback—are critically important.

Small groups become effective when they develop a group synergy through a common group understanding. That common understanding and synergy are made possible through effective listening that incorporates individual ideas in new ways into a common group concept. To take advantage of everyone's input and generate new ideas we, as a group, must be good listeners. Without careful listening, a group is simply made up of individuals with independent and often competing or conflicting ideas. The goal of small group communication is to create and develop ideas together. Listening plays a key role in achieving that goal. If no one is listening effectively, the group fails to achieve the larger unity for which it was convened. In organizations, successful high-performance teams have "an open communication structure that allows all members to participate. Individuals are listened to regardless of their age, title, sex, race, ethnicity, profession or other status characteristics" (Wheelan, 1999, p. 42).

Research indicates, however, that even though about half of our communication time is spent listening (DuBrin, 2000), most of us are not very good listeners (Alessandra & Hunsaker, 1993). Many physicians do not listen carefully enough to their patients' stories to make accurate diagnoses (Kolata, 2005). Indeed, most of us listen at a 25% effectiveness level, which means we miss about 75% of the messages (Reece & Brandt, 2005). In addition, what I hear may not be the 25% you thought was the most important part of what you were saying. Ineffective listening interferes with communication. In groups, it becomes an even greater obstacle because we are listening to several people providing different messages.

Why are we such poor listeners? Some scholars have suggested that even though we have all been encouraged to talk, few of us have been taught how to listen. As Johnson (1996, p. 91) put it, "No parent waits eagerly for a child to learn to listen. Rather, the emphasis is on learning to talk." We tend to believe that talking is the same thing as communicating. Yet, as the expression goes, "God gave us two ears and one mouth."

We often incorrectly identify talking with leading and listening with following. Yet, listening is an important skill. The following funny story, or "tall tale," makes the point. Visit www.snopes.com/military/lighthouse.asp for the rest of the story. Is anybody listening or just talking and repeating the story?

Canadian authorities to U.S. Navy ship: Please divert your course 15 degrees to the south to avoid a collision.

Americans: Recommend you divert your course 15 degrees to the north to avoid a collision.

Canadians: Negative. You will have to divert your course 15 degrees to the south to avoid a collision.

Americans: This is the captain of a U.S. Navy ship. I say again, divert YOUR course.

Canadians: No, I say again, divert YOUR course.

Americans: This is the aircraft carrier USS *Lincoln,* the second largest ship in the United States 92 Fleet. We are accompanied by three destroyers, three cruisers, and numerous support vessels. I demand that you change YOUR course 15 degrees north. I say again, that is one five degrees north, or countermeasures will be taken to ensure the safety of this ship.

Canadians: This is a lighthouse. Your call.

The Influence of Culture on Listening

Listening is also influenced by culture. Understanding the cultural influences on our *listening styles* is important to developing an intercultural sensitivity and communication competence. To be successful in communicating with people having other cultural orientations, a person must take into account the likely differences in cultural expectations of the participating individuals as listeners and be able to respond to their communication within the context of their listening habits and cultural norms (Imhof & Janusik, 2006).

A number of studies have shown the influence of culture on listening. Harris (2004) examined Mexican listening styles, and Veenstra (2004) investigated the listening styles of modern Arab men. Both studies show the importance of understanding the historical background and cultural values of a community and how it affects listening behavior. Imhof's (2003) study comparing German and American participants suggests that German participants often place more emphasis on their listening behavior than Americans do. Imhof and Janusik (2006) suggested that their German participants conceptualize listening as interactive and focused on the person in a way that supports monitoring the conversation. Their American participants conceptualize listening as a sustaining activity that affects the listener's knowledge structure and set of attitudes. Dragan and Sherblom (2008) reported a comparison of the listening styles of respondents from countries of the former Soviet Union (culturally influenced by the Soviet ideology of collectivism) and native-born American participants (culturally influenced by American individualism). They report that the individualism–collectivism dimension of culture has an important effect on listening styles. In general, the post-Soviet collectivist-influenced group chooses significantly more people-oriented and less action-oriented listening styles than the American individualist-influenced group does. The American group is generally more action oriented in their listening style than the post-Soviet group. So culture matters, and listening styles should be taken into account when working in a group.

Listening as a Critical Leadership Skill

Mediators, negotiators, and other individuals who are trained to work through problems must first learn to listen effectively. In negotiator training seminars, the negotiator trainees often are reminded that they have never learned anything while they were talking and that they cannot succeed in a negotiating session until they fully understand the other side (Asherman & Asherman, 1990). When they are talking, they are sending messages but are not developing much insight into how other people think or feel.

In *The Seven Habits of Highly Effective People,* Covey (1989) identified one of the seven habits as "Seek first to understand, then to be understood" (p. 235). Ineffective people, he explains, are eager to be heard but often do not take the time to understand the other person's perspective before speaking. Highly effective people place understanding the other person first, and that understanding comes only through listening.

Motivation

No one becomes a better listener without the motivation to do so. Essentially, we all ask, "What's in it for me?" In small groups, the listening payoff is clear. Effective listening, with the consequent synergy of shared ideas, allows for successful solutions to problems, the achievement of goals, and the personal satisfaction of a job well done.

The rewards of effective listening include many life-enhancing experiences, such as learning, building relationships, being entertained, enjoying conversations, making intelligent decisions, saving time, settling disagreements, getting the best value, preventing accidents and mistakes, asking intelligent questions, and making accurate evaluations (DuBrin, 2000; Recce & Brandt, 2005). Good listeners get a great deal more out of small group membership and are more appreciated by their fellow members.

Listening has been shown to be a important skill for successful managers, supervisors, and professional employees as well. Listening takes up more than 60% of an average day on the job (Peters, 1987), but effective listening is difficult, and "only about one-third of employees say that their managers listen to them" (Sweeney & McFarlin, 2002, p. 294).

Good listening is a complex process, and numerous ways exist to parse it into its component parts. In this chapter, we present several ways of looking at the listening process. First, we examine the four components of listening: hearing, interpreting, evaluating, and responding. Then we examine active versus passive listening.

The Four Components of Listening

> "I know that you believe that you understand what you think I said, but I am not sure you realize that what you heard is not what I meant." *(attributed to Robert McCloskey)*

Listening is a complex process that involves four sequential components experienced in rapid succession. We must sense or hear the message, interpret or provide meaning to the message, evaluate the content of the message, and retain and respond to the message in the context of an ongoing communication event. Each of these components is itself a complex process. For this reason, a more detailed examination of each follows.

Sensing (Hearing the Message)

Hearing the sounds, and even being able to repeat the words, is not the same thing as *sensing*, or hearing, the message. Hearing is the involuntary "physiological process of receiving aural stimuli" (Johnson, 1996, p. 91). Thus, the act of hearing the sounds is nonselective. Sensing or hearing the message, on the other hand, is a voluntary act whereby we choose certain sounds and noises to pay attention to, while avoiding others. This is an important part of listening and happens as a result of our decision to attune to certain messages. Hearing and listening to the message are influenced by selective attention and the amounts of external and internal noise.

Selective Attention.   Choosing one message over another is called *selective attention*. The messages we attune to are the ones that have some "preprogrammed" importance for us. If I am an avid football fan, I will be drawn toward football-related messages. If I'm interested in social or environmental issues, I will tune in to those. If I am a blogger, I will selectively attend to messages related to blogging. If I am committed to social justice, I am more likely to pay attention when equal-rights issues are discussed. On the other hand, if I do not follow the soap operas on TV, I am not likely to pay attention to someone discussing the latest gossip about one of the stars.

There are several reasons we engage in this practice of selective attention, as indicated in Table 7.1. To start, some things are simply more important to us. For example, when someone calls our name, we are more likely to respond. With the barrage of stimulation that assaults us from all directions in our daily lives, we must learn to discriminate those stimuli that are necessary either to our survival or to our well-being from those that make little difference to us in our ongoing lives. Because we cannot

TABLE 7.1   Reasons for Selective Attention

1. Some things are more important than others.
2. We are more likely to listen when the content supports our point of view.
3. Messages contradicting what we believe are likely to be rejected.
4. Expertise or understanding can decrease interest in other viewpoints.
5. Difficult material may be ignored.

possibly process all the stimulation that surrounds us, we have learned to pay attention to those stimuli that are familiar to us and that have particular significance for us. These can range from issues of crucial importance to those that appear trivial. They can include basic survival, our jobs, our relationships, popular cultural icons, or any number of other stimuli in our environments.

Because small groups are convened for any number of purposes, we may be called on to listen to discussions ranging from subjects in which we have little or no interest, to those in which we have strong feelings or feel particularly expert, or to those that excite great controversy. In each of these cases, we are presented with particular challenges to our ability to listen carefully and to contribute meaningfully to the group discussion.

In addition, small groups are frequently made up of individuals from a variety of backgrounds, experiences, and points of view. If we have been asked to join a group convened to come up with solutions to a given problem in our community, we are more likely to pay attention to, and to side with, individuals, arguments, or examples that support our point of view on the issue than to those that oppose it, particularly if the topic is a controversial one. In a sense, we put "emotional cotton" in our ears when certain topics are broached. Even when we are ready to listen, anger, frustration, or hostility may interfere and make us defensive rather than good listeners.

When messages contradict or challenge our way of thinking, we may tend to reject them. Prejudices, stereotypes, and preconceived ideas can prevent us from fully hearing issues and alternative viewpoints on topics. If we hold preconceived ideas about the place of women in our society, assume that older people have little to contribute to the economic base of our society, make assumptions about the general characteristics of people based on their racial or ethnic backgrounds, hold stereotypes about gay people, or believe adamantly in one side of an issue, such as the right to die or the right to choice, then it becomes difficult for us to hear other people's views on these topics when they oppose or even question our own.

In addition, we make conscious decisions to pay attention to some messages and ignore others. As we become more expert in a particular subject, we may tend to dismiss what we consider unsophisticated viewpoints. This can become a problem in small groups, when ideas are weighted toward the opinions of the "experts" and miss the potentially broader and sometimes innovative views of those on the "outside" of the issue.

Finally, difficult material may discourage us from listening carefully. If we believe we do not understand the issue in question, we may simply drop out of the discussion, assuming we have nothing to offer to it anyway. This robs the group of our potential input from a fresh perspective, while robbing ourselves of an opportunity to learn something new and perhaps beneficial in some way. In a small group, members with particular expertise need to take responsibility for clarifying the issues and helping all members overcome the barriers to understanding, but they must also be open to listening to new and innovative approaches to the issue under discussion.

Noise.   *Noise* is a useful term for the interference that occurs between the spoken message and hearing it. There are two types of noise: external and internal. *External noise* includes distractions that make it difficult to hear the other person. For a small group, these can include extraneous sounds like a telephone ringing; bad acoustics;

poor visibility between the speaker and the listener; an uncomfortable physical environment; other people talking, coughing, or moving around; or any number of other physical distractions. Comedian George Carlin's quip "Aren't you glad the phone wasn't invented by Alexander Graham Siren?" alludes to the distraction and irritation caused by certain sounds. Remember the last beautiful spring day when you were sitting in a hot, stuffy classroom and you could hear music and people having fun outside? That is the essence of external noise.

Internal noise includes a preoccupation with personal issues, charged-up emotional states, stereotyping and prejudice toward the sender or toward his or her message, or distractions from other aspects of our lives. All of these interfere with our hearing. We are not blank slates that unconditionally accept all incoming verbal and nonverbal messages. If we do not make a conscious effort or are not trained in active listening, we frequently allow noise to interfere with our hearing.

Interpreting the Message

Assigning meaning to someone's message is a complex task. In hearing the message and choosing to pay attention, we accept the message into our memory system. *Interpreting* the message is the next step. Our goal should be to understand the other person's meaning. We are all limited in our perspective and understanding by our perceptions of others' verbal and nonverbal communication. As I listen to someone else, I filter my interpretation of her or his message through my own attitudes, assumptions, needs, values, past and present experiences, knowledge, expectations, fears, goals, educational background, and emotional involvement. Thus, we each bring our own particular limitations to hearing and accurately interpreting someone else's message.

A much cited story provides an example of the preconceptions we frequently bring to our interpretations. A little boy is involved in a serious automobile accident in which his father, who was driving the car, is killed instantly. The boy is rushed to the hospital in critical condition. The emergency room doctor takes one look at the boy and shouts, "Oh, my God. It's my son!" How is this possible? For some of us, the answer is not immediately apparent. Our implicit assumption that doctors are ordinarily men can make the interpretation process difficult. In this case, the doctor is the boy's mother. Recognizing our assumptions and interpretations can be tricky business.

During a job interview, the interviewer tells the interviewee that "only the top 10% get jobs with this company." Is the interviewer boasting, trying to show the exclusiveness of the company, explaining how selective the process can be, letting the interviewee know there is little chance of being hired, or making the chance to be hired seem like an honor? There are many possible interpretations of this type of statement. As the interviewee, we will likely to adopt the one that reflects our own prior experiences and sets of assumptions. This interpretation will, in turn, likely influence our interview performance. This is true in small group discussions, as well.

Although we all use preprogrammed assumptions to interpret and understand communication events, we can retrain those assumptive bases. For example, customer service personnel in some companies are trained to see a complaint or problem as just an opportunity turned upside down (Zemke & Schaaf, 1989). The staff are trained to

Successful group decision making requires outstanding teamwork and common goals.

accept criticism of their organization as valued input, rather than to react defensively. Thus, our interpretation of others' messages can be consciously affected by our attention to our own assumptive bases. The more we learn to move beyond our unexamined assumptions and the more we allow ourselves to understand others' perspectives, the more accurate or mutually beneficial our interpretations of their messages can become.

Evaluating the Message Content

This stage involves forming an opinion or making a judgment regarding the messages. We are asking ourselves if the "facts" support the points being made or justify the positions being taken. It is a quality-control step, which poor listeners frequently overlook in their rush to judgment. Too often, we don't stop to make certain that all the information is carefully gathered and weighed.

When we serve on a jury, we are admonished by the judge to refrain from making any final decision until all the evidence has been heard. This is a reminder of the importance of the evaluation stage of listening. *Evaluation* is the process of taking in various inputs, filtering out those that we consider unimportant, interpreting those that are important in our view, and then making decisions about how to deal with them. In the decision-making process, it is important not to evaluate before collecting enough information.

Memory: Retaining and Responding to the Message

Everyone in good mental health has two types of *memory*. *Short-term memory* is our working memory, and it lasts from 1 to 60 seconds and decides which incoming messages should be preserved. If we do not recognize the messages as important, they are dismissed. Through our selective attention, we may concentrate on certain types of messages. If we are distracted by external or internal noise, however, there is a good chance we will temporarily lose a portion of the message, and unless there is some compelling reason to retain the input, the message may be easily overridden by competing stimuli. In the first meeting of a small group, we may be so intent both on making sure others perceive us well and on monitoring our own external performance that we do not concentrate on introductory information given during the meeting. In so doing, we may effectively undermine the good impression we wanted to make.

If we are stimulated to process and store particular bits of information, those bits gain access to our *long-term memory*. Although this part of our memory is relatively unlimited in its capacity, the message must first gain entry. Often, we must hear something several times before it gains access to our long-term memory. The first component of listening is that of acting on which messages to admit to our short- and long-term memory bases. Selective attention, external and internal noise, and our memory system all play important roles in our ability to hear the message.

Each of the four components of listening plays a vital part in how well we participate in small groups. As we have shown, each component can be either a building block or a barrier in our listening process, and active, effective listening is key to the success of small groups.

Active Listening

Active listening is hard work. When we engage in active listening, we respond verbally and nonverbally to the other group members, letting them know we are paying attention. We become part of the transaction and take responsibility for understanding their meanings. These active listening behaviors and skills are not intuitive and do have barriers to their effective achievement. We present some of those barriers (Golen, 1990).

Barriers to Active Listening

Lack of Interest.   The first barrier has to do with *lack of interest* in the subject matter, either because we find it inherently uninteresting or because we have determined it is too difficult for us to understand. This can lead to boredom, impatience with the speaker, daydreaming, or becoming preoccupied with something else instead of listening. To work with this barrier and contribute meaningfully to the group process, we need to find areas of interest. We may even tell ourselves that since we are there at that moment, we might as well pay attention to the content of the discussion.

Distracting Delivery.   A second barrier to good listening is *distracting delivery*—our tendency to judge the speaker's personal characteristics. If someone fidgets, refuses to be efficient in his or her comments, seems disorganized, speaks in an accent or cadence different from our own, dresses in an unusual way, or behaves in any number of other ways distracting to us, we may become impatient and inattentive or begin concentrating on the speaker's mannerisms or delivery, rather than on the message (Pearson & Davilla, 1993). We need to remember, however, that it may be the least likely person who offers the greatest insight on a particular issue. All too often, we miss that when we allow ourselves to be distracted by superficial aspects of a person's presentation style. We need to remind ourselves to judge content, not delivery, and we need to exercise patience, allowing the other person to develop her or his ideas before rejecting them based on irrelevant criteria.

External and Internal Noise.   External and internal noise is the third barrier. As we discussed earlier under Noise, this can prevent us from hearing the messages conveyed during a small group session. During any conversation, a phone ringing, a lawn mower running, or someone hammering nearby is a distraction. Whether the noise is external or internal, it is up to each of us to make an effort to hear past it—to concentrate on the message. We might remind ourselves that the information we miss by being distracted will have to be regained sometime in the future. Essentially, not listening at this moment is an opportunity lost that will require our time and energy later. In a group, it may be difficult to recreate the messages that are missed, since the dynamics of the group process are difficult to recreate.

Arrogance and Disrespect.   The fourth barrier relates to our emotional responses to behaviors that show *arrogance* or *disrespect*. People with know-it-all attitudes or who use generalizations such as "you always" or "you never" may create hostility in us. If we are attacked personally or treated with disrespect, we are less likely to listen carefully to what is being said. This behavior may be difficult for individual group members to deal with effectively, but a strong group leader should be able to moderate that kind of behavior in the interest of the group as a whole. In the case of behaviors that are simply annoying, each of us as group members must try to overlook and to see through them to the contributions the individual is making to the group process.

Preprogrammed Emotional Responses.   A fifth barrier to effective listening, *preprogrammed emotional responses,* occur when a group member touches on an issue to which we have a strong emotional reaction. Group members may refuse to maintain a relaxing and agreeable environment for the speaker or refuse to relate to and benefit from the speaker's ideas, may disagree or argue outwardly or inwardly with the speaker or become emotional and excited when the speaker's views differ from their own, and the discussion can quickly degenerate into an argument of already established biases, rather than airing different points of view. Frequently, the more important the topic, the more likely group members are to respond from a preprogrammed point of view than from a rational response to the issue at hand. When this happens, we are best advised to sit back, relax, and hear the other person out. If we have really listened carefully, we may find points on which we can agree. If not, we have still heard the speaker and can make a relevant reply based on what was really said, rather than on our preprogrammed emotional reaction.

Ambushing.   This sixth barrier often comes hand-in-hand with the fifth one. We disagree with the individual and simply wait for a chance to interrupt or debate. We rehearse our own rebuttal while the individual is speaking and wait for the chance to ambush. Some listeners listen intently for points on which they can disagree and then just wait for their chance to attack the speaker.

Listening for Facts.   A seventh barrier to effective listening is getting past our training in school, which was to listen only for the facts in order to recall them for a test. In a small group discussion, delivering a series of facts is not the sole purpose of communication. Rather, the purpose is to achieve some degree of mutual understanding. Deliberative listening, or listening only for facts, can actually blind us to the overall point being made by the sender. Understanding comes from sensing the other person's point, not just from developing a catalog of the facts presented. Thus, effective listening looks for the overall themes that encompass the facts and the reasoning behind them.

Faking Attention—Pseudo-listening.   The eighth barrier to effective listening—*faking attention*—may also have its genesis in our school training. Often, usually some time around second or third grade, we are singled out by a teacher who admonishes us to "Pay attention!" After that, we become quite adept at faking attention, and before long we may fake more than we listen. The only solution to this problem is to recognize it and work at really listening.

Thought Speed.   *Thought speed* is the ninth barrier to careful listening. Because we can think three to four times faster than anyone can talk, our temptation is to make use of the "free" time by allowing ourselves to wander around mentally. We may formulate our responses to what we think is being said, we may be triggered into thoughts on totally unrelated subjects, or we may simply feel bored and stop listening altogether. We can, however, train ourselves to use our thought energy to concentrate more fully on what is being said and intended—listening carefully to the phrasing of the message, observing the manner of presentation, and looking for any other clues that may be apparent in the delivery of the message. This concentration is a clear competitive advantage that effective listeners can use.

Other Barriers.   Other barriers to active listening include laziness or tiredness (avoiding a subject because it is complex or difficult or because it takes too much time) and insincerity (avoiding eye contact while listening and paying attention only to the speaker's words, rather than to the speaker's meaning).

Active Listening Response Methods

Active listeners take advantage of the opportunity to listen carefully and understand each person during a group discussion. This enables them to participate more effectively and offer constructive feedback during the process. Four response methods that active listeners use are paraphrasing, expressing understanding, asking questions, and using nonverbal communication.

Paraphrasing. Considered one of the secrets of effective listeners, *paraphrasing* is stating in our own words what we think the speaker intended to say. The description should be objective. Essentially, we are responding to the verbal and nonverbal signals given by the speaker.

Among other things, paraphrasing is an excellent way to fight daydreaming. If we are concentrating on developing an internal summary of another individual's thoughts and ideas, we do not have time to daydream (Dobkin & Pace, 2006). We can paraphrase verbally to the speaker or simply paraphrase internally by mentally summarizing the other person's points.

In addition, in group meetings there is a tendency for the discussion to go off on tangents. Thus, a second value of paraphrasing lies in its ability to bring the discussion back to the points being made at that time and to put group members back on the same track. A simple comment such as "So I understand that what you are concerned about is . . ." allows a clear response by the speaker. Whether he or she says yes or no, everyone is back talking about the same issue. Used in this context, paraphrasing is a no-lose technique, and it helps the group stay focused.

Finally, paraphrasing can move emotional issues from the personal back to the objective. If one of the group members has been complaining that "You never listen to my comments about . . . !" a careful restatement, such as "Okay, what I hear you saying is . . ." can allow the other group members to focus on the crux of the problem. The complaining member is treated with respect, and the discussion is turned toward something that involves content, not emotion.

Expressing Understanding. At times, it may seem more appropriate to focus on the feelings of the speaker, rather than to restate the content of the message. This type of statement *expressing understanding* allows the group to assess more accurately how well the speaker's feelings have been perceived and understood, and this may permit the speaker to view her or his own feelings more accurately, as well. "You sound hopeful about . . ." allows the speaker to clarify or modify his or her meaning and the group to better understand the totality of the message. To enhance clarity, we should note the nonverbal communication of the speaker, as well as the actual statements. This is more than saying, "I know how you feel."

Asking Questions. Part of paraphrasing and expressing understanding is the effective use of *questions*. This is a skill rarely taught and frequently used in ways that discourage, rather than enhance, discussion. Questions can be seen as challenges to our honesty or position on an issue, or they can be seen as manipulative. A question such as "You don't really believe those people, do you?" does not invite an open discussion of the respondent's point of view. In a small group, the goal of questioning should be to clarify the other person's perspective, open up the discussion, or follow up on a previous idea. It should not be used as a thinly veiled attempt at putting the respondent on the spot. Combined with paraphrasing and expressed understanding, questions allow the listener to both indicate an interest and clarify the message. A simple "Do you mean . . . ?" may clear up any possible misunderstandings.

Using Nonverbal Communication.   Since more than 50% of all meaning is communicated nonverbally, effective listeners make use of nonverbal gestures. Making eye contact, nodding our heads, and sitting in an attentive manner all indicate that we are interested and listening, and they encourage the speaker to continue talking. Fidgeting, frowning, looking at our watches, reading our own notes, or behaving in other distracting ways gives the opposite message.

Feedback: Responding to the Message

Listening is an active process, and *feedback* is a vital part of that process. Since we cannot *not* communicate, no response is nonetheless a response. After carefully listening to the message as openly and completely as we can, we are in a position to respond to what was communicated. We should respond nonverbally during the message with good eye contact and some head nods. Feedback plays an important role in the effective listening process, but it is intricately tied to the first three components of listening: hearing the message, interpreting it, and evaluating its content. The most effective feedback indicates to the sender that we are listening to the content of the message, interpreting it accurately, and understanding it.

Feedback is vital to any group process committed to improving itself, for it is the only way to know what needs to be improved. Giving and receiving feedback should be more than just a part of a team member's behavior; it should be part of the whole group's culture. It has two purposes. One is to support the other group members verbally and nonverbally. The other is to focus on the content of their messages, rather than on their attitudes or attributes. Effective feedback furthers the quality of the group discussion. Group members who learn to diagnose the group's process and task concerns, and to be adaptive in producing effective solutions, can develop an understanding of the knowledge and skills necessary to successfully perform their group tasks (Salas, Nichols, & Driskell, 2007).

Providing Constructive Feedback

Offer *constructive feedback* that uses descriptive statements without judgment, exaggeration, labeling, or attribution of motives. State the facts as specifically as possible. Tell how the behavior affects you. Say why you are affected that way and describe the connection between the facts you observed and your feelings. Let the other person respond. Describe the change you want the other person to consider. Describe why you think the change will alleviate the problem. Listen to the other person's response. Be prepared to discuss options and to compromise to arrive at a solution, rather than argue specific points. For example, "When you are late for meetings, I get angry because I am a busy person and dislike wasting time sitting and waiting for you to arrive. Is there another time that we could schedule our meetings so that you could get here on time?" will probably be more effective than "You are always late for meetings. I'm tired of you being so irresponsible and wasting my time like that. When will you ever grow up, learn to take your commitments seriously, and take some responsibility for being places on time?" Table 7.2 offers guidelines for providing effective group feedback.

Talk First About Yourself, Not the Other Person.   Use "I" not "you" as the subject of your feedback statement. Speak for yourself. Be careful about statements such as "The group feels" or "The group doesn't like . . ." Encourage others to state their own complaints.

Phrase the Issue as a Statement, Not a Question.   Questions appear controlling and manipulative and can cause people to become defensive and angry. Consider the difference between "Can you stop so that we can get down to business?" and "I would like to get on with our meeting and business."

Restrict Your Feedback to Things You Know for Certain.   Do not present opinions as facts. Speak only of what you saw and heard and what you feel and want.

Provide Positive Feedback as Well as Negative.   Many people take good work for granted and give feedback only when there are problems. People are more likely to pay attention to your complaints if they have also received your compliments. It is important to remember to tell people when they have done something well. Help people hear and accept your compliments when giving positive feedback. People sometimes feel awkward when told good things about themselves and will fend off the compliment or change the subject. Reinforce the positive feedback and help the person hear, acknowledge, and accept it.

Some additional positive ways of providing effective feedback include acknowledging the need for feedback, giving both positive and negative feedback, and understanding the context in which feedback is given. To provide constructive feedback, do not use labels, exaggerate, or be judgmental, and speak only for yourself. Think ahead of time about what you want to say, and plan out carefully how you will phrase it sensitively.

Understand the Context.   An important characteristic of feedback is that it is always in a context. You never simply walk up to a person, deliver a feedback statement, and then leave. Before you give feedback, review the actions and decisions that led to that moment. Determine if the moment is right. You must consider more than your own need to give feedback. Constructive feedback can happen only within a context of listening to and caring about the person. Do not give feedback when you do not know much about the circumstances of the behavior or will not be around long enough to follow up on your feedback. "Hit and run" feedback is not fair.

Don't Use Labels.   Describe the behavior. Be clear, specific and unambiguous. Labels such as "fascist" "male chauvinist pig," or "unthinking politically correct clone" will be taken as insults rather than as legitimate feedback.

Be Careful Not to Exaggerate.   Be exact. An exaggeration will invite an argument from the feedback receiver rather than dealing with the real issue. Saying, "You're always late for meetings" invites a defensive response of "Well, not always" or "I'm not usually very late," rather than a thoughtful one.

Do Not Be Judgmental.   Evaluative words such as *good, bad,* and *should* make implicit judgments that make the content of the feedback difficult to hear.

TABLE 7.2   Guidelines for Providing Effective Group Feedback

1. Feedback should be descriptive, not evaluative. It should describe our interpretation of the other person's message. The focus should be on what we think we heard, rather than on our perception of the quality of the statements. "That's stupid" is clearly a poorly phrased feedback statement.
2. Effective feedback should be designed to clarify the process. The feedback should be understood by both parties and, if possible, the rest of the group.
3. Effective feedback should take into account the needs of the group, not just our own feelings. Is providing feedback useful to the group purpose?
4. Effective feedback should be directed toward helping to move the group process along. Simply making judgments rarely helps the group. The feedback should be constructive for everyone, not a show of one-upmanship.
5. Effective feedback should be well-timed. We should distinguish what is better left unsaid, or said later in private, from what is relevant and timely now but will be irrelevant or unproductive if said later. Group work is a process, and "when it's over, it's over." Timing is important, and some issues cannot or should not be revisited.
6. Effective feedback should not be stored up so it can be "dumped" later. Sandbagging, or waiting until we can score, will subvert the group process.
7. Effective feedback should be tentative. Regardless of how astute we are as listeners, we cannot know for certain what others really mean or why they act as they do. We can practice introducing our responses with tentative phrases like, "It seems to me . . ."
8. Effective feedback should be honest. Manipulative or political actions in a group identify *us,* not the person toward whom we have directed our attack, as the problem.

Receiving Feedback

When you are *receiving feedback,* the first thing to do is to breathe. Receiving feedback is stressful, and our bodies react by getting tense. Taking slow, full, deep breaths helps our body relax and allows our brain to maintain greater alertness. Listen carefully. Do not interrupt or discourage the feedback giver. Ask questions for clarity or for specific examples. Acknowledge the feedback. Paraphrase the message in your own words to let the person know you heard and understood what was said. Acknowledge the valid points and agree with what is true. Acknowledge the other person's point of view and try to understand his or her reaction. Then take time to sort out what you have heard.

There may be a time when you receive feedback from someone who does not know feedback guidelines. In these cases, help your critic refashion the criticism so that it conforms to the rules for constructive feedback.

Summary

Listening and feedback are vital group communication skills. We are not naturally proficient at either of these. Hearing and listening are not the same thing. To learn to listen, we must understand the process.

There are four components to listening: sensing, which involves understanding the roles of selective attention, external and internal noise, and short- and long-term memory; interpreting, which means assigning specific meaning to what we paid attention to; evaluating, which involves placing importance on certain issues; and responding, which involves providing feedback.

Active listening involves becoming part of the communication transaction and taking responsibility for understanding the speaker's intentions. It means learning to overcome the barriers to effective listening to which many of us are subject and responding appropriately to what is being said. Small groups are most effective and produce the best results when members listen and respond with care to one another's input.

DISCUSSION QUESTIONS

1. In what ways is listening important to effective group and team communication?
2. What's in it for you or your group and team members to be good listeners? Can you add some additional items beyond the ones discussed in this text?
3. Explain selective attention. Why do we engage in selective attention?
4. What are some examples of internal and external noise in your small group and team communication classroom?
5. Think of a recent situation in which you found listening difficult. Which of the four phases presented the most difficulty for you? Why? How did you overcome the difficulty?
6. How can paraphrasing be used for effective listening? Provide three specific examples.
7. How can expressing understanding, asking questions, and nonverbal communication be used for effective listening? Provide an example for each concept.
8. What are the guidelines for giving feedback?
9. How can you give positive feedback?
10. When you receive feedback, what are the important concepts to remember?

REFERENCES

Alessandra, T., & Hunsaker, P. (1993). *Communicating at work*. New York: Simon & Schuster.

Asherman, I., & Asherman, S. (1990). *The negotiation sourcebook*. Amherst, MA: Human Resource Development Press.

Covey, S. R. (1989). *The seven habits of highly effective people*. New York: Simon & Schuster.

Dragan, N., & Sherblom, J. C. (2008). The influence of cultural individualism and collectivism on US and Post Soviet listening styles. *Human Communication, 11,* 177–192.

Dobkin, B. A., & Pace, R. C. (2006). *Communicating in a changing world: An introduction to theory and practice*. New York: McGraw-Hill.

DuBrin, A. J. (2000). *Applying psychology: Individual and organizational effectiveness* (5th ed.). Upper Saddle River, NJ: Prentice-Hall.

Furmanek, B., & Palumbo, R. (1991). *Abbott and Costello in Hollywood*. New York: Putnam.

Golen, S. (1990). A factor analysis of barriers to effective listening. *Journal of Business Communication, 27,* 25–36.

Harris, J. A. (2004). Listening in the global business community: Spotlight on Mexico. *Listening Professional, 3,* 1–35.

Imhof, M. (2003). The social construction of listener: Listening behavior across situations, perceived listener status, and cultures. *Communication Research Reports, 20,* 369–378.

Imhof, M. & Janusik, L. A. (2006). Development and validation of the Imhof-Janusik listening concepts inventory to measure listening conceptualization differences between cultures. *Journal of Intercultural Communication Research, 35*(2), 79–98.

Johnson, D. (1996). Helpful listening and responding. In K. M. Galvin & P. J. Cooper (Eds.), *Making connections: Readings in relational communication.* Roxbury, MA: Roxbury Publishing.

Kolata, G. (2005, November 30). When the doctor is in, but you wish he wasn't. *New York Times,* pp. A1, A16.

Pearson, J. C., & Davilla, R. A. (1993). The gender construct. In L. P. Aaliss & D. J. Borisoff (Eds.), *Women & men communicating: Challenges and changes.* Orlando, FL: Harcourt Brace Jovanovich.

Peters, T. (1987). *Thriving on chaos.* New York: Knopf.

Ray, R. G. (1999). *The facilitative leader.* Upper Saddle River, NJ: Prentice-Hall.

Reece, B. L., & Brandt, R. (2005). *Effective human relations: Personal and organizational applications* (9th ed.). Boston: Houghton Mifflin.

Salas, E., Nichols, D. R., & Driskell, J. E. (2007). Testing three team training strategies in intact teams. *Small Group Research, 38*(4), 471–488.

Sweeney, P. D., & McFarlin, D. B. (2002). *Organizational behavior: Solutions for management.* Boston: McGraw-Hill Irwin.

Veenstra, C. (2004). Listening between Arabs and Americans. *Listening Professional, 3,* 5–30.

Wheelan, S. A. (1999). *Creating effective teams.* Thousand Oaks, CA: Sage.

Zemke, R., & Schaaf, D. (1989). *The service edge.* New York: New American Library.

CHAPTER 8

Group Evolution: Teams

CHAPTER OUTLINE

Organizations and Teams

Teams
  Parallel Teams
  Self-Directed Work Teams

Summary

Discussion Questions

References

CHAPTER OBJECTIVES

- Explain employee involvement as a part of team development.
- Define teams.
- Discuss the importance of teams.
- Identify the characteristics of parallel structures.
- Explain the limitations of parallel teams.
- Outline the characteristics of self-directed work teams.
- Discuss the benefits and costs of self-directed work teams.

KEY TERMS

Esprit de corps
Functional groups
Individual rewards
Not invented here (NIH)

Parallel teams
Segmentalism
Self-directed work teams
Self-managing work teams

Silos
Team facilitators
Teams

In our team-obsessed age, the concept of the dream team has become irresistible. But it's brutally clear that they often blow up. Why? Because they're not teams. They're just bunches of people. . . . You cannot assemble a group of stars and then sit back to watch them conquer the world. You can't even count on them to avoid embarrassment. The 2004 U.S. Olympic basketball team consisted entirely of NBA stars; it finished third and lost to Lithuania. There was only one Dream Team, and that was the 1992 U.S. Olympic basketball team, Michael Jordan, Magic Johnson, Larry Bird, Charles Barkley, Patrick Ewing—it was a one-time event. (And remember, Bird and Magic, the veteran co-captains, both had reputations as team players.) For the rest of us, putting together a few talented people who will work honestly and rigorously for something greater than themselves—that's more than enough of a dream.

(Colvin, 2006, pp. 88, 92).

In contrast, the 2008 U.S. basketball team had a riveting victory over Spain 118–107 to capture the gold without being a Dream Team. "As hokey as it may sound, the Americans leaned the value of teamwork."

("U.S. golden, beats Spain in finals," 2008, p. C1).

Senge, Kleiner, Roberts, Ross, and Smith (1994) traced the origin of the word *team* to the Indo-European word *deuk*, which means "to pull." The modern sense of the team, meaning a group of people pulling and acting together, emerged in the sixteenth century.

Team: <u>T</u>ogether <u>E</u>veryone <u>A</u>chieves <u>M</u>ore

There Is No "I" in "Team"!

When the drill instructor begins counting, you've got three minutes to make the bed—hospital corners and the proverbial quarter bounce. When you're done, you're told to get back in a line. The goal is to have every bed in the platoon made. So I made my bed, then I stood on the line. I was pretty proud, because when three minutes were up, there weren't more than ten men who had finished. "Ahead of the pack," I thought. But the drill instructors weren't congratulating us. Everyone's bed has to be made. So rip off the sheets and do it again.

I ripped off the sheets again, and again, and again. Finally one of the drill instructors looked me in the eye. "Your bunkmate isn't done. What are you doing?" I thought, "What am I doing?" Standing on line thinking I'd accomplished something, while my bunkmate struggled.

Together my bunkmate and I made our beds about twice as fast as we did alone. Still, not everyone was finishing. Finally, we realized, "Okay, when we're done we've got to go help the bed next to us, and the bed down from that," and so on. I went from thinking, "I'll hand my bunkmate a pillow, but I'm not going to make the bed for him" to making beds for anyone who needed help. That first lesson was an epiphany for me: "You can't survive in the Marine Corps without helping the guy next to you." There is no "I" in "team"!

Source: Westerman, 2006, p. 106

From these origins, Senge and colleagues defined a team as "any group of people who need each other to accomplish a result" (p. 354).

How does a group become a team? When there is consensus on the group's purpose, task, operating procedures, or process, groups develop a sense of synergy that moves beyond individual efforts, or even those of the group as a whole, to a new level of creativity and task accomplishment. While sports might provide an obvious example of teamwork, "in high pressure workplaces, such as nuclear plants, aircraft cockpits, or the military, teamwork is essential to survive" (Appleby & Davis, 2001, p. B2). An equally stressful environment, health-care organizations, "increasingly rely on interdisciplinary teams for comprehensive diagnosis and treatment of patients" (Ellingson, 2003, p. 93). Fast-paced sports or stressful environments offer dramatic examples of the importance of teamwork. Moreover, as we observed earlier in this book, the majority of U.S. corporations use teams that have provided significant gains in productivity, effectiveness, and employee satisfaction with their jobs (Shockley-Zalabak, 2002).

Organizations and Teams

If teams are implemented and supported effectively, they improve quality, enhance creativity in solving important issues, and increase employee involvement (Baldwin, Boomer, & Rubin, 2008; Sweeney & McFarlin, 2002). Cummings and Worley (2005) reported that: "a manufacturing and service technologies continue to develop—for example, just-in-time inventory systems, lean manufacturing, robotics, and service quality concepts—there is increasing pressure on organizations to implement team-based work designs" (p. 230). Teamwork concepts are not limited to for-profit organizations, however. In fact, the principles of involvement through teamwork have also been applied with success to voluntary organizations, ranging from school committees to community groups (Denhardt, Denhardt, & Aristigueta, 2009). Throughout our professional careers, we will take part in a variety of committees and teams, and a high level of participant involvement will lead to better results. Although we concentrate on organizations in this chapter, the importance of involvement, teams, and self-management applies to all types of groups.

Organizations frequently use the label teams for group activities unrelated to actual team processes. An upper-level manager might call her or his support group a team even though they function independently, with one member, for example, focusing on accounting, another on human resources, and a third on purchasing. Even more important, no one sees the interdependence between the functions of the various departments or divisions. Many assembly plants, fast-food outlets, and other organizations call their groups of employees teams. Actually, each member has specific tasks to carry out and rarely, if ever, has any input on any major decisions, nor are they involved in solving problems. The correct label is *functional groups,* since they carry out functions in the context of a group of people. A functional group often becomes a semipermanent group that is assigned the task of completing a variety of organizational purposes (Griffin, 2005). However, this involves job assignments, not the ability to develop a proactive team environment. The distinguishing characteristic of a team is

TABLE 8.1 Keys to Team Effectiveness

Clear mission, vision, goals, purpose. Team members understand and agree on the goals and the direction being pursued by the team.

Effective communication. All members are included in discussions. Efforts are made to be sure that certain communication processes succeed in providing information, reasons, and understanding. Verbal, nonverbal, and digital communication processes are monitored, evaluated, and improved.

Limited size. Normally, the larger the group (more than 10), the more complex the process becomes. Ideally, 5 to 10 team members should compose the team.

Skill levels appropriate for the complexity of team actions. Team members are well trained and have a commitment to continuous learning.

Trust. Proactive processes are encouraged to develop trust among team members, including telling the truth, fulfilling obligations, and standing by the other team members.

Appropriate and supportive external leadership. Supervision understands and accepts that the locus of control has shifted from management to the team.

Defined roles and responsibilities. Team members understand what is expected of them and how to carry out their responsibilities.

Links between team activities and rewards. The relationship is clearly defined, so team members receive rewards for their group-oriented actions.

the degree of interdependence between members (Harris & Nelson, 2008). Members of a temporary committee or ad hoc group rarely develop a strong sense of overriding purpose or a commitment to the other group members.

Nevertheless, we have indicated throughout this book, many dramatic examples of successful teamwork in organizations. Between 70% and 82% of all U.S. firms have teams, and the number is increasing (Sweeney & McFarlin, 2002). This makes "teamwork skills one of the most commonly required skills in the work environment" (de Janasz, Dowd, & Schneider, 2002, p. 311). The keys to team effectiveness are explained in Table 8.1.

Teams

Teams are formal work groups consisting of people who work together to achieve common group goals. Often, they are ongoing groups of individuals who coordinate their activities, even when they are not in constant contact. Special task groups, intact work groups, new work units, or participants from various parts of the organization assigned to achieve a common goal are additional examples of teams (McShane & Von Glinow, 2000). Teams function as a unit, "often with little or no supervision, to carry out work-related tasks, functions, and activities" (Griffin, 2005, p. 620). Teams, themselves, rather than a team leader, control the group process. When team members are actively involved, there is a marked increase in understanding, shared vision, collaborative team strategy, buy-in to the implementation process, and use of the knowledge of the participants. "One terrific example of adaptive teamwork can be found at Southwest Airlines" (Baldwin, Boomer, & Rubin, 2008, p. 257), the most consistently productive, profitable, cost-efficient, and customer-praised airline because of the best on-time performance, baggage handling, and customer satisfaction. Teams can effectively improve processes, increase creativity, make higher-quality decisions, improve communication, reduce turnover, increase employee morale, and respond to global competition (de Janasz et al., 2002).

Teams provide four advantages over individuals in organizations. First, they spawn *espirit de corps,* or a sense of groupness and community. Faced with the myriad changes occurring in organizations, teams often provide an important support system for members. Second, teams can increase the potential for innovative approaches to problems or improvements as demonstrated earlier in this text. Teams also develop a collective memory about how to work effectively together, which is the third advantage. Finally, there is a team's collective knowledge and working habits, which can lead to better judgments and outcomes than individuals operating independently (Baldwin et al., 2008; Harris & Nelson, 2008). However, teams are not always the best design for work. Some organizations or tasks do not lend themselves well to a team culture (Patterson, Grenny, Maxfield, McMillan, & Switzler, 2008).

For our purposes, teams are: (a) groups seeking solutions to particular problems or (b) groups implementing existing organizational goals (e.g., functional teams, task forces, specialized work groups, project teams), which represent parallel teams and the semiautonomous, self-directed, or self-managing teams in which members are expected to coordinate their work, set their own norms, follow a schedule, and undertake numerous other responsibilities. Table 8.2 shows the movement from traditional groups to teams and to self-directed teams.

Parallel Teams

Your organization may request that you join a problem-solving team. Your membership will be in addition to your regular duties. In other words, this is a *parallel team,* one that functions parallel to your ongoing responsibilities. You bring some expertise or professional interest in the issue, but you are not relieved of your current work demands. In most cases, these groups are advisory, and the power to implement the proposed solutions remains with the manager. The team's degree of authority, or its ability to implement proposed solutions, is low (Sweeney & McFarlin, 2002). Management maintains a high level of involvement, and the team has little control over the resources needed to actually follow through. The team's vision or mission is set by management, not by the team itself.

Parallel teams have three specific limitations: individual rewards, inappropriate management styles, and segmentalism. Because these barriers can be overcome by moving toward self-directed units or self-managed teams, they warrant further analysis.

Individual Rewards.   The reliance on *individual rewards* is counterproductive to a team-centered orientation (Cohen & Fink, 2001). Many organizations reward individual performance rather than focus on the team's output (Anderson & Anderson, 2001).

TABLE 8.2   The Evolution of Teams: From Involvement to Self-Direction

Groups	Teams	Self-Directed Teams
Traditional Groups	*Enlightened Leadership*	*Shared Leadership*
Group/team leader/manager	Leader facilitates meetings	Everyone shares leadership
Sets agenda	All members contribute to success	Members set guidelines for success
Directs problem solution	Members take responsibility	Working procedures decided by team
Establish limits and uses rules	Everyone helps with agenda	Meetings owned by members
Controls disruptive behavior	Members' needs recognized	Members are accountable
Task focus priority over member focus	Members control disruptive behaviors	

Underdeveloped Group Involvement ⟶ *Traditional Teamwork* ⟶ *Self-Directed Team*

Team Stage 1	Team Stage 2	Team Stage 3	Team Stage 4
Unempowered	Somewhat unempowered	Somewhat empowered	Empowered
Members do as told	Team/group somewhat parallel to organization structure	Team parallel to, integrated part of, organization structure	Team independent
Members execute leader's directions	Members react, request, make suggestions	Members participate in setting agenda and direction	Members take responsibility for process
High leader control, plan, direct	Less leader control, more leader coach, counsel, open communication	More participant control, critical thinking, involved team members	Control planning, leader facilitates and teaches others to lead themselves

Unfortunately, this can lead team members to focus on their own rewards rather than on team success. In education, the competition for grades provides a useful example. When assigned to a group project, some students have little incentive to devote a great deal of time to this three- to four-month team assignment. Others worry more about their individual grade than the group's success. So the group rarely evolves into a team because the rewards are unclear.

Little in our training teaches us how to focus on the team rather than on our individual rewards. Even training in athletics or interscholastic events (such as debate) does not prepare us for teamwork in an organization (Bolman & Deal, 2003). Although wins and losses are readily apparent in competitive activities, teams in organizations must labor as a group to accomplish goals that might take months or years to fulfill. In addition, the rules or measurement for success are clearer in competition—such as time available, roles (quarterback, second affirmative speaker, coach), and time span (season). Effective teams are built on trust, which takes time to develop (Covey, 2006).

As long as team members cannot identify a clear, positive consequence for becoming a team player (e.g., recognition or rewards based on the team's success), parallel teams will find themselves limited in success.

Inappropriate Management Styles. Second, many managers and supervisors are ill equipped to encourage team building. This is true for two reasons. They fear a loss of power, and they are more comfortable managing than leading a team.

Loss of Power. Often, managers and supervisors view employee involvement in the decision-making process as a threat to their own power and authority (McShane & Von Glinow, 2000). This perceived loss of power has led first-line supervisors to resist team efforts.

Managing Versus Leading. Underscoring the difference between managing and leading has become a popular means for focusing on productive and counterproductive behaviors (Harris & Nelson, 2008). Managing is required to plan, budget, organize, and control. Someone must schedule the group meetings, set the agenda, and perform other mundane duties. Overreliance on these managerial tools, however, tends to sabotage employee involvement. A well-intentioned manager might design an agenda that excludes important information, topics, or input. Too little time might be allocated for a full discussion of the issues. As we discovered earlier, both agendas and time allocation are important issues, but they can also be used to limit the group's synergy or success.

Leading involves developing strong subordinates and group members (Kotter, 1990). Although the leader bears the responsibility for implementing effective team-building concepts, overreliance on the leader for heroic attempts at motivating and developing individuals is counterproductive (McShane & Von Glinow, 2000). Leaders need to empower teams by strengthening the team's control throughout the decision-making process (Haris & Nelson, 2008).

Autocratic management and heroic leadership can be significant impediments in the team-building process. If team-building efforts are to be successful, supervisors and managers will assume entirely different roles from their traditional ones. Instead of being the boss, reward dispenser, and coordinator, managers and supervisors become liaisons, linking pins, and facilitators. Power has thus shifted through the empowerment process, and leading—rather than managing—becomes the expected behavior. Without proper training, managers and supervisors will conduct business as usual, rather than deal with the uncertainties inherent in employee involvement through teams.

The most important behaviors for managers and supervisors as *team facilitators* are to encourage open communication; team problem solving; team decision making; self-management; cross-training and performance monitoring; listening, sharing information, giving verbal and written feedback, and attending to nonverbal clues; working through conflicts and developing a climate of teamwork; and continuously learning, while tolerating ambiguity and uncertainty (Hackman & Johnson, 2000). Two conclusions are clear from this list. First, few individuals can accomplish all of these behaviors, so shared leadership within the group is important. Second, some training in group process is critical for successful group leadership. Unfortunately, too few managers and supervisors have learned the basics of effective facilitation.

Segmentalism. The tendency of separate units within the same organization to be indifferent to the success of other units of the organization, or to compete with those units, is called *segmentalism* (Griffin, 2005). As organizations undergo change, a high degree of concern for the success of an individual organizational unit over the success of other entities can diminish any successful team efforts (Beitler, 2006)). Often referred to as *silos,* these units see attempts to increase cross-functional activities as a threat to the unit's autonomy. Units or groups isolate themselves and focus on problems that are unique to their areas of interest (e.g., shipping, marketing, public relations). Intrinsic to this response is the belief that external rewards will diminish because the perceived payoff or benefits will be shared by other units. Even when these issues are not critical, many managers are not eager to give up what they perceive as their power or control. In the past, these orientations have proven to be powerful deterrents to effective team building (Kanter, 1983; Sweeney & McFarlin, 2002).

NIH (not invented here) provides an excellent example of an unwillingness to accept outside information, which limits cooperation. The CEO of Apple Computer announced during the 1990 corporate reorganization that NIH would no longer be tolerated (Buell, Levine, & Gross, 1990). His reason was simple—"a house divided cannot stand." Apple's subunits were spending their energies competing internally by rejecting ideas from other units because they were "not invented here." Apple's potential synergy was reduced because of a lack of common interest or collaboration.

Self-Directed Work Teams

Parallel teams serve numerous purposes, despite their inherent limitations. Experiences in parallel teams can lay the groundwork for self-directed units (McShane & Von Glinow, 2000).

Characteristics of a Self-Directed Work Team. Parallel teams place the power to make and implement decisions and solutions with the manager or person in charge. *Self-directed work teams* (SDWT) have control over resources use and decision implementation. As such, SDWT are self-regulating. After sufficient training and experience, team members work together to complete a total job or project. The team leads itself. As discussed earlier in this text, at Nucor Steel, the largest U.S. steel producer and recycler, a team-based approach is utilized: "Team members meet among themselves to figure out supply-flow problems, quality issues, vacation schedules, and even disciplinary actions" (Parker, 2005, p. 5D). Whole Foods stores are organized into SDWT that are responsible and accountable for their own performance: "The central idea is giving the group responsibility for a meaningful whole—a product, subassembly, or complete service—with ample autonomy, resources and collective responsibility for results" (Bolman & Deal, 2003, p. 149). "At Whole Foods, the basic organizational unit is not the store but the team. Small, empowered work groups are granted a degree of autonomy nearly unprecedented in retailing" (Hamel, 2007, p. 122). There are roughly eight teams in each store that oversee departments ranging from checkout to produce to seafood. Whole Foods represents the radical decentralization achieved with self-directed work teams.

The power of shared responsibility is impressive. Team members become part of the solution, not symptoms of the problem, when they have an active role in deciding the team's direction. Examples of companies that have successfully used SDWT include Harley-Davidson, where teams spearheaded a return to profitability; Johns Hopkins Hospital, where patient volume increased and turnover decreased; and Hallmark cards, where there was a 200% reduction in design time (de Janasz et al., 2002). SDWT share common boundaries that surround the team's activities, interdependent tasks, articulated purposes, and well-understood, personally owned goals. The Running with a Telephone Pole box provides good example.

Running with a Telephone Pole

Running five miles while carrying a telephone pole is a grueling task—made more so when it's a race between your six-man team and several others. The only instructions: move our telephone pole along the route, don't let it touch the ground, come in first. "It pays to be a winner," shouted the instructor, a phrase . . . that let us know there was a reward for coming in first. The race began immediately, so we had to come up with the best technique on the fly. There was no time to discuss a strategy or organize our process. My team struggled at first, but our approach evolved quickly. We had four guys carrying the pole and two resting by jogging alongside. When we switched off, we decided, it should be the two guys hurting the most—not necessarily the two who had been carrying the longest—who got to rest.

Nobody, especially a type A Recon Marine, wants to be the person who's "not carrying his weight." But some of these guys were simply workhorses—they could run forever with this thing—and some of us could not. We were learning to put team success ahead of our own egos. That was the only way we could move the fastest as a team and win the race.

Source: Westerman, 2006, p. 106

Overcoming the Barriers to Building a Self-Managing Team.   First, *self-managing work teams* help overcome the impact of individualized rewards because self-managing work teams are designed to create member interaction and interdependence. In the companies cited earlier regarding the effectiveness of self-managing work teams, employees are also better paid, because they are rewarded on a team success basis (Cummings & Worley, 2005; Griffin, 2005). Rather than viewing colleagues as competitors, individuals have powerful incentives for working together to maximize success. In addition, self-managing work teams provide a group identification and increased job satisfaction (Denhardt et al., 2009; McShane & von Glinow, 2000). Task excellence is achieved because employees identify with the issues and the solutions. Being part of the solution, individuals feel a greater incentive and obligation to guarantee successful implementation. For example, at Worthington Industries, an Ohio-based steel processor

> "When an employee is hired to join a plant-floor team, he works for a 90-day probationary period, after which the team votes to determine whether he can stay. The system works because much of the team's pay is based on performance, so members are clear-eyed and unsparing in evaluating a new candidate's contribution." (Colvin, 2006, p. 88)

Second, the *role of managers and supervisors is dramatically different* in the self-managing work team. In traditional organizations, leadership is based on the manager's having the decision-making power, the information, the responsibility for distributing rewards, and in many cases, the expertise. The result is that the manager tells people what to do and becomes an administrator, rather than a leader. Shared responsibility and control take the place of the traditional manager's carrying the responsibilities and burdens of managing performance alone. The primary roles for the manager are those of facilitator and coach. The self-managing work team leader constantly asks, "How can each problem be solved in a way that further develops the team's commitment and capabilities?" These team leaders learn to empower others, move decisions to the proper level, provide a vision and communicate it, and build trust and openness.

Third, self-managing work teams *overcome segmentalism.* Subordinates' and managers' perspectives are broadened beyond a narrow concern for a specialized area. Instead, team members identify with the problems associated with the overriding issues of productivity and quality. In addition, learning to solve problems as they develop makes each team member increasingly better qualified to solve future problems.

Seven conclusions point to the benefits and costs of self-managing work teams. Self-managing work teams are touted as solutions to a wide variety of organizational issues and these seven specific benefits have been shown consistently: (1) improvement in work methods and procedures, (2) gains in attraction and retention of employees, (3) increases in staffing flexibility, (4) increases in service and product quality, (5) improvements in output, (6) enhanced quality of decision making, and (7) reductions in supervision and staff support, since the team carries out most support activities such as retrieving supplies, getting information, and scheduling activities (Cummings & Worley, 2005; Harris & Nelson, 2008).

These factors lead to better productivity. Teams set the production goals, which tend to be higher. Feedback is employed effectively to improve performance. Cross-training enhances the ability of team members to help out and replace one another. The cost of labor is reduced 20% to 40%, in many cases. There are, however, drawbacks to these team approaches as well. If self-managing work-team programs are to be implemented successfully, costs and pitfalls must be considered carefully. There are at least five costs that occur in many self-managing work-team programs: (1) increased training costs, including the use of staff or outside consultants to facilitate implementation; (2) unmet expectations for organizational change; (3) conflicts between participants and nonparticipants, occurring if only a few teams are formed; (4) time lost in team meetings and a slower decision-making process; and (5) resistance to the change by some staff-support groups.

In addition, there are seven possible pitfalls: (1) insufficient training or training that is too late for the teams, (2) management that is too impatient for results, (3) failure to acknowledge that people will test the system, (4) trying to implement when the technology for a particular change is insufficiently known, (5) inadequate time allowed for the experience to gel before it 1s evaluated, (6) inappropriate boundaries chosen for team membership or responsibilities, and (7) a corporate culture that is radically against the self-managing team philosophy.

TABLE 8.3   Ethics for the Team-based Workplace

The Association for Business Communication adopted a set of professional ethics and code of conduct that was approved by its board of directors on October 19, 2005. Those professional ethics are summarized in brief here and available in their complete form on the association Web site. The guiding ethical principles are truthfulness, honesty, and fairness; confidentiality; integrity; respect for others; and professional and social responsibility.

Truthfulness, Honesty, and Fairness: truthful, factual, well-balanced, forthright, honest, and accurate communication; avoid deception; strive for consistency, transparency, and fairness.

Confidentiality: respect rights to privacy and personal conversations; do not divulge information, concepts, or findings when serving as referees.

Integrity: avoid conflicts; do not knowingly act in ways that jeopardize our own or others' professional welfare.

Respect for Others: civility, respect, intellectual freedom, and courteous and civil discourse; value diversity, practice inclusiveness, and treat others with respect.

Professional and Social Responsibility: remain competent and truthful; use talents for the good and welfare of our social communities; encourage others to uphold ethical standards; assist others in professional development; uphold dignity and credibility.

Source: Adapted from the Association for Business Communication Professional Ethics and Code of Conduct (available at www.businesscommunication.org/about/Code_of_Ethics.html).

Thus, self-managing work teams require a substantial investment in time, forethought, and commitment to be successful. Implementation can be difficult, but the successes of self-managing work teams make this approach to organizational transformation exciting and important.

Under the very best of circumstances, change is difficult. In the attempt to redefine employment relations, identifying and pursuing common interests is a vital component. A learning experience that requires management and employees alike to reconsider many underlying—and often incorrect—assumptions, might be the most important outcome of any self-managing work team process. Consider the team ethics described in Table 8.3.

Summary

We have discussed three issues: first, the importance of considering means for increasing employee involvement through the use of groups; second, the role of problem-solving groups as parallel organizational structures, and the successes and inherent limitations to their use; and third, groups and teams that utilize shared power and responsibility. Our summary of the successes of self-managing work teams points to one viable alternative to traditional group structure. Because self-managing work teams require a significant structural and psychological change, the basic concepts behind the self-managing work team are outlined.

Too often, organizations have rewarded values such as "If it ain't broke, don't fix it." However, by passing managerial power to self-managing work teams, new values can be encouraged, such as "Do your job well and find ways to constantly improve it!" Constant innovation and quality improvement are ends sought by most organizations.

The goal is to create group and work environments in which power, knowledge, information, and rewards are shared. By assuming more responsibility, group members become self-managing through their work teams. Although implementation can be difficult, the rewards can be remarkable for the organization and its members.

DISCUSSION QUESTIONS

1. What is an example of an employee involvement program? Why would employee involvement be beneficial to an organization?
2. What is the difference between groups and teams?
3. Define *parallel team structure*. Will these types of teams be limited in their effectiveness in organizations? Why or why not?
4. Define *self-managing work team*.
5. What are some of the pitfalls for self-managing teams? Why should these be considered before adopting this process?

REFERENCES

Anderson, L. A., & Anderson, D. (2001). *The change leader's roadmap: How to navigate your organization's transformation.* San Francisco: Jossey-Bass/Phiffer.

Appleby, J., & Davis, R. (2001, March 1). Teamwork used to be a money saver, now it's a life saver. *USA Today,* pp. 1B–2B.

Baldwin, T. T., Boomer, W. H., & Rubin, R. S. (2008). *Developing management skills: What great managers know and do.* Boston: McGraw-Hill.

Beitler, (2006). *Strategic organizational change: A practitioner's guide for managers and consultants* (2nd ed.). Greensboro, NC: PPI.

Bolman, L. G., & Deal, T. E. (2003). *Reframing organizations: Artistry, choice, and leadership* (3rd ed.). San Francisco: Jossey-Bass.

Buell, B., Levine, J. B., & Gross, N. (1990, October 15). Apple: New team, new strategy. *Business Week,* p. 88.

Cohen, A. R., & Fink, S. L. (2001). *Effective behavior in organizations: Cases, concepts, and student experiences.* Boston: McGraw-Hill Irwin.

Colvin, G. (2006, June 12). Why dream teams fail. *Fortune,* pp. 87–92.

Covey, S. M. R. (2006) *The speed of trust: The one thing that changes everything.* New York: Free Press.

Cummings, T. G., & Worley, C. G. (2005). *Organization development and change* (8th ed.). Florence, KY: Thomson South-Western.

Denhardt, R. B., Denhardt, J. V., & Aristigueta, M. P. (2009). *Managing human behavior in public and nonprofit organizations* (2nd ed). Thousand Oaks, CA: Sage.

de Janasz, S. C., Dowd., K. O., & Schneider, B. Z. (2002). *Interpersonal skills in organizations.* Boston: McGraw-Hill.

Ellingson, L. L. (2003, May). Interdisciplinary health care teamwork in the clinic backstage. *Journal of Applied Communication Research, 31,* 93–117.

Griffin, R. W. (2005). *Management* (8th ed.). Boston: Houghton Mifflin.

Hackman, M. Z., & Johnson, C. E. (2000). *Leadership: A communication perspective* (3rd ed.). Prospect Hills, IL: Waveland.

Hamil, G. (2007, October 1). Break free! *Fortune,* pp. 119–126.

Harris, T. E., & Nelson, M. D. (2008). *Applied organizational communication: Theory and practice in a global environment* (3rd ed.). New York: Lawrence Erlbaum Associates.

Kanter, R. M. (1983). *Change masters: Innovation for productivity in the American corporation.* New York: Simon & Schuster.

Kotter, J. P. (1990). *A force for change: How leadership differs from management.* New York: Free Press.

McShane, S. L., & Von Glinow, M. A. (2000). *Organizational behavior.* Boston: McGraw-Hill.

Parker, V. L. (2005, July 24). "Team-based" management gaining popularity. *Tuscaloosa News,* pp. 1D, 5D.

Patterson, K., Grenny, J., Maxfield, D., McMillan, R., & Switzler, A. (2008). *Influencer: The power to change anything.* New York: McGraw-Hill.

Senge, P. M., Kleiner, A., Roberts, C., Ross, R. B., & Smith, B. J. (1994). *The fifth discipline fieldbook: Strategies and tools for building a learning organization.* New York: Doubleday.

Shockley-Zalabak, P. (2002, April). Protean places: Teams across time and space. *Journal of Applied Communication Research, 30,* 231–250.

Sweeney, P. D., & McFarlin, D. B. (2002). *Organizational behavior: Solutions for management.* Boston: McGraw-Hill.

U.S. golden, beats Spain in finals. (2008, August 25). *Tuscaloosa News,* pp. C1, C4.

Westerman, J. (2006, June 12). From Wharton to war. *Fortune,* pp. 105–106.

CHAPTER

9

Decision Making and Problem Solving

CHAPTER OBJECTIVES

- Explain the importance of defining the problem.
- Discuss internal and external constraints.
- Identify the process of developing alternatives.
- Determine what issues must be considered in making the choice or decision.
- Outline the implementation stage process.
- Examine the decision–evaluation step.
- Describe the influences on the decision-making and problem-solving processes.
- Explain a benefit of computer-mediated group decision making.

KEY TERMS

Alternatives	External constraints	Internal constraints
"Black Swan" phenomenon	Feedback loop	Problem solving
Constraints	Five W's and the H	T chart
Decision making	Initial decision	Unintended consequences

"Would you tell me, please, which way I ought to go from here?"
"That depends a good deal on where you want to get to," said the Cat.
"I don't much care where—" said Alice.
"Then it doesn't matter which way you go," said the Cat.
"—so long as I get somewhere," Alice added as an explanation.
"Oh, you're sure to do that," said the Cat, "if you only walk long enough."

(The complete illustrated works of Lewis Carroll [*Alice's Adventures in Wonderland*],
Guiliano, 1982, pp. 39–40).

"On January 15, 2009, a US Airways plane with an engine failure crashed into the Hudson River. All 150 passengers and 5 crew members came out of the plane alive. Later news reports revealed that if it weren't for Chesley Sullenberger, the pilot who completely kept his cool while maneuvering the plane into the water, this miraculous story could have easily been another senseless tragedy on the news. The rest of us will probably never have to face a plane crash—let alone maneuver a crashing plane safely into a river. However, chances are that we will be facing other life challenges that demand all our inner resources and perhaps surprise us with strengths we never knew we had." (Chopra, 2009).

Landing a passenger jet safely in the Hudson River after running into a flock of geese and losing power in both engines is an amazing feat. It requires a series of small decisions made by a group of talented and dedicated people working together toward a common goal. Jeff Skiles, the co-pilot, was flying the plane at the time of the bird strike. The plane had been airborne for less than 3 minutes and flying at an altitude of only 3,200 feet. A flock of geese flew straight at them, struck the jet, and took out the engines. There was a thump, the smell of burning birds, and silence as both engines went dead. Skiles kept trying to restart the engines and began to check off emergency landing procedures while Sullenberger, the pilot, made contact with the air traffic controller to say that they needed to return to LaGuardia Airport. The controller alerted LaGuardia's air traffic control tower, which stopped all departing flights in anticipation of their emergency return. Minutes later, Sullenberger indicated that they were unable to make it to LaGuardia. The controller asked if he wanted to go to Teterboro Airport in New Jersey, which was closer to their location. The pilot said yes, and the controller alerted air traffic control at Teterboro before Sullenberger told the controller that they couldn't make it there either. As the pilot advised the passengers that they were going down and to brace for impact, air traffic controllers watched the plane clear the George Washington Bridge by less than 900 feet and glide into the Hudson River. Alert commuter ferry boat operators changed their scheduled runs to arrive at the side of the plane within minutes. Flight attendants worked to claim passengers and lead an organized evacuation of the plane. Hospitals made preparations, and police and ambulances arrived on the scene. Sullenberger is reported to have walked the aisles twice to make sure everyone evacuated the plane safely (Batty, 2009).

Landing the plane in the Hudson and safely evacuating all of the passengers and the crew required a small group decision-making process involving a series of steps. That is the nature of small group decision-making and problem-solving processes. They are complex processes involving a series of choices. An effective process means not jumping to a conclusion but considering the potential for a set of alternatives and finally arriving at the best possible solution given the set of circumstances. Landing the plane in the Hudson resulted from a series of decisions: trying to restart the engines, attempting to return to LaGuardia, considering landing at Teterboro, and finally thinking of the Hudson as the only open space within reach to set the plane down. It required a series of conscious choices to be made while considering the constraints of a complex environment and a multitude of possible consequences.

Decision Making and Problem Solving

Decision making and problem solving involve making choices. *Decision making* involves choosing among two or more alternatives to solve the problem. A problem describes a gap between the current situation and a desired solution. *Problem solving* involves the generation of alternatives aimed at moving from an existing state to a preferred state. Both processes result in a choice, even if that choice is not to make a choice. Although decision making and problem solving can be complex processes, they can be described in six discreet, interrelated steps. We can follow these six steps to effective decision making and problem solving:

First, we **Define** the goal. To do this we have to understand what makes achieving this goal a problem. What are the obstacles that make it difficult to achieve?

Second, we **Examine** the constraints preventing our achievement of the identified goal. These constraints are often complex in nature and must be discussed thoroughly to be fully understood.

Third, we **Consider** the possible alternatives for responding to the problem within the constraints.

Fourth, we make an **Initial** decision after considering the possible alternatives. It is important that this be only an *initial decision,* that is open to discussion, reevaluation, and change. We need to take time to think about the best option, which may not be an ideal one, and to think about the less desirable aspects of it as well as its positive attributes. The best solution may not be a single alternative but a combination of alternatives.

Fifth, **Develop** a plan of action to implement the decision. This may be a simple, direct plan, or it may be a more complex set of processes and procedures. Developing this specific step-by-step action plan may also cause us to reevaluate or modify the initial decision.

Sixth, the final step is to **Evaluate** the results and consequences of the decision. This completes the *feedback loop* that informs our decision making the next time.

Each of these stages has a connection to every other stage, forming a negotiated interaction among them. The problem exists only within a given context and a set of desired goals. The context and goals relate to the implementation of the solution and may relate to the constraints we have identified as important to the decision. The alternatives we develop and consider depend on our definition of the problem, the goals we hope to achieve, the constraints we have established, and the context in which we expect to implement the solution. Beneath the surface of a decision lies a complex pattern of assumptions and expectations that give substance to the meaning and consequences of that decision.

DECIDE: The Stages of Decision Making and Problem Solving

Define the Goal, Understand the Problem

Most problems are problems precisely because they are not easily understood or solved. As H. L. Mencken, a famous American editor and political commentator, said, "There is always an easy solution to every human problem—neat, plausible and wrong" (Boone, 1992, p. 86). To reach a desirable and effective solution, we need to clearly understand what it is we want to achieve. Without a clear goal in mind, we are like Alice in Wonderland when she came upon the Cheshire Cat.

If we do not know where we want to go, it does not really matter how much effort we put into making our decision. Therefore, our first step in understanding a problem is to clearly define our goals and the criteria we will use to recognize and evaluate our achievement of those goals.

Once we have established our goals, we then need to understand what it is that stands between us and them. Getting to the root of what it is that is keeping us from our desired outcome is not always easy or obvious. What may initially appear to be the obstacle may simply be a symptom of a deeper underlying issue that, without resolution, may continue to create the undesirable effects we had hoped to overcome. For example, I may see myself as overweight and out of shape. I know how to lose weight: Eat less. I know how to get in shape: Work out three to five times a week for at least an hour. These solutions appear straightforward, but they may not address the underlying problem: Why have I gotten myself into habits that make me overweight and out of shape? Do I perpetuate life situations and attitudes that lead to my using food as a coping mechanism or to exhaustion as an excuse to avoid exercise? Are there other underlying problems that need to be addressed before I can effectively address my health or fitness problem? What at first appears to be the problem may simply be a symptom. Attempting to solve that issue merely glosses over the deeper problem, which will continue to manifest until we address its root cause. Individuals and groups have a tendency to follow the path of least resistance when trying to make a decision. A quick-fix diet or a membership in the local gym might seem to solve the overweight and out-of-shape problem. However, if I was not working out before, why would starting now actually work? Easy solution, yes. Correct solution, perhaps. However, expediency in resolving a problem can often lead to hasty decisions when we pick the most obvious decision rather than the best one (Beach, 1997).

To really solve problems, our challenge is to first come to understand the deeper levels of the real problem to be solved. We may or may not be aware of the hidden agendas we carry around with us that keep us from seeing and addressing these underlying issues. In addition, it may appear inefficient or even threatening for us as a group to spend valuable time and energy looking beneath the surface when we have immediate goals to reach or needs to attend to. However, real and effective solutions depend on appropriately defining the underlying issues.

Asking questions is at the heart of group decision making. Asking questions is essential to identifying the problem to be solved and to gathering the relevant information to solve it. Six types of questions, sometimes known as the *five W's and the H,* are important to ask. They are shown in Table 9.1. Asking these questions helps focus our attention to address a problem.

When the United States launched the *Challenger* spacecraft on January 28, 1986, there was strong evidence available indicating that it might explode (Kruglanski, 1986). That information was ignored, discredited, and downplayed by decision makers (Gouran, Hirokawa, & Martz, 1986). At each successive level of the decision-making process, decisions were made to either discount or not pass along the relevant information: "In short, it appears that the decision makers responsible for the *Challenger* launch, while still concerned about safety, were also influenced by the objective of maintaining their launch schedule" (Hirokawa, 2003, p. 130).

In response to the 1986 disaster, NASA created a safety office. However, on February 1, 2003, the *Columbia* shuttle broke apart while trying to return to earth, killing the seven astronauts aboard. The subsequent inquiry revealed that many of the same decision-making issues that caused the *Challenger* disaster still remained (Eisler, Watson,

TABLE 9.1   Ask: Who, What, Why, When, Where, and How

Ask:

For whom is it a problem?

What is the problem?

Why is it a problem?

When is it a problem?

Where is it a problem?

How is it a problem?

& Levin, 2003; Levin, 2003). In a safety meeting prior to the *Columbia* launch, a fateful decision was made to go ahead despite the revelation that a large chunk of foam came off during a mission in late 2002 (Watson, 2003a). The investigating group's final report of the incident concluded that "NASA's overconfident management and inattention doomed *Columbia* every bit as much as the chunk of foam that struck the shuttle with deadly force" (Dunn, 2003, p. A3).

As we noted earlier, what at first appears to be a problem might actually be a symptom. With NASA, the lack of a safety office was not the problem. Instead, the problem was the culture and attitudes of the agency itself, since the newly created safety office (1986) was quickly underfunded and ignored (Eisler et al., 2003; Watson, 2003b).

In a less tragic example of poor decision making, the Coca-Cola corporation introduced "New Coke," apparently expecting it to become an overnight taste sensation. Coca-Cola was forced to reverse its decision quickly, however, and reintroduce "Coke Classic" when sales dropped off and consumers protested (Whyte, 1991). In these situations, highly skilled individuals and groups made decisions with negative impacts on their long-term goals and with consequences for large numbers of people. They made these decisions because they failed to adequately address the larger contexts and dynamic interactions surrounding their decisions—the weather at the time of the *Challenger* launch, which exacerbated the problem with the faulty O-rings; the inherent tendency of foam to dislodge during shuttle launch, which was underplayed with *Columbia*; and the taste desires of the consumers of Coca-Cola. In hindsight, we can see that misreading the information on the initial problem allowed NASA and Coca-Cola to ignore critical information.

If the decision-making processes had been working effectively, the larger issues surrounding the goals and immediate problems would have been openly discussed, with the problem definition expanded, the constraints acknowledged, and possible alternative solutions sought. More fully conscious decisions could have been made, incorporating an understanding of the possible or likely consequences of the decisions taken and predicting a better outcome.

Examine the Constraints

Constraints are an inevitable element of any decision-making process and may be of two types: external or internal. *External constraints* are those imposed on the decision-making process, such as the time, money, energy, knowledge base, or other resources that the group needs for the decision-making process and to implement a solution. *Internal constraints* are those integral to the problem. They may have caused the initial problem, or they may have to do with limitations on the implementation, such as government regulations, the physical location, technical or design difficulties, or other constraining factors and circumstances. Specific questions to identify constraints include the following:

How does the problem relate to our stated goals?

Will resolving it ensure that our goals are met?

When, how, and by whom was this problem brought to our attention?

What difficulties are being created by it?

What harm or lack of benefit important enough to justify investigation does it create?

What, if any, aspects of the problem or the solution are potentially catastrophic? (Earthquakes, tidal waves, and outbreaks of botulism are all events that occur rarely, but when they do they can be devastating. If some aspect of the problem or the solution has a large negative potential and occurs even once, is that too often?)

What are the other harms that must be considered?

What are the benefits that are being denied?

What has been violated by a deviation from standard procedures?

When does the problem occur? When does it not occur?

What locations, people, and situations are most likely to have the problem?

What other problems consistently (always or almost always) co-occur with this problem? Can these be related somehow? Do we have the correct cause and effect?

Once the group has asked and answered all the questions it can on its own, it then must analyze what else it needs to know to more fully understand and define the issue and develop meaningful alternative solutions. Some additional questions follow:

What are we trying to evaluate, understand, and comprehend?

What data will help—samples, surveys, books, articles, research, interviews, site visits?

How will the data be recorded, shared, synthesized?

What special skills are needed to gather the information?

What obstacles to gathering the information exist? Time, expertise, availability?

Who else can be included in the discussion?

How did we get our information? Is it first- or secondhand? Is it rumor or verifiable?

How current, representative, and respected are our sources?

How complete is the picture? Are there obvious gaps?

Consider the Alternatives

Developing *alternatives* is frequently the most creative and exciting part of the process. It can also be the most difficult and frustrating. It involves gathering as much information from as many sources as possible, digesting and synthesizing that information, and forming it into a workable shape that responds to the problem at hand. An essential part of this exploration of possible courses of action is bringing into focus the unintended consequences, along with the scope of a proposed solution and its long- or short-term goals and expected results. This requires critical thinking—that is, the ability to manage, integrate, and organize complex information.

Critical thinking is a key element to successful group decision making (Kayes, 2006). Every possible alternative should be examined. Frequently a solution is derived from a far-out idea that becomes the key to a difficult problem. For example, suggesting that the United States abandon its space program may not be a popular idea, but raising the issue could help a decision-making group grapple with the underlying reasons for the disasters—the flights themselves—and to develop some alternatives. Developing alternatives increases the statistical chance that a group will isolate the most significant issues and locate the best solution (Herek, Janis, & Huth, 1987; Katzenback & Smith, 1993).

In 1982, Johnson & Johnson faced a major disaster—seven deaths in 2 days from the ingestion of cyanide-laced Extra-Strength Tylenol (Trujillo & Roth, 1987). Four years later, in February of 1986, a 23-year-old New York woman died after ingesting two Extra-Strength Tylenol capsules, and cyanide was found in the body of a Nashville man and in his bottle of Tylenol capsules (Benson, 1988). Johnson & Johnson took an almost unthinkable set of actions—far from normal for a profit-making organization. In spite of the costs and logistical hurdles, it discontinued production of over-the-counter capsules and replaced 15 million capsule products already on the market. The company's CEO, James Burke, appeared on television on *The Phil Donahue Show,* spoke at the National Press Club, and held press conferences to confront negative news coverage. The company wanted to calm public fears, distinguish the contaminated Tylenol capsules from caplets and other Tylenol products, and assert that the capsules had been contaminated after they left the manufacturing and distribution facilities. As a result of these efforts, Johnson & Johnson and Tylenol emerged from this crisis with an effective response that saved the company's reputation and maintained the product's market share (39% of the market share 12 weeks after the second crisis, close to their 42% all-time market high), dramatically demonstrating how well groups can solve problems when they engage in an open decision-making process (Benson, 1988).

The group must reexamine its original goals and evaluation criteria in light of the expanded understanding of the problems and constraints. It then decides what expectations or criteria are relevant or possible to apply to the final decision and to its evaluation. The group might start with visualizing the ideal solution. What would be included in this outcome, and what could be excluded? Next, because the ideal may not be workable or practical, the group must decide what must be present at a minimum to make it acceptable. One way of arriving at these solutions is to brainstorm all the criteria that the group thinks essential or important to the final resolution, such as the following:

A solution must not exceed a particular cost ceiling.

A solution must be cost effective.

A solution must be acceptable to particular groups.

A solution must be acceptable to particular individuals in positions of power.

A solution must be capable of quick implementation.

A solution must be easy to maintain and administer.

A solution must be a useful base for future planning.

A solution must be easily justified to a given audience.

A solution must meet certain regulatory standards.

A solution must provide recreational opportunities for particular groups.

A solution must be accessible or usable by handicapped people.

A solution must . . .

Once a variety of alternative solutions have been placed in discussion, the focus shifts to the possible consequences—intended and unintended—of each of the alternatives. This is sometimes more difficult than we at first think. There may be hidden effects and unintended consequences in areas we may not be taking into account. *Unintended consequences* are those results that occur because of the decision but were not expected or planned. Even small decisions can have large unintended consequences. For example, in July 2003, an 86-year-old retiree drove his car through an open-air market in Santa Monica, California, killing 10 people and injuring dozens more. The California Highway Patrol commissioner immediately called for legislation to require road testing for drivers age 75 and older (Barnhill, 2003). On the surface, tougher testing for older drivers makes sense. Twenty states and the District of Columbia already require some type of special relicensing requirements for older drivers. However, what if a large number of the 18.9 million drivers age 70-plus ceased to drive as a result of this testing? There may be a positive benefit in highway safety, but an unintended consequence would be that someone would have to drive as many as 18.9 million more people around. This would require families, communities, and others to adjust their lives. Additional taxi and bus services would be required. This does not mean that testing and relicensing is inappropriate, but it does illustrate what happens when we make small changes within a system. All consequences must be considered. Being aware of the possibilities and then weighing the likelihood and seriousness of each, should it occur, is important. Remember that before they happened, the *Challenger* and *Columbia* space shuttle disasters were considered highly unlikely by NASA.

Taleb (2007) describes the *"Black Swan" phenomenon* as a rare, hard-to-predict, large-impact consequence that is beyond the realm of our normal expectations. The term *Black Swan* comes from the assumption that all swans are white. Taleb suggests that we give up that assumption and, although we cannot predict a Black Swan event and consequence, we build a robustness into our decision-making processes to reduce the negative effects of those events should they occur. We can do this at the same time that we build toward maximizing the consequences of more frequently occurring positive outcomes. In other words, we must take both positive and negative possibilities into account in our decision making. We must consider all of the possible unintended consequences that we can and then weigh those consequences against the more likely possibilities in our decision-making process. As individuals and as groups, we may not always make the right decisions, but when we consider all of the possible outcomes before making those decisions, we are more likely to make better ones.

Initiate a Decision

After defining the goals and the underlying problem to be addressed, coming to an understanding of the constraints on solving the problem and examining alternative solutions and their likely consequences, we are ready to decide which of the available alternatives best meets our goals. Our choice needs to take into account the costs and consequences of our best long-term solution and compare them with the less ideal, but perhaps more affordable or more easily implemented and maintained, solutions. Restating the original objective is one way to make certain the group does not travel too far from its original purpose (Schultz, Ketrow, & Urban, 1995).

If I want to lose weight and develop a healthy exercise regimen but find that my underlying problem relates to my current work situation, it may be that the ideal solution is to quit my job and go to a high-cost therapeutic retreat. For obvious reasons, this may not serve the other interests of my life and may not be realistically possible. Rather than opting for this life-changing solution or no solution at all, I may do better to plan a staged, long-term solution that incorporates all of the complexities and constraints of my life. I can then implement a strategy that will take me where I want to go in discreet and achievable increments. On the other hand, I may be able to renegotiate some of those external constraints as well. If, for example, I have a spouse or partner who can take over some of the responsibility for earning the family income, freeing me to pursue a more satisfying, if less-well-paying, job, I might be able to consider my choices in a different light. Changing the focus of the problem and the constraints on the alternative solutions makes our choices and the possibilities for their implementation different. In most decision-making and problem-solving situations, there are a number of interrelated and negotiable possibilities. This is important to keep in mind when trying to solve what appear to be insurmountable problems. Groups have to look for ways to evaluate choices in realistic scenarios, without giving up or accepting an all-or-nothing solution.

In addition, we need to keep in mind that our larger choices are ultimately constrained by the small choices we have made at each step along the way, including the sets of priorities we have chosen to follow. The choice we make incorporates all the previous choices we have made both consciously and unconsciously. We can probably never make perfect choices all of the time, but we improve our odds of making good choices based on the available information and through the effective use of the decision-making process.

Once the goals have been refined in light of the information and data that have been gathered and analyzed, the group is able to search for alternative solutions. Members should be encouraged to be as creative as possible, drawing from one another's ideas and insights. The group can use any number of techniques in developing this list of alternative solutions (see Chapter 11). When the list is developed, the group must then go back and examine each of the alternatives it is considering for any possible consequences—intended or unintended—of their implementation. The group should keep a careful record of this discussion of the alternatives. Some piece of an alternative discarded along the way may prove useful when combined with another.

When the list of alternatives and their foreseeable consequences has been developed, it is time to choose which one best fits the goals and solves the problems the group has outlined. Each alternative should be discussed in relation to how well it fits within the parameters established for the decision. Some questions the group might ask themselves include these:

How well does the alternative meet the goals we have established? Does it meet the most important ones?

How well does it solve the problem?

Which parts of the problem will be solved?

Which will be left unsolved?

Is that acceptable?

Do the advantages of this solution outweigh any possible disadvantages?

Are there reasons why this solution will not be implemented?

If it is implemented, will it be easy or difficult to maintain?

Are there concomitant problems that should be addressed?

Is this solution going to drain away important resources (money, personnel, time) from other problems?

Will this solution affect individuals or groups not considered in this discussion or have other unintended consequences?

Are there ways in which this alternative ignores important research data or other information obtained by this group?

Is this alternative justifiable to those who will be asked to pay for it or who will be affected by it?

A group can use a *T chart,* in which the advantages of each alternative are listed on one side and the disadvantages are listed on the other side (see Figure 9.1). This

FIGURE 9.1   T Chart for Assessing Alternative Solutions

Advantages	Disadvantages

gives the group a way to answer the simple question, "Do the advantages outweigh the disadvantages?"

To initiate the decision once the list of alternatives has been generated, the group can

1. Assign an A to the top one-third of the items that are absolutely essential for the decision to be acceptable.
2. Assign a C to the bottom one-third of the items that are not really critical. In any problem-solving situation, there are numerous nonessential or cosmetic items that do not need to be considered at that moment.
3. The middle one-third automatically receive a B.
4. Go back to the B's and force them into the A column or the C column.
5. Forget the C's and eliminate them from discussion.
6. Prioritize the A's and you have developed a good starting point for developing the essential criteria.

Using the A list, the group can now refine its goals and evaluation criteria, writing them down to clarify them and to ensure that all members understand and agree with the decision on them. This is an essential part of the process, and it is important to document it. It will form the basis for making the choice from alternatives and for evaluating the implementation of that choice. When each alternative has been weighed and the decision made, the group must develop a strategy for the implementation of that decision.

Develop an Action Plan

Yogi Berra is credited with saying, "When you come to a fork in the road, take it!"

The decision-making group may not be responsible for the actual implementation of the decision, but it is responsible to design a strategy that helps ensure that it is implemented, because a solution that is not implemented is not a solution; it is just a good idea. As we have noted earlier, the implementation stage is frequently where the decision-making process breaks down. Although the difficulties in this stage should have been anticipated earlier in the process, there may be various reasons why they may not have been adequately addressed.

The implementation plan frequently is ignored or given inadequate attention in the decision-making process. Assume for a moment that a state's legislature decides that relicensing will be required for all older drivers. How would it be done? Who would pay for the additional personnel at the motor vehicles department? What provisions would be made to guarantee fairness, to counter lawsuits arguing age discrimination, and to review and rectify any unfair decisions? These and many more questions will need to be faced in the implementation process, and the implementation process itself may modify the decision. Elaborate reports generated for government agencies or private corporations that have taken months of time and great financial investment to produce are often shelved because those charged with the implementation are not vested in the project or because implementation is too costly or requires infrastructure that is not in place. Everyone feels cheated, and the process itself takes on an expectation of failure.

The group can begin by asking itself a few questions:

Are there adversarial groups or individuals who will try to block the implementation of this decision? Can we alter the solution to gain their allegiance? If not, can we safely ignore or go around them?

Have each of the implementation steps been considered carefully, including who does what, when, where, and how (person, activity, time, place, and method)?

Evaluate the Results and Consequences

The decision-making/problem-solving process is not finished until we have seen whether it has accomplished its goals or has had better or worse consequences than we expected. After the fact, NASA was forced to examine its decisions on the *Challenger* and *Columbia* launches and examine its decision-making process, as well. Had this evaluation occurred as part of the initial decision-making process, the disasters might have been averted. Large decisions are the result of many small ones made throughout the entire decision-making process. Each phase of the process opens certain sets of possibilities, while closing others. To learn from our decision-making process, we need to examine the outcomes in terms of both those we expected and those we did not expect, and we need to understand when we predicted accurately, as well as when we went wrong in not predicting actual consequences and limitations.

The decision-making process is most effective when we take the evaluation stage into account in the beginning, as we are defining the problem. Part of an effective evaluation is to set up a procedure for measuring the success of our outcome as it relates to the definition of the original problem. We should be able to say at the beginning of the process that a given desired outcome will be apparent if it meets certain specific criteria. These criteria become the basis for the evaluation.

In addition, to be able to replicate and understand the process itself, we should document it at each step along the way so we can rethink our solution if it is flawed. The composition and working relationships of the group or team, the goals we identify, the ways we define the problem, the reasons for narrowing or expanding its scope, the constraints we choose to consider and why, our information-gathering tools and strategies, the alternatives we develop and pursue or decline to pursue and why, our choice of a solution and the reasons for it, the implementation process we develop and propose, the implementation process that actually takes place, the results of the implementation, and, finally, the effects of the process itself on the outcome all need to be examined. Evaluating our decisions and the processes we used to make them helps us avoid repeating disastrous decisions, while giving us the tools to replicate positive ones. Table 9.2 summarizes the six steps of this decision-making and problem-solving model.

TABLE 9.2 Six-Step DECIDE Model of Decision Making and Problem Solving

Define the goal and understand the problem.

Identify the problem and specify its symptoms.
Gather information on the size and scope of the problem.
Research out the seriousness, urgency, and implications of the problem.
Look for causes and underlying conditions of the problem.

Examine the constraints preventing goal achievement.

Identify the criteria that would indicate successful achievement of the goals.
Rank order the criteria in importance, and specify criteria that must be met.
Identify which criteria must be met and which are less essential.
Refine the goals, based on criteria, to be satisfactory, realistic, achievable.

Consider the alternatives for responding to the problem and constraints.
Suggest as many alternative solutions as possible.
Refine and combine alternative solutions.

Initiate a decision by thinking through the advantages and disadvantages of each option.

Evaluate the alternative decisions or solutions using the goal criteria.
Rank order the solutions based on how well they meet the criteria.
Does a single solution or a solution combination meet all criteria that must be met?
If not, reevaluate solutions and goals. Are goals achievable? Other solutions?
If yes, does the solution meet goals that should and can be met?
If not, is there another solution or set that can meet these criteria as well?
Does the solution create additional problems? How can they be resolved?

Develop a decision plan of action to implement the best option.
Identify criteria and method to evaluate the decision once it is implemented.
Develop a procedure for implementing the solution that best meets criteria.
Do the decision and solution accomplish the goals?

Evaluate the results and consequences of the decision, completing the "feedback loop."

Evaluate the decision or solution: for the evaluation.
Evaluate the implementation: Is it achievable? Is it too expensive? Does it take too long?
Implement an ongoing evaluation plan that occurs at regular intervals.

Context Influences on Decision-Making and Problem-Solving Groups

Although the stages of the decision-making process form the structure that shapes it, the interaction among the stages gives the decision-making process its energy. Making decisions in groups and teams helps us address the underlying interrelationships of the problems and issues to be resolved by making it possible to examine a problem from multiple and often discrepant perspectives. This examination helps develop solutions that take into account the complex environment of the problem and its solution. When NASA sent the Hubble telescope into orbit, it initially did not work. The NASA corporate culture has been blamed, in large part, for this setback, as that culture encouraged individuals to make autonomous decisions without seeking or paying attention to dissenting opinions of an expert group (Capers & Lipton, 1993; Stein & Kanter, 1993). As with the *Challenger* and *Columbia* disasters, extremely bright and dedicated NASA scientists, engineers, and managers made a poor decision. That decision might have been avoided if they had made use of the wider range of information, expertise, and perspectives available to them.

Group Composition

Deciding the makeup of a decision-making or problem-solving group or team itself is a significant part of the group process. The membership should reflect the larger social and organizational environment in which the group takes part, as well as the nature of the problem and the context in which it occurs. A Native American reservation economic development group clearly should include those expected to implement the solution and those expected to be affected by it. The community group charged with developing solid waste disposal options would do well to include at least one or two members with some knowledge of the technical, market, and cost aspects of the problem, as well as members with an understanding of the social and political characteristics of the community to be served. Informed human resources managers recognized some time ago how ironic it was for managers to try and make decisions regarding what motivates employees (Harris & Nelson, 2008). Since these groups have different jobs, skills, and working conditions, the best decision-making group would consist of representatives from all sides, including the employees to be motivated.

Group Process

The group should consider at least four issues, as shown in Table 9.3, before it can effectively begin the task at hand. First, it needs to address the external constraints on the group process itself. These include the time frame for completing the task, the time and commitment each of the members has to give the group, the knowledge and understanding individual members bring to the problem at hand, the availability of outside sources for technical expertise, and any other relevant concerns. Each group has its own strengths and weaknesses, and it is wise to understand and take these into account to make the best use of everyone's time, abilities, and interests.

TABLE 9.3   Four Preliminary Steps

1. External constraints on the process—What are the limitations?
2. Procedural issues—How to run the group?
3. Voting or consensus—How will decisions be made?
4. Ethical decisions—What are the possible ethical dimensions of the decisions?

Second, the group needs to decide how it will run itself. Will it elect a chair and someone to keep the minutes of the proceedings, or will there not be formal group leadership? Who will be in charge of setting the agenda for meetings? Who will call the meetings, and how frequently does the group need to meet? If the group is within an organizational context, these decisions may be made by those who have established the group and charged it with a given responsibility. If the group is not already structured, however, it may fall to the members themselves to decide how best to meet their goals. Group dynamics may evolve over time with shared decision-making and problem-solving successes and failures. Leadership may shift and change according to topics under consideration, or leadership may be stable. It may be based on personality or expertise. Ways of dealing with disruptive members may be formally addressed or informally handled as situations arise, or the issue may be left unaddressed. Whatever the decisions made about group leadership, structure, and process, those decisions can become critical to the overall success or failure of the group effort.

Third, the group must decide how the outcome of the problem-solving process itself will be determined—whether by a majority vote or by overall consensus (Wood, 1992). These two methods are quite different and may make a great deal of difference in the acceptance and effectiveness of the implementation of the decision. Voting yes or no on a particular issue indicates how the group members think, but obtaining consensus among the group members enhances their commitment to the decision (Ellis & Fisher, 1994). The nature of the problem to be addressed may dictate whether consensus is possible, desirable, or necessary; whether a vote by a two-thirds majority or by 51% of the members will suffice; or whether the leader of a subgroup should make a particular decision. Once these aspects of the process have been adequately addressed, the group is ready to move on to the issues at hand. Table 9.4 outlines the consensus process.

Finally, a group should consider the ethical dimensions of its decision-making discussion behaviors and the outcomes of its decisions and implementation strategies. Group members' commitment to tell the truth, engage in fair play, keep their promises, help one another, and act reciprocally will stimulate a more engaged and productive group decision-making process. Considering the ethical dimensions of alternative

TABLE 9.4   The Consensus Process

Consensus Includes	Consensus Does Not Include
1. Seek everyone's ideas—Prevent groupthink and take advantage of all ideas.	1. Voting—It creates a win/lose outcome since the minority is told it does not matter.
2. Listen—Work toward understanding of other group/team members.	2. Majority rule—People not included in the outcome have little motivation to help carry out the decision.
3. Discuss ideas—Encourage and explore differences.	
4. Do not expect to get all you want—A group/team should work toward integrating everyone's ideas and needs.	3. Bargaining—Consensus seeks the best outcome, not a compromise.
5. Reach an agreement that everyone can live with—Avoid win/lose perspectives.	4. Minority rule—If you disagree with the proposal, offer a viable alternative or let the process continue.

TABLE 9.5   Ethical Behaviors in Decision-Making and Problem-Solving Groups

1. **Fidelity:** Keep your promises.
2. **Veracity:** Tell the truth.
3. **Fair Play:** Do not exploit, cheat, or "freeload" on others.
4. **Gratitude:** Express thanks, reciprocate.
5. **No Maleficence:** Do not cause pain or suffering to others through verbal assault.
6. **Beneficence:** Help others achieve their goals and the group's goals.
7. **Reparation:** Repair harms to others that are your fault, even when inadvertent.
8. **Do Not Kill:** Respect others and their ideas.
9. **Do Not Deprive of Property:** Do not take other's ideas or intellectual property as your own.
10. **Do Oppose Injustices:** Consider the group and the effect of its decisions and solutions.
11. **Do Promote Justice:** Work toward improvement.

See Kienzler (1997) for more information on the set of ethical principles adapted here for small groups.

solutions and their impact can help a group make better choices among the potential alternatives. Kienzler (1997) suggested a list of 11 ethical principles, presented in Table 9.5, that can help a group make ethical decisions.

Benefits of Decision Making in Computer-Mediated Groups

Groups do not always make the best decision even when they have enough information to do so. Often groups fail to make an unbiased assessment of the information on its merits, choosing instead to rely on members' initial preferences and on initially shared information. The proportion of group members who share the information before the discussion begins, rather than the quality of the information itself, often affects the subsequent group decision (Klocke, 2007). Even though only the inclusion of new and relatively unshared pieces of pertinent information is likely to produce a group decision of higher quality than an individual decision, shared information has a higher probability of being mentioned in the group discussion, while unshared information is relatively neglected. This is often a problem for decision-making groups that meet face-to-face. Groups who make their decisions through computer-mediated communication (CMC), however, appear to have a better chance of overcoming this bias. CMC groups, who have an adequate time allowed for their decision-making process, have been shown to be more active and equal in their group participation, to use unshared information in the group discussion more effectively, and to engage in an overall better decision-making performance (Berry, 2006; Campbell & Stasser, 2006). There may be several reasons for this outcome. A text-based CMC medium provides a means for relatively synchronous, anonymous group communication with reduced social cues of power and status and an enhanced means of group memory provided by the series of typed messages that can be reviewed. Campbell and Stasser (2006) suggested that each of these characteristics of the communication medium enhances the CMC group's decision-making process. Berry

(2006) credits the ability of members to post their comments at once without interrupting each other and the tendency of members to be more active and equal in participation within the group. In general, it appears that the CMC medium can have a positive influence on certain aspects of the small group decision-making process.

Summary

Two assumptions underlie our discussion: that the group is formed with a particular problem or issue to resolve and that there are particular results or goals that it hopes or expects to achieve. Research shows that groups are more successful at achieving their goals when they approach a problem systematically and rationally (Hirokawa, 1983). Understanding the decision-making stages can help groups structure their process. Although the individual stages of the decision-making process can be described separately, they are, as we have noted, interrelated. In defining the problem, understanding the constraints, searching for alternatives, deciding on a solution, and understanding the consequences of the implementation of that solution, a group moves back and forth between stages, balancing each stage against the others, while keeping the goals in mind.

We may find that what initially was presented as the problem is, in fact, only a symptom of the underlying problem. By carefully articulating the expected outcome or goals we hope to achieve, we can reexamine the original issue or problem which we are presented. Throughout the process, these goals can provide structure and order to the discussion and keep the decision-making process on track. They can act as directional signs and allow us to measure our progress as a group. They can also give us a sense of closure when we are finished. The first step, therefore, in solving the problem for which a group has been convened is to understand clearly the goals to be achieved.

In discussing the goals, the group must understand the internal constraints under which it is operating—whether financial, technical, political, environmental, or other constraints. Within that context, the group will want to decide which goals are the most important, which are necessary, which would be desirable, and which might be excessive, for the given purpose and set of circumstances. For example, if our initial stated goal is to close, cover, and secure our town dump, as required by state environmental regulations, we might be tempted to expand that goal to create a park or recreational area on top of the old dump site. This has been done in some other communities, but is it practical for ours? Will our citizens value it enough to pay for the extra cost of bringing the site to that standard and then maintaining it as a park in the future? On the other hand, as the costs of waste disposal escalate, we might be tempted to scale back our dump closure plans to simply closing the gates and hoping that the environmental regulators do not bother us about it. In that case, we might find in a few years that the runoff from the site pollutes neighboring wells and water supplies, leading to lawsuits and a requirement that the town supply clean water to the affected residents. In considering our goals, therefore, we need to think through the potential effects of their implementation. The scope of the goals dictates the scope of the problem to be resolved.

DISCUSSION QUESTIONS

1. Why is defining the problem important to effective decision making?
2. Distinguish between internal and external constraints. Provide an example of each one from your own experience.
3. Why should you be careful about accepting the first answer to a difficult problem? What decision-making principle does this highlight?
4. What constraints do we face when we make a final choice?
5. What actions should be considered when implementing a decision?
6. What elements are important for an effective evaluation stage?
7. What is meant by concurrence seeking? Why would a group be prone to trying to achieve concurrence seeking?
8. Do you agree with the conclusion that groups are more successful when they approach a problem systematically and rationally? Why or why not?
9. Briefly outline the systematic problem-solving approach provided in this chapter.

REFERENCES

Barnhill, W. (2003, September). New focus on older drivers. *AARP Bulletin,* pp. 10–11.

Batty, D. (2009, January 19). *Guardian.* Retrieved May 19, 2009, from guardian.co.uk.

Beach, L. R. (1997). *The psychology of decision making: People in organizations.* Thousand Oaks, CA: Sage.

Benson, J. A. (1988). Crisis revisited: An analysis of strategies used by Tylenol in the second tampering episode. *Central States Speech Journal, 39*(1), 49–66.

Berry, G. R. (2006). Can computer-mediated asynchronous communication improve team processes and decision making? *Journal of Business Communication, 43*(4), 72–93.

Boone, L. E. (1992). *Quotable business.* New York: Random House.

Campbell, J., & Stasser, G. (2006). The influence of time and task demonstrability on decision-making in computer-mediated and face-to-face groups. *Small Group Research, 28*(3), 271–294.

Capers, R. S., & Lipton, E. (1993). Hubble error: Time, money and millionths of an inch. *Academy of Management Executive, 7*(4), 41–62.

Chopra, M. (2009, January 28). *The survivor's club.* Retrieved May 19, 2009, from www.huffingtonpost.com.

Dunn, M. (2003, August 27). Investigators issue scathing report of NASA's management. *Tuscaloosa News,* p. A3.

Eisler, P., Watson, T., & Levin, A. (2003, August 27). Report flays NASA culture. *USA Today,* p. 1A.

Ellis, D. G., & Fisher, B. A. (1994). *Small group decision making: Communication and the group process* (4th ed.). New York: McGraw-Hill.

Gouran, D. S., Hirokawa, R. Y., & Martz, A. E. (1986). A critical analysis of factors related to decisional processes involved in the *Challenger* disaster. *Central States Speech Journal, 37,* 119–135.

Guiliano, E. (1982). *The complete illustrated works of Lewis Carroll.* New York: Avenel Books.

Harris, T. E. & Nelson, M. D. (2008). *Applied organizational communication: Theory and practice in a global environment.* New York: Lawrence Erlbaum Associates.

Herek, G., Janis, I. L., & Huth, P. (1987). Decision-making during international crisis: Is quality of process related to outcome? *Journal of Conflict Resolution, 31,* 203–226.

Hirokawa, R. Y. (1983). Group communication and problem solving effectiveness: An investigation of group phases. *Human Communication Research, 9,* 291–305.

Kayes, D. C. (2006). From climbing stairs to riding waves. *Small Group Research, 37*(6), 612–630.

Kienzter, D. S. (1997). Visual ethics. *Journal of Business Communication, 34*(2), 171–187.

Katzenbach, J. R., & Smith, D. K. (1993). *The wisdom of teams: Create a high-performance organization.* Boston: Harvard Business School Press.

Klocke, U. (2007). How to improve decision making in small groups. *Small Group Research, 28*(3), 437–468.

Kruglanski, A. W. (1986, August). Freezethink and the *Challenger. Psychology Today*, pp. 48–49.

Levin, A. (2003, August 27). Board found agency full of flaws. *USA Today*, p. 5A.

Schultz, B., Ketrow, S. M., & Urban, D. M. (1995). Improving decision quality in the small group: The role of the reminder. *Small Group Research, 26*, 521–541.

Stein, B. A., & Kanter, R. M. (1993). Why good people do bad things: A retrospective on the Hubble fiasco. *Academy of Management Executive, 7*(4), 58–62.

Taleb, N. N. (2007). *The Black Swan: The impact of the highly improbable*. New York: Random House.

Trujillo, N., & Roth, E. L. (1987). Organizational perspectives for public relations research and practice. *Management Communication Quarterly, 1*, 218–224.

Watson, T. (2003a, May 15). Probe slams NASA safety. *USA Today*, p. 1A.

Watson, T. (2003b, June 24). Records show NASA safety office cuts. *USA Today*, p. 3A.

Whyte, G. (1991). Decision failures: Why they occur and how to prevent them. *Academy of Management Executive, 5*(2), 23–31.

Wood, J. T. (1992). Alternative methods of group decision making. In R. S. Cathcart & L. A.

CHAPTER

10

Creativity in the Small Group Process

CHAPTER OUTLINE

CHAPTER OBJECTIVES

- Understand creativity.
- Explain creativity as a new way of seeing.
- Outline the perceptual, cultural, and emotional barriers to creativity.
- Demonstrate the use of idea needlers and manipulative verbs.
- Examine the importance of association, metaphors, and analogy for creativity.
- Discuss ways of solving problems creatively.
- Provide the elements of a creative group climate.
- Review and explain Gibb's group climate factors.

KEY TERMS

Algorithms	Empathy	Openness
Analogy	Equality	Paradigmatic thinking
Association	Evaluation	Paradigms
Climate	Heuristics	Perceptual barriers
Creative abrasion	Idea needlers	Sharing
Creativity	Manipulative verbs	Spontaneity
Cultural barriers	Metaphors	
Emotional barriers	Neutrality	

Tough problems of all kinds can be resolved because one universal principle is at the core of learning to think like a genius: you've got to break the rules. . . . Einstein was a great problem solver because he was a superb rule breaker. It is a common trait of genius, and a skill that can be learned and cultivated. We can all think like Einstein if we just learn to break the rules. "Common sense is the collection of prejudices acquired by the age eighteen"—Albert Einstein.

(Thorpe, 2000, pp. 3–4).

Groups need to accomplish more than reproducing the existing system. They must create something new. This creative process is facilitated by a creative group interaction. This chapter focuses on the concepts behind group creativity. It defines *creativity* and examines some of the myths surrounding it, exposes some of the barriers to creativity, provides techniques for increasing creativity, identifies the steps for solving problems creatively, and outlines the requirements for a creative climate.

What Is Creativity?

When what you do is new, different, and helpful, it shows creativity (Goman, 2000). Several definitions of creativity follow: "Creativity is . . . going beyond the current boundaries of technology, knowledge, social norms or beliefs . . . [or] seeing and acting on new relationships, thereby bringing them to life" (Anderson, 1992, p. 41). "Creativity . . . involves the power to originate, to break away from the existing ways of looking at things, to move freely in the realm of the imagination, to create . . . new ideas and strong feelings" (Sacks, 1995, pp. 241–242). In summary, creativity is "any form of action that leads to results that are novel, useful, and predictable" (Denhardt, Denhardt, & Aristigueta, 2009, p. 57).

Trying something new, invoking new perceptions, or providing a new response are creative approaches to problem solving. If you drive a new route to work to avoid a traffic jam, you are being creative. Adding a new spice or other nonstandard ingredient to the chili recipe is a creative act. Creative ideas enhance and expand the possibilities of a product, a way of doing something, or a way of seeing things. After all, what is an Egg McMuffin but egg, cheese, ham, and a muffin (with lots of cholesterol)? Sometimes

Teamwork is a creative process

"boldly going where no one has gone before" is a group's goal, but more often the desired outcome is finding a better, more creative solution to a mundane problem.

Albert Einstein is credited with having said that "Imagination is more important than knowledge"; "Our thinking creates problems that the same type of thinking will not solve"; "Everything should be made as simple as possible, but not simpler"; and "To raise new questions, new possibilities, to regard old problems from a new angle, requires creative imagination and marks real advance" (Grogan, 2004; Morgan, 1993; Vergano, 2005). Imagination, insightful understanding, and creativity are at the core of these statements.

In our thinking and behaving, we sometimes find ourselves locked in boxes of closed perspectives with actions that prevent us from discovering insights or developing solutions. As a simple example, it took years before someone asked the obvious question, "Why do freezers have to lie on their sides instead of standing up like refrigerators?" The first freezer was prone, so subsequent freezers were also made prone, but now we have upright freezers. Bose asked a similar question about the size of the traditional speaker: "Why so huge?" Now we have excellent small speakers.

What makes creativity possible is the concept of an underlying system, or ground, beneath the surface of our perceptions of apparently disparate and unrelated phenomena. Because of this unifying ground, there are innumerable ways of getting to the same place (see equifinality, in Chapter 2). Einstein's famous statement "God does not play dice with the universe" suggests his assumption of an underlying, although not necessarily apparent, pattern or system. Problems do not occur randomly or in isolation. A systematic and open-minded approach to small group problem solving should yield answers to the underlying causes and consequences of a problem, directing us toward a simple, but not simplistic, solution. Often, this means unlocking ourselves from our habitual ways of thinking. Ariely, in *Predictably Irrational* (2008), observed, "We are far less rational in our decision making than standard economics assumes. Our irrational behaviors are neither random or senseless—they are systematic and predictable" (p. 42). This observation underscores the need to look for underlying patterns that lead to errors in our thinking.

In popular myth and fiction, creativity is often associated with people who are considered unusual. We tend to imagine that creativity is linked to an impoverished antisocial individual locked away in a top-floor garret, finally emerging after years of experimentation with a grand invention. At the very least, we see a MacGyver-like character creating simple and innovative solutions to complex problems, using only the minimal materials at hand. In the real world of everyday life however, creativity is much less dramatic and much more common.

As indicated earlier, we are all creative. "The typical brain consists of 100 billion cells, each of which connects and communicates with up to 10,000 of its colleagues . . . [which] forge an elaborate network of one quadrillion (1,000,000,000,000,000) connections. . . ." (Pink, 2006, p. 13). This chapter will provide tools for more effectively using that network of brain cells for solving problems in teams and groups.

Creativity Means a New Way of Seeing

Creativity is the result of looking at things and seeing them in a new way, synthesizing two or more previously unrelated phenomena or modifying something that already exists. One way to understand creativity is to draw the distinction between *heuristics* and *algorithms*. A task is heuristic if it involves learning by doing, perhaps through trial and error. It is algorithmic if it imposes a straightforward, tried-and-true solution. Most tasks, even mundane ones, such as driving to work, completing a research paper, or arranging a room, do not have single, precise formats or answers. They show equifinality—many different ways to reach a workable solution—and are therefore open to creative solutions. We all engage in creative problem solving on a daily basis. If you change your study habits and the result is a better grade, you have been creative. When you rearrange your room or apartment so there is better access to certain areas, you have been a creative problem solver.

Creative individuals generate ideas *and* make something happen as a result. For example, a plain iron bar was worth $5. When someone took that iron bar and forged horseshoes from it, the value increased to $11. At some point, it was also used to make needles, and the price rose to $3,285. Someone else decided to make watch springs from it, and its value went to $250,000. The ability to see the same iron bar and realize its many uses is creativity. In this case, it meant the difference between $5 and $250,000 (de Janasz, Dowd, & Schneider, 2002).

Guidelines for creative problem solving include keeping an open mind; withholding premature judgments; looking at problems in new ways and as opportunities, rather than as obstacles; accepting different opinions; avoiding too heavy reliance on logic; allowing for ambiguity; being willing to break the rules and "draw outside the lines"; and asking why and what if (Denhardt et al., 2009).

Reviews of business success stories reveal several attributes of creative people. Why, for example, do some people want a lime with their Corona beer? A time-honored Mexican custom, perhaps? No, the Corona-and-lime ritual dates back to 1981, when, on a bet with his buddy, a bartender put a lime into the neck of a Corona to see if he could begin a trend—success! (Lindstron, 2008) Among their characteristics, innovative individuals tend to see combinations not obvious to everyone else. For example, "it was Craig McCaw's gift . . . to look across the traffic jams and see a nation of people talking on car phones. In September of 1994, Mr. McCaw made himself $800 million by selling McCaw Cellular Communications Corp., Kirkland, Wash., to New York–based AT&T Corp. for a total of $11.5 billion" (Bowers & Gupta, 1994, p. A1). Other innovative people simply spot the obvious and look at it in a new way. Quicken, the successful and profitable personal-finance software, is based on the simple principle that most people hate to balance their checkbooks. Scott Cook, a former brand manager at Procter & Gamble, observed this and came up with a solution. "People don't buy technology," Mr. Cook suggested. "They don't say, 'Fill 'er up. I'll take 10 gallons of technology.' They buy what technology does for them" (Bowers & Gupta, 1994, p. A13). Entrepreneurs who strike it rich are the ones who take existing concepts and find new ways of utilizing them. Google thrives on a creative atmosphere that encourages off-the-wall thinking and experimentation. Engineers at Google are required to spend 20% of their time pursuing their own ideas (Lashinsky, 2006). Organizations must be creative to survive in the 21st century (Robinson & Stern, 1997; Senge, Keliner, Roberts, & Smith, 1999; "The creative corporation toolbox," 205).

Creative thinking is available to all of us, but too often, we stifle it in ourselves. One advantage of working in a group is being able to take advantage of the creative processes of a number of people working simultaneously. People think, make decisions, and solve problems in different ways. A group can explore and take advantage of those alternative approaches to a problem or a decision and thereby develop creative new insights, decisions, and solutions.

Barriers to Creativity

In general, we limit our creativity because we lack self-confidence, fear taking risks, feel a need to conform, do not feel we are in an environment that encourages creativity, or find ourselves locked into our habitual ways of looking at the world—our *paradigms*. Table 10.1 lists some common blocks to creativity and possible responses to them. These blocks to our creativity can often be traced to our social training, beginning at a very young age.

The vast majority of our education and acculturation has been based on learning the right way to do something. Rarely are we rewarded or provided positive recognition for being wrong or marching to the tune of a "different drummer." Being different can mean we will be ostracized. Perception, culture, and emotion stand as barriers to the free use of our creative imaginations.

TABLE 10.1   Common Blocks and Creative Responses

Blocks	Creative Responses
That's impossible.	See the ways in which it is possible.
It's not exactly right.	Assume no solution is perfect.
I might appear foolish.	So did Albert Einstein.
Let's get serious.	Then, when do we get to have fun?
That's not logical.	Neither is the theory of light as both wave and particle.
That's not practical.	Who says?

Perceptual Barriers

Perceptual barriers are those characteristics that blind us to the hidden dimensions of an issue. Perceptual barriers include difficulty in isolating the problem, narrowing the problem so much that we see only the immediate issue and not the larger context, over-looking "trivia" that may be at the base of the problem, overlooking the obvious or failing to investigate it fully, accepting superficial similarities with our prior experiences as indicative of sameness, inadequately defining terms or isolating attributes, and failing to distinguish between cause and effect (Denhardt et al., 2009).

Many of these perceptual barriers result from *paradigmatic thinking*. As Marshall McLuhan stated, we shape our tools and then our tools shape us. Our tendency is to define issues in terms of the ways we have already defined them. The following exercise illustrates this concept. Put nine dots on a piece of paper (as shown Figure 10.1). Connect all nine dots using four straight lines without lifting your pen or pencil from the paper. The solutions are revealed later in this section. (The secret is to try thinking outside the box.)

FIGURE 10.1   The Nine-Dot Puzzle

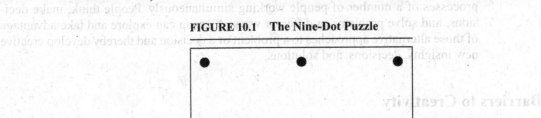

A paradigm is the preformed model we use for our thinking. It is the container within which acceptable discourse about an issue is defined. Thomas Kuhn (1962) outlined the impact of paradigms on how we think. Although Kuhn was focusing on scientists when he explained how their paradigms, or views of the world, limit their scopes of inquiry, the paradigmatic box that encloses our thinking applies to all of us. We each use paradigms to understand and respond to the problems, people, and ideas we encounter on a daily basis.

A paradigm, however, will blind us to certain facts, ideas, and problems, because we have come to accept it without question. In our search for understanding, we want certainty, but being certain means we have not left room for doubt in our world. To be creative, we must be willing to challenge the current paradigms, to see outside our boxes, or views of the world, and to open ourselves up to other options.

The letters Q W E R T Y U I O P form a familiar pattern for anyone using a computer keyboard. They are the top row of letters, and they have appeared on typewriters since the 1870s (Oech, 1992). The original manual typewriters could not respond as quickly as an operator could type, so the keys would jam. Sholes & Co., a leading typewriter manufacturer, decided to slow down the operators by making the keyboard more difficult to use. This inefficiency was created by including the *O* and *I*, the third and sixth most frequently used letters, in the top row, thereby slowing down the operator. This pattern worked to resolve the original manual typewriter problem and has remained on the keyboard since, despite its built-in inefficiency.

As you can see by looking at Figure 10.2, the answer to the nine-dot exercise is not all that difficult, if you go outside the box established paradigmatically around the nine dots. Alternately, all nine dots can be connected with one line—just use a very broad felt-tipped marker and cover all nine dots in one sweep. Other creative solutions include bending the paper in a circular form so that you can move your pen or pencil around the paper and connect all nine dots, or folding the paper so that all nine dots are on top of each other and pushing the pencil through the page, so that the pencil pierces all nine dots. One line and all nine dots are then connected.

The following is another creativity exercise (Mattimore, 1994). Which of the following numbers is most different from the others?

1) Three
2) Thirteen
3) Thirty-one

Most people have difficulty with this exercise. The number that is really different is 2, since it is an even number, while the other five numbers are odd, but we tend not to see the 2 as a number since it is separated with a closing parenthesis from the other numbers. We tend to define the problem in a standard, paradigmatic manner. By assuming the 1), 2), and 3) are simply organizing symbols, we miss the obvious—three additional numbers.

Paradigmatic thinking creates blinders on our thinking, leading us to assume we are inherently not creative people. When we are in trouble, however, we all find we have the ability to be creative.

FIGURE 10.2   The Nine-Dot Solution

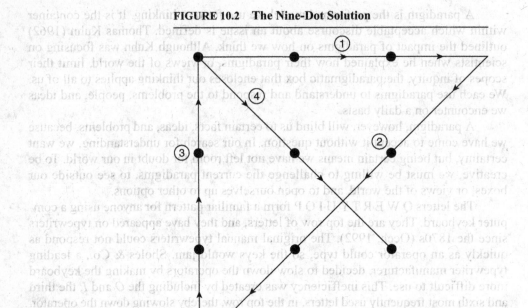

Cultural Barriers

Behind perceptual barriers are additional barriers formed by cultural expectations. Our basic social and emotional needs are met through our membership and acceptance into a cultural network. The barriers presented by our cultural system are based on the expectation of conformity with rules and standard norms of thinking, behavior, and interaction. *Cultural barriers* include a requirement for conformity, an expectation of practicality and efficiency, particular arenas for competition or cooperation, an expectation of politeness and of following rules for social order, a reliance on statistical proofs, a dependence on generalizations, a trust in the power of reason and logic, a belief in an either/or perspective on issues, and a reliance on expert knowledge.

We learn early that playing by the rules will ensure us a place in the game. We were also taught in our early schooling to stay in line, not to cheat, and not to talk out of turn (and to raise our hands). But when we become too orderly, we lose the ability to see things from a different perspective. The nine dots and the "2)" examples make that point.

Our experiences in school and in the work world also teach us that life, after all, is serious business, but to move beyond "business as usual," we need to relax and play with things, words, ideas, and concepts. Sometimes we need to be bold and "just do it." Although society places a great deal of emphasis on seeing things as they are, creativity involves seeing things slightly differently. For instance, write down all the uses you can think of for a Styrofoam coffee cup. Can you name 100? It's not hard, if you realize the cup can be used to mold (as a cookie cutter or to make sand castles), for packing (break it up), and to store things (nails, pennies). Some groups have used the cup for pets (to hold fish), telephones, and for numerous other nonstandard uses. Just because the cup was designed for coffee does not limit its potential for other creative uses.

Like individuals, organizations can develop working habits that restrict creativity. Different divisions or departments focus on their expertise and areas of responsibility, which can lead to perceptual barriers. *Creative abrasion* is being used by some organizations to overcome this limitation. This involves bringing people with different skills, ideas, and values together to generate new ideas, problem-solving approaches, and products: "This process breaks traditional frames of thinking by having diverse perspectives rub creatively against each other to develop innovative solutions" (Cummings & Worley, 2005, p. 506). In addition, organizations often turn to outside consultants who offer different perspectives regarding issues or problems (Davenport, Prusak, & Wilson, 2003). Both approaches allow individuals to open a window to different ways of viewing a problem.

Some of our most creative moments occur when we are willing to play, question, challenge, and enjoy solving problems (Mattimore, 1994; Thompson, 1992). Being naive or a little disrespectful of the "way things have always been done" can pay off when we confront serious issues.

Emotional Barriers

In addition to and closely associated with perceptual and cultural barriers to creativity are the personal, *emotional barriers* we place in the way of our creative abilities. There are risks and hard work associated with "going out on a limb" and trying something new. We may have to take more time than we would like, we may make a mistake, and we may risk the censure of our peers by looking foolish or being judged incompetent.

Creativity can appear to be a chancy pursuit, so we tend to be very tentative in our attempts. We often seek the approval of others for our ideas, rather than risk being wrong. Most significant inventions throughout history have been initially rejected by the majority of people. Although our schooling and upbringing have emphasized being careful to find the right answers before we raise our hands, creative answers require a willingness to take a chance, to think out loud, and to risk being wrong. If we miss the target on the first try, we can practice, and eventually we will be on target and find appropriate answers. Fear of making a mistake often causes us to limit our creativity. In a sense, we have lost our right to be wrong.

Because our society rewards being "right" and having particular knowledge, we are sometimes caught in the net of our own expertise. If we know too much about a subject, we may lose our ability to see new and different approaches and concepts. All too often, we assume that the current standard of knowledge and ways of doing things are the best. There are numerous examples of highly placed people being overly certain. To name only one, in 1899, the director of the U.S. Patent Office said that "everything that can be invented has been invented" and requested that the Patent Office be dismantled and that he be transferred to a new position in government. Today, the average American automobile contains as much information-processing computing power as was on board the *Apollo* moon-landing craft in 1969, and more than a 1970s mainframe computer (Davis & Davidson, 1991).

We also frequently assume that only large research organizations or experts with particular qualifications can come up with innovative and relevant ideas. When we think of grand inventions, we imagine the Apple Computers, Sonys, or Whirlpools of the world, but "two-thirds of all inventions are created by individuals on their own time or by small organizations" (Thompson, 1992, p. 190). We are all familiar with the concept "nothing ventured, nothing gained." Creativity requires that we risk something to find a better solution. As Picasso said, "Every act of creation is first of all an act of destruction." We must be willing to destroy some of our preconceptions. Picasso's experiments with new ways of seeing, challenging the traditional Western view of what constituted a suitable viewpoint for paintings, gave us Cubism and other innovative ways of viewing reality (Fargis, 1998). We need to be willing to challenge existing paradigms in order to open the door to creativity.

Techniques for Encouraging Creativity

Although we are all naturally creative, we tend to squelch our abilities in our efforts to conform to social expectations. Four specific techniques can help us find ways of opening ourselves up to our creativity. These are idea needlers, manipulative verbs, association and metaphors, and analogy.

Idea Needlers

In a vein similar to the Styrofoam cup exercise, imagine how many uses there are for baking soda. A few years ago, we might have limited its use to a cooking ingredient. Now it is used to keep refrigerators odor free, to clean carpets, and to brush teeth. There are probably many other uses for baking soda that you can think of. "Tea bags" are now used for instant coffee, premeasured doses of medicine, and numerous other applications. What if you wanted to question the design of the typical college classroom or the arrangement of the chairs in the classroom? The *idea needlers* in Table 10.2 are designed to help us raise the questions that enhance our ability to discover ideas.

These idea needlers offer us the opportunity to use a different perspective, or lens, to view the problem.

Manipulative Verbs

When we decide to alter, multiply, eliminate, divide, or transpose, we are using *manipulative verbs* to change the way we view a particular process. Changing a verb can alter the sense of a statement and can have a dramatic effect on preconceived meanings:

TABLE 10.2   Idea Needlers

How much is the result of custom, tradition, or opinion?	Can motion be added to it?
Why does it have this shape?	Will it be better standing still?
How would I design it, if I had to build it in my home workshop?	What other layout might be better?
What if this were turned inside out? reversed? upside down?	Can cause and effect be reversed? Is one possibly also the other?
What if this were larger? higher? longer? wider? thicker? lower?	Should it be put on the other end or in the middle?
What else can it be made to do?	Should it slide instead of rotate?
What other power would work better?	How could it be described by what it is not?
Where else can this be done?	Has a search been made of the patent literature? of trade journals?
What if the order were changed?	Could a vendor supply this for less?
Suppose this were left out?	How could this be made easier to use?
How can it appeal to the senses?	Can it be made safer?
How about extra value?	How could this be changed for quicker assembly?
Can this be multiplied?	What other materials would do this job?
What if this were blown up?	What is similar to this but costs less? Why?
What if this were carried to extremes?	What if it were made faster?
How can this be made more compact?	What motion or power is wasted?
Would this be better symmetrical or asymmetrical?	Could the package be used for something afterward?
In what form could this be: A liquid, powder, paste, or solid; A rod, tube, triangle, cube, or sphere?	If all specifications could be forgotten, how else could the basic function be accomplished?
	Could these be made to meet specifications?
	How do non-competitors solve problems similar to this?

"A baseball or softball manager can shuffle the team's batting order 362,880 times by merely rearranging his or her starting players" (Osborne, 1963, p. 273). Table 10.3 shows some manipulative verbs that can be used to rephrase questions in ways that can transform our thinking about a problem or issue. Whatever the problem area, changing keywords can open up possibilities for ways of seeing an issue that might never have occurred before.

TABLE 10.3   Manipulative Verbs

magnify	complement	minimize	submerge	modify	add
alter	soften	adapt	fluff up	combine	lighten
substitute	bypass	reverse	subtract	divide	stretch
multiply	repeat	eliminate	thicken	separate	protect
subdue	extrude	invert	repel	distort	symbolize
transpose	segregate	unify	integrate	squeeze	
rotate	abstract	flatten	rearrange	freeze	

Association and Metaphors

Robert Frost once said, "an idea is a feat of association." When we use concepts such as "most like" or "least like," we are using *association*. *Metaphors* associate unlike phenomena and help us visualize concepts. When Shakespeare called the world a "stage," he made clear his idea of life and of society. There are numerous ways to include metaphors in creative thinking. Metaphors such as "a breath of fresh air," "the new kid on the block," "an interesting window on the world," or "back to square one" all provide expanded insights into meaning beyond the literal definitions of the words. In addition, "metaphors play a critical role in the communication process. They are the best devices to use when describing abstract concepts and expressing emotions" (Johnson & Hackman, 1995, p. 100).

Particular terms carry connotations we associate with prior experiences and previously heard uses. When we talk about "eradicating poverty," we associate the term with other things we have worked at "eradicating," such as tuberculosis, hunger, other diseases where the attempts did not succeed. Perhaps we find *eradicate* is too strong a word for what we consider possible. Can we "alleviate" poverty? What are other problems we have alleviated? The associations may or may not involve the same subject or class of subjects. We may associate herds of elephants or horses, packs of dogs, or flocks of chickens with a particular group of people or with the clouds in the sky. Try looking at the descriptions in Table 10.4 and see if they free up your conception of groups.

Analogy

The use of *analogy* is similar to that of association and metaphor, but it is understood here to refer to the ways in which we broaden our senses of what is actually possible. Tunnel vision limits our perspective to a small set of ideas and frequently hampers our quest for creativity. The use of analogies, a comparison between things that are similar in some respects but quite different in others, helps open our perceptions to other useful concepts. For example, when Procter & Gamble tried to solve the problem of how to package delicate potato chips, they found themselves limited to the traditional "bag full of air" answer. Then they considered other fragile and brittle items. The most obvious analogy was dried leaves. A new way of packaging potato chips came about

TABLE 10.4   Concepts of Groups

A shrewdness of apes	A down of hares	A leap of leopards
A murder of crows	A drift of hogs	A nest of vipers
An unkindness of ravens	An exaltation of larks	A parliament of owls
A crash of rhinos	A gam of whales	A pitying of turtle doves
A charm of finches	A grist of bees	A rafter of turkeys
A covey of quail	A kindle of kittens	A smack of jellyfish

when the group asked, "Is there a time when leaves are *not* fragile?" A walk through the woods showed that wet leaves are not fragile, and they conform to the mold they land on (a branch, rock, or pile). So, the answer was to package potato chips when they are wet, conform them to a preset form, and then dry them. The ultimate product was Pringles potato crisps.

Dr. Rene Lanennec, the inventor of the stethoscope, got his inspiration from observing children sending signals to each other by tapping on the end of a log. Henry Ford visited a slaughterhouse and was inspired to produce a better way to mass-produce cars. Willis Carrier was watching water condensing on the side of a glass and got the idea for an air conditioner. Eli Whitney found a means for inventing the cotton "gin" (short for en*gine*) when he saw a cat reaching through a fence trying to grab a chicken (Mattimore, 1994). Thus, idea needlers, manipulative verbs, association, and analogy are four techniques that tap into our creative potential.

Tapscott and Williams, in *Wikinomics* (2006), explore the world of open sourcing that is, releasing problems to the collective knowledge of the Web—which increases accessibility to the collective capability via the Web, providing an important argument for increasing "ways of looking at problems." Collective knowledge, expert viewpoints, capability, and resources have been used by organizations ranging from YouTube to Proctor & Gamble, leading to significant improvements in innovation, profits, and success. This provides a pragmatic application of the four techniques just discussed.

Organizations train group creativity by presenting building materials and asking the participants to design an "award-winning" structure. This group is part of the Management Development Project at the University of Alabama

Solving Problems Creatively

When you are unable to think of a creative idea, consider these five suggestions:

      1. *Trigger your unconscious:* Take a rest from consciously thinking about the problem you're trying to solve. You can get insights while you're working out, walking, playing cards, or taking a shower.

      2. *Loosen your mind:* Let your mind wander a little. You'll go back to the task at hand relaxed and refreshed.

      3. *Break down the problem into a series of doable tasks:* The problem can be broken down into either a set of questions to be answered or a series of small problems that can be solved one at a time.

      4. *Do some research:* Look for other examples of the same type of problem somewhere else. Most problems have been faced in some way by someone else somewhere. As we have heard time and again, "there is nothing new under the sun." Search for alternative solutions by looking in other locations.

      5. *Ask yourself questions:*
        a. What are the different parts of the problem?
        b. Does one part hold the key to other parts?
        c. Can I apply knowledge from other situations to this one?
        d. Would exaggerating the problem make the solution more apparent?
        e. What is the normal situation? Are there alternatives?

A Creative Group Climate

We have now examined the issues surrounding creativity, in general. Group creativity, however, frequently depends on the *climate* of the group process itself. A supportive climate increases the probability that individuals and groups will be creative and successful in reaching their goals. The cornerstones of a creative climate are mutual trust, respect, and commitment. Group leaders, facilitators, and members must address the fundamental issues of openness and sharing, if a creative group climate is to be cultivated.

Openness

Maintaining *openness*—a supportive communication climate—during the problem-solving process is vital for creativity. People have emotional and safety concerns, such as, "How open and honest can I be in this situation?" "Will anyone use what I say against me?" "Will others be honest about their feelings and opinions?" "Are my goals compatible with those of the others?" "Can I freely express my wishes and fears?"

Sharing

Sharing relevant information, resources, and responsibility is a cornerstone of a creative climate. Information and responsibility must be shared to ensure that trust will not be manipulated. Without trust, we can become defensive and ruin the possibilities for creative interaction. We generally want to know how we fit in, what is acceptable behavior, what our roles and responsibilities are, how we can contribute, and what others expect from us.

Some groups feel good, and we are happy to be members of them. Other groups feel tense or hostile, and being a member is distasteful and hard work. These feelings are based on the dynamics of supportive and defensive climates generated in the group. Jack Gibb (1961) defined strategies that create a supportive group climate versus those that create a defensive one. The difference between these two types of climate lies in how we communicate, not the content, goal, or purpose of what we communicate.

We discuss the six comparisons Gibb made to help explain the difference between defensive and supportive communication. These comparisons are evaluation versus description; control versus problem orientation; strategy versus spontaneity; neutrality versus empathy; superiority versus equality; and certainty versus provisionalism. In the last category, we discuss the effects of group climate through reciprocity.

Gibb's Communication Climate Comparisons

Evaluation Versus Description.   *Evaluation* places us in a hierarchic relationship, with the evaluator assuming a position of superiority. This immediately throws off the balance of communication and sets up a backdrop for tension. When someone is blaming us or letting us know he or she is judging what we say or do, we become defensive. Comments such as "If it weren't for your lack of interest, we'd be doing much better" make most of us defend ourselves rather than listen. At their best, evaluation and judgment teach us to avoid future criticism. At their worst, they lead us to avoid the situation, person, or problem. What evaluation usually does not do is cause us to voluntarily alter our behavior. When such evaluation is delivered in front of the rest of the group, it is threatening and may cause us to become even more defensive. In addition, the rest of the group is likely to respond by becoming uncomfortable and defensive.

Fortunately, we can avoid that response by describing the same situation with neutral statements of fact. By doing so, we have a very good chance of gaining the support of the other group members. If it really is my fault that the group is not progressing, a simple description without demanding that I accept guilt will allow me to hear the message. Stick to the observable facts. Since our goal should be to make the group work effectively as a unit, little can be gained by ostracizing individual members through evaluation.

To guarantee that our comments are seen as supportive, rather than as simply critical, we need to "own" the statements and take responsibility. Saying, "I think we should end the meeting now, so we can go watch the game; we can finish the report later when we don't have other distractions" is vastly different from "None of you seem to care about this report, since all you want to do is watch the game." As with feedback, it is important to be specific in our comments and avoid making value judgments. Saying, "I wouldn't have to repeat myself time and again if you would just pay attention like any adult" is not as likely to make someone listen more closely to my message as saying, "Apparently I am not being clear. What can I do to make the process work better?" Clearly, the real issue is our own perception regarding the other group members. Do we see them as needing our judgment, or do we see them as colleagues for whom we have respect and compassion?

Control Versus Problem Orientation. Issuing orders or making it clear that we have the power to control others' behavior creates defensiveness. When we attempt to change the attitudes of other group members or to restrict their freedom, we will likely encounter some resistance. Group members are well aware of where power lies and will resist our claiming it.

In the case of small groups, the point is to solve a problem using the input of all members. It is not intended as a forum for a power play. Orienting the group discussion toward the problem allows a "we" orientation rather than an "us versus them" orientation. In many organizations, there is a great deal of discussion regarding empowering employees through creating a team spirit and a group orientation (Phillips & Wallace, 1992). Unfortunately, many managers and supervisors still believe that telling others what to do is the best way to achieve results (Harris & Nelson, 2008). In small groups, there is frequently pressure to "cut to the chase" and produce results. Rather than one individual succumbing to the temptation to take charge and orchestrate the process, however, the end results are better served by describing the problem and letting the group take responsibility for the outcome.

Strategy Versus Spontaneity. The use of gimmicks or manipulation to get what we want may seem strategic in ensuring a particular outcome from the group process, but it rarely sets the tone for a cooperative, supportive group climate. Our natural resistance to high-pressure sales comes from our dislike of being manipulated. If the gimmicks do work and we feel we have been manipulated, we are not likely to forgive or forget. At that point, the game is on, and the only issue is who wins which round. Missing from this game is the goal of the group!

Spontaneity, on the other hand, is a willingness to be honest and direct. Gibb proposed that we remain open and responsive to the group process as it unfolds. Rather than trying to plan how we are going to achieve our own goals (strategy), we should be open to the fresh ideas that evolve in the context of the ongoing group process (spontaneity).

Neutrality Versus Empathy. If we come to our group meeting feeling distraught because our apartment caught fire, our computer was ruined, and we lost all our possessions, and our group's only response is, "Too bad," or "That is a problem. Now let's get on with our important group work," we will not feel supported. We are looking for empathy, and we are receiving neutrality. When people are detached from our needs or seem indifferent, they are expressing *neutrality.*

The opposite of neutrality is empathy. *Empathy* expresses a concern for group members as people, not just as other group participants. Empathy acknowledges others as worthwhile and involves a sensitivity toward others, a willingness to suspend judgment, and an attempt to respond to their needs. Simple supportive statements such as "I'm really sorry. Is there anything we can do? If you are unable to fully participate today, we understand" express interest, show concern, and ensure the best possible continued participation of each member in the group process.

Superiority Versus Equality.   In any group, there are bound to be discrepancies in experience, training, particular knowledge, status, or power. Although these may be apparent on the surface, for the group to work effectively, as we have discussed earlier, we need the input of all members. When some members perceive themselves or others to be superior in some way, they may shut those with less power, influence, or expertise out of the process, to the detriment of all.

A sense of *equality,* on the other hand, sets the stage for an effective group process. A simple question such as "What do you think?" indicates our interest in the other member's perspective. In addition, as we have noted earlier, it is sometimes the most unlikely person who offers the most creative insights. To shut that person out of the discussion robs us of the value of her or his input. To the extent that we are all vested in the outcome of the group process, we should encourage equal participation from each of the members.

Certainty Versus Provisionalism.   Many of us have areas in which we believe we have particular knowledge or expertise. However, in a group process, we need to be aware that others may hold their own quite different understandings with equal assurance. As we have discussed under "Active Listening" (see Chapter 7), arrogance and disrespect most often serve the opposite purpose from what we have in mind, creating defensiveness in the other group members and undermining the group process. Labeling other group members as wrong, foolish, or naive is clearly counterproductive to achieving the group's task or social-facilitation goals. To the extent that we refuse to listen to others and are unwavering in our positions, there is little hope for productive group discussion.

On the other hand, if we state our positions provisionally, admitting a willingness to hear the views of others, we are more likely to be heard by them, as well. It is important to keep in mind that if the object was for us to come up with the solution on our own, we would not need to bother convening a group.

Summary

Creativity is an important skill for small group and team problem solving success. Creativity means a new way of looking at issues and problems. Perceptual, cultural, and emotional barriers can restrain our creativity.

Four specific techniques for encouraging creativity—idea needlers, manipulative verbs, association and metaphors, and analogy—are presented to enhance group creativity. In addition, five steps are offered to become more creative.

The idea of a creative group climate is introduced through an examination of openness, sharing, and Gibb's communication climate comparisons.

Gibb's six dichotomous categories allow us to see the difference between defensive and supportive communication. Supportive communication fosters a climate for creative problem solving. When people feel defensive, they are likely to retaliate. If my contributions or personal attributes come under attack, I am likely to respond in kind. On the other hand, if I feel valued and appreciated for my contributions and for who I am, I am likely to respond in positive ways and support the other members of my group. Ultimately, membership in a small group should bring us joy, make us feel worthwhile, and open us to new challenges and opportunities. Positive group climates benefit all members and foster creativity.

All of these issues affect group climate. When group members listen attentively and supportively, group climate and the potential for creativity is enhanced. When group members show disrespect and lack of interest, members become defensive, and creativity is discouraged.

DISCUSSION QUESTIONS

1. Provide an example of creativity from your own experience. How does it fit with the chapter's discussion of creativity?

2. What guidelines exist for creative problem solving?

3. What is meant by thinking outside the box? Getting outside of our paradigm?

4. Name five cultural barriers to creativity. Why do you think these would keep a group from being creative?

5. Individually, or as a group, find examples of emotional barriers limiting creativity.

6. Identify five metaphors that are used to describe five different majors or concentrations of study on your campus. For example, being a premed is a "bear." Why are metaphors useful in creativity?

7. What are some ways of solving problems creatively?

8. What actions can be taken to develop a creative group climate?

9. What central issues or themes are present across Gibb's six group climate comparisons? What characteristics do the six dichotomous categories share? How do they differ?

10. Individually, or as a group, develop a scenario in which defensive communication occurs. Develop a second scenario in which the same goals are sought but supportive communication is used.

REFERENCES

Ariely, M. (2007). *Predictably irrational: The hidden forces that shape our decisions.* New York: Simon & Schuster.

Anderson, J. V. (1992). Weirder than fiction: The reality and myths of creativity. *Academy of Management Executive, 6*(4), 40–47.

Bowers, B., & Gupta, U. (1994, October 19). New entrepreneurs offer simple lesson in building a fortune. *Wall Street Journal,* pp. A1, A13.

Cummings, T. G., & Worley, C. G. (2005). *Organizational development and change* (8th ed.). Mason, OH: South-Western.

Davenport, T. H., Prusak, L., & Wilson, H. J. (2003). *What's the big idea: Creating and capitalizing on the best management thinking.* Boston: Harvard Business School Press.

Davis, S., & Davidson, B. (1991). *2020 vision.* New York: Simon & Schuster.

de Janasz, S. C., Dowd, K. O., & Schneider, B. Z. (2002). *Interpersonal skills in organizations*. Boston: McGraw-Hill.

Denhardt, R. B., Denhardt, J. V., U Aristigueta, M. P. (2009). *Managing human behavior in public and nonprofit organizations* (2nd ed.) Thousand Oaks, CA: Sage.

Fargis, P. (Ed.). (1998). *The New York Public Library desk reference* (3rd ed.). New York: Macmillan.

Gibb, J. (1961). Defensive communication. *Journal of Communication, 11,* 141–148.

Goman, C. K. (2000). *Creativity in business: A practical guide for creative thinking*. Menlo Park, CA: Crisp.

Grogan, D. W. (Ed.). (2004). 100 years of genius without limitations. *Discover, 25,* 9.

Harris, T. E., & Nelson, M. D. (2008). *Applied organizational communication: Theory and practice in a global environment*. New York: Lawrence Erlbaum Associates.

Johnson, C. E., & Hackman, M. Z. (1995). *Creative communication*. Prospect Heights, IL: Waveland.

Kuhn, T. S. (1962). *The structure of scientific revolutions*. Chicago: University of Chicago Press.

Lashinsky, A. (2006, October 2). Chaos by design. *Fortune*, pp. 86–98.

Lindstrom, M. (2008). *Buy-ology: Truth and lies about why we buy*. New York: Simon & Schuster.

Mattimore, B. W. (1994). *99 percent inspiration: Tips, tales & techniques for liberating your business creativity*. New York: AMACOM.

Morgan, G. (1993). *Imaginization*. Newbury Park, CA: Sage.

Oech, R. V. (1992). *A whack on the side of the head*. Menlo Park, CA: Creative Think.

Osborne, A. F. (1963). *Applied imagination* (3rd ed.). New York: Charles Scribner's Sons.

Phillips, D., & Wallace, L. (1992). *Influence in the workplace: Maximizing personal empowerment*. Dubuque, IA: Kendall/Hunt.

Pink , D. H. (2006). *A whole new mind: Why right-brainers will rule the future*. New York: Riverhead.

Robinson, A. G., & Stern, S. (1997). *Corporate creativity: How innovation and improvement actually happen*. San Francisco: Berrett-Koelhler.

Sacks, O. (1995). *An anthropologist on Mars*. New York: Alfred A. Knopf.

Senge, P., Keliner, A., Roberts, C., & Smith, B. (1999). *The dance of change: The challenges of sustaining momentum in learning organizations*. New York: Doubleday/Currency.

Tapscott, D., & Williams, A. D. (2006). *Wikinomics: How mass collaboration changes everything*. New York: Portfolio.

"The creative corporation toolbox." (2005, October 10). *Business Week*, pp. 72–77.

Thompson, C. C. (1992). *What a great idea!: Key steps creative people take*. New York: Harper Perennial.

Thorpe, S. (2000). *Learning to think like Einstein*. New York: Barnes & Noble.

Vergano, D. (2005, March 8). Einstein, icon for all time. *USA Today*, pp. 1D–2D.

CHAPTER

11 *Group Process and Presentation Techniques*

CHAPTER OBJECTIVES

- Describe the goals and uses of brainstorming.
- Explain focus groups and their uses.
- Outline the nominal group technique.
- Illustrate why and how to use the Delphi technique.
- Describe the use of synectics.
- Explain the use of buzz sessions.
- Provide an example of idea writing.

- Show how to use role-playing and listening teams to develop an issue.
- Apply RISK and PERT to develop a solution to a problem.
- Demonstrate flowcharts, fishbone diagrams, and Pareto's principle.
- Describe small group presentation formats.

KEY TERMS

Brainstorming	Idea writing	Role-playing
Buzz sessions	Ishikawa diagrams	Six Sigma
Colloquium	Listening teams	Symposium
Delphi technique	Nominal group technique	Synectics
Fishbone diagrams	Panel	Total Quality Management
Flowcharts	Pareto's principle	(TQM)
Focus group	PERT	
Forum	RISK procedure	

Modern aviation is extremely safe. When crashes occur, they are rarely a result of one catastrophic event. Instead, they are the accumulation of seven consecutive human errors sometimes brought on by poor weather, being behind schedule, overwork, and pilots who have not flown together before. Usually, seven consecutive human errors are involved with one error being magnified by the second error. "These seven errors, furthermore, are rarely problems of knowledge or flying skill. . . . The kinds of errors that cause plane crashes are invariably errors of teamwork and communication."

(Gladwell, 2008, p. 184).

Avoiding a possible plane crash presents a hypothetical, and statistically unlikely, problem for most of us. What this issue does highlight for groups and teams is that group processes and presentations are a key step toward success. There are a number of techniques that can (a) prevent the accumulation of errors leading to a poor conclusion, (b) enhance your group's creativity, (c) facilitate its problem-solving process, and (d) provide a method by which the group can present that information to a larger audience in a persuasive manner. Solving problems effectively requires an appropriate mind-set—viewing problems as opportunities or challenges and looking for solutions. A disciplined approach to clarifying the problem through a variety of tools and identifying and implementing appropriate solutions is critical, as the aviation example shows (Gladstone, 2008; Thompson, 1999). Brainstorming is a productive group-creativity-enhancing process (Jana, 2009). Specific group techniques for gathering information, developing insights within the group, and working through sticking places in the group discussion process include focus groups, nominal group technique, the Delphi technique, synectics, buzz sessions, idea writing, and listening teams. Flowcharts, fishbone diagrams, and use of Pareto's principle are additional techniques that can help groups organize the problem-solving process. RISK and

PERT are processes that help groups systematically go through a complex implementation procedure to meet a goal. These are not just hypothetical approaches. They are used widely in organizations to increase the quality of the products we purchase and can help a group find better solutions. The forum, panel, colloquium, or symposium formats can help organize a group's presentation to, and interactive discussion with, a larger audience.

Brainstorming

Brainstorming is one of the most popular and useful techniques for creative problem solving. If you have a concept and are trying to develop as many insights as possible during a group meeting, brainstorming can help. Four guidelines are helpful in facilitating brainstorming:

1. The more ideas, the better. Quantity is desirable.
2. All ideas are welcome. The wilder the idea, the better.
3. No criticism of ideas at this stage. "Freewheeling" is welcome.
4. Hitchhiking on ideas, using someone else's idea as a springboard for additional thoughts, and combining and improving on ideas are encouraged.

Brainstorming can be fun, and we can all enjoy the process of being creative. If the group is critical and non-supportive, however, the process will not work. The key to successful brainstorming is establishing a climate that encourages individuals to act in an open manner. If done well, brainstorming can produce a large number of original ideas. When the creative brainstorming process is complete, we will need to sort through these ideas to discover which ones are usable and which are creative but perhaps not very practical. It is important that the prioritizing step follow the brainstorming session and not to stifle the free flow of ideas. One method for sorting ideas, after the brainstorming session is complete, is to use the ACB sorting method (shown in Table 11.1). The ACB method assigns ideas equally to one of three piles. If there are 45 items, assign an A to the 15 best ideas. Put a C on the 15 least usable. The remaining 15 ideas are assigned B's, since they fall in the middle. Now go back and separate the B's into the A or C category. Store the C category ideas for later use. Go back to the A category and prioritize the ideas in terms of their importance, urgency, or applicability

TABLE 11.1   ACB Idea Sorting Method

1. Assign an A to the best one-third of the ideas.
2. Assign a C to the least usable one-third of the ideas.
3. The middle one-third automatically receive a B.
4. Go back to the B's and separate them into the A or C category.
5. Store the C category ideas for later use.
6. Prioritize the A's in terms of their importance, urgency, or applicability to the problem at hand.

to the problem at hand. The ideas are now organized, and possible resolutions can be discussed by the group.

What is the payoff? Research in organizations has uncovered shared feelings of optimism and excitement as an outcome of some barriers being overcome, encouraging a more creative climate (Paulus & Dzindolet, 1993). At GlaxoSmithKline, a pharmaceutical firm, brainstorming has been used successfully to help project teams think of innovative actions for existing action plans (Denhardt, Denhardt, & Aristigueta, 2009). Best Buy and Whirlpool place select teams together in a sequestered apartment for 10 weeks to utilize *extreme brainstorming,* allowing team members to operate continually in finding creative approaches to significant issues (Jana, 2008). Sequestering is not necessary for successful brainstorming, but commitment to finding better alternatives is required.

Westin Hotels examined more than 500 possible names generated through brainstorming, focus groups, and employee suggestions, before it branded its new chain "Element": "The aim was to find a name that was simple, modern and not too literal" (Yancey, 2006, p. 2D). Even the smallest details were considered. For example, the letter *t* was curved at the bottom so it would not be perceived as a cross, which could be misinterpreted.

Creative Decision-Making Techniques

Using different types of formats and approaches to deal with different types of issues and different group contexts can enhance the creativity of small group discussions, decisions, and solutions. Focus groups, nominal group technique, the Delphi technique, synectics, buzz sessions, idea writing, role-playing, and listening teams each have applicability to different settings and for solving different types of problems.

The secret to being an effective group is to use the approaches and techniques most appropriate to the particular circumstances facing the group at that time. We are unlikely to use all these techniques in the same group with the same issues, but being aware of a number of strategies provides us with a repertoire from which to choose an appropriate one. If group discussion and decision-making and problem-solving processes have become stalled, more and more of the same process can only give us more and more of the same result. If two meetings a week do not move the group toward solving the problem, why would three or four meetings work better? If the discussion or decision-making format we are using as a group has reached an impasse, continued discussion using the same format is probably not useful. The following techniques offer different approaches to dealing with particular group circumstances.

Focus Groups

There is an old axiom regarding problems: If you want to know the answer, ask the people involved. They may not know the answer, but they know what matters to them and can provide valuable insights regarding the possible success of any solution (Cummings & Worley, 2005). When you are attempting to find detailed, thorough, and unstructured answers to problems, a *focus group* can be the vehicle for understanding people's values, interests, and attitudes.

In a focus group, a facilitator introduces an issue or topic and asks the group to discuss it. Later, the responses are carefully examined to identify major themes. Often, the meeting is tape-recorded so the entire discussion can be replayed and analyzed later. The facilitator asks questions and helps the group explore issues through discussion.

Focus groups have been used in advertising and marketing for years as a way to ask a cross-section of potential users how they feel about a product, packaging, promotion, or service. The use of focus groups has been extended to include morale problems in organizations, menus for cafeterias and vending machines, arguments to be used by lawyers when approaching a jury, customer responses to products or campaigns, and political campaign issues. The focus group is a highly adaptive technique that encourages a freewheeling discussion on a particular issue. The key is to: (1) make certain to explore the major issues surrounding a problem, decision, or concern and then (2) organize those issues by theme in an explicit and useful manner. Focus groups can yield impressive results since they provide an additional avenue to creativity (Yartnoff, 1999). To obtain the best results, ask open-ended questions that elicit thoughtful responses, do not try to force the focus group toward a particular solution or allow the group to focus on a particular solution instead of the problems. Listen to all the answers. Focus groups allow us to understand what individuals actually involved in the issues think. As with most group processes, structure makes the focus group more effective. A focus group generally follows the seven steps outlined in Table 11.2 (Simon, 1999).

Nominal Group Technique

Research indicates that we can produce better ideas when we work in the presence of others. In addition, the group setting allows for a more balanced participation than simply asking for individual input. However, participation by group members is frequently not equal. Some members are quiet while others talk a lot. If the participants have different

TABLE 11.2   Seven Key Steps for Focus Groups

1. Define the purpose of the focus group. Ask questions such as "What do we want to achieve?"
2. Plan ahead for the session. Why are you having this meeting, and when will it occur?
3. Identify and invite the participants. If you have an intact group, then this is fairly easy. Otherwise, choosing the right participants will often decide your success.
4. Provide an overview to your participants so they know why they are attending. Once again, if this is an intact group, provide a reason for the focus group.
5. Generate the questions to be asked. This is not an open-ended forum. Instead, you are trying to determine specific information.
6. Develop a script or a plan of action so you are certain you obtain the necessary information in the time available.
7. Interpret and report the results.

Note: In many situations, professional facilitators are used.

opinions and goals, not all perspectives and concerns may be heard with equal results. When the input of all parties is needed, the nominal group technique offers a viable alternative method for obtaining it. The *nominal group technique* is a highly structured meeting agenda that allows everyone to contribute in a relatively equal manner and without having that contribution interrupted by evaluative comments from others. This approach allows controversial issues to be examined and provides a numerical rating of assigned priorities to the ideas and alternatives suggested by members (McShane & Von Glinow, 2000). The nominal group technique typically includes four steps:

1. Participants work alone and respond in writing with possible solutions to a stated problem. This silent, independent generation of ideas in writing is the key to airing a broad range of ideas on the topic.

2. Each member reads his or her ideas aloud in a round-robin fashion without any criticism or discussion. This round-robin sharing of ideas means that each participant contributes a single idea at a time, which is then recorded on a large flip chart. Discussion of the ideas is not permitted until all have been read and the idea sheets taped to the wall so that they can be seen by the whole group. The group facilitator continues to request ideas from participants until all ideas have been recorded or the group reaches a consensus that they have produced a sufficient number of ideas to discuss.

3. The ideas on the list are now discussed and clarified as to their meanings, but with no evaluative comments allowed. The participants discuss each idea on the list until they are clear about the meaning of all suggestions. This can be done in a serial manner. If there are too many ideas to be effectively covered, the facilitator can instead identify and suggest key issues or themes running through the ideas that need to be clarified. During this step, members may also discover that two or more ideas listed on the chart mean essentially the same thing and decide to combine them.

4. Members then rank order the ideas by importance, which is done by individual, secret ballot. The results of this ballot are tabulated and recorded on the flip chart. The results and any follow-up discussion of the voting pattern suggest the group's orientation and possible solutions to the problem.

When issues are too controversial or too complex for a full and open verbal group discussion, the nominal group technique can be useful. For example, if everyone in a group wants to install a computer system but no one can agree on the brand, the nominal group technique can provide an efficient means for involving all interested parties and can facilitate a faster solution. The phrasing of the question or problem to be addressed, however, is important. For this computer system example, a question of "Which computer system should we purchase?" is not an appropriate nominal group technique question. A more worthwhile question would be to ask, "What functions must the new computer system perform?" or "What software must the new computer system run?" The nominal group technique could be an efficient and useful means of obtaining a group-prioritized comprehensive list of the computer functions or software. Because the nominal group is highly structured, a greater likelihood exists that there will be a strong orientation to accomplishing the group's task and a lessened chance for conflict. This task orientation also means that there will be less group cohesiveness because the technique minimizes social interaction (McShane & Von Glinow, 2000).

Nominal group technique is a highly structured format that provides a guarantee that everyone can participate. It makes public, in a written form, the choices of the group, and all interested parties are allowed to watch the decision-making process as it unfolds.

Delphi Technique

Sometimes, a group does not need to meet face-to-face. At other times, it is simply not practical to have everyone get together. The *Delphi technique* is a written survey method for gathering opinions without holding a group meeting. It is a method that was designed by the RAND Corporation to aid in its ability to predict technological innovations, and it has since been used by groups for many purposes (DeWine, 2001). A large number of people can be included, and distance is not a factor. When you want to solicit a variety of inputs, and especially when you need input from people who are at a distance, the Delphi technique offers a solution.

An initial survey is distributed, and the written results are tabulated. These results are then sent back to the original respondents along with additional follow-up questions. A Delphi procedure might start with the formulation of the issues, asking participants to describe and clarify the issue that should be under consideration and how it should be stated. Second, it can solicit options. Given the issue, what options are available? Third, it can help determine initial positions on the issue—which issues everyone agrees are important and should be pursued and which are unimportant and should be dropped from discussion. A focus can then be placed on those issues that show disagreement among the respondents. Fourth, the reasons for these disagreements can be explored and the underlying assumptions, views, or facts being used by individuals to support their respective positions made clear. Fifth, the underlying reasons can be evaluated and the arguments that are used to defend positions can be compared to one another on a relative basis by the group. Finally, the group can reevaluate the options based on its view of the underlying evidence and assessment of each position. The process is summarized in Table 11.3.

On the negative side, the technique can be cumbersome. Mailing, analysis, ranking, reporting, and follow-ups must all occur at each step, but the technique provides a means to incorporate the ideas of various individuals without having a meeting. The best use for the Delphi technique is "for complex issues and questions that require much thoughtful consideration" (DeWine, 2001, p. 180). A positive aspect is

TABLE 11.3 Six Steps of the Delphi Technique

1. Deciding to administer a questionnaire
2. Selecting a group to respond—normally experts or highly involved individuals
3. Formulating the questions
4. Producing the questionnaire
5. Setting a deadline for returning the questionnaires
6. Receiving and analyzing the questionnaires

that it incorporates the value of a nominal group technique, allowing equal participation from all individuals. And the process requires good organization and highly motivated participants, or little participation will occur.

Synectics

Synectics is a formalized technique for group process design that helps groups tackle difficult problems creatively. It asks group members to use analogies to break their existing patterns of thinking and to develop analogies regarding particular concepts in order to see another aspect of a problem (Gordon, 1961). This process requires a skilled facilitator, since the group is attempting to use analogy, metaphor, and fantasy chaining to deal with a real issue, but the goal is to generate new, creative ideas.

The process begins with a review of the "problem as given" as stated by the client or agency for whom the group is trying to solve the problem. An analysis follows in which group members ask "how" and "what" questions of the client, such as "How is the problem a problem for you?" "What have you done to try to solve it?" "What is desired from this group?" (Chilberg, 1989). While listening to the client's responses, group members write ideas based on their perceptions of the client's explicit and implied desires, goals, and problems. Next the group lists these ideas on a flip chart or board in the form of "how to" statements (such as, "The problem is *how to* provide easy yet restricted access to particular areas of the building"), and the client is asked to offer a solution to each. For those ideas, representing aspects of the problem for which the client is unable to provide a solution, participants are asked to think metaphorically about the problem or to build analogies from other processes. These are listed for the group and are built on through a process of group brainstorming. The object is to use analogy and metaphor to create new ways of approaching and thinking about a problem and to use fantasy chaining to elaborate on those new ideas. Fantasy chaining is a process through which one member builds upon the analogy or metaphor suggested by another. Another group member then builds upon their extension of that metaphor, or takes it in a new direction. The process is ongoing and involves the group in a collaborative, creative activity that is both fun and productive.

For example, imagine you are trying to design a car's interior. What possible insights to that design could be offered by thinking of it as a living room, a bedroom, a park, a football stadium, a glass jar, or other type of space? Once an analogy is developed, the group can brainstorm the attributes of the space and develop them through group fantasy themes. (Perhaps it should be thought of as a multifunction sports arena rather than a football stadium and useful for baseball as well as football.) This step of visual analogy begins the process of redesigning the car interior. Synectics is a useful technique when a group has run out of creative ideas, become mired in controversy over how to view something, or is just stuck in its problem-solving processes. It can provide a useful, energizing (and fun) interlude to reinvigorate the problem-solving process and a creative approach to finding a solution to an otherwise seemingly impenetrable problem. In organizations, it has been used for creating improvements by reducing the number of steps employees must take to complete tasks. Group participants are asked to imagine they are part of a manufacturing process. As they go through the daily routines, they discover innovative solutions to creating a more effective process (Weitz, 1995). Because the group members are not actually engaging in the work routine, they are more likely to see unnecessary work habits that make the job harder for the employees and reduce effectiveness because their imagining of the process provides a unique perspective.

Buzz Sessions

When you have a large number of participants and want to encourage participation by each member, breaking participants into groups of approximately six members each can be a solution. These group events, called *buzz sessions,* are designed to create spontaneous small group discussions of a specific problem or question. The groups are given the topic for discussion, and a time limit is announced. After the time is up, a spokesperson from each group reports to the larger group. The responses are summarized on a master list, and the key issues can then be identified and discussed by the larger group.

Because you are dealing with a large number of individuals, careful design is necessary. First, identify the issue and frame it as a target question (e.g., "What should be done to reduce the number of accidents that have occurred?"). Second, designate leaders who will facilitate the discussion and place the group responses on flip charts or some other highly visible display. Provide a time limit for the groups to buzz and discuss the issues. Usually 5 to 10 minutes per issue is adequate. Finally, ask the designated leaders to make reports and present the results to the larger group of the whole. The dynamics of not allowing long-term group process opens the door to a variety of ideas and invites input from all participants while limiting the time required for the process.

Idea Writing

Idea writing also typically divides a large group into small working groups but differs from buzz sessions in that it provides those smaller groups with a written task, rather than an oral discussion. Each participant in the small group responds in writing to a stimulus question and then places his or her response on a pad in the center of the group. These pads are then passed to the right around the group, and each participant reacts, in writing, to what is written on each of the other pads. When the pads travel around the circle and reach their authors once again, the participants read the comments made in response to their initial statements, and the small group discusses the principal ideas that emerged through the written interaction. The group then summarizes the discussion and can report conclusions, points of agreement, points of disagreement, and those points needing further discussion to the larger group. Idea writing can provide more balanced input from group members than oral discussions and may work better than buzz sessions if there are dominant and quiet members in the groups or if the topic for discussion is an emotional or controversial one.

Role-Playing

Role-playing allows participants to experience and discuss dimensions of a problem or a sensitive issue that they may not normally experience. Then group members can present, analyze, and suggest solutions. The role-playing technique is most useful for a problem involving human relationships and generally involves a five-step process. First, the problem must be identified. Second, members of the group need to come up with a plot, setting, and characters to participate in the problem situation. Third, members choose or are assigned roles to play; non-players are involved as observers. Fourth, players present their interpretation of the problem. Fifth, players and non-players discuss what occurred during the role-playing and analyze alternative approaches to the same situation.

Listening Teams

Listening teams are used to encourage active participation in the process of listening to difficult or challenging information. Listening teams are formed when a moderator or leader divides a group into teams prior to a lecture or presentation. Each team is then assigned a specific listening task, such as quality issues, cost, and participant satisfaction, in order to focus on very specific parts of the difficult material. After the presentation, members of each team are given time to take notes, discuss, and organize their thoughts. The team members then serve as resources for the larger discussion of issues that follows.

Problem-Solving Tools

Three problem-solving tools, flowcharts, fishbone diagrams, and Pareto's principle, can be used effectively to clarify underlying issues, goals, and problems and to develop alternatives. For example, Hospital Corporation of America used flowcharts, fishbone diagrams, and Pareto charts to reduce the cost of antibiotics to the hospital by 44.5% and to patients by 45% (Cummings & Worley, 2005).

Flowcharts

Flowcharts give a visual description of a process across time or transactions, showing the actual ordering of the steps of the process in an ongoing situation. The flowchart can then be compared to a more ideal order or sequence. In a proposed scenario, flowcharts can be used to compare different ways of accomplishing a given task.

There are several different types of flowcharts, depending on the process to be mapped. Deployment flowcharts show who does what, when, in the process. They can be used in small groups for assigning group roles and responsibilities as a way of ensuring that each member knows what is expected of her or him, when it is expected, and by whom. Top-down flowcharts are designed to show the major steps in a work process. Those steps are ordered across the top, with the substeps within each of them connected with sequence arrows underneath the major steps. Detailed flowcharts show the sequential order of occurrences and decisions in a work setting, such as the flow of people, products, services, or paperwork. Figures 11.1 and 11.2 are two examples of detailed flowcharts.

FIGURE 11.1   Flowchart: Seeking Employment

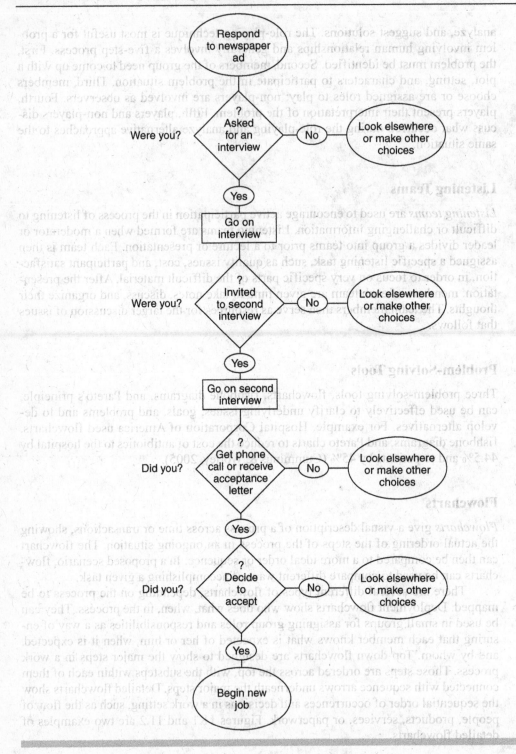

Respond to newspaper ad

Were you?   **? Asked for an interview**   No → **Look elsewhere or make other choices**

Yes ↓

Go on interview

Were you?   **? Invited to second interview**   No → **Look elsewhere or make other choices**

Yes ↓

Go on second interview

Did you?   **? Get phone call or receive acceptance letter**   No → **Look elsewhere or make other choices**

Yes ↓

Did you?   **? Decide to accept**   No → **Look elsewhere or make other choices**

Yes ↓

Begin new job

FIGURE 11.2   Flowchart: From Bed to Work

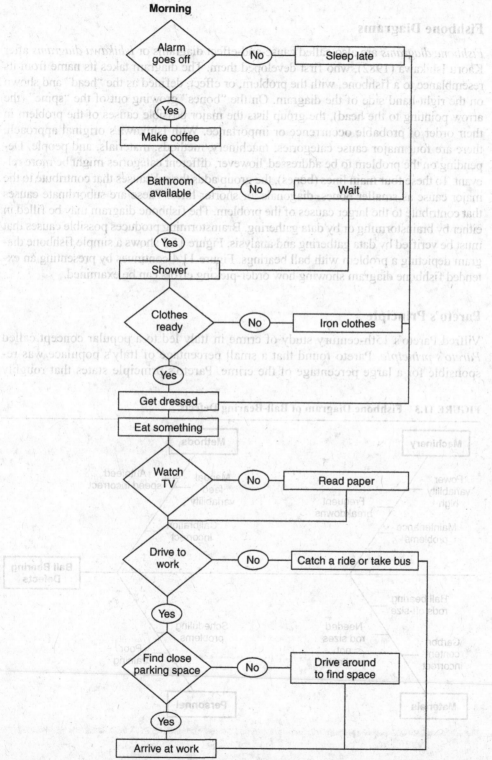

Fishbone Diagrams

Fishbone diagrams are also called cause-and-effect diagrams or *Ishikawa diagrams* after Kaoru Ishikawa (1982), who first developed them. The diagram takes its name from its resemblance to a fishbone, with the problem, or effect, defined as the "head" and shown on the right-hand side of the diagram. On the "bones" growing out of the "spine" (the arrow pointing to the head), the group lists the major possible causes of the problem in their order of probable occurrence or importance. With Ishikawa's original approach, there are four major cause categories: machinery, methods, materials, and people. Depending on the problem to be addressed, however, different categories might be more relevant. To these four main lines (bones), the group adds the subcauses that contribute to the major cause as smaller bones, diagonals, or shorter lines. These are subordinate causes that contribute to the larger causes of the problem. The fishbone diagram may be filled in either by brainstorming or by data gathering. Brainstorming produces possible causes that must be verified by data gathering and analysis. Figure 11.3 shows a simple fishbone diagram depicting a problem with ball bearings. Figure 11.4 continues by presenting an extended fishbone diagram showing how order-picking errors can be examined.

Pareto's Principle

Vilfred Pareto's 15th-century study of crime in Italy led to a popular concept called *Pareto's principle*. Pareto found that a small percentage of Italy's populace was responsible for a large percentage of the crime. Pareto's principle states that roughly

FIGURE 11.3   Fishbone Diagram of Ball-Bearing Defects

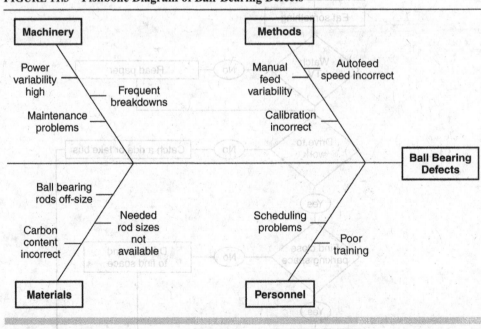

FIGURE 11.4   Fishbone Diagram of Order-Picking Errors

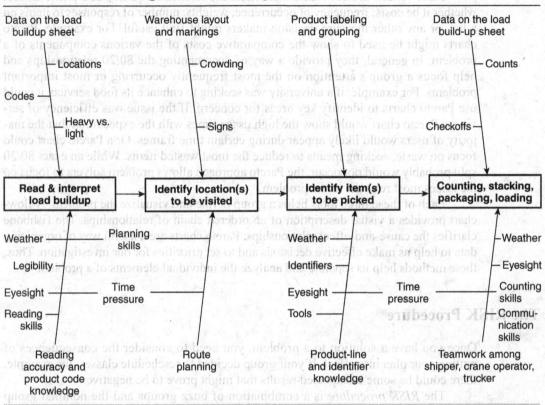

80% of all problems can be traced to approximately 20% of all possible causes. In general, around 80% of all positive results are produced by 20% of the efforts. Approximately 80% of a company's profits come from 20% of its products. For example, companies have found that "20% of customers often generate 150% of the company's total economic profit, while the worst 20% can lose 75% of the profits" (Selden & Colvin, 2003, p. 123). The 80/20 rule holds for a number of issues. Research indicates that approximately 80% of sales come from 20% of customers; 80% of washing comes from 20% of our wardrobe; 80% of file usage comes from 20% of files; 80% of complaints come from 20% of customers; 80% of sick leave is taken by 20% of employees; 80% of dirt is on the 20% of the most used floor area; 20% of car parts will cause 80% of problems; 20% of people in volunteer groups do 80% of the work.

Pareto's principle provides a useful tool for setting priorities in our decision-making process. The complexity of the small group process makes it easy to be side-tracked by issues that can be expected to make little, if any, appreciable difference in the outcome. It is useful to remember that our focus should be on the 20% of information that will provide 80% of the expected benefit and the 20% of the problem that is critical to be solved.

Pareto charts are bar charts that reflect the relative frequency of a phenomenon, whether it be costs, frequency of occurrence, weights, number of responses to items on a list, or any other measure decision makers might find useful. For example, Pareto charts might be used to show the comparative costs of the various components of a problem. In general, they provide a way of documenting the 80/20 relationships and help focus a group's attention on the most frequently occurring or most important problems. For example, if a university was seeking to enhance its food service, it could use Pareto charts to identify key areas for concern. If the issue was efficiency of service, a Pareto chart would show the high usage times with the expectation that the majority of users would likely appear during certain time frames. Or a Pareto chart could focus on waste, seeking means to reduce the most wasted items. While an exact 80/20 split probably would not occur, the Pareto approach allows problem solvers to focus on the issues most relevant to the problem.

Each of these three tools helps a group define and visualize the problem. A flowchart provides a visual description of an ordered chain of relationships. The fishbone clarifies the cause-and-effect relationships. Pareto charts are a useful way of organizing data to help us make effective decisions and to set priorities for our investigation. Thus, these methods help us separate and analyze the individual elements of a problem.

The RISK Procedure

Once you have a solution to a problem, you need to consider the consequences of putting your plan into effect. If your group decided to reschedule classes, for example, there could be some unexpected results that might prove to be negative.

The *RISK procedure* is a combination of buzz groups and the nominal group technique. The meeting leader presents a solution in detail, and the meeting participants are encouraged to think of any risks or problems that might be created by the change. These concerns are compiled on a flip chart. As with brainstorming, all ideas should be welcomed, since the most obscure ones may generate the most serious consequences or spur someone else in the meeting to identify another problem.

The list is compiled and presented later in the meeting or at the next meeting. Using the ACB method of sorting items, the approach used in brainstorming (or some other means of differentiating the important from the less important problems), a final list of problems that represents potential roadblocks is compiled and prioritized.

PERT (Program Evaluation and Review Technique)

Once the solution has been identified, the actual implementation remains. The program evaluation and review technique, *PERT,* is a systematic approach for designing the solution steps. This planning system involves eight steps:

1. Identify the final goal of the decision-making process. How will the solution look when it is implemented?

2. List all the events that must occur before the final goal is achieved. Brainstorm to develop this list.
3. Put the steps in chronological order.
4. Use a flow diagram to show how the events will occur.
5. Determine the specific activities that must occur to accomplish each step or stage.
6. Specify the time needed for each event and the end product.
7. Decide whether the deadlines are feasible and if the goals can be met in the time specified.
8. Determine a critical path for the events that must occur and assign responsibility for accomplishment of each step and event within that path to a particular individual or group.

Once responsibilities have been assigned, write down a full timetable with specific deadlines and follow-up. A program is only as good as its actual implementation.

How These Techniques Are Used

Total Quality Management (TQM) and Six Sigma are two examples of how these creative decision-making techniques are used in organizations. For example, almost all consumer products in the 21st century have a higher quality than their counterparts made 10 or 15 years earlier (Cummings & Worley, 2001). When faced with quality issues, organizations began to understand that using the traditional problem-solving approaches was inadequate for achieving quality. A popular phrase in organizations is that "more and more of the same can only give you more and more of the same"—freely interpreted, inadequate quality cannot be fixed by using the same approaches. We examine two of the most successful uses of the techniques we just covered in this chapter.

Total Quality Management (TQM) involves a comprehensive intervention that focuses all the organization systems on the continuous improvement of quality (Cohen, Fink, Gadon, & Willis, 2001). In many cases, teams are used to focus on the needs of internal (other departments and interacting units) and external customers to guarantee quality. When TQM was first introduced, teams would examine past problems and use these creative approaches to find solutions. Now, in those companies experiencing the greatest successes, the emphasis has shifted from fixing problems to looking toward proactive problem anticipation and prevention (Cummings & Worley, 2001). TQM involves training in brainstorming, flowcharts, fishbone diagrams, and other problem-solving procedures as the first step in the long-term process of continuous improvement. A study of 54 firms of different sizes showed that TQM adopters outperformed those that did not utilize TQM (Powell, 1995). The most important finding, however, was that those successful firms focused more on changing the culture by increasing the use of teams, empowerment, and commitment rather than concentrating on the techniques themselves (Powell, 1995). Without the increased use of individuals and teams involved in the actual problem solving, the techniques simply are not as effective.

In addition, organizations are turning to *Six Sigma,* which is a process that aims to reduce deviations (that is, quality errors) to 3.4 defects per 1 million instances,

TABLE 11.4 Does Achieving Six Sigma Really Matter?

99% effective means achieving three or four Sigma. However, if only three or four Sigma is achieved, rather than Six Sigma (99.999%), the following would result:

✓ 20,000 lost articles of mail per hour
✓ 5,000 incorrect surgical operations per week
✓ two short or long landings per day at each major airport
✓ 200,000 wrong drug prescriptions each year
✓ no electricity for almost 7 hours each month

which translates to a 99.9997% level of perfection. If applied to brewing coffee, this would mean there would only be 3.4 sour pots of coffee per 1 million brewed. If applied to your college experience, it would essentially eliminate all typos for all your papers—except 3.4 times (3.4 words) per 1 million.

Sigma is a letter of the Greek alphabet used as a symbol by statisticians to mark a bell curve showing the likelihood that something, such as the pot of coffee, will deviate from the norm: "The Six Sigma movement attempts to insert the science of hardnosed statistics into the foggy philosophy of quality" (Jones, 1998, p. 2B). According to Defeo (1999, p. 11), "Getting Six Sigma started begins with the formation of Six Sigma teams." Is it important? Clearly, it depends on how much impact this level of quality will have on the organization's effectiveness (Griffin, 2005). Table 11.4 shows why increasing quality is important.

Some of the results are impressive. At Dow Chemical Company, each "Six Sigma project has freed up an average of $500,000 in the first year" (Ardnt, 2002, p. 72). Allied Signal discovered a way to recycle 200 million pounds of stained carpet a year, translating into $30–$50 million savings a year. The list of successes is extensive. At the same time, it is a complicated process involving training in the group process, creative problem-solving techniques, and statistical analysis. Currently, "the best organizations operate at about Three to Four Sigma, which translates into about 6,200 defects per million" (Defeo, 1999, p. 12), which are the differences demonstrated in Table 11.4. The benefits of Six Sigma include increased motivation, morale, pride, production, and profitability (Defeo, 1999). However, without proper training in the techniques included in this chapter plus a strong emphasis on statistical analysis, Six Sigma probably will not realize its full value. As with the other methods discussed, Six Sigma should be applied to those issues where errors need to be substantially reduced or virtually disappear (Griffin, 2005). When used incorrectly, Six Sigma is akin to killing a fly with a sledgehammer—it might not be worth the energy.

Formats for Group Presentations

A group often finds that it needs to present its conclusions, findings, recommendations, or a summary of its discussion to a larger audience. Several formats are conducive to group discussions and presentations. Forum, panel, colloquium, and

Group presentations must be well prepared and organized

symposium formats can help organize a group's discussion and facilitate a group's interaction with a larger audience.

The Forum

The *forum* provides a format for speaking and listening to a larger audience. It is a form of public discussion in which the full audience participates, examining a topic or problem after a short presentation by the group. The audience members give reaction speeches one at a time and in an orderly fashion. A moderator selects the speakers, or they may be ordered by speakers lining up at a microphone located in front of the audience. Sometimes, time limits are imposed on the speakers, and, on occasion, a moderator who believes that one view has been overly represented by a series of speakers while another view has been left silent may call for a representative of the opposing view to speak. Speakers present and support arguments, take positions, take issue with what has been said, ask and answer questions, and respond to comments. Open town meetings and a public "hearings" are examples of forums. Often a forum is used in conjunction with other public discussion formats, such as a panel–forum or symposium–forum format, with the purpose of presenting information or a proposal and then soliciting public reaction to the proposal. An audience can receive diverse perspectives from experts as well as an opportunity to obtain additional information from knowledgeable and interested stakeholders. It provides an important opportunity for an audience to give verbal expression to its thinking and provides an opportunity for correcting intentional or inadvertent bias, distortion, or misunderstanding surrounding an issue. A good forum ensures that all parties, opinions, objections, views, preferences, and perspectives can be heard.

The Panel

A *panel* is a public format in which a group of four to eight experts discusses a problem or decision in front of an audience. This discussion often follows the problem-solving format but uses an informal, sometimes humorous, style of interaction to keep the audience's attention and to effectively share information that may be technical in nature. The moderator starts the meeting; explains the format to the audience; orients the audience to the topic or problem to be discussed; introduces the speakers, perhaps mentioning their expertise and perspective (for example, if they represent a particular group, cause, or company); keeps time; and sometimes summarizes the speakers' positions. The panel format provides no direct interaction between the panel of experts and the audience, but it is often followed by a moderated question-and-answer or a forum session. The panel should not normally run longer than an hour and may provide another half hour to an hour for questions or for a forum discussion.

Planning a panel is important. The panel must agree on basic definitions, parameters of the problem to be discussed, the questions or issues to be considered, speaker time limits, and the order of the speakers. There should be no big surprises for the speakers on the day of the presentation, and the presentation should not turn into a debate. An effective panel is collaboratively informational to the audience rather than argumentatively confrontational among the speakers.

The Colloquium

A *colloquium* is a form of public discussion in which a group of three to six experts, usually chosen for their divergent views, discusses a problem, following the problem-solving format, in front of an audience with a moderator facilitating their interaction. The purpose of a colloquium is to identify, develop, and work through possible solutions to a problem for the benefit and with the participation of the audience. The moderator should open the colloquium, introduce the problem, introduce the discussion group, describe the format for the discussion, and moderate the interactions throughout the session. The moderator may have to explicitly encourage audience participation by inviting the audience to ask questions or make comments at points in the discussion. The moderator must also work to keep the discussion focused and moving.

A colloquium frequently opens with short position or opinion statements by the experts and then shifts to a more interactive public discussion of the issues with audience participation, shifting back to comments by one or more of the experts, and returning again to audience comments, so that the discussion is carried on both in front of and with the participation of audience members.

A colloquium normally lasts at least an hour but not more than 2 hours. A good moderator must sense the flow of the discussion to ensure not cutting it off too soon, allowing all parties, perspectives, and opinions, to be heard but also not allowing it to drag on repetitiously and become tedious or boring. Achieving a sense of closure is important.

The Symposium

A *symposium* provides a format for a series of two to six brief speeches made on different aspects of a complex and difficult problem. The speakers are typically experts in different areas related to a problem, and the purpose of the symposium is to present complex technical information to the audience about the problem. The speeches are well prepared, practiced, and polished presentations that are uninterrupted by the audience and presented by skilled public speakers. The symposium should not run longer than an hour and is often followed by a half-hour forum to allow audience questions and discussion of the issue.

Planning prior to the symposium determines how the speakers will divide the topic, the order in which they will speak, and the time allocated for each speech. The speakers and moderator are often seated on a platform, or behind a table and lectern, providing a more formal public-presentation setting. The moderator introduces the session, addresses the important issues surrounding the topic, introduces the speakers, outlines how the topic will be approached by the speakers, and provides a summary at the conclusion of the symposium. If a forum discussion follows the symposium, the moderator facilitates that session as well.

Summary

We have discussed brainstorming, eight group decision-making techniques that are useful in appropriate circumstances, and three problem-solving tools. In line with our goal to increase creativity in decision making and problem solving, changing the way we approach a decision, a problem, or a solution can enhance the outcome quality, moving beyond standard ways of looking at issues, overcoming creativity blocks, and seeking new insights. Brainstorming and the specialized approaches outlined here offer ways to make a group more effective. Creative group structuring and processing can bring different answers and understanding to many issues. The forum, panel, colloquium, and symposium provide different formats for presenting and discussing those understandings.

DISCUSSION QUESTIONS

1. What is a focus group? How does it differ from a standard group? What topics on your campus would benefit from a focus group discussion?

2. Outline the nominal group technique. Why should it be considered a tool in small group decision making and problem solving?

3. What do you see as the benefits and weaknesses of the Delphi procedure?

4. Handling large groups can be difficult. What are buzz groups, and how can they be used? How can idea writing be used with large groups?

5. Design a role-play of a difficult small group interaction. Present and discuss it.

6. Discuss the issue of course registration and textbook purchasing. Define the problem.

    a. Develop a flowchart of the problem.

    b. Develop a fishbone diagram of the cause–effect relationships.

    c. Apply Pareto's principle to the problem.

    d. How have these techniques assisted in understanding the problem and possible solutions?

7. Distinguish among a forum, panel, colloquium, and symposium as a means for making a public presentation. Which one would you prefer to use? Why?

REFERENCES

Arndt, M. (2002, July 22). Quality isn't just for widgets. *Business Week,* pp. 72–73.

Chilberg, J. C. (1989). A review of group process designs for facilitating communication in problem-solving groups. *Management Communication Quarterly, 3*(1), 51–70.

Cohen, A. R., Fink, S. L., Gadon, H., & Willis, R. D. (2001). *Effective behavior in organizations* (7th ed.). Boston: McGraw-Hill Irwin.

Cummings, T. G., & Worley, C. G. (2005). *Organizational development and change* (8th ed.). Florence, KY: South-Western.

Defeo, J. A. (1999, July). Six Sigma: Road map for survival. *HRFocus,* pp. 11–12.

Denhardt, R. B., Denhardt, J. V., & Aristigueta, M. P. (2009). *Managing human behavior in public and nonprofit organizations* (2nd ed.). Thousand Oaks, CA, Sage.

DeWine, S. (2001). *The consultant's craft: Improving organizational communication.* Boston: Bedford/St. Martin's.

Gladwell, M. (2008). *Outliers: The story of success.* New York: Little, Brown.

Gordon, W. J. J. (1961). *Synectics.* New York: Harper & Row.

Griffin, R. W. (2005). *Management.* Boston: Houghton Mifflin.

Ishikawa, K. (1982). *Guide to quality control* (2nd rev. ed.). Tokyo: Asian Productivity Organization.

Jana, R. (2008, October 28 & 30). Real life imitates real world. *Business Week,* p. 42.

Jones, D. (1998, July 21). Firms aim for Six Sigma efficiency. *USA Today,* pp. 1B–2B.

McShane, S. L., & Von Glinow, M. A. (2000). *Organizational behavior.* Boston: Irwin McGraw-Hill.

Powell, T. (1995). Total Quality Management as a competitive advantage: A review and empirical study. *Strategic Management Journal, 16,* 15–37.

Selden, L., & Colvin, G. (2003, July). Increasing innovations: What customers want. *Fortune,* pp. 122ff.

Thompson, C. B. (1999, September). Problem solving tools to improve productivity. *Journal of Property Management,* pp. 11–16.

Weitz, A. J. (1995). Change: How to remove the fear, resentment, and resistance. *Hospital Management Quarterly, 17*(2), 75–79.

Yancey, K. B. (2006, September 16). Could you name a new hotel chain? *USA Today,* p. 2D.

Yartnoff, L. B. (1999, July). Focusing in: How to use focus groups to find out what customers want. *International Banking,* pp. 46–49.

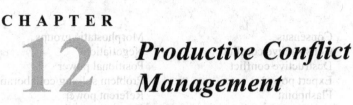

CHAPTER
12 *Productive Conflict Management*

CHAPTER OBJECTIVES

- Define conflict as a communication process.
- Explain how conflict is a consequence of actions.
- Differentiate between destructive and constructive conflict.
- Identify sources of conflict.
- Describe six styles of conflict management.
- Demonstrate negotiation as a strategy.
- Provide examples of the types of power.
- Explain how to make conflict strategies work.

KEY TERMS

Accommodation

Avoidance

Avoidance power

Charismatic power

Conflict

Competition

Compromise

Conflict-management styles

Consensus

Constructive conflict

Destructive conflict

Expert power

Flashpoint

Interdependence

Interpersonal linkage power

Morphogenic groups

Morphostatic groups

Negotiation

Positional power

Problem solving/collaboration

Referent power

Reward–punishment power

Scarce resources

In essence, the postmodern view bids disputants to do several things: (1) consider that your protracted conflict is a signal that you and your opponent have probably become identified with the poles of the conflict; (2) consider that the relationship in which you find yourself is not the inconvenient result of the existence of an opposing view but the expression of your own incompleteness taken as completeness; (3) value the relationship, miserable though it might feel, as an opportunity to live out your own multiplicity; and thus, (4) focus on ways to let the conflictual relationship transform the parties rather than on the parties resolving the conflict.

(Kegan, 1994, p. 320).

For most of us, conflict evokes images of winning and losing, with one or both of the parties ending up frustrated and demoralized by the situation. However, the Chinese character for conflict consists of two superimposed symbols graphically showing conflict's two sides: opportunity as well as danger (Hocker & Wilmot, 1991). *Conflict* is inevitable in decision-making groups, and many scholars have changed from a perspective that emphasizes the negative aspects of conflict to one that focuses on encouraging constructive outcomes and benefits (Wood, 2004). When handled skillfully through a group's communication processes, conflict can be constructive and beneficial and can lead to high-quality outcomes, increased group morale, better perspective-taking skills, and enhanced relationships. Constructively engaging in conflict can help produce the energy needed by a small group to develop new and creative ideas. For conflict to be constructive, however, all parties must emphasize a mutual respect and collaborative orientation, rather than engaging in aggressive behavior, a lack of respect, and a competitive orientation.

Stephan (2008) articulated a number of psychological and communication processes that facilitate conflict resolution. One important psychological process is to develop an emotional empathy—that is, the capacity to feel the emotions of the other members of the group. Expressing positive feelings and attitudes toward them, and conveying a concern for their welfare is an important component. A second is to show a cognitive empathy by understanding the position of the other person and being able to articulate the situation from that person's perspective. A third is to focus on a mutual interdependence, the pursuit of common goals, and an equality of person in the communication. The communication processes of conflict resolution include an ability to work through disagreements and build trust by (1) engaging in critical self-reflection and examining one's own ideas, experiences, and perspectives; (2) being actively involved in the group interaction through sharing, inquiring, and showing interest in the ideas of others; (3) employing genuine self-disclosure; (4) expressing a level of comfort with the emotions of others; and (5) participating in attentive listening to the perspectives expressed by others, appreciating those differences, accepting them, and respecting them.

This chapter explores the nature of conflict as a communication event within the interactions of small groups. It suggests strategies for conflict resolution and investigates the power dynamics that underlie the expression of conflict. Our objective is to explore the positive expression of dissent within group decision-making processes and the development of more functional and less contentious problem-solving conflict-management tactics and strategies.

Defining Conflict

"Conflict is a disagreement between two or more parties" (Ayoko, Callan, & Hartel, 2008, p. 123). Task conflict describes disagreements about the tasks to be performed by a group. Relationship conflict depicts incompatibilities among group members. Task conflict involves differences in viewpoints, ideas, and opinions among group members and has been shown to encourage greater group understanding of complex issues, confidence in their task, innovation in their approach, willingness to reevaluate their positions, reduction in complacency, effectiveness in outcomes, and ability to produce higher quality decisions (Ayoko et al., 2008; Kotlyar & Karakowsky, 2006). Relationship conflict is found in personality clashes and interpersonal friction, produces personal frustration, and reduces group cohesion, commitment, satisfaction, efficiency, and performance. Relationship conflict among group members negatively affects a group's ability to realize its potential for effective decision making (Rau, 2005). The intensity of the conflict within the group depends on the number of people affected by it and the degree of interdependence in the relationships among those in conflict. If one party does not depend on the other, that party will not necessarily become engaged in the conflict (Ayoko et al., 2008).

Conflict can be painful and costly in terms of emotional energy, and if nothing is to be gained by engaging in it or lost by avoiding it, people are likely to not engage in it. On the other hand, those who have the most to gain or lose are the most likely to want to engage in the conflict. Each of the parties to the conflict perceives that the other is in some way interfering with his or her ability to achieve what he or she needs, wants, or expects, such as a desirable outcome, respect, freedom to do something, or avoidance of some loss. Thus, conflict occurs among people who are dependent on each other and who perceive themselves to have mutually incompatible goals.

Conflict Within Systems

Conflict consists of the substance of the issue around which a disagreement takes place and the pattern of interactive communication between the participants engaged in the dispute. The substance and pattern of the conflict are inextricably linked through the communication process. It is the pattern that gives meaning to the substance and the substance that manifests the pattern. In small group conflict, however, it is the pattern of the conflict, rather than the substance of the matter over which the conflict is engaged, that determines the quality of the outcome for the group. Regardless of the issue under dispute, if the participants are open to new perspectives and are committed to maintaining their relationships and resolving their disputes, they are more likely to find a satisfactory solution. On the other hand, if they feel little or no relational concern and are afraid of giving up their positions, they are less likely to achieve a satisfactory outcome.

The conflict communication process itself sets in motion a series of actions and counteractions that creates patterns of thinking, behaving, and relating to others. When no new patterns or ways of thinking and interacting are introduced, the group can stagnate in its conflict. Groups in which no new input is accepted and used are known as *morphostatic groups*. They become a non-changing system, simply maintaining the status quo or expending energy trying to avoid the conflict. Groups that are open to change, accepting new ideas and ways of interacting, are called morphogenic groups. *Constructive conflict* can happen only in *morphogenic groups,* having members who are willing to examine their assumptions and perspectives and to offer new patterns of response. This openness fosters creativity and synergy within the group and helps facilitate the group's progress through the conflict.

Conflict Within Small Groups

As members of a group, we are interdependent. Our group process is intended to result in an outcome in which we all participate in creating. The extent to which we all are invested in the group and participate in it, however, is also the extent to which we are likely to find ourselves in conflict. Conflict happens at all phases of the group process, from organizing the group and deciding on the procedural mechanisms through the definition of the problem to the details of specific tasks and issues. If there is no conflict, the group may either be so homogeneous that few, if any, new and creative ideas can emerge, or it may be suffering from an unhealthy pressure for conformity and a tendency toward groupthink.

Whether conflict is constructive or destructive depends on several factors, including the origin, or *flashpoint,* of the conflict, as well as the orientation of the group members toward communication patterns of conflict resolution. When the flashpoint for the conflict resides in the substance of the particular issues under consideration, task conflict, it has one of the essential ingredients for engaging in constructive conflict management. On the other hand, when the flashpoint resides in the interactive pattern itself, such as when some members are less vested in the process than others or when the group has developed a history of conflict patterns regardless of the substance of the issue, then it has the potential of becoming *destructive conflict*. Group members who do not feel they have as much to gain as others do can use avoidance or other destructive strategies. Likewise, unresolved "personality clashes" or relationship conflict can hinder attempts at constructive conflict management. Although the issues of the conflict may vary, a satisfactory resolution often depends on seeking to understand and address the origins of the conflict and on defining the issues, while simultaneously engaging in appropriate conflict-resolution communication strategies.

The Substance of Conflict

Assuming that the members are invested in the group, that they feel empowered, and that there is a diversity of viewpoints and experiences, we have issue-based conflict. If we do not agree with other group members about the particular issues of concern, and if we are reasonably invested in our own perspectives, we are likely to come into conflict with those who oppose us or see things differently. In constructive issue-based conflict, the causes and substance of the conflict can be sought through a discussion of the issues under dispute rather than as due to inherent personality problems, the group's relationship history, or preexisting conditions. Toyota credits "lots of conflict" over how it produces its cars as a major contributor to its enviable position as a quality producer of motor vehicles (Ward, 1998). The result has been the production and sale of over 1,000,000 Toyota hybrid synergy-drive cars such as the Prius and Camry worldwide (www.toyota.com, July 18, 2008). The substantive influences that lead to conflict can be found in at least three sources.

One source of conflict is the perception of *scarce resources,* including a lack of time; need to prioritize; insufficient information; inadequate space; limited rewards; limited access to financial, informational, or other resources; competition for leadership positions; or any other perceived limitations to the full and fair treatment of the group process and issues under consideration.

A second source of conflict is diversity in the backgrounds, cultural values, and orientations of group members, including religious, political, or socioeconomic values; differing interests and abilities; varying amounts and types of knowledge, experience, or expertise with the subject at hand; different information or perspective about the subject; differing perceptions of one's own or another's relative status or power (including unresolved rivalries for status or power); and differences in orientation, knowledge, and relationship to the group process, goals, or issues under discussion.

Our differing cultural backgrounds provide perhaps the most apparent examples of our diversity and can affect how we approach conflict. Group members from collectivist cultures, in which individual goals are not as important as the group goal, are more likely to avoid conflict with other group members (Cai & Fink, 2002). This means that even if two individuals from different cultural backgrounds perceive the same conflict, their *conflict-management styles* may cause them to act differently. At the same time, individuals from collectivist cultures can be just as competitive as those from individualist cultures with people outside the group (Chen, Chen, & Meindl, 1998). The differing attitudes, perceptions, and values of different generations working together can cause conflict in the group as well (Zemke, Raines, & Filipczak,

2000). In addition, organizations may have cultural norms that "influence the types of conflicts that occur and the ways in which they may be dealt" (DeVito, 2004, p. 314). In groups and teams at work, or in other group settings, understanding the influence of diverse backgrounds on conflict is important.

A third source of conflict is variation in our orientations toward task accomplishment, including divergent definitions or understandings of the breadth or depth of the subject at hand; the group process that is best used to engage it; differences in levels of commitment to the process and group project; differing degrees of importance placed on a need for timeliness in the completion of the task; divergent values regarding the necessity of optimization of a solution; and differences in attitude, understanding, and approach to the group process and task.

As these three sources demonstrate, assumptions about group interaction patterns themselves can become the substance of conflict. There are a number of other potential sources of conflict in any particular group as well, but to the extent that they are acknowledged and addressed as issue-based conflicts, they can be managed productively by the group, with all members working to achieve something in common and with the overall outcome being the best possible one under a given set of circumstances.

Whether conflict is managed constructively or destructively depends on several factors, including the group members' levels of engagement in the process, their attitudes toward conflict in general and toward the specific conflict, the amount of time and energy group members are willing and able to commit to resolving the conflict, their degree of respect for the other parties in the conflict, the value members place on their interpersonal relationships, and the level of skill members have in communicating their way through the conflict.

Patterns of Conflict Management

No one pattern of conflict management is suitable for all conflict situations, on all occasions, at all times, or in all contexts. Some conflicts are simply more important than others, and we need to use our time and energy resources carefully and productively to resolve them. However, when we see conflict as a dance, rather than as a war, we are all better served (Hocker & Wilmot, 1991). Constructive conflicts share the elements of mutual interpersonal concern, expression of interdependence, and an assumption of equifinality. Mutual interpersonal concern means that productive conflict focuses on the critical evaluation of the ideas rather than the personalities. *Interdependence* means working together as a team in the evaluation of those ideas rather than working separately or at cross-purposes. Equifinality means recognizing that there is more than one way to reach a successful resolution. Conflicts are seen as an opportunity for dialogue rather than as a debate (Zornoza, Ripoll, & Peiro, 2002).

Dysfunctional conflict refuses, avoids, or suspends the evaluation of ideas and focuses attention instead on a group member's behavior, abilities, or personality (Witteman, 1991). Destructive conflict is based in a lack of concern for the relational elements of the interaction, focusing instead on a feeling of individual independence and

FIGURE 12.1 **Five Styles of Conflict Management**

Low—Assertiveness—High
Concern for self
Get the task done

Compete
Tough battler
Power—We/They
Win/Lose

Collaborate
Problem Solver
Integrator—Us
Win/Win

Compromise
Conciliator
Lose/Lose

Avoid
Impersonal complier
Avoider—Withdraw
Lose/Win

Accommodate
Friendly helper
Suppressor—Harmony
Lose/Win

Low—Cooperativeness—High
Satisfy others
Prosocial

rightness and an assumption of a zero-sum game of winners and losers: for one participant to win, the other must lose.

Many of us use a limited number of conflict-management styles or orientations to respond to conflict (Shockley-Zalabak, 2002). Our styles are based on the degree to which we maintain an underlying set of assumptions about the need to maintain our relationships through cooperation with others and the importance of accomplishing the task at hand (Lulofs & Cahn, 2000). As shown in Figure 12.1, a two-dimensional conflict-management style grid can be developed that shows the effect of various degrees of emphasis on how we view cooperation with others and task accomplishment.

Problem solving/collaboration is the style that seeks to maximize the gain for all participants. It is high on both relationship and task orientations. Smoothing (or *accommodation*) is the style that gives in to others to avoid conflict. It is high on the relationship orientation but low on task. *Compromise* is the style that assumes that each side gives in enough to resolve the issue and move on. It is at the middle of the continuum on both orientations, with some concern with relationships and some with task, but overall with a more practical and less idealistic orientation to conflict. *Competition* is a style dedicated to winning and can become destructive when it means winning at any cost. It is low on relationship orientation and high on task. *Avoidance* is the style that concedes before the conflict is even engaged. It is low on both relationship and task orientations. Orientations that value both relationship and task set the stage for constructive conflict management and have the potential for a satisfactory resolution. Those orientations that do not value either relationship or task often result in destructive conflict patterns within the group and a resolution that is unsatisfactory for at least one or more of the participants. Perpetually avoiding, engaging in too much competition, compromising too quickly, or accommodating to avoid controversy by smoothing over difficulties can all develop into dysfunctional group conflict patterns.

Since small groups are interactive systems, understanding how conflict management takes place in them is more complicated than simply understanding the conflict-management styles of the individual members. Superimposed on these individual styles are six comparable group conflict-resolution strategies. Each of these has both constructive and destructive applications, depending on the overall conflict orientation of the group and of each of the individuals within it. Thus, the processes of conflict management and resolution take place in a complex environment and are neither straightforward nor easy to accomplish. We consider these styles in the order in which we have presented them for the individual styles: collaboration (as consensus) negotiation, accommodation, compromise, competition, and avoidance (Harris & Nelson, 2008).

Collaboration (and Consensus)

The ideal conflict-resolution strategy for any group is one of win–win, or *consensus* (collaboration). Consensus takes time, energy, and commitment. It is appropriate for the most important conflicts, but it may not be worth the effort for side issues or matters of relatively small consequence. Consensus requires carefully defining the issues; discussing group-process strategies for communication; agreeing on the parameters of a good solution; being open, careful, and considerate; listening to all perspectives; and being willing to take the time and energy needed to forge solutions from the best parts of the perspectives offered. This strategy assumes that "none of us is as smart as all of us are together." While the collaborative style is commonly referred to as "win–win," that does not mean the absence of conflict. In fact, collaboration can involve strong disagreements, but they focus on the problem-solving issues not personalities or positions (McNary, 2003).

Collaborative communication entails the participation of all members, with each stating his or her point of view as clearly and concisely as possible, while listening attentively to those of others. Once all initial perspectives have been presented and understood, the conflicting viewpoints are engaged, with each side presenting the rational basis of its point of view. Each party remains open to being convinced by the more compelling aspects of another's argument. The ultimate resolution will most likely combine elements of all or most perspectives, mixing and reshaping the best parts of each to form a new and more creative whole than any individual original part. The resolution should reflect the process itself, as well as the substance of the ideas discussed, with each member contributing to the forging of a final solution. That solution will ideally satisfy all participants, with each having been heard and feeling validated by the process, whether or not his or her own initial ideas were ultimately used. In fact, cooperative team experiences "reduce prejudice, increase acceptance of others, and heighten morale" (Tjosvold, 1995, p. 89). While competition has been assumed to increase productivity, collaboration leads to "higher achievement and productivity, especially on more complex tasks and problems that benefit from the sharing of information and ideas" (Tjosvold, 1995, p. 89). Collaboration is less likely to result in destructive conflict when it is done fairly and when all members feel empowered through the process, but collaboration also may involve some negotiation as described in the next section.

Safety is so much a part of the culture at Nucor Steel Tuscaloosa that it is put before quality, cost, productivity, and profit. This is backed up with the Weekly Central Safety Committee, comprising all managers and a cross-section of supervisors and hourly team members, where the message is consistently reinforced that "Nothing is more important than safety. . . . Nothing!"

Negotiation

Negotiation, as a conflict-resolution strategy, involves forging a resolution between opposing points of view, assuring that each side "wins" and gets the benefits most important to its overall goals. As a strategy, it is frequently associated with a more formal determination to enter into bargaining than is collaboration. It usually follows an impasse in discussion, when disagreements seem irresolvable and neither side seems willing or able to make enough concessions to reach a satisfactory resolution. Depending on the depth of the impasse, an impartial mediator may be needed to help the parties find areas of mutual agreement. This mediator may be another member of the group who understands the issue and its different perspectives and who can help the parties better understand each other.

Negotiation is not a binding arbitration through which a resolution is imposed by a third party. In negotiation, the parties must resolve their differences and arrive at a solution themselves. Negotiation implies a commitment to the process and to both sides bargaining with openness and fairness in a good-faith effort to reach a mutually acceptable agreement.

Successful negotiation depends on planning and strategy. It may entail choosing one member from each side to represent that point of view in the presentation of the arguments. Negotiating also requires (1) a thorough acquaintance with all sides of the issues under consideration; (2) a strong rationale for one's own particular point of view, including appropriate documentation; (3) a list of those parts of the issue that can be conceded without harming the essence of one's desired benefit; (4) a good understanding of the other's point of view, how they are likely to argue it, and what they might be willing to concede without losing the essence of their benefit; and (5) a respect for the other party and its viewpoint. A successful outcome will leave all parties satisfied that they got what they most needed or wanted and that the resolution is fair to them all.

Negotiation, however, can also be handled destructively when members use manipulative strategies, such as starting from the extreme end of their own conflict continuum; denigrating the other's perspective; refusing to listen carefully; exaggerating the value of their concessions, while minimizing those of the other; concealing pertinent information; arguing forcefully, right or wrong; and stonewalling, or being willing to take as long as necessary to win (Hocker & Wilmot, 1991).

Adopting a strategy of negotiation represents a new level of seriousness in the discussion. The important part of negotiation, as with all aspects of constructive conflict management, is to achieve what is best for the overall group effort, without sacrificing the personal relationships that bind the group together (Fisher, Ury, & Patton, 1991).

Accommodation

Accommodation as a strategy implies giving up all or most of one's own position (or benefit) for the sake of others. It involves a primarily one-sided concession and is most constructively used within a context of collaborative conflict management, with the intention being to reduce interpersonal tension for the sake of the overall task and the group process. When used to move beyond insignificant or superficial conflicts to save energy and group harmony for the more important issues, accommodation has a positive effect and can be considered constructive. For example, if most members of the group want to meet in the evening and one member prefers days, that member might be willing to go along with the evening time, if she or he possibly can, in order not to derail the group process over a relatively minor point. If, however, this member gives in on most of the important issues that involve conflicting points of view just for the sake of group harmony, that member may eventually end up feeling resentful and angry and may withdraw altogether from the group discussion process. In that case, the group loses the value of that member's unique perspective.

Trading accommodation on one point to win favor for another may have positive or negative consequences on the group process. If done in the spirit of constructive compromise, it may enhance the group effort. If, however, it is done in such a way that it pits one issue against another and builds coalitions that divide the group, it may have a long-term negative impact. For accommodation to work well, it needs to be used for the benefit of the overall process. It should not result in the group's losing the benefit of opposing points of view and the synergy that results from constructive conflict. The effect of destructive accommodation is similar to that of destructive avoidance, in that it assumes a limited "pie" that must be divided and forfeits the value of unique perspectives that might add to creative problem solving and enhanced solutions.

Compromise

Compromise, too, can be used as a conflict-management strategy within either a constructive, collaborative orientation or a destructive, competitive one. When we decide to split the difference, we are using compromise. This strategy is appropriate when there is insufficient time or energy to work toward consensus and when it is generally agreed that the issue is not worth the use of that time or energy. Compromise can also be used when there are no realistic ways of "expanding the pie" and no easy agreement about its division. When each participant is oriented to the common good, each may be willing to concede some of his or her potential gain to move ahead with the group process. In the example of the waste management community group, those members who would prefer to send all the refuse to the waste-to-energy plant and save the town the difficulty of storing and managing recyclable goods may have to compromise with those who would prefer to recycle everything but the most useless parts of the waste stream. Realistically, the group may decide to send all but a few categories of recyclable goods to the energy plant. In that way, each side may give up part of its perceived ideal solution to meet the larger and more realistic group goals of staying within funding limits and making the solution as easy as possible for the town to administer. Neither group gets all that it wants, but both get some of it, and the solution may, in its implementation, be an optimal one. It is constructive compromise if the process has been handled fairly and with respect for the losses felt by those who have offered some of their own perceived benefit for the common good.

As with competition, however, compromise can be destructive if some members feel railroaded. When power is used irresponsibly to force some members to give up part of their positions in the name of compromise, those who feel they have not willingly participated in the choice are apt to feel disempowered and resentful. Regardless of how "efficient" this kind of power use may appear at the time, it can often backfire at a later point when cooperation and agreement are most needed among group members. Thus, compromise should truly be compromise, with each member feeling empowered in the concession to benefit what all have agreed is the larger good.

Competition

Competition has a win–lose orientation. It is marked by self-interest, rather than mutual interest, and by an assumption of a limited resource and limited possibilities for gain. Although it can be associated with destructive conflict management, there are many times and places where "healthy competition" can be seen as constructive and productive. Competition, embedded in an overall orientation of mutual respect and interdependence, when the limits on the competitive forum are clear and when everyone can agree on playing by the rules of the game, can lead to an efficient allocation of scarce time and other resources. It can also be fun and invigorating, much like being involved in playing or watching a football game, or a vigorous debate. A decision to use competitive strategies in a small group is appropriate when there is limited time or resources and when the larger goals of the group are enhanced by its use. It is a decision best made by mutual consent, whether implicit or explicit.

Constructive competitive communication in small groups includes making careful rationales for disagreements based on the substance of the issue at hand, while refraining from personal attacks. Using competition to assign leadership roles may be the most efficient way of allowing a group to assess the suitability of one or another person for particular responsibilities. When candidates debate their points of view on the relevant issues and maintain civility and respect for one another, the competitive process can energize discussion around group issues and can ensure a measure of group cohesiveness. The group's assumption is that one candidate will win in the final vote or by consensus. The other candidate has, however, been able to state a position and be heard. That member will, as a likely consequence, assume more authority within the group. The competition is also expected to be bounded by the "rules of the game" and not expected to spill over into the subsequent group process. In another example, if there is a limited amount of money to be distributed among various intragroup projects, that allocation may be best decided through a competitive process, with each party putting forth its most convincing arguments for its need for a portion of the money. Allocations may then be discussed until a decision is reached as to which parties should receive which portions of the funding. Depending on the importance of the distribution scheme to the overall goals of the group, the decision may be made by a vote (competition), by compromise, by accommodation, or by consensus (collaboration), thereby embedding the competitive strategy within another overall strategy. However, it is decided, some parties may "win" and others "lose," but when the process is working as it should, the larger goals of the group are served. The key to constructive resolution of conflict resides, finally, in maintaining mutual respect among the group members themselves regardless of the immediate issues in conflict.

In its destructive guise, enmeshed within a context of lack of relational concern, the competitive communication style may ignore the rules of fair play and may include personal attacks involving any of the following tactics: confrontational remarks (such as pointing out another individual's errors in thinking or logic, rather than focusing on the issue), personal criticism (such as criticism of the other's characteristics or behaviors), personal rejection (such as antagonism toward the person, rather than toward the substance of the issue), hostile imperatives (such as demands, threats, assignment of blame), hostile questions (such as asking leading or rhetorical questions), presumptive remarks (such as attributions of thoughts or feelings to the other), or denial of one's own responsibility in the area of the conflict (Hocker & Wilmot, 1991).

Therefore, in a small group, in which members are interdependent and mutual respect and trust are essential to optimizing solutions, competition needs to be handled carefully and with full awareness of the dangers it can pose. The rules of the competitive strategy, as well as the value of the personal relationships, must be made explicit.

Avoidance

The avoidance strategy entails withdrawing from the conflict. If avoidance is due to an individual's lack of information, understanding, or any particular opinion on the substance of the conflict, it can be a constructive strategy. The group process is rarely well served when conflict is not constructively engaged in an informed way. On the other hand, when avoidance is the result of feeling disempowered or disengaged, it can negatively affect the group process.

Destructive avoidance in the form of missing group meetings or refusing to participate in the discussion and work robs the group of individual perspectives and energy and impoverishes the decision-making process. When it leads to festering resentments on the part of the avoiding member, or among the other group members, and to members expressing dissatisfaction with the group process, within or outside the group, it can hamper or actually derail the entire group effort. This aspect of avoidance is discussed further in the section on avoidance power.

When avoidance takes the guise of moving the subject of discussion off the point of conflict, it may temporarily ease some tension; but at best, it keeps the group from working through its disagreements and arriving at a constructive resolution. Conflict is usually resolved only by working through it, rather than by suppressing, avoiding, or exploding it. If it is not satisfactorily resolved, it may fester beneath the surface of any resolution and may later disrupt the outcome.

Groups will develop their own norms (see Chapter 3) on how to handle disputes (Kuhn & Poole, 2000). As you can well imagine, these norms can be quite complex since they are dependent on the combination of the individual styles that are being used to influence the other group members. Some groups tend to avoid issues or disagreements, while others distribute group rewards in a manner similar to the competitive style with winners and losers. Groups seeking to effectively manage conflict with an integrative approach, which utilizes collaboration, make more effective decisions than those groups using the avoidance or competitive approaches (Kuhn & Poole, 2000). But not all issues deserve the time and energy required for collaboration.

Conflict is healthiest when group members face it directly and choose an appropriate strategy for dealing with it. In that way, it serves the larger purposes for which groups are convened—the creative solutions resulting from synergy. Table 12.1 identifies some of the ethical principles involved in productive conflict management.

Power in Group Conflict

Although power dynamics are integral to the group process at all levels, they are frequently most apparent at points of conflict. As power ensures each of us access to the resources needed to maintain life and well-being, it is an essential tool for our survival. To the extent that it is exercised in a social context, we recognize it, respond to it, accept it, and use it through communication. We grant power to others and, in turn, are granted power by others in the groups in which we interact (McShane & Von Glinow, 2000). Although we all hold power in many different forms, we translate it into different currencies, or values, when we trade, spend, or use it in a group. Because groups are systems of interdependent relationships and every part affects every other part, even those who withdraw and refuse to participate are exercising power and influencing the group interaction. When I "take my marbles and go home," I change the possibilities for the group interaction. Power, therefore, underlies most of our group communication patterns and, by extension, our conflicts.

There are at least seven types of power available for use in groups: expert power, interpersonal linkage power, reward and punishment power, positional power (sometimes called legitimate power), referent power, charismatic (or personal) power, and avoidance power (French & Raven, 1968; Harris & Nelson, 2008; Raven, 1993).

TABLE 12.1   Ethics for Productive Conflict Management

The Institute for Global Ethics outlines a set of ethical values based on principles of compassion, fairness, honesty, respect, and responsibility. These ethical principles are summarized here and adapted as guidelines for engaging in productive conflict management.

Compassion

Our group's reality can be defined by our caring relationships.
Time is valuable and can be used to make connections with others in the group.
Our humanity increases when barriers are reduced between ourselves and others.
We can gain strength from our relatedness to others and from joining a larger human endeavor.

Fairness

No individual is more important than another.
Time is valuable to both self and others.
The dignity of self and others must be honored.
Human cooperation and competition occur but should occur within bounds of fairness.
Humans should restrain from self-interest to achieve the greater good.

Honesty

Truth is essential and valued.
Open, honest, intimate communication is preferred.
Competition and cooperation occur, but both should be open.

Respect

The value of both self and others should be considered paramount.
It is important to consider the time, space, and energy needed to manage conflict.
Others have an inherent integrity and are ends in themselves, not a means to one's own ends.
A collaborative model is possible and desirable.

Responsibility

The world is defined by the commitments I make.
Time (mine and others') is important and should not be wasted.
An ethic of care is important for myself and others.
An attitude of ownership and accountability is preferred.
Responsibility means looking beyond myself, overcoming ambivalence, and contributing.

Source: Summarized and adapted with permission from Ingbar (2005).

Expert Power

Expert power is generated by having an ability to access particular information that is valued. To the extent that a group has a problem to solve that involves an understanding of technical, regulatory, political, or other specialized information, those with that information will be in a position to exercise their power to guide and influence the group discussion and decision making. For example, in the community group looking for solutions to its solid waste disposal problem, a trash hauler for the community may have expert power. That person knows the amount and content of the trash that needs to be disposed of, and this information becomes a vital element in the decision-making process. As with any type of power, however, it is important for the group and person to keep that expertise in perspective and not let it override the larger goals of the group process. It frequently is easy for those who hold expert power to abuse it by directing it, consciously or unconsciously, toward some measure of personal gain. It is also easy for less-informed group members to enhance expert power by giving more support than is warranted to the expert's opinions.

Interpersonal Linkage Power

Those members in a group who have personal access to people or information sources that can be useful to the group bring a particular type of power to the group process. Their *interpersonal linkage power* allows them to engage the services of individuals, groups, and organizations, or to gain access to resources not generally available to others in the group, and that may enhance the group's ability to achieve its goals. In the community group, a member who knows someone in a neighboring community group engaged in a similar task may be in a position to help forge an intercommunity agreement on trash hauling or recycling. If such an agreement potentially reduces the waste disposal costs for both communities by increasing overall volumes and thereby giving added "weight" to the communities' negotiations with their markets, the person responsible for this possibility holds substantial interpersonal linkage power within the group. An office secretary may have interpersonal linkage power in a group when he or she can prevail on office contacts to do mailings or research for the group. This power, as with any of the other types of power, can have multiple levels of influence and strength.

Reward–Punishment Power

Those who can effectively reward or punish other members of the group hold another type of power. To the extent that we can effectively praise or humiliate fellow group members, we all hold this *reward–punishment power*. However, we usually think of it as the ability to materially affect another's well-being in terms of financial rewards or punishments, personal relationship rewards or punishments, or other rewards or punishments that we consider particularly meaningful. If one of the drivers for the trash hauler is also a member of the group, he may feel intimidated about disagreeing with the trash-hauling boss, for fear of losing his job. Additionally, this person may go out of his way to support the boss in the hope of getting a raise. Likewise, in an organizational small group, the administrative assistant or secretary may hold this power. To the extent this person controls the flow of information and access to needed administrative services in the office, maintaining good relations with her may be key to doing one's job effectively on a day-to-day basis. When participation in groups is based on regard for reward and punishment power, effective group process may be sacrificed. This type of power, therefore, must be used with great care and with a sense of responsibility.

Positional (Legitimate) Power

Those granted power by others for specific purposes or because of the responsibilities of their position within the group may be said to have positional or legitimate power. Their authority may be limited to particular aspects of the group process, or may be broader. Somewhat like expert power, this power may translate into leading discussions and making or contributing to particular types of decisions. Its use can move the group process in particular directions and can substantively shape the outcome. If the head of an organization is also a member of the small group, the other members may defer to that person because of her position, regardless of how well she understands the particular issues being discussed. This represents an unfortunate use of *positional power*. In the community group, the town accountant knows the condition of the town's finances and may be able to offer insight into current financial arrangements and obligations. Although this may be a more legitimate use of positional power, because this person may know what has been done and how it has been accounted for, he may not be the best person for anticipating new ways of raising money or reallocating existing funds. Administrative assistants and secretaries also often have positional power because of their valuable knowledge and access to particular information. The elected chair of the group also holds positional power. As with all types of power, positional power is legitimized by others' perceptions of its value and worth.

Referent Power

Referent power, the power conferred by affiliation with respected groups or people, can be used in certain contexts to enhance personal power in a group situation. It may be used to add to credibility and, therefore, provide those members more influence in the overall group process. In the community group, a member who is a personal friend of the head of the state environmental regulatory commission has referent power, which may appear to be more influential than it actually is or should be. In a group of executives, a person who holds a degree from a prestigious school may hold referent power, if the other group members assume that this person has superior knowledge, whether or not that particular knowledge bears on the issues under discussion.

Charismatic (Personal) Power

Charismatic or personal power resides in particular personalities to which others are attracted. It is elusive in that it is difficult to define, but we recognize it when we see it or feel it. There are those who become "opinion leaders" by virtue of their personal charm and characteristics, rather than principally because of their knowledge or expertise. *Charismatic power* is resident in many individuals in everyday life, and we sometimes refer to them as "natural leaders." Well-known charismatic personalities are the Reverends Martin Luther King Jr. and Jesse Jackson. President Ronald Reagan is also considered by many to have been a charismatic leader. When used responsibly, charismatic power can be beneficial to group process, ensuring that all members are respected and heard and that fairness prevails. When used irresponsibly, it can further disempower weaker members of a group.

Avoidance Power

Avoidance power may be used when members believe they have little or no power in a group or when they believe they have little to gain from group membership. They may refuse to participate in the process, while at the same time resenting their exclusion from it. Avoidance power may be manifest by being late for or absent from meetings, not fulfilling group obligations, refusing to share information or ideas, or sniping at others' ideas within the group. This power may also translate into denial and equivocation (such as refusing to take responsibility for actions or statements), topic management (such as shifting the topic to one with which the person feels more comfortable), noncommittal remarks (such as irrelevant or abstract comments), or irreverent remarks (such as making joking comments at inappropriate times). By engaging in any of these behaviors, these members may effectively keep the group from optimizing its creativity (Hocker & Wilmot, 1991).

Avoidance power in a small group may be felt in numerous more subtle ways, including draining group energy from the task at hand through the group's ongoing attempts to engage and involve the member in the process, draining energy by requiring other members to do larger portions of the work, losing the benefit of that member's contributions to the group effort, and causing resentment among other members, thereby weighing down their own creative energy and preventing them from optimizing solutions.

In the community group, if the trash hauler feels she is not fully appreciated, she may subtly or directly refuse to share information about the quantity and quality of the community's trash, leaving the group to scramble for indirect ways of estimating this information. If the avoiding members show their resentment by criticizing the group effort outside the group, they may derail the results of the group process when it comes to adopting proposals the group puts forth. If, for example, members talk to other community residents about the negative aspects of the process, it might sabotage the community support necessary to implement the proposal. Avoidance power can be highly destructive and insidious in its effects on the group and its achievements.

On the other hand, avoidance power should not be attributed to members who simply choose not to participate in some aspect of the discussion or process. They may think they have nothing of substance to offer on a particular point. Lack of full participation may have roots in something other than avoidance power.

Power in Context

It is frequently tempting to criticize participants for their abuse of the power they hold. However, as members of small groups, we must take responsibility for the power we grant to or permit others to have, as well as for that we take ourselves. Expert power is only as forceful as other group members allow it to be. Avoidance power may be the only perceived route left to a member others have effectively shut out of the process. We are agents of and respondents to power, and we have power and choice in both. As such, we are each responsible for the part we play in the use and abuse of power in our groups.

Too often, power is seen as a pie with a limited number of slices, but power is not finite. All people have power, and any individual may simultaneously employ several types of power in any particular group. Power resides in relationships, rather than in individuals. It is relative to the group. The trash hauler in the community group has expert power in that group, but his or her expertise in that area may have little value to a group setting up a children's day-care center. Each individual brings a set of experiences, habits, knowledge, and other values to every interaction. The interaction and the context in which it takes place determine the relative power and value of the individuals' participation. A person who feels disempowered in one group may be highly valued and empowered in another. For example, an artist may feel out of her or his element in a meeting of industry executives discussing plant and equipment investment but may be a highly valued member of a creative design team. Thus, power is resident in relationships and relational contexts. In effective groups, members pursue mutual influence, which leads to a higher level of success because there is a synergetic process occurring (Murrell & Meredith, 2000).

Effective leadership can help ensure the empowerment of all group members. Empowerment may take many forms, but first and foremost it assures a sense of worth and dignity for each individual. A group leader may empower members to make decisions and act on their own, taking responsibility for various parts of the group process (Scott & Jaffe, 1991), or that leader may exercise more hierarchical power; but for the group process to be effective, all members must feel empowered to contribute, whether they agree or disagree with the group leader or with each other. When a group is based on mutual respect, with all members feeling empowered, conflict can be handled constructively, enhancing the overall creative process.

Summary

Conflict is an important part of the group process. When we perceive incompatible goals, scarce rewards, or interference from another party, we have conflict. Conflict can be seen as the key, in some cases, to achieving the best possible solution in a group decision-making process. To the extent that it enlivens us and sharpens our focus on the issue, it can expand the possibilities for creative solutions to problems. For conflict to work constructively, however, we need to focus on issues and carefully delimit goals and expectations. Conflict should be considered part of the decision-making process, with its explicit and implicit parameters. When conflict is engaged constructively, it can enhance group cohesion, while reducing tension.

Essential to making any conflict-management strategy work is consensus among group members as to which strategies are appropriate for which conflicts. This means the group must make initial decisions about the overall priorities of the decision-making process, including an explicit understanding of the constraints on the process itself.

Each group must wrestle with small and large conflicts. The members must determine which issues are the most important and most worthy of the time and energy it takes to achieve consensus. Some will need to be handled quickly and efficiently, in order to save the time and energy required for the more important ones. If it is critical to the group's ongoing mission that consensus be achieved around particular issues, it might be worthwhile for the group to allow the extra time needed to build that consensus.

Underlying successful conflict management, regardless of the particular strategy used, is the honoring of interpersonal relationships and mutual respect, as well as the responsible use of power. Both these prerequisites take intention and focus, along with an awareness of the cost of disregarding them. Resolving differences can be difficult and fraught with pitfalls. It is not necessarily easy or natural but is rather a learned skill. It is frequently easy to succumb to anger, frustration, resentment, hurt feelings, or any number of other personal emotional reactions in the heat of conflict. It is in these instances that practice and learned conflict-management behavior can be most useful. Several particular communication strategies help ensure constructive conflict management.

As difficult as the process of managing conflict may be, the only way around it is through it. If a fire burning a pile of refuse is doused before the refuse is thoroughly burned, the pile may smolder and reignite later. If the fire is allowed to burn unchecked or is fueled with gasoline, it may leap out of its boundaries and cause unintended harm. On the other hand, if it is allowed to burn within the allowable perimeters, the refuse is consumed, and the problem is satisfactorily resolved. Keeping the fire under control takes planning and a certain amount of time, energy, and focus. It means staying with the heat until it has run its course. So, too, when conflict is engaged constructively, it resolves the issues under dispute and moves the process further ahead. When all the parties to a conflict adopt positive communication strategies, the outcome has a good chance of being a successful one, with a satisfactory outcome for all participants.

Conflict plays a key role in the functioning or lack of functioning of groups. When it is handled constructively, with careful attention to the patterns of communication interaction, it contributes to the creativity and synergy of group process; when handled destructively, it undermines the group's best efforts. Table 12.2 lists some important behaviors to constructive conflict management.

TABLE 12.2   Constructive Conflict Management

---

1. Maintain a commitment to the importance of positive group relationships.
2. State positions directly and honestly.
3. Listen attentively to diverse opinions.
4. Accept responsibility for one's own thoughts and feelings.
5. Address the issues, not the personalities.
6. Communicate understanding of the other persons and their perspectives.
7. Use supportive, rather than defensive, communication strategies.
8. Look for areas of agreement that underlie the disagreement.
9. Focus on particular aspects of the issues, rather than on hardened positions.
10. Generate as many alternatives as feasible before coming to a final resolution.
11. Insist that solutions be based on predetermined objective standards.

DISCUSSION QUESTIONS

1. Define *conflict*. What do you think are its key factors or characteristics?

2. Distinguish between substance and pattern in a conflict.

3. What is the difference between a morphostatic system and a morphogenic system? Provide an example of each from your own experience. Which group would be easier to work with in problem solving? Why?

4. Why are flashpoints occurring in the interactive pattern of a group more difficult to resolve or deal with than those that occur in the substance of the issue?

5. How do scarce resources, diverse backgrounds, and varying orientations to task accomplishments influence the substance of conflict?

6. How are assertiveness and cooperativeness used in determining conflict style? Outline how they create the five conflict-managing styles discussed in this chapter.

7. Briefly outline an example of collaborative conflict resolution that you have engaged in. Contrast that with a competitive conflict. Which was more satisfying to you? To the other party?

8. What are the important elements in a successful negotiation strategy?

9. Distinguish between accommodation and avoidance. Provide an example of how to use each strategy effectively in a small group discussion.

10. What should be the key factors in deciding to use compromise?

11. What are some examples of constructive competitive communication in small groups?

12. Provide an example of the seven types of power in small groups.

REFERENCES

Ayoko, O. B., Callan, V. J., & Hartel, C. E. J. (2008). The influence of team emotional intelligence climate on conflict and team members' reactions to conflict. *Small Group Research, 39*(2), 121–149.

Cai, D. A., & Fink, E. L. (2002). Conflict style differences between individualists and collectivists. *Communication Monographs, 69,* 67–87.

Chen, C. C., Chen, X. P., & Meindl, J. R. (1998). How can cooperation be fostered? The cultural effects of individualism–collectivism. *Academy of Management Review, 23*(3), 285–304.

DeVito, J. A. (2004). *The interpersonal communication book* (10th ed.). Boston: Allyn & Bacon.

Fisher, R., Ury, W., & Patton, B. (1991). *Getting to yes: Negotiating agreement without giving in* (2nd ed.). Boston: Houghton Mifflin.

French, J. R. P., & Raven, B. (1968). The bases of social power. In D. Cartwright & A. Zander (Eds.), *Group dynamics.* New York: Harper & Row.

Harris, T. E., & Nelson, M. D. (2008). *Applied organizational communication: Theory and practice in a*

global environment. New York: Lawrence Erlbaum Associates.

Hocker, J. L., & Wilmot, W. W. (1991). *Interpersonal conflict* (3rd ed.). Dubuque, IA: William C. Brown.

Ingbar, J. (2005). *Organizational ethics: Where values and cultures meet.* Camden, ME: Institute for Global Ethics (www.globalethics.org).

Kegan, R. (1994). *In over our heads.* Cambridge, MA: Harvard University Press.

Kotlyar, I., & Karakowsky, L. (2006). Leading conflict? Linkages between leader behaviors and group conflict. *Small Group Research, 37*(4), 377–403.

Kuhn, T., & Poole, M. (2002). Do conflict management styles affect group decision making? *Human Communication Research, 26*(4), 558–590.

Lulofs, R. S., & Cahn, D. D. (2000). *Conflict: From theory to action* (2nd ed.). Boston: Allyn & Bacon.

McNary, L. D. (2003, April). The term "win–win" in conflict management: A classic case of misuse and overuse. *Journal of Business Communication, 40,* 144–159.

McShane, S. L., & Von Glinow, M. A. (2000). *Organizational behavior*. Boston: McGraw-Hill Irwin.

Murrell, K. L., & Meredith, M. (2000). *Empowering employees*. New York: McGraw-Hill

Rau, D. (2005). The influence of relationship conflict and trust on the transactive memory. *Small Group Research, 36*(6), 746–771.

Raven, B. H. (1993). The bases of power: Origins and recent developments. *Journal of Social Issues, 49*(4), 227–251.

Scott, C. D., & Jaffe, D. T. (1991). *Empowerment*. Menlo Park, CA: Crisp.

Shockley-Zalabak, P. (2002). *Fundamentals of organizational communication: Knowledge, sensitivity, skills, values* (5th ed.). Boston: Allyn & Bacon.

Stephan, W. G. (2008). Psychological and communication processes associated with intergroup conflict resolution. *Small Group Research, 39*(1), 28–41.

Tjosvold, D. (1995). Cooperation theory, constructive controversy, and effectiveness: Learning from crisis. In R. A. Guzzo, E. Salas, & Associates (Eds.), *Team effectiveness and decision making in organizations* (pp. 79–112). San Francisco: Jossey-Bass.

Ward, A. C. (1998, July–August). Another look at how Toyota integrates product development. *Harvard Business Review*, pp. 36–49.

Witteman, H. (1991). Group member satisfaction. *Small Group Research, 22*(1), 24–58.

Wood, J. T. (2004). *Communication mosaics: An introduction to the field of communication*. Florence, KY: Thomson Wadsworth.

Zemke, R., Raines, C., & Filipczak, B. (2000). *Generations at work: Managing the clash of veterans, Xers, and Nexters in your workplace*. New York: AMACOM.

Zornoza, A., Ripoll, P., & Peiro, J. M. (2002). Conflict management in groups that work in two different communication contexts: Face-to-face and computer-mediated communication. *Small Group Research, 33*(5), 481–508.

CHAPTER 13
Leadership in Small Groups

CHAPTER OBJECTIVES

- Explain the characteristics of leadership.
- Identify the attributes of leaders.
- Differentiate among theories of leadership.
- Outline the premises behind the leadership-style theories.
- Explain the Managerial Grid and its applications.

- Describe transactional and transformational leadership.
- Discuss leadership by adaptation.
- Present three characteristics of leaders.
- Describe the different processes for becoming a leader.
- Explain the tasks of group leaders.
- Discuss the influences of leaders on group structure.
- Identify leadership limitations.

KEY TERMS

Action mediation	Emergent group leader	Opportunism
Appointed group leader	Impoverished management	Paternalism/maternalism
Authority–compliance	Interdependence	Style theories
Autocratic system	Laissez-faire system	Team management
Communication competence	Leader-as-coach	Trait theories
Country club management	Leader-as-conductor	Transformational leaders
Credibility	Leader-as-technician	Transactional leaders
Democratic system	Managerial Grid	Universal theories
Elected group leader	Middle of the road	Vision

Money's Nice, but a Good Boss Is Better

When it comes to sizing up the quality of their workplaces, federal workers value strong leadership and straight answers from their bosses more than pay and benefits, according to a comprehensive study of the federal workforce. What separates agencies in the minds of their employees is the senior leadership, how well or poorly it shares information with subordinates, and the training and opportunities it provides workers, according to the federal survey results of the Partnership for Public Service, a nonpartisan group devoted to improving public service.

(Vogel, 2009)

Leadership, whether expressed by an individual or engaged in collectively by the members of a group, is about developing dreams, visions, goals, and objectives that help focus a group's energy to engage in its task and accomplish its mission. Leadership is often associated with the symbols, speeches, and insights presented at critical turning points in the thinking of a group, movement, or larger community. These insights make a group's goals and objectives real and achievable; but the essence of leadership itself is the conception and articulation of the group's vision (Northhouse, 2004).

Recognizing Leaders

Lee Iacocca, former CEO of the Chrysler corporation, articulates nine characteristics that he calls the test of a true leader. He says these characteristics are not complicated or fancy, but just clear, obvious qualities that are necessary for every leader. He defines these characteristics as the "9 C's"—(1) curious, (2) creative, (3) communicate, (4) character, (5) courage, (6) conviction, (7) charisma, (8) competence, and (9) common sense (Iacocca, 2007). Table 13.1 lists these important "9 C's."

Leadership is "the process of influencing others to understand and agree about what needs to be done and how to do it, and the process of facilitating individual and collective efforts to accomplish shared objectives" (Yukl, 2006, p. 8). A good leader serves as a catalyst for the group process (Northhouse, 2004). She or he encourages group members to engage in productive interaction, interpret ambiguous information and confusing events, make sense of uncertainties, and achieve shared objectives (Raes, Glunk, Heijltjes, & Roe, 2007).

An effective leader listens and is sensitive to the diverse and subtle influences on a group's ability to work productively. An effective leader helps focus and shape the group's discussion, is able to make sense of apparently disparate ideas, and encourages group members to express their contradictory viewpoints, stimulating the benefits of conflict among diverse perspectives. An effective leader enables and motivates a group to stay on track, to remain energized and empowered, to resolve conflicts constructively,

TABLE 13.1   Lee Iacocca's Nine C's of Leadership

Curiosity	Listen to people outside the "yes" crowd. Read widely and voraciously. Step outside your "comfort zone" to hear different ideas. Put ideas to the test.
Creative	Go out on a limb. Try something different. Think outside the box. Things change. Be creative to handle that change.
Communicate	Face reality with straight talk. Begin with the truth even when it's painful, not with denial or dishonesty.
Character	Consider the reasons for action and the difference between right and wrong, and have the courage to do the right thing.
Courage	Swagger isn't courage, and neither is tough talk, posturing, or bravado. Courage means making a commitment to sit down and negotiate.
Conviction	Have the passion to really get something done, and then spend the time and energy necessary to accomplish it.
Charisma	Cultivate the ability to inspire people. It is based on trust. It's not flashy but earned through commitment, honesty, and communication.
Competence	Know what you are doing. Surround yourself with people who know what they are doing. Be a problem solver.
Common Sense	The only things you have going for you as a human being are your ability to reason and your common sense.

and to make creative decisions to reach desirable outcomes. An effective leader is the person the group looks to when it has reached an impasse, needs guidance in setting a new direction or staying on course, or needs order restored to an unruly group process. An effective leader may be autocratic or democratic and collaborative in style, but she or he elicits respect from group members and gives respect in turn.

A leader may take on the role of a coach who leads the debate team to a successful outcome, the captain of a winning sports team, the person who keeps a group of stranded hikers from panicking and hiking around in circles, or the person who holds a small group together until it has completed the task for which it was convened. Leaders are the ones who shoulder the largest responsibility for a group's success and accept the biggest burden of blame when a group or team fails to meet its goals or has unfortunate outcomes.

Because leaders are a part of the systems in which they participate, however, their leadership abilities are influenced by the groups they lead and the context within which they lead them. Many different types of people have been highly effective leaders in different types of situations and contexts. Like power, leadership exists in the context and in the relationships among people as much as in the abilities of the individual. Most of us recognize a good leader when we see or work with one in a given context, but that same person might not be equally effective with another group or in another situation. A person who understands the ways of the wilderness and how to survive for days in the wild with little or no food or other supplies may be a good leader for a group of stranded hikers. Those same skills would probably not be as useful for the leader of a group planning a strategy for putting together a bid on a prime industrial development site. Although we can frequently point to particular individuals as leaders, it is not always as easy to define leadership in such a way that we can anticipate who will make a good leader and who will not, under specific set of circumstances.

In general, we can say that a good leader is one who is successful in helping the group accomplish the goals it set out to accomplish, and a poor leader is one who fails to do that. Leadership exists in the set of behaviors that brings a group closer to achieving its goals (Pavitt, High, Tressler, & Winslow, 2007). "Leaders deserve to be so called only when they have been key players in acts of leadership" (Clark & Clark, 1990, p. 20). Their leadership is defined by the context and consequences in which it is enacted. It is in the act of carrying out leadership that a leader is recognized, rather than by any particular abstract characteristic.

Leaders Function Within a System

Leaders play key roles in the systems in which they participate. Their effect on the patterns of interaction within their groups and between their groups and the external environments in which they are located are often influential in determining the outcome of the group process.

Groups as systems are as successful as their ability to process new information and find new ways of approaching problems—their ability to be morphogenic (take in, process, and transform information and procedures), rather than morphostatic (resisting change and maintaining the status quo). This ability entails responding to the substance of internal and external environments within which the group operates, the issues for which the group is convened, and the complex interactions between people, issues, multiple environments, and group dynamics.

Leaders act as arbiters of these interfaces, serving as communication links between the group and its external environment and between the group members and the process in which they are engaged. A leader must have the skills and knowledge to gather information from the environment and decode those factors that are helpful and relevant to the group process and the ability to translate and encode that information into forms that are useful to the group. A leader acts to facilitate the process and procedure of the group, manage the substance of the task, and maintain the group cohesiveness and morale. This requires taking on the procedural roles of coordinator, orienter, and procedural technician; the substantive roles of initiator, opinion giver, and elaborator; and the maintenance roles of encourager, harmonizer, and compromiser (Pavitt et al., 2007). Effective leaders must negotiate context and action. In context mediation, the leader "must collect and form detailed impressions about the environment" (Barge, 1994, p. 12). In *action mediation,* the leader must remove environmental obstacles through appropriate behaviors (Barge, 1994). The wilderness leader mediates between the wilderness and the group that is unfamiliar with it. She or he assesses the situation (context mediation) and develops strategies for helping group members understand that situation, reducing any possible negative effects on the group, and encouraging appropriate behavior (action mediation). For the leader to be effective in this role, however, he or she depends on the group's cooperation and trust in his or her ability. Good leadership is an interactive system that requires a "reciprocal relationship between leaders and followers" (Barge, 1994, p. 19). Leader effectiveness "is not merely a function of leader behavior, but rather a joint function of leader behavior and situational requirements" (Vecchio, Bullis, & Brazil, 2006, p. 408). Leaders must display warmth and supportiveness while being directive and monitoring group member commitment and competence (Vecchio et al., 2006). Within this context, leaders must work to encourage trust and cooperation within the group (Roussin, 2008).

Theories of Leadership

A traditional approach to leadership relied on mechanistic metaphors for breaking leadership down into its component parts. Current theories encompass a much broader and more continuous scope of attributes, behaviors, and patterns of interaction. Early theories were based on hierarchic models from industrial organizations. In these contexts, leaders oversaw production employees and were expected to maintain efficiency and discipline against what were assumed to be the natural instincts of employees to avoid work. Leaders gave orders, and workers were expected to follow them. Workers were not expected to be creative in their thinking or to have ideas for improving their methods of working. The leaders of these groups of workers were expected to be rigid and authoritarian (Barge, 1994). Changes in organizational expectations, however, have brought comparable changes in leadership expectations.

When we examine leadership today, it appears to be more of an art than science. It is useful, nonetheless, to try to describe the traits and behaviors that effective leaders share. Although leadership has been the subject of a great deal of communication research, no one theory has fully explained it. On the other hand, several perspectives taken together can contribute a great deal to our understanding of it.

Most traditional descriptions of leadership define it according to trait theories, personal characteristics associated with an individual person, or style theories, the behaviors a person manifests. The *trait theories* assume that certain physical and psychological characteristics predispose some people to leadership (Hackman & Johnson, 2000). The *style theories* assume that particular kinds of behavior (e.g., task-oriented or relationship-oriented behaviors) underlie leadership ability.

In terms of leadership styles, Gastil (1994) argued that neither a democratic nor an autocratic leadership style is necessarily more efficient or productive. However, he suggested that some benefits of a democratic style of leadership are in giving group members responsibility, which improves the general abilities and leadership skills of group members, assists the group in its decision-making processes, and helps group members share important leadership functions.

Superimposed on these two types of theories are the two dimensions of universality and situational dependence. *Universal theories* posit that particular traits or styles characterize leaders across most situations; situational theories posit that any given traits or styles are unique to specific situations (Barge, 1994). The four resulting categories defined by traits, styles, universal theories, and situational factors produce a grid that encompasses most of the leadership theories: universal trait theories, universal style or behavior theories, contingency trait theories, and situational behavior theories (Barge, 1994). Universal trait theories posit particular personal characteristics that leaders in most circumstances share. Universal style theories posit particular behaviors in which effective leaders generally engage. Contingency trait theories posit the idea that different personal characteristics are appropriate to leaders in different types of situations, and situational behavior theories suggest the idea that leaders adapt behaviors to the requirements of particular circumstances.

Managerial Leadership Grid Theory

Of particular interest among the style (or behavior) theories are those based on results of leadership studies conducted at Ohio State University during the 1950s. These studies found that a concern for task (substance, object mediation) and a concern for relationships (pattern, action mediation) were often associated with leadership. These two concerns formed the basis for many follow-up studies, including those by Robert Blake and Jane Mouton, who developed the now well-known *Managerial Grid* (Blake & Mouton, 1985/1964). This grid places a concern for people on a vertical axis and a concern for task on a horizontal axis, defining a two-dimensional space.

The Managerial Grid characterizes a total of seven leadership styles. The first five are team management, authority–compliance, middle of the road, country club management, and impoverished management, according to the point along each of the axes at which a leader's behavior falls (Blake & McCanse, 1991; Blake & Mouton,

1985). These dimensions also correspond to the conflict-management styles presented in Chapter 12 and shown in parentheses in the list that follows. Blake, Mouton, and Allen (1987) added two additional leadership styles—paternalism/maternalism and opportunism. Each of these seven leadership styles is located on the grid and assigned a value of 1 (least) to 9 (most) on each of the two axes of concern for people and concern for task, as indicated in Figure 13.1.

1. *9,9 Team Management (Collaboration).* The leader demonstrates a high degree of concern for both people (9) and task (9). The group members work together with mutual respect and a strong goal orientation. The group has a good chance for a successful outcome. This orientation takes time and commitment from both the leader and the group members, but when time and energy permit, it is clearly a superior group decision-making method.

2. *9,1 Authority–Compliance (Competition).* The leader is concerned with completing the task (9) but shows little interest or regard for relationships (1). Group members are not expected to participate in the decision making. Depending on the overall context of the group and the task at hand, this may be highly efficient and productive or may lead to feelings of disenfranchisement by the group, causing the group to not support the decisions. In either case, it does not allow for the creative decision making that results from group synergy.

3. *5,5 Middle of the Road (Compromise).* Although not strongly committed in either direction, the leader shows a moderate concern for interpersonal relationships (5) and a moderate concern for the task at hand (5). Without a strong commitment to results, the outcome is not likely to be optimal, but it may satisfy everyone somewhat. If time and energy constraints are the deciding factor, this may be the most practical course.

4. *1,9 Country Club Management (Accommodation).* The group leader is more concerned about interpersonal relationships (9) than about accomplishing the task (1). When the group is convened for the sake of enjoyment or personal contact, this is an appropriate style. If, however, it is trying to find a solution to a problem, this is an inefficient way to go about it. On the other hand, if the group and the leader prefer to feel good about each other, while agreeing that the leader should take sole responsibility for making decisions, this style may work well.

5. *1,1 Impoverished Management (Avoidance).* With a low concern for both people (1) and task (1), the leader does not try to influence group members and cares little for whether they achieve their goals. This style is used by leaders who are overworked, do not care about this particular project, or have "retired on the job." This style is not helpful to the group's interpersonal relationships or goal accomplishments.

6. *9+9 Paternalism/Maternalism.* As in the team management style, the leader shows a high level of concern for both people (9) and task (9). However, rather than assuming the group has its own stake in the outcome and is working for intrinsic rewards, the leader assumes the group is burdened by the task and requires extrinsic rewards. In this case, the leader pushes the group to get the job done and then rewards the members in ways he or she has available, through salaries, benefits, or working conditions, if they are employees, or through other benefits, if he or she has a different relationship with the group. Drawbacks are that group members

FIGURE 13.1 Managerial Leadership Grid

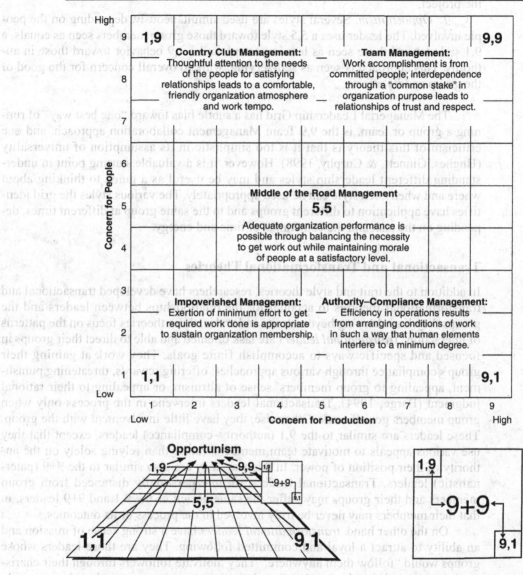

High

9 **1,9**   **9,9**

Country Club Management: **Team Management:**
Thoughtful attention to the needs   Work accomplishment is from
8   of the people for satisfying   committed people; interdependence
relationships leads to a comfortable,   through a "common stake" in
friendly organization atmosphere   organization purpose leads to
7   and work tempo.   relationships of trust and respect.

Middle of the Road Management
5   **5,5**
Adequate organization performance is
4   possible through balancing the necessity
to get work out while maintaining morale
of people at a satisfactory level.

Concern for People

3
Impoverished Management: **Authority–Compliance Management:**
Exertion of minimum effort to get   Efficiency in operations results
2 required work done is appropriate   from arranging conditions of work
to sustain organization membership.   in such a way that human elements
interfere to a minimum degree.

1   **1,1**   **9,1**

Low
1   2   3   4   5   6   7   8   9
Low   **Concern for Production**   High

Opportunism

1,9   **9,9**   1,9
                              9+9
5,5   9,1

1,1   **9,1**

                                        1,9
                                     9+9
                                        9,1

People adapt and shift to any Grid style needed to gain   **9+9: Paternalism/Maternalism**
the maximum advantage. Performance occurs according   Reward and approval gain loyalty
to selfish gain. Effort is given for advantage or personal   and obedience to work requirement.
gain.   Failure leads to punishment.

Source: The Leadership Grid figure, Paternalism figure, and Opportunism figure, from *Leadership Dilemmas—Grid Solutions,* by Robert R. Blake and Anne Adams McCanse (Formerly the *Managerial Grid* by Robert R. Blake and Jane S. Mouton). Houston: Gulf Publishing, (Grid figure: p. 29, Paternalism figure: p. 30, Opportunism figure: p. 31). Copyright 1991 by Scientific Methods, Inc. Reproduced by permission of the owners.

may simply work for a price and never develop loyalty or commitment and pride in the project.

7. *Opportunism.* Several styles are used simultaneously, depending on the people involved. The leader uses a 5,5 style toward those group members seen as equals, a 9,1 style toward those seen as less important, and a 1,9 behavior toward those in authority. This approach is seen as self-serving, with no overall concern for the good of the group and its efforts.

The Managerial Leadership Grid has a subtle bias toward "one best way" of running a group or team, is the 9,9 Team Management collaboration approach, and one criticism of this theory is that it is too simplistic in its assumption of universality (Hughes, Ginnett, & Curphy, 1998). However, it is a valuable starting point in understanding different leadership styles and may be useful as a guide to thinking about where and when each style can be used appropriately. The various styles the grid identifies have application to different groups and to the same group at different times, depending on the task and the constraints of time and energy.

Transactional and Transformational Theories

In addition to the trait and style theories, researchers have developed transactional and transformational theories to account for the relationships between leaders and the groups they lead. Moving beyond traits and styles, these theories focus on the patterns of interaction. *Transactional leaders* are task oriented and able to direct their groups in focused and specific ways to accomplish finite goals. They work at gaining their group's compliance through various approaches: offering rewards, threatening punishment, appealing to group members' sense of altruism, or appealing to their rational judgment (Barge, 1994). Transactional leaders intervene in the process only when group members get off track. Otherwise, they have little involvement with the group. These leaders are similar to the 9,1 (authority–compliance) leaders, except that they use various appeals to motivate team members, rather than relying solely on the authority of their position of power. In this way, they are also similar to the 9+9 (paternalistic) leaders. Transactional leaders are interpersonally distanced from group members and their groups may suffer the same deficit as the 9,1 and 9+9 leaders, in that their members may never be truly involved in the process or its outcomes.

On the other hand, *transformational leaders* have a strong sense of mission and an ability to attract a loyal and committed following. They are those leaders whose groups would "follow them anywhere." They motivate followers through their charismatic power, their inspirational vision, their ability to express complex ideas in easily understood ways, and their individualized attention to followers. These leaders both represent and shape the group members' perceptions of the task or mission and motivate them to aspire to a set of goals, rather than relying on explicit instructions or extrinsic rewards and punishments (Barge, 1994; Hackman & Johnson, 2000). Transformational charismatic leaders effectively represent and define the key attributes of a group's identity, articulating a psychological purpose to the meaning of the group and its task (Schyns & Felfe, 2006). In contrast with those leaders who simply

Dr. Martin Luther King Jr., a transformational leader, at the front of a voting rights march from Selma, Alabama, to the state capital in Montgomery

manage the group process by administering, within a system, by following the rules, the transformational leader empowers the group to accomplish tasks through proactive communication and mutual trust (Bennis & Nanus, 1997). Transformational leaders include political and religious leaders, as well as some who lead dynamic organizations.

Leadership by Adaptation

Despite the appeal of many theories of leadership, defining leadership in a way that encompasses all situations remains elusive: "Implicit within all leadership theories is the notion that leaders are most effective when they can dissect the demands and constraints of a situation and perform the required actions to take advantage of a situation's opportunities and overcome its constraints" (Barge, 1994, p. 57). Because groups are dynamic systems, leaders need to be able to adapt their styles and behaviors to the needs of the particular group within a context. Ellis and Cronshaw (1992) suggest that leaders are more effective when they develop a social intelligence that allows them to monitor situations and adapt their leadership behaviors as required.

Leadership, therefore, is more often found in the interactions of the group and in its process than solely in the traits and qualities of the individuals enacting it. This is true in multiple forms of leadership, from the formal leadership that emerges or is imposed on the group to the intuitive "dance" the leader engages in to maintain the group dynamic: "Effective leadership, research suggests, is remarkably chameleonlike . . . [it] is a function of the situation in which it is found" (Kotter, 1988, p. 21). There is no "single comprehensive list of leadership qualities and . . . . no single path to leadership," but adaptability is a key characteristic of effective leadership (Clark & Clark,

1990, p. 70). Thus, despite the plethora of theories on leadership, its actual manifestation is frequently hard to predict but highly evident when we experience it. It happens within the context of the group and is dependent on the group's responses to it.

A Leader

Lao Tsu is credited with the saying:

> The wicked leader is he whom the people despise.
> The good leader is he whom the people revere.
> The great leader is he about whom the people say, "We did it ourselves."

Leaderless Groups

Leaderless groups, defined as "groups that do not have a designated person with continuing authority over the other members and responsibility for maintaining the group," have existed for decades (Counselman, 1991, p. 243). Many experts, however, have expressed skepticism over the viability and productivity of truly leaderless groups. Yalom (1985) suggest that most so-called leaderless groups in fact have unofficial leaders in the more experienced or expert group members who informally fulfill the leadership functions. Others have cautioned that a leaderless group soon becomes "leadershipless"—that is, develops a lack of clear focus or structure and finds it difficult to maintain group norms. Without a clearly defined, shared sense of purpose and a consistent, commonly agreed-upon set of norms, a group may find itself constantly negotiating how it will do things rather than engaging in an efficient performance of its tasks. Leaderless groups have been known to dissolve in disappointment when members' behaviors, such as lateness to meetings, absences, and the expression of hostile feelings, coupled with the refusal by one or two group members to discuss group dynamics, have gone unchecked (Counselman, 1991). This is not to say that leaderless groups cannot work. To be effective, however, group members must cooperatively take on the leadership functions of (a) continuing to reaffirm the group's task, process, and vision; (b) repeatedly emphasizing the need for a safe group climate in which to engage in their work; and (c) maintaining the group's norms and boundaries between permissible and impermissible behaviors. Whether one person fulfills these functions or the group as a whole shares responsibility for them, these leadership functions are necessary to effective group processes.

Three Characteristics of Leaders

Regardless of the particulars of any one theory of leadership, there are generally at least three characteristics we expect leaders to manifest: vision, credibility, and communication competence. Vision provides the direction for the group process; credibility, the reason for the group to follow that direction; and communication competence, the means for communicating that direction to the group. Each of these contributes to the ability of a leader to influence the group process.

Vision

True leaders are expected to do more than simply conduct meetings, control agendas, and keep track of events. A key piece of leadership is the ability to hold onto an overall *vision* while moving a group through the process necessary to achieve that vision. Leaders need to set long- and short-term goals, focus attention on relevant activities, manage conflict, and empower other group members to contribute to the creative process (Bennis & Nanus, 1997).

The wilderness leader sets the goal of getting the group safely out of the wilderness. To achieve that goal, he must keep the group safe and healthy for as long as it takes to find the way out. This may mean he will need to find sources of potable water and ways of feeding and sheltering the group within the constraints of the natural environment, while maintaining the group's morale. Keeping the goal in sight, while keeping the group on track toward accomplishing it, can be a complex task.

Credibility

Effective leadership depends on the group's willingness to follow. This willingness is generally based on the group's perception of the leader's abilities and credibility (Hackman & Johnson, 2000). Without the group's trust and confidence, the most visionary leader is paralyzed in her attempts to direct the group toward the stated goals and visions. The wilderness leader would be powerless to help the group if members did not participate in the process. If they do not believe in the leader's ability to help them find the way to safety, or if they do not trust him to keep the group's welfare as a priority, they are not likely to follow his advice and instructions. Thus, vision without credibility may prevent the most insightful and creative leader from being effective.

Credibility is a complex phenomenon. It is made up of several factors: competence (knowledge and expertise in a topic), character (honesty and trustworthiness), composure (ability to remain calm under stress), sociability (likableness), and extroversion (degree of interest in others) (Barge, 1994). Each of these builds a base of power and is activated by the perceptions of the value of that power by the members of the group. Those leaders who are perceived to have a relevant power base, as well as the best interests of their group at heart, will have influence in their groups. Leaders who are perceived to lack such a power base or who are perceived to be manipulative or dishonest will have a harder time gaining compliance from their group.

Communication Competence

Another important piece of group leadership is *communication competence* (Drucker, 1998). For a leader to be effective, he or she must be able to translate his or her relevant knowledge, skills, and situationally appropriate behavior to group members in ways they can understand and trust. Communication competence includes the ability to decode and understand messages coming from the environment—both within the group and from outside it—and to encode and interpret that information for the group members or for those relevant others outside the group. A leader must be able to communicate in a way that "upholds and 'fits into' the existing cultural value system or transcends that system by articulating an alternative value system" (Barge, 1994, p. 238). As such, leaders must be able to understand their environment and interpret it in a way that makes sense to group members (Buckingham & Coffman, 1999).

Before going on a whitewater rafting trip, the river guide explains to the rafters what to expect and how to respond to a given set of commands that the guide will issue when they reach the white water. Before they get into the raft and follow the instructions, though, the rafters need to believe that the guide knows the river and how to interpret the currents, eddies, and falls; that she or he is able to maneuver the raft safely through or around the rapids, cares about the rafters' well-being, and is able to tell them what, when, and how to do things effectively in a way they can understand. In addition, regardless of how well the guide knows the river and techniques for paddling it, if something unexpected happens when they are out on a treacherous stretch of the river and the guide tells the rafters to do something that they have not previously been told to expect, the guide will need to be able to communicate the rationale for that different command, either verbally or nonverbally, in a way that makes sense to the rafters. Leaders must be able to communicate their overall vision, have credibility among their followers, and be trustworthy in the situation at hand.

Communication competence also frequently includes an ability to manage ambiguity and uncertainty. A leader must be able to "read" the group, as well as the environment in which it operates, and know when to reduce and when to heighten uncertainty. On the river, the raft guide needs to reduce uncertainty enough to allay the fears of the rafters and keep them calm so that they are able to enjoy the trip and not panic or cause harm to themselves or to fellow rafters. However, the rafters must also understand the dangers of the river, not become too relaxed and casual in the raft, and be prepared for the unexpected. A mix of certainty and uncertainty is required for a fun and safe trip.

The leader of a real estate development group preparing a bid on a prime piece of land balances certainty and uncertainty in the process of putting together a successful bid. Although it is certain that the group needs to offer enough money to outbid the competitors, while keeping its bid low enough to assure that it can make a profit from its development, there is some uncertainty about the exact dollar amount that will accomplish both requirements. The leader may want to reduce uncertainty and streamline group discussion by relying on parallels with prior development to the extent possible, but he or she may also want the group members to struggle with the unknown aspects of this particular case, to make sure they are not overlooking something crucial and expensive. The leader thus needs to balance the efficiency and comfort associated with reducing uncertainty with the risks of conflict and becoming engaged in a time-consuming discussion associated with raising the levels of uncertainty. Managing the mix of certainty and uncertainty appropriately in a group is the task of a good leader and a test of his or her communication competence.

Choosing a Leader

Because small groups are convened for a variety of purposes, within diverse contexts, and with a variety of people, talents, time, energy, and tasks, many factors influence the quality and type of leadership needed for an effective group process. Some small groups are formed for a limited purpose, for a limited period of time, with limited resources, and expecting limited commitment from members. Such a group may simply need a leader who can keep the process on track. It may want to leave most of the decision making to one person, with only a nod of approval from the other members. Other groups have broader tasks and more complex goals. Those may benefit from a more collaborative leadership style. Leaders may be appointed or elected, or they may emerge during the group process. Leadership may also be shared among group members.

Appointed Leaders

For many groups formed within an organizational context, the leader is appointed by a manager in the larger organization. An *appointed group leader* may set up the group, call the first meeting, set the agenda, establish group norms and expectations, establish relationships with outside sources of power, and act as an arbiter of the group process. This may be someone with position or referent power in an organization or someone with particular expertise in the area under investigation. An appointed leader with a respected base of power can be beneficial in setting a positive tone for the group process. In addition, a well-connected leader with interpersonal linkages or positional power may make it easier for the group to obtain information and resources needed for the task (Harris & Nelson, 2008). A leader who commands respect based on the group's perceptions of her or his power may be able to empower group members and manage conflict more effectively than someone not as well perceived.

One drawback to an appointed leader is the tendency such leaders may have to exert their power and control over the group process, thus diminishing the potential contributions of other members. When members feel barred from participating fully, they may use their own avoidance power, with the adverse impact associated with a loss of their input. Even when a leader is benevolent and caring in his or her assertion of power and control, the group may feel disempowered and lose motivation and a sense of shared responsibility for the outcome. Control of group process is a difficult balance to hold. Any leader may be tempted to exert more control than is warranted, but those who are appointed may be more inclined to move in that direction than those who are more democratically chosen.

Elected Leaders

An *elected group leader* is one the group chooses through its own formal processes. The group may choose a leader based on his expertise with the task at hand, on his known ability to lead a group process, or because of his perceived power in some other area. Elected leaders share some characteristics with appointed leaders, in that their position within the group is formalized, and their relationship to other members is as the "first among equals." Even when leaders are chosen simply for the convenience of having someone call the meetings and set the agenda with no other formal power in the group, the position itself frequently enhances the perceived power of the person who is chosen. An elected leader is inherently more accountable to the group members than is an appointed one and may be less likely to abuse that power, but most of us can probably cite instances in which democratically elected leaders have taken inappropriate liberties with the exercise of power.

Emergent Leaders

An *emergent group leader* is one who "starts out as any other member of a group of peers, but . . . . gradually emerges as leader in the perceptions of the other members by providing leadership services" that the group values (Brilhart & Galanes, 1995, p. 161). There are two types of emergent leaders: those who emerge from a leaderless group of peers and those who emerge alongside an existing leader to meet particular needs.

In studying leaders who emerge from leaderless groups, researchers at the University of Minnesota found that certain actions make some members of a leaderless group more likely than others to become the group leaders (Bormann, 1975; Geier, 1967). Group members who are reticent or lack information or those who are bossy and dogmatic are eliminated as candidates for leadership early in the process. Those members who speak frequently, are well informed, and support democratic group process remain in consideration. It is from this group that the leader will likely emerge: "The Minnesota Studies show that leaders emerge through a method of residues in which group members are rejected until only one remains" (Beebe & Masterson, 1990, p. 253).

On the other hand, in a group with an appointed or elected leader, a member with expertise in the particular area under consideration may emerge as her skills are increasingly called on during the group process. If a small group has been convened to develop a marketing strategy for electronic parts, an executive from the marketing group might be appointed the initial group leader. As the discussion develops, another individual may emerge as especially knowledgeable about the market niche for these particular component parts. If that person gains the respect and trust of the group, the members may turn increasingly to her to take over the group process (Cummings & Worley, 2001). This latter type of emergent leadership is similar to the type associated with shared, or facilitative, leadership.

Shared (Facilitative) Leadership

As its name implies, shared, or facilitative, leadership is based on a collaborative group effort, with members sharing power as the task dictates. As the group members become increasingly empowered, leaders become facilitators, rather than directors or managers. Increasing numbers of organizations have turned to self-managing work teams and problem-solving groups (Harris, 1992–1993). In these cases, a team is put together with the empowerment of group members as a primary goal (Cummings & Worley, 2001). As the group progresses toward greater empowerment, the leader's role

TABLE 13.2   Advantages and Disadvantages of Shared, Facilitative Leadership

Advantages	Disadvantages
1. Provides a broader range of information on the problem, alternatives, and recommended solution.	1. Less personal accountability for group's decision; a bad group decision is still a bad decision.
2. Lends a more creative approach to problem solving; uses expertise, information, and member knowledge.	2. Takes group's energy and focus away from task; if getting the job done is the only issue, not worth the time.
3. Gives members an increasing awareness of leader's problems and hurdles.	3. Increases opportunity for disagreement over issues.
4. Increases commitment to issues and solution.	4. Takes more time.
5. Enhances morale.	5. Allows strong voices to dominate.

shifts from direct to indirect involvement. Rather than being in charge, the leader becomes a facilitator who empowers other members to carry out the responsibilities and functions. The facilitative leader regards power as something to be shared with group members. This empowerment of group members often leads to better long-term results. Rather than a leader eliciting responses from group members, or trying to instill motivation in each person, individuals contribute freely, because each person has some ownership in the group process.

As Table 13.2 indicates, there are advantages and disadvantages to this type of group leadership. To the extent that group members are committed to the process and share in the responsibility, as well as in the power, the process is well served. Two principle disadvantages to this type of leadership are that conflicts may be more difficult and time-consuming to resolve if no one member is empowered to mediate them and that chaos might ensue if there is no one person overseeing the accomplishment of specific tasks and coordinating overall results. However, with a cohesive group and a well-defined task and set of goals, this type of leadership may work well.

Issues of Gender and Race

Koch (2005) argues that gender is an important socially constructed and contextually dependent influence on the dynamics of group leadership. She reports that females in leadership positions often receive two to three times more negative emotional affect in their groups than do male leaders. However, she finds that female leaders receive two to three times more emotional affect displays overall and are, at the same time, often rated as more competent by their groups than the male leaders. The male leaders are rated as equally competent by the men and women in their groups, but the female leaders are rated, in general, as higher in competence by the males in their groups than by the female group members. She interprets these results as indicating that (a) a group led by a woman may feel freer to be more affectively expressive than a group led by a man, and (b) a differential standard of competence expectations may exist based on a comparison between generalized social–cultural stereotypes and the individual group leader's specific abilities demonstrated in the group.

Ellis, Ilgen, and Hollenbeck (2006) identified a similar type of socially constructed bias in group member evaluations based on the race of a group leader. They found that members of a group with a Black leader who performs well are more likely to attribute the leader's performance to personal ability and effort than are members of a group with a White leader who performs well. Groups that perform poorly are equally likely to blame external causes for their performance, rather than leader behavior, regardless of the race of the leader. They conclude that this represents a subtle bias in group member expectations that affects their perceptions and overall ratings of their group leaders. No doubt more research will be done in this area, but the results of these two studies suggest how leadership is socially constructed and evaluated by small group members.

Leaders of Technologically Mediated Groups

Hoyt and Blascovich (2003) argue that the growing number of geographically disperse organizations, and the increasing use of technologically mediated virtual work group meetings, places new demands on leadership practices. In their study of group leadership in an immersive virtual environment, they show a need to develop group trust and values congruence among members for the group to be productive. In addition, two leadership styles, transactional and transformational, produce different types of productivity in these task groups. Transactional leadership facilitates the greatest quantitative productivity for groups. However, transformational leadership provides more intellectual stimulation, better qualitative group performance, greater satisfaction among group members with the leadership, and an enhanced group cohesiveness. Leadership style is an important influence on the productivity of these technologically mediated groups.

Tasks of Group Leaders

In a small group, someone needs to do the mundane tasks of scheduling and organizing meetings. In addition, at least three meeting duties usually are performed by group leaders: facilitating the meeting, empowering members to ensure full participation, and managing conflicts.

Facilitating Meetings

Although a highly motivated group or team might be able to proceed effectively toward its goals during a meeting, one person usually needs to accept the primary responsibility for facilitating that process—making sure the discussion gets started, that issues are engaged and resolved in satisfactory ways, and that the larger goals of the group are kept in view. During a lively discussion, it may fall to the leader to keep the group on task. Although the leader may want to see the group explore as many relevant side issues as possible in specific areas, it is important to balance the time and energy the group spends on individual discussion points with the available time and resources the group has at its disposal. Some issues will warrant a larger share of the group's resources than others, and it becomes the leader's task to make sure that time and energy are appropriately allocated.

Empowering Group Members

In complex problem-solving tasks, a leader plays an important role empowering group members, encouraging full participation and consideration of all points of view, and developing the synergy for creative problem solving. In any group, there are usually those who feel entitled to expressing their opinions and contributing their perspectives and those who feel more reticent and feel their viewpoints may not be as valuable as those of others. For a group to gain the benefit of each member's unique contribution, a leader must encourage those who feel disempowered and estranged from the process to become involved. Engaging all group members, while avoiding making them or others uncomfortable, is the hallmark of a skillful leader.

Managing Conflict

Intrinsic to open discussion is the management of conflict. Conflict is an inevitable part of full participation by diverse participants. Knowing when to relieve and when to stimulate conflict is important to creative problem solving. When group members become so vested in ownership of their viewpoints that they dig in their heels and refuse to listen to others, a leader may need to back the group away from the point of conflict and search for common ground. However, if group members are reluctant to speak their minds for fear of causing disharmony or being thought foolish or uninformed, a leader may need to probe the divergent views to begin a full and open discussion of all aspects of an issue. Only through exploring as many perspectives as possible can the group forge an optimum solution. Thus, it is the leader who must coordinate the group process, knowing when to soothe and when to challenge group members.

Influences on Group Leadership

External Context

The system within which a group is formed is one of the factors that determines the style of leadership appropriate to that group. A group may be formed within the context of a *democratic,* an *autocratic,* or a *laissez-faire* system. A cooperative art gallery or natural foods store is frequently formed as a democratic organization. A small group formed within such a context would be influenced by that type of interaction and will likely expect collaborative decision making and leadership. On the other hand, many traditional manufacturing organizations are autocratic. They are based on hierarchic, top-down management, and a small group formed within that context may be influenced in its interactions by that larger system, with an assumption of formal leadership roles and the final authority to make decisions resting with the group leader or manager. In another context: a farmers' market often is held within a laissez-faire system in which a municipality sets aside a given area on certain days of the week for farmers to come and sell their produce. The farmers may not have any formal relationship to the system or to one another, aside from coming when they have something to sell. A small group of farmers formed into an association to decide where certain booths should be set up might have very little structure in its organizing and leadership processes, yet it may be efficient in its decision making.

Nature of the Task

In addition to being influenced by the context in which they are formed, groups are also influenced by the nature of the task for which they are convened. If the task is a straightforward one with an obvious best choice or with a choice that requires more administrative work than decision making, it might fall to a designated leader to come up with an answer with very little group input. For example, a small group from the food co-op convened to find the best prices and sources for oats and wheat might ask one person to do the research and come back to the group with a proposal for the group to accept or reject. On the other hand, a group of automobile workers convened to decide how best to form work teams to accomplish a new task may need creative thinking from each member and may choose to develop a collaborative solution. In these cases, the task may override the orientation of the larger system in the group's decision-making format. An example of this can be seen in many U.S. industry attempts to increase quality in the production process (Caroselli, 1992). Traditionally, industry management has dictated how quality is to be obtained and told employees what they must do to achieve the goal. Missing from this formula has been the involvement of the employees who do the actual work. For many employees, these quality mandates have been no different from any other management exhortations, such as cost cutting, reorganizing, safety rules, and summer schedules. However, once organizations began involving employees in deciding how best to resolve quality issues, listening to the employees and taking into account their experience, knowledge, and perceptions through group meetings, they experienced an immediate increase in quality. When employees' input was sought and incorporated into the development of a quality-improvement strategy, they felt a sense of ownership and a resulting commitment to implement their solutions (Kearns, 1990).

Interdependence of Group Members

Another factor in the type of leadership that groups need or want is the degree of *interdependence* between members. The more invested individual members are in the outcome of the group process, the more democratic they are likely to want the process to be. The less invested the members are, the more willing they are to let the leader make the decisions or to make no decisions at all. If the farmers at the market decide the location is not working for them, they might form a group to find a new location. Because they are each invested in the outcome, they may impose a structure on the group to ensure that all options are considered and that the needs of each farmer are taken into account.

According to Barge (1994, p. 181), "Leadership becomes more relevant and important to people in times of perceived crisis and turmoil" than at times when things are going relatively smoothly. In addition, within any group, certain tasks may require quick and decisive attention, while others warrant longer time for thoughtful consideration. An effective group leader helps the group make those distinctions and saves valuable time and energy for the important group issues. In general, the leader's task is to coordinate and communicate. This involves listening and responding, allowing for creative discussion and conflict, keeping the group on track, and maintaining civility throughout the process.

Leadership Styles

As in any human endeavor, maintaining balance within a dynamic, changing, morphogenic environment is a challenge not always successfully met. Although small groups are often best served by various participatory styles of leadership, research indicates that American leaders often tend to be a cross between John Wayne and the Lone Ranger (Bradford & Cohen, 1984; Harris & Nelson, 2008). Americans frequently tend to take as a leadership model that of the heroic, autocratic leader in a hierarchic system. We often look to the leader to solve problems or to oversee group efforts. The leader becomes the center of attention and is expected to run the show. Two specific types of heroic, autocratic leadership behaviors often prevail—the leader-as-technician and the *leader-as-conductor*. Another alternative is the leader-as-coach approach.

Leader-as-Technician

In a group set up to solve a problem with technical issues underlying it or with requirements for specialized knowledge or experience, we are apt to look to someone with expertise in that area to lead the process—the *leader-as-technician*. It becomes the tendency of the group to defer to that person whenever a difficult decision comes to the fore. If, for example, a group is convened to examine alternatives to traditional and expensive health-care options for an organization's employees, the group may look to a health-care provider to lead the discussion. When the topics under consideration move toward a discussion of the merits of various options for treatment of specific types of physical or psychological impairment, group members may turn to this leader for insight and direction. Soon it becomes apparent that it is easier and more efficient to simply ask the leader to determine the best course of treatment for various anticipated ills. As we have discussed in earlier sections, this may be efficient for technical concerns or for issues having little consequence, but when the issues involved are broad ranging and of relatively high importance to a number of people, the larger, less specifically technical aspects of these issues need to be considered as well.

It must be remembered that those with technical expertise, regardless of how deep or broad, are likely to be biased toward a particular point of view. It is easy to forget that most group members probably have some health experience of their own and may be able to offer insights from the perspective of a consumer that the health-care provider is apt to overlook. However, when group members think they do not have particular knowledge of the immediate issues under discussion, they may feel disempowered and become increasingly disengaged from the process. It is easy to see how the "expert" as the leader of this discussion could take the acknowledgment of her or his expertise as a cue to control the discussion and the eventual outcome of the decision-making process. As in any group process, the responsibility for leadership and the results of decision making are shared by group members, whether or not they acknowledge their part in it. Each member has the power and responsibility to participate in the leadership of the group.

Leader-as-Conductor

As part of the Western orientation toward hierarchic leadership models, we often assume that the leader should orchestrate the entire group process—the leader-as-conductor. While it is important and necessary to coordinate group efforts, the balance between micromanagement on the one side and laissez-faire non-management on the other is difficult to attain and maintain. Too often, in the U.S. model, leaders tend to err on the side of micromanagement of the group process. An obvious example is the designated leader who spends all his or her time looking over the shoulders of the group members, checking on every detail. More subtly, high-control managers may so closely define the group process that members are not free to pursue leads they find interesting or promising in unanticipated ways. In either case, jobs or other aspects of the group process that might have engaged individual creativity and commitment become routine and predictable, and group members may lose their motivation.

Our responses as group members and group leaders are embedded in our cultural paradigms and are therefore frequently difficult to see. Consequently, groups are often poorly formed and lack the training to take responsibility for the group process. Although it takes time, when groups are carefully formed and initiated with a view toward the goals expected to be achieved, and when group members are empowered by effective leaders, the result usually produces a positive effect on the decision-making process.

Leader-as-Coach

Effective coaches use problems as opportunities to build skills, morale, and experience (Harris & Nelson, 2008). A *leader-as-coach* explains, demonstrates, and leads, rather than ordering or cajoling. A coach focuses on the positive aspects of accomplishments while providing open and honest critical feedback. A coach relates one-on-one, person-to-person, to negotiate values, develop opportunities, facilitate change, stimulate innovation, and encourage trust. Peters and Austin (1985) identified at least five coaching roles. The first is to orient and educate when goals, roles, or conditions change and new skills are needed. The second is to sponsor and encourage when an individual has an outstanding skill and can make a special contribution. The third is to offer special encouragement and to make simple, brief corrections. The fourth is to counsel when problems interfere with work or damage performance, and to respond to setbacks. The fifth is to confront recurring problems and issues that are not resolved and that can have a long-term negative impact on the individual, the group, and the task. Coaches take a positive approach, focus on possible solutions rather than problems, treat others as equals, are supportive rather than judgmental, and help set realistic goals.

Summary

Effective leadership of small groups is as varied as the groups themselves and the contexts in which they are formed. Transformational or collaborative leadership styles have an appeal, but there are times and places in which other types of leaders may be more effective or efficient. When at sea, a ship is necessarily run as a hierarchic system. During a storm or in the midst of a tight docking maneuver, there is no time to sit and collaborate on a course of action. On the other hand, a democratically run food co-op would not so readily tolerate a leader who took on the authority of the captain of a ship.

The leaders of small groups have as their principal task that of ensuring that the group process moves toward a solution to the problem for which the group was convened. The more complex the problem and the more diverse the group, the more difficult and complex the role of the leader. If the task is a routine one or one on which little depends, the leader's role may be minimal. If the task is large, complex, and has possible far-reaching consequences, the role of the leader may be critical to ensuring the best outcome.

Although our underlying bias throughout this book is toward collaborative group work, there are contexts and tasks for which other decision-making strategies are more appropriate. Group leaders must be alert to these distinctions and guide the group toward the most efficient use of its time and energy. Some groups look to leadership for direction, others expect to be self-directed, and still others are ambivalent and unsure of their role in the process. Whether leaders are appointed, elected, or emerge, they become responsible for managing and defining, or helping the group define, the process, the goals, the tasks, and the patterns of interaction.

DISCUSSION QUESTIONS

1. What is the relationship between being a leader and the system in which a leader participates?

2. Provide an example from your own experience of a good leader. How well does your example fit with the definition of a good leader? How does it fit and how does it differ?

3. How do leaders act as arbiters of the interfaces between the group and the system?

4. Explain the dimensions of universality and situational dependence.

5. Outline the seven options for leadership styles provided by the Managerial Grid. What elements determine each of these options?

6. Distinguish between transactional and transformational leaders. Provide an example of each type of leader.

7. How can leaders be similar to chameleons? Explain.

8. Define vision and credibility as important characteristics for leaders.

9. Explain communication competence.

10. Leaders can be chosen, can be appointed, can be elected, can emerge, and may share responsibility. Provide an example of each type of leader from your own experience.

11. What are the three primary influences on group structure?

12. Why do leaders become technicians or conductors?

REFERENCES

Barge, J. K. (1994). *Leadership*. New York: St. Martin's Press.

Beebe, S. A., & Masterson, J. T. (1990). *Communicating in small groups: Principles and practices* (2nd ed.). Glenview, IL: Scott Foresman.

Bennis, W., & Nanus, G. (1997). Toward the new millennium. In G. R. Hichman (Ed.), *Leading organizations: Perspectives for a new era* (pp. 5–7). Thousand Oaks, CA: Sage.

Blake, R. R., & McCanse, A. A. (1991). *Leadership dilemmas—Grid solutions*. Houston: Gulf.

Blake, R. R., & Mouton, R. R. (1985). *The Managerial Grid III: The key to leadership excellence*. Houston: Gulf. [Originally published 1964]

Blake, R. R., Mouton, J. S., & Allen, R. L. (1987). *Spectacular teamwork*. New York: John Wiley.

Bormann, E. G. (1975). *Discussion and group methods: Theory and practice* (2nd ed.). New York: Harper & Row.

Bradford, D. L., & Cohen, C. J. (1984). *Managing for excellence: The guide for developing high performance in contemporary organizations*. New York: John Wiley.

Brilhart, J. K., & Galanes, G. J. (1995). *Effective group discussion* (8th ed.). Madison, WI: WCB Brown & Benchmark.

Buckingham, M., & Coffman, C. (1999). *First break all the rules: What the world's greatest managers do differently*. New York: Simon & Schuster.

Caroselli, M. (1992). *Quality-driven designs*. San Diego: Pfeiffer.

Clark, K. E., & Clark, M. B. (1990). *Measures of leadership*. West Orange, NJ: Leadership Library of America.

Counselman, E. F. (1991). Leadership in a long-term leaderless women's group. *Small Group Research, 22*(2), 240–257.

Cummings, T. G., & Worley, C. G. (2001). *Organizational development and change* (7th ed.). Florence, KY: South-Western.

Drucker, P. F. (1998). *Peter Drucker on the profession of management*. Boston: Harvard Business School Press.

Ellis, R. J., & Cronshaw, S. F. (1992). Self-monitoring and leader emergence. *Small Group Research, 23*(1), 113–129.

Ellis, A. P. J., Ilgen, D. R., & Hollenbeck, J. R. (2006). The effects of team leader race on performance evaluations. *Small Group Research, 37*(3), 295–332.

Gastil, J. (1994). A meta-analytic review of the productivity and satisfaction of democratic and autocratic leadership. *Small Group Research, 25*(3), 384–410.

Geier, J. C. (1967). A trait approach to the study of leadership in small groups. *Journal of Communication, 17*, 316–323.

Hackman, M. Z., & Johnson, C. E. (2000). *Leadership: A communication perspective* (3rd ed.). Prospect Heights, IL: Waveland.

Harris, T. E. (1992–1993). Toward effective employee involvement: An analysis of parallel and self-managing teams. *Journal of Applied Business Research, 9*(1), 25–33.

Harris, T. E., & Nelson, M. D. (2008). *Applied organizational communication: Theory and practice in a global environment*. New York: Lawrence Erlbaum Associates.

Hoyt, C. L., & Blascovich, J. (2003). Transformational and transactional leadership in virtual and physical environments. *Small Group Research, 34*(6), 678–715.

Hughes, R. L., Ginnett, R. C., & Curphy, G. J. (1998). Contingency theories of leadership. In G. R. Hichman (Ed.), *Leading organizations: Perspectives for a new era* (pp. 141–157). Thousand Oaks, CA: Sage.

Iacocca, L. (2007). *Where have all the leaders gone?* New York: Scribner.

Kearns, D. T. (1990). Leadership through quality. *Academy of Management Executive, 4*(2), 86–89.

Koch, S. C. (2005). Evaluative affect display toward male and female leaders in task-oriented groups. *Small Group Research, 36*(6), 678–703.

Kotter, J. P. (1988). *The leadership factor*. New York: The Free Press.

Northhouse, P. G. (2001). *Leadership theory and practice* (3rd ed.). Thousand Oaks, CA: Sage.

Pavitt, C., High, A. C., Tressler, K. E., & Winslow, J. K. (2007). Leadership communication during group resource dilemmas. *Small Group Research, 38*(4), 509–531.

Peters, T., & Austin, T. (1985). *A passion for excellence: The leadership difference*. New York: Random House.

Raes, A. M. L., Glunk, U., Heijltjes, M. G., & Roe, R. A. (2007). Top management team and middle managers. *Small Group Research, 38*(3), 360–386.

Roussin, C. J. (2008). Increasing trust, psychological safety, and team performance through dyadic leadership discovery. *Small Group Research, 39*(2), 224–248.

Schyns, B., & Felfe, J. (2006). The personality of followers and its effects on the perception of leadership. *Small Group Research, 37*(5), 522–539.

Vecchio, R. P., Bullis, R. C., & Brazil, D. M. (2006). The utility of situational leadership theory. *Small Group Research, 37*(5), 407–424.

Vogel, S. (2009, May 20). Money's nice, but a good boss is better. *Washington Post,* www.washingtonpost.com.

Yalom, I. (1985). *The theory and practice of group psychotherapy*. New York: Basic Books.

Yukl, G. (2006). *Leadership in organizations* (6th ed.). Upper Saddle River, NJ: Pearson Education.

CHAPTER

14 Observing and Evaluating a Small Group

CHAPTER OUTLINE

Systematic Feedback

Success and Failure

Observer–Member Scales
   Rating Scales
   Post-Meeting Evaluation Forms

Observer Feedback Guidelines

Individual Role Behavior

Verbal Interaction and Content Analysis

Ethical Reflection

Summary

Discussion Questions

References

CHAPTER OBJECTIVES

- Describe four ways of learning how to make small groups successful.
- Discuss the design, types, and uses of rating scales.
- Describe post-meeting evaluation forms.
- Explain the key question regarding information usefulness.
- Outline observer feedback guidelines.
- Describe the evaluation of verbal interactions and content analysis.

KEY TERMS

Content-analysis procedures
Espoused ethics
Ethics-in-use
Formative evaluations
Informal roles

Likert scale
Maintenance-oriented roles
Observer feedback
Post-meeting evaluation forms
Rating scales

Self-centered roles
Summative evaluations
Systematic feedback
Task-oriented roles
Verbal interaction analysis

246

Faced with growing problems and shared threats, concerned groups of citizens pull together, form associations and networks, and pursue shared objectives of peace and sustainability.

Business leaders recognize the groundswell of change in the thinking and expectations of their clients and customers and respond with goods and services that meet the shift in demand.

(Laszlo, 2006, p. xxiii).

For small groups to know they are effective, they must have some means of evaluating their success or failure. During the group process, members must decide what specific activities should be continued, stopped, or altered. Just completing a project on time does not make a group successful. The process of the group must be evaluated, as well as the short- and long-term consequences of implementing its solutions.

This chapter examines the value of systematic feedback and offers some techniques for evaluating small groups.

Systematic Feedback

Feedback, when done well by focusing on specific behaviors and actions, can have a positive effect on a group and on individual performance. Feedback is meant to guide future behavioral change for group members. However, compliments such as "That was very good" or criticisms such as "You needed more preparation" leave the receivers little to consider in terms of improvements (Baldwin, Bommer, & Rubin, 2008).

There are four ways of obtaining feedback to improve a group's future success. The first is to read a great deal about groups and teams. Although reading and research can provide theories and insights, they offer no practical experience. We can discover why groups and teams are important and what made a particular team successful, but we may lack the ability to apply this information to a new situation.

The second method is participation in small groups. By using intuition and a gut feeling about effectiveness, we can evaluate and adjust during and after the group process. Although we learn by doing, our ability to observe our actions while we are simultaneously engaging in those activities is limited. We may also be engaged in counterproductive small group behaviors and never realize it, because the group continues to be successful in spite of itself. When new demands are placed on our small group abilities, our old behaviors, such as leadership and empowerment behaviors, may no longer suffice. Since we need theories and principles to guide our behaviors, combining the first two steps can be helpful, but even then, we may not know how well we are doing.

A third approach is to obtain external evaluation and advice. This is a useful addition to the first two approaches, if the observer is equipped with tools and knowledge to effectively provide feedback. An observer, however, must provide more than an overall evaluation that it "went pretty well."

A final source of feedback is our own reflection and analysis. In some cases, the straightest route to finding out how well a group did is to ask the members. The group is in the best position to know if goals and objectives have been completed. As a group member, we can give and receive *systematic feedback* to and from other group participants. A combination of all these techniques can provide the most comprehensive view for the evaluation and can reflect the participants' reactions to the process as well as external measures of effectiveness (Phillips & Stone, 2002).

Success and Failure

Although being less than perfect is failure to some individuals, and not "getting by" is failure to others, improvement can occur in either situation if we are aware of the causes and cures for the failure. One sage observer stated that the person who makes no mistakes usually makes nothing. Another concluded that failure is a success if we learn from it. Recognizing failure is one of the surest routes to success, if we examine why we failed.

Since successful small group behaviors require specific actions and behaviors, when we begin the process of becoming more effective in groups we are unlikely to be resounding successes every time. Sound, well-targeted feedback can help the process and provide guidelines that focus on improvement efforts in terms of specific, behavioral activities.

To become an effective group member and leader, we need to maximize the amount of input we receive (Northhouse, 2004). Individual and group feedback, both internal and external to the group, can provide valuable information and opportunities for growth.

Observer–Members Scales

Group members can act as participant observers, or outside observers can be used. In general, members should not evaluate a meeting, one another, or themselves while participating. If you are directly involved in the work, you will probably not be, nor should be, a dispassionate observer, and you may not be able to concentrate on the team's work while attempting to effectively evaluate. Two very different skills are involved here—participation and evaluation. Not only is it difficult to concentrate on the group process while we are evaluating (it is difficult to do two things well at once), but while evaluating, we may give off nonverbal signals that lead other members to think we are not interested or are critical of them, the group, or the process.

When appropriate, consultant observers not directly involved with the group work can provide excellent insights. Recognizing this as an important source of growth and development, corporations systematically offer evaluations of a specific team's process by outside observers to help the team develop.

The focus of the evaluation should be on the skills desired by the group members and the fundamental skills required by all groups. A review of the previous chapters will provide some topics. Some examples of topics include content (knowledge of issues, how well researched), critical thinking skills (ability to examine the issues beyond the obvious or apparent, willingness to listen to others), higher-order thinking skills (integrate knowledge, understand impact of different ideas), organization (understanding and use of forming, norming, storming, and performing phases), communication (verbal, nonverbal, feedback, clarity), problem solving (definitions, common ground), and solutions (complete, clearly articulated, future actions specified). As these examples make clear, evaluations should be for specific group activities.

When outside observers are not available, many team development programs suggest appointing a group member to be an observer. This task is handed around among the group members. We learn about a process when we are asked to evaluate it, so the group or team can benefit, and each member becomes more insightful. In addition, we often can learn about how to improve our own performance by observing others.

Longstanding groups can set aside specific times to periodically analyze their group process. Increasingly, professional teams earmark the last 10 minutes of any team meeting for reflecting time, giving the group a chance to review its process. This ongoing team development facilitates continued growth.

The quality of any of these approaches to evaluation, however, will be enhanced with specific tools, and the list of items that can be analyzed is limited only by the time available.

Rating Scales

When we ask "How well did we do?" we are setting the stage for the effective use of *rating scales*. With our small group, we can ask questions ranging from "How well did the group analyze the topic?" to "How fully did all members participate?" Responses may be "very well," "adequately," or "poorly." Depending on the degree of specificity desired, you can make the scale more precise, such as using a *Likert scale* with a 1 to 5 or a 1 to 7 rating, equating the numbers with terms such as *very adequate, moderately adequate, unsure, moderately inadequate,* and *inadequate.* Likert scales are popular and easy to use, as shown in this example.

Likert Scale Example

"The group worked well together" (check one):

Strongly agree   _____
Moderately agree   _____
Agree somewhat   _____
Unsure   _____
Disagree somewhat   _____
Moderately disagree   _____
Strongly disagree   _____

The list of questions should be adapted to the particular activity you wish to evaluate and may include leadership, group climate, nonverbal communication, or organization of the problem and solution analysis. A simple, quick, and all-purpose rating scale could include issues such as clarity of problem analysis, equality of participation, listening to one another, and willingness to engage in dialogue and closure.

A scale allows observers and members to provide feedback that can be translated into some definable measure. The results, if gathered from a variety of sources, can also be tabulated to obtain a total score.

The topics included in the rating scale should be relevant to the expected behaviors for a group or team. Each group will have specific concerns that can be included in the rating scale. Possible topics can include any issues addressed in this text, including verbal and nonverbal communication, balanced participation, focus on group success, cohesiveness, stages, utilizing diversity, listening and feedback, decision making, problem solving, creativity, conflict management, and leadership. Table 14.1 shows typical areas of concern, but any of the issues examined in preceding chapters would be appropriate for use on a self-evaluation rating scale as well.

To be most effective, the rating scale should cover a variety of topics. Sometimes these are developed into a Likert scale approach, mentioned above, with the seven categories of strongly agree (7), moderately agree (6), agree somewhat (5), unsure (4), disagree somewhat (3), moderately disagree (2), and strongly disagree (1). Sometimes, for simplicity, evaluation rating scales are reduced to five categories indicating strongly agree (5), mildly agree (4), uncertain (3), mildly disagree (2), strongly disagree (1). Alternately, unique scales are developed to measure something particularly important to the group process, as shown in the following example.

TABLE 14.1   Rating Scale Topics—Possible Areas of Concern

Amount of participation by the members
Role acceptance by members—Do members do what needs to be done?
Leadership qualities and leaders' abilities to handle disagreements and conflicts
Appropriateness of leadership
Quality of research
Shared research activities and their success
Communication skills, including listening, feedback, and clarity
Internal process issues, such as clarifying and summarizing
Creative processes and actions
Willingness and ability to confront issues
Civilized disagreement that took advantage of diversity of ideas
Appropriate decision-making approaches, such as consensus
Quality of climate
Balancing of participation to allow all members to take part
Shared leadership and/or responsibility
Other issues

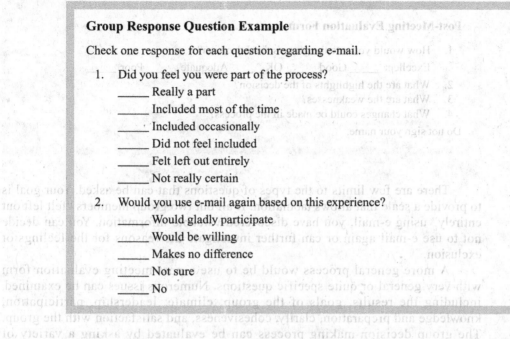

Group Response Question Example

Check one response for each question regarding e-mail.

1. Did you feel you were part of the process?
    _____ Really a part
    _____ Included most of the time
    _____ Included occasionally
    _____ Did not feel included
    _____ Felt left out entirely
    _____ Not really certain

2. Would you use e-mail again based on this experience?
    _____ Would gladly participate
    _____ Would be willing
    _____ Makes no difference
    _____ Not sure
    _____ No

Rating scales used by the group members or outside observers offer a systematic feedback mechanism. The value of ratings lies in the specificity of the information they provide. Rather than just saying something was good or bad, a scaling device provides a relative comparison. When we combine several forms together, we have a broad-based set of information.

Post-Meeting Evaluation Forms

Post-meeting evaluation forms are questionnaires that seek specific feedback from participants about a particular activity or meeting. This feedback is intended for internal group consumption in an effort to improve the quality of the group process. Rather than finding out at the end of the process that no one thought the meetings were useful, the evaluation forms offer immediate opportunities to improve. Specific issues such as leadership, listening, nonverbal interactions, member participation, and climate can be analyzed.

The most important characteristic is that the forms are completed anonymously by members. The results are tallied and reported to the group as soon as possible. As with the individual rating scales, the post-meeting evaluation forms can be tailor-made to the group's needs. If a group spends a great deal of time on e-mail, they might include questions regarding the format of the e-mail, such as, "Was there timely response by other members?" or "Were messages clear?" A brief example of a post-meeting set of evaluation questions follows in the box.

Post-Meeting Evaluation Form

1. How would you rate the group's final decision?
   Excellent _____ Good _____ OK _____ Adequate _____ Poor _____
2. What are the highlights of the decision?
3. What are the weaknesses?
4. What changes could be made in the process?

Do not sign your name.

There are few limits to the types of questions that can be asked. Your goal is to provide a scale that allows tabulation. If all but two group members "felt left out entirely" using e-mail, you have discovered valuable information. You can decide not to use e-mail again or can further investigate the reasons for the feelings of exclusion.

A more general process would be to use a post-meeting evaluation form with very general or quite specific questions. Numerous issues can be examined, including the results, goals of the group, climate, leadership, participation, knowledge and preparation, clarity, cohesiveness, and satisfaction with the group. The group decision-making process can be evaluated by asking a variety of specific questions using a scale from 1 to 7, with 1 being not at all and 7 being a great deal.

Here are some sample questions:

1. How clearly did the group analyze the problem?
2. How well did the group analyze its goal or objective?
3. How clearly was the problem articulated?
4. Was creativity encouraged?
5. Did the group take time to let the analysis develop?
6. Did the group consider all possible solutions?
7. Were the positive consequences outlined?
8. Were the negative consequences outlined?
9. Was sufficient information used in the process?

A team effectiveness critique could include specific interaction issues. In this case, providing specific directions to evaluators on the meaning of key terms will prove useful (Beebe, Mottet, & Roach, 2004).

For example:

1 = Very poor. The group/team failed to demonstrate behaviors, and/or behaviors were demonstrated without proficiency. This requires careful and specific improvement.

3 = Adequate. The group/team demonstrated some behaviors, and all demonstrated behaviors were moderately proficient. This requires some careful attention to improvement.

5 = Excellent. The group/team demonstrated all important behaviors with proficiency. This requires no additional attention.

The most important characteristic of any evaluation form is *the usefulness of the information to your group or team*. The nine items on the Sample Feedback Form shown in Figure 14.1, for example, might be relatively meaningless in a different context. Remember that some of the issues an effective team can be rated on goals and objectives, high standards of performance, broad-based participation by all members, conflict-management skills, problem recognition, decision making by consensus, climate, synergy, cohesiveness, positive working atmosphere, constructive criticism, individual recognition, hidden agendas, valuing others, clarity of roles by members, and flexibility.

FIGURE 14.1 Sample Feedback Form

Team: _____ Date: _____

Instructions:

Please indicate your assessment of your team.

Circle one of the numbers from 1 to 7 for each of the nine areas of concern.

1. Goals and Objectives

There is a lack of commonly understood goals and objectives.				Team members understand and agree on goals and objectives.		
1	2	3	4	5	6	7

2. Utilization of Resources

All member resources are not recognized and/or utilized.				Member resources are fully recognized and utilized.		
1	2	3	4	5	6	7

3. Trust and Conflict

There is little trust among members, and conflict is evident.				There is a high degree of trust among members, and conflict is dealt with openly and worked through.		
1	2	3	4	5	6	7

4. Leadership

One person dominates and leadership roles are not carried out or shared.				There is full participation in leadership, and leadership roles are shared by members.		
1	2	3	4	5	6	7

(continued)

FIGURE 14.1 (*continued*)

5. Control and Procedures

There is little control, and there is a lack of procedures to guide team functioning.

There are effective procedures to guide team functioning; team members support these procedures.

| 1 | 2 | 3 | 4 | 5 | 6 | 7 |

6. Interpersonal Communication

Communication among members is open and participative.

Communication among members is guarded and closed.

| 1 | 2 | 3 | 4 | 5 | 6 | 7 |

7. Problem Solving/Decision Making

The team has no agreed-upon approaches to problem solving and decision making.

The team has well-established and agreed-upon approaches to problem solving and decision making.

| 1 | 2 | 3 | 4 | 5 | 6 | 7 |

8. Experimentation/Creativity

The team is rigid and does not experiment with how things are done.

The team experiments with different ways of doing things and is creative in its approach.

| 1 | 2 | 3 | 4 | 5 | 6 | 7 |

9. Evaluation

The group never evaluates its functioning or process.

The group often evaluates its functioning and process.

| 1 | 2 | 3 | 4 | 5 | 6 | 7 |

A excellent group or team exercise is to develop a set of criteria specific to the group. Few activities can be as educational as a group discussion regarding what factors are most important to your particular group. The resulting feedback from the evaluation is customized and, therefore, made immediately useful to the group. As a starting place, take any combination of the standard feedback instruments provided in this chapter and pick the items most salient to your group or team. If you are involved in a semester-long project, consider using *formative evaluations,* which are done during the process, in addition to *summative evaluations,* which are done at the end. The goal should be to continually improve how the group is functioning as well as completing its tasks. How we view the group process at the end can be quite subjective. It is important to provide continual feedback, so that the group can modify its activities to increase success (Crews & North, 2000). Often, open-ended questions such as "How effective is the group?" "How can the group improve?" and "What needs to change to improve the group?" can help keep the group on track.

Observer Feedback Guidelines

Obtaining individual *observer feedback* on the group process is also useful. When you are asked to provide individual written or oral feedback, observe the following guidelines:

1. Avoid generalizations such as "well done." The more *specific* the feedback, the better.

2. Focus on *behaviors* that can be changed.

3. *Do not debate or argue* with the group you are evaluating. Your evaluation is meant to be useful to the group. This is not a forum for your ideas or analysis. Provide your observations, insights, or opinions, but do not demand that the group accept them.

4. *Do not micromanage* the group process. As an observer, your job is not to go over every detail of the process. Choose specific areas and develop them well. In general, a full analysis of two or three items will be much more useful than covering everything.

5. *Remember your role.* An evaluator should function as a facilitator and developer. What will your comments do to enhance the group process? How can the individuals and the group utilize the comments? Avoid statements that say "I didn't like" without providing specific explanations regarding the value of the "liking."

6. *Accentuate the positive aspects.* Always start with the positive and try to spend most of your time finding things the group did right.

7. End with *specific suggestions* for improvement.

8. Be *clear and concise* if you present your ideas orally or in writing.

9. *Compliment in public and criticize in private* is an accepted practice in most professional settings. This rule of thumb definitely applies to small group settings.

10. In an organizational setting, developing positive relationships during the feedback process will repay itself time and again. The goal is not to find fault, blame individuals, or criticize the effort. Your job is to help the group or team develop and improve.

Individual Role Behavior

As discussed earlier (see Chapter 3) our group role behavior falls into three broad classifications—task, maintenance, and self-centered. *Task-oriented roles* assist the group in accomplishing its goal. *Maintenance-oriented roles* focus on the social aspects. *Self-centered roles* are concerned with individual needs. These are *informal roles* that develop *during* the group transactions.

You can use these categories in a single evaluation sheet or let the group decide which ones need to be highlighted. Some honest questioning, looking out for alternative concerns, and reminding the group of past events can be quite useful. In the end, avoid a cookie-cutter approach to group evaluation.

Once again, the most effective device for your team or group might be a combination of the standard issues and your own group's interests.

Verbal Interaction and Content Analysis

Two additional devices that can be useful for group process evaluation are the *verbal interaction analysis* and *content analysis procedures*. The verbal interaction analysis traces the number of times members address one another. If a group has five members, put the names in a starlike diagram reflecting the seating pattern used in the discussion. The first time Tom speaks to Sheila, draw an arrow from Tom to Sheila. As everyone begins participating, draw the arrows as they apply. When Tom speaks to Sheila a second time, mark the arrow. As Figure 14.2 demonstrates, the markings begin to show the interaction patterns. Not only does this analysis indicate who might not be participating, but it also shows who has emerged as the leader during this particular discussion. We can also decide if someone is dominating the discussion.

Content analysis is used to analyze the type of comments made. You also can keep track of how often they are made. Any of the lists we have suggested can be used for a content analysis evaluation. If you want to know who displayed the most leadership behaviors, develop a list of desired leadership activities and then keep track of how often each group member engages in these activities. The list of individual behaviors

FIGURE 14.2   Verbal Interaction Talk Patterns

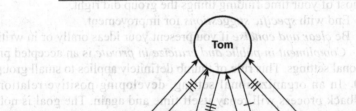

would also work for content analysis. Verbal interaction and content analysis processes allow observers to be very specific in analyzing particular behaviors.

There is a "deep belief in Western cultures of the value of quantitative forms of measurement, at the expense of other forms of assessment" (Senge et al., 1999, p. 284). However, using qualitative measures linked to some common themes, as addressed in this text, is also valuable. Quantitative measures can be simpler to examine and calculate, but qualitative measures are often richer in content. An excellent alternative to ensure a degree of usefulness in the feedback is to schedule a debriefing session for the intact group or team with an external evaluator. Self-examination and evaluation, without placing too much emphasis on individual behavior, can be insightful. Having a skilled external facilitator present can make the process go more smoothly and the result more worthwhile.

Ethical Reflection

You can keep a journal of the group process. The value of an ongoing journal of activities derives from the fact that we tend to forget important milestones as the process moves forward. When we go back to earlier records, we can recover important insights regarding missed opportunities.

Finally, ethical decision-making behaviors provide an excellent opportunity for reflection. Paul and Strbiak (1997) followed a framework provided by Argyris and Schon (1974) in developing a model for evaluating a communicator's ethical decision-making behaviors. Their model can be adapted to small groups by analyzing and comparing a group's espoused ethics and ethics-in-use. *Espoused ethics* are the ethical principles a group states as governing its actions. The group's *ethics-in-use* are the ethical principles that appear to actually underlie the group's behavior and can be inferred from observing its behaviors. A group's actual behavior is ethical when it is congruent with the espoused ethics of the group. Evaluating a group's ethical behavior requires asking the group to articulate a set of ethical principles it believes should govern its actions and then having the group review its actions, decisions, and solutions to determine how well those behaviors align with the original or espoused set of ethical principles. A lack of clear ethical behavior promotes distrust, which ultimately will diminish or destroy group actions (Covey, 2006).

Summary

Anything worth doing is worth doing well. Systematic feedback is the key to successful group processes. Observer/member scales are an excellent means of focusing on specific areas for improvement. Rating scales allow a broad range of analysis of concepts ranging from individual actions to leadership effectiveness. Individual role behaviors can be the basis for feedback. Verbal interaction and content analysis can focus on particular behaviors.

We all hope our groups will be successful, but to get the most from our group experiences, we need to incorporate learning. Elbert Hubbard, an American writer, is credited with saying that "A failure is a person who has blundered but is not capable of cashing in on the experience" (Boone, 1992, p. 239). Or, to put it another way: There are no mistakes, only opportunities. The only difference between ability and luck may be the ability to avoid a mistake and repeat a success a second time. These comments suggest the importance of feedback and learning as we develop small group communication skills.

DISCUSSION QUESTIONS

1. What are the four ways of learning about how to make small groups successful? Which ones have you used? Were they successful in teaching general group effectiveness concepts?

2. Why use a consultant or an observer for a small group?

3. How can a rating scale be used to evaluate a small group?

4. What issues would be useful to include on a rating scale?

5. How can post-meeting evaluation forms be used? What are their most important characteristics?

6. Discuss the guidelines for providing observer feedback to a group.

7. How can an observer utilize interaction between group members to provide feedback?

8. What are some examples of espoused ethics versus ethics-in-use?

REFERENCES

Argyris, C., & Schon, D. A. (1974). *Theory in practice: Increasing professional effectiveness.* New York: Wiley-Interscience.

Baldwin, T. T., Bommer, W. H., & Rubin, R. S. (2008). *Developing management skills: What great managers know and do.* Boston: McGraw-Hill.

Beebe, S. A., Mottet, T. P., & Roach, K. D. (2004). *Training and development: Enhancing communication and leadership skills.* Boston: Pearson.

Boone, L. E. (1992). *Quotable business.* New York: Random House.

Crews, T. B., & North, A. B. (2000). Team evaluation (Part 2 of 2). *Instructional Strategies, 16*(2), 1–4.

Covey, S. M. R. (2006). *The speed of trust: The one thing that changes everything.* New York: Free Press.

Laszlo, E. (2006). *The chaos point: The world at the crossroads.* Charlottesville, VA: Hampton Roads.

Northhouse, P. G. (2004). *Leadership: Theory and practice* (3rd ed.). Thousand Oaks, CA: Sage.

Phillips, J. J., & Stone, R. D. (2002). *How to measure training results.* New York: McGraw-Hill.

Senge, P., Kleiner, A., Roberts, C., Ross, R., Roth, G., & Smith, B. (1999). *The dance of change: The challenges of sustaining momentum in learning organizations.* New York: Doubleday.

C H A P T E R

15

Computer-Mediated Small Group Communication

CHAPTER OUTLINE

Using Technology to Communicate
Computer-Mediated Communication (CMC)
Group Performance in CMC
Social Networking Through Facebook

Influences of the CMC Medium on Communication
Social Presence
Some Effects of CMC on Group Processes

Choosing a Medium for the Effective Use of CMC
Choosing a Medium for the Communication Task
Finding a Language Demand–Technology Fit

Matching Media Richness to the Communication Function

Adopting Effective Group Communication Strategies for CMC
Facilitating Effective CMC Group Communication
Leading a CMC Group Meeting

Summary

Discussion Questions

References

CHAPTER OBJECTIVES

- Define computer-mediated communication (CMC).
- Describe audio- and videoconferencing.
- Discuss the effects of CMC on group processes.
- Explain the concept of social presence and the influences of media richness and synchronous communication.
- Describe methods for choosing an appropriate communication medium by the communication task, language demand–technology fit, and the communication function.
- Discuss group process and leadership responsibilities for effective small group CMC.

KEY TERMS

Asynchronous communication
Audio-conferencing

Audio clipping
Audio delay

Computer-mediated
communication (CMC)

259

Computer ethics
Communication function
Communication task

Face-to-face (FTF) groups
Media richness
Social presence

Synchronous communication
Videoconferencing

The Moto Razr V3 ultrathin cellphone with its anodized aluminum finish and sil-ver, black, or magenta color was created by a development team in virtual secrecy, even within Motorola. The team of electrical engineers, mechanical engineers, and industrial designers brought diverse expertise to the project and each member offered his or her particular talent, experience, and perspective. Together, they designed, fashioned, and produced one of the most successful cellphones ever created. Incred-ibly, Motorola sold almost as many Razrs in 2005 and 2006 as Apple sold iPods! Well, "Hello, Moto!"

(Lashinsky, 2006).

Using Technology to Communicate

Technology affects our communication, our relationships, and our lives. It is not a ques-tion of if we will use technology to communicate with each other; it is a question of when, how, and how well. *Computer-mediated communication (CMC)* moves commu-nication a step beyond time and space, allowing it to be "instantaneously asynchro-nous" or "nearly synchronous" and geographically prolific by co-occurring in multiple geographic locations at once. From a human communication perspective, CMC is a so-cial and psychological phenomenon, not just a technological one (Shedletsky & Aitken, 2004).

To stay competitive in today's electronically connected economy, corporations are using communication technology to connect geographically dispersed group members (Cummings & Worley, 2005; Friedman, 2005). For example, MySQL, the $40 million computer software maker, employs 320 workers in 25 countries, most of whom work from home. The technologies used by today's corporate workers include e-mail to share documents as attachments; websites to post company information; electronic bulletin boards and blogs to carry on group discussions; computer mes-saging and group chat software; *audio-conferencing;* webcams and videoconferenc-ing software; YouTube for digital video presentations; Facebook and other social networking sites; and meeting as groups of avatars in virtual worlds like Second Life. Effectively managing these technology-connected work teams requires a new set of management and communication skills to keep employees feeling connected and valued (Hyatt, 2006).

To be effective with the medium, we must understand something about the technology and its multiple influences on small group communication. We must plan for its use and adopt strategies for being effective in that communication (Rogers, 1999). Hacker and Steiner (2001) suggested that we need more than access to the Internet to become successful users of it. We need the opportunity to develop our skills and comfort level with the medium, overcoming our anxieties and developing a positive motivation based on our perception of the tangible benefits to be gained in our interpersonal, work-related, financial, and social interests. In this chapter, we explore some of the ways groups use communication technologies, the communication challenges posed by these technologies, and the ways in which groups communicate effectively while using them.

Computer-Mediated Communication (CMC)

Computer-mediated communication (CMC) describes communication that takes place through a variety of media and provides distributed group members with video, audio, and text-based messaging capabilities (Graetz, Boyle, Kimble, Thompson, & Garloch, 1998). These facilities include computer and audio and *video conferencing* systems, blogs, instant messaging, computer chat rooms, electronic mail, bulletin boards, Facebook, Second Life, Twitter, YouTube and other social networking facilities. Many of these CMC systems have software, sometimes called groupware, specifically designed to help groups discuss issues, make decisions, and communicate effectively.

Although some early authors limited the use of CMC to text-based computer-mediated message systems (for example, Walther, 1996), we include audio- and video-conferencing systems in our discussion of CMC because these systems are becoming increasingly available and useful to groups in their decision-making and problem-solving communication, and because they are increasingly used in combination with text-based systems.

CMC, whether text, audio, or video based, has an effect on the communication in a group. CMC group members tend to focus more on the task and instrumental aspects of the process than on the personal and social aspects of the group. Thus, they tend to be more content oriented and less social–emotional in their communication style than face-to-face groups are (Walther, 1996). Individuals in CMC groups tend to feel more anonymous in their participation and to detect less individual personality in the other group members. They frequently participate more equally, and low-status members often contribute more freely. They also communicate more uninhibitedly, sometimes generating more negative messages and experiencing more difficulty in attaining a group consensus. Although CMC groups sometimes have a higher level of conflict, they can also display positive effect and frequently engage in less argumentation. They are less likely to have an emergent leader and are more likely to have a decentralized and less permanent leadership. CMC groups also tend to deemphasize personal relationships and experience less interpersonal attraction (Conrad & Poole, 2002). However, they can develop interpersonally positive relationships when groups continue to meet over time (Conrad & Poole, 2002; Rains, 2005).

Metzger and Flanagan (2002) report that people in general are more active in their use of CMC than they are when using more traditional communication media such as books, magazines, newspapers, telephones, and television. People report their CMC to be more goal directed and intentional. They use CMC to purposely seek out specific types of information and entertainment rather than to casually browse or "surf the Web" just to pass the time.

Cai (2004) reported that computer use serves different functions than more traditional media. His research showed that people who gave up the use of the computer for a day did not increase the amount of time they watched television or used other media. Giving up television viewing for a day, however, significantly increased the time they spent using other, more traditional media such as the radio, VCR, and telephone. Warren and Bluma (2002) in their study of 180 children, reported that the average grade-school child logged on less than three times a week from home, but only a small minority of the parents they surveyed used an Internet filter. Most reported making rules about Internet surfing, and more than 70% of the computers the children used at home were located in an open family area such as the kitchen, dining room, or living room. College and university students use computer-mediated communication in chat rooms, instant messaging, and e-mail largely to develop and maintain personal relationships. Collectively, these findings suggest that computer use, with its qualities of interactivity, hypertextuality, synchronous multimedia, and relative lack of gatekeeping, serves a different function than other, more traditional communication media. Small groups use CMC in different ways to fulfill different communication functions, as well.

Group Performance in CMC

The networked-conferencing model of computer-mediated communication (CMC) appears to enhance the small group communication process in a number of ways. CMC has been shown to facilitate active participation and collaboration among team members and to increase the equality of participation among group members (Schrire, 2004, 2006). CMC helps foster a positive team-building environment that promotes group member engagement and collaborative problem solving (Gaimster, 2007). CMC groups often participate in a more collaborative analysis, evaluation, and resolution of the problem and engage in vigorous debate, showing greater interactivity and cognitive effort among the group members as they work toward a solution (Vess, 2005). Throughout these decision-making processes, group members are more equally active in their participation and negotiation (Wood & Fassett, 2003). Newer forms of CMC that provide a greater sense of *social presence* enhance these positive aspects of the medium even more. Sherblom, Withers, and Leonard (2009) show that groups meeting in Second Life, an online three-dimensional virtual world, are both task efficient and relational in accomplishing their group's goals. Although they can experience technical challenges with the Internet, in accessing Second Life, and in coping with the extra effort and reduced nonverbal cues of communicating through text chat, group members find Second Life to be an effective medium for group communication. Group members are able to develop a sense of social presence within their working group, engage in appropriate social–emotional communication among members, and develop interpersonal working relationships. Second Life is particularly useful for group discussion, separating personal communication from discussions of task, and fostering a professional

A Small Group Meeting in Second Life
(Photo: Sherblom, 2009)

orientation to group participation, collaboration, and brainstorming. Facilitating speaker turn taking and developing good listening habits among group members can become issues for the group, but for communicators who consciously work through the communication medium to achieve their goals, group collaboration, team building, and problem solving have been shown to be facilitated and enhanced by the medium.

CMC groups often generate more unique ideas than *face-to-face (FTF)* groups but also take longer to reach consensus (Olaniran, 1994). CMC appears to reduce group members' abilities to criticize and informally pressure one another to conform to a particular idea or way of thinking during the group discussion. CMC groups are less likely to reach consensus than FTF groups in a short amount of time and may be less likely to discuss some of the important attributes of problem-solving cases but, given time, can arrive at quality decisions (McGrath & Hollingshead, 1994).

Bordia (1997) reviewed the ways in which CMC groups differ from FTF groups. CMC groups generally take longer to complete a task, and within the same time period produce fewer remarks than FTF groups do. However, CMC groups usually perform better than FTF groups on idea-generation tasks, and there is greater equality of participation in CMC groups. When time is limited, CMC groups perform better than FTF groups on tasks that are less involving but worse on tasks requiring more social–emotional interaction. Given enough time, CMC groups can perform as well as FTF groups in developing social–emotional relationships. There is reduced normative social pressure in CMC groups, and the perception and understanding of other group members is often poorer in CMC groups. When time is

TABLE 15.1   Computer Mediated Communication (CMC) Compared to Face-to-Face (FTF) Group Discussion

1. CMC groups take longer to complete a task.
2. In a given time period, CMC groups produce fewer remarks than FTF groups.
3. CMC groups perform better than FTF groups on idea-generation tasks.
4. There is greater equality of participation in CMC groups.
5. When time is limited, CMC groups perform better than FTF groups on tasks that are less involving.
6. When time is limited, CMC groups perform worse on tasks requiring more social–emotional interaction, but given enough time CMC groups perform as well as FTF groups.
7. There is reduced normative social pressure in CMC groups.
8. Perception (understanding) of other participants and task is poorer in CMC groups.
9. In CMC, when time is limited, the communication partner is perceived less charitably.
10. CMC groups have a higher incidence of uninhibited behavior and a sense of anonymous deindividuation.
11. CMC group members evidence less attitude change.

Source: Bordia (1997).

limited, other group members are less charitably perceived. CMC groups have a higher incidence of uninhibited comments, which appears to come from a sense of anonymous deindividuation. CMC group members also show less attitude change resulting from their discussions. These differences are listed in Table 15.1.

Social Networking Through Facebook

A social networking site like Facebook can be used by groups to maintain both the social and task aspects of their relationships. Use of Facebook is known to positively influence an individual's social–psychological well-being, self-esteem, and sense of satisfaction with life. A positive relationship between Facebook use and the ability to maintain personal and social relationships is also suggested (Ellison, Steinfield, & Lampe, 2007). Facebook can help a group develop strong positive interpersonal attitudes among its members and facilitate their sense of psychological closeness through the sharing of personal stories, beliefs, comments about oneself, and responses from other group members. Mazer, Murphy, and Simonds (2007) show that using Facebook in this way can facilitate immediacy, self-disclosure, and humor, and can stimulate motivation and commitment among group members.

Audio- and Videoconferencing.   A number of electronic meeting systems—both professional and personal computer-based web-based systems such as Yahoo! Messenger, Windows Live Messenger, and Second Life—provide audio- and videoconferencing facilities. These systems allow computer users to communicate verbally using headsets, microphones, speakers, and an audio connection or interact visually through webcams (or video cameras), as they engage in text-based chat, and exchange text and graphic information.

The quality of the audio is important. Poor audio quality, whether due to a lack of vocal intelligibility, *audio delay,* or *audio clipping,* is distracting to participants and problematic to holding an effective group meeting. Some systems can make speaker intelligibility difficult if all participants are not equally well heard. Some speakers' voices may be too soft to be adequately carried by the system or may become garbled because of their distance from the system's microphone. Audio delays can occur when an audio signal must travel over a long distance from one meeting site to another. In face-to-face meetings, we anticipate simultaneous verbal and nonverbal responses to our comments and are accustomed to very short pause intervals between conversational utterances (100 milliseconds). In audio- and videoconference meetings, when the geographical locations of groups are distant, even a fast communication medium may not provide this instantaneous response. Relatively short audio delays can interfere with the smooth flow of a meeting, causing participants to become impatient and ill at ease. Audio delays can also create a perception that participants at the distant location are not well prepared for the meeting or that they are cognitively slow and verbally inarticulate. Audio clipping occurs when a participant's microphone fails to pick up the beginning of an utterance or drops the end of the utterance. This can happen in systems using voice-activated microphones that turn on and off with the presence of sound. In these systems, single-word responses may be lost. Participants who interrupt one another, talk over one another, cough, move chairs, or even attempt to provide vocalized support for an idea or comment may make it impossible to hear a speaker's complete utterance. Each of these audio problems can create a challenge to holding a productive CMC meeting, as they distract participant attention and make concentration on the meeting topic difficult.

In addition to poor audio quality, video image is a communication challenge for videoconferencing. The video picture of participants' faces may not be large enough, refined enough, or updated by the technology quickly enough to accurately provide the subtle facial cues participants need for smooth turn taking. A lack of clarity in this nonverbal communication can make videoconferencing susceptible to pragmatic conversational difficulties such as determining a speaking order or identifying who is speaking, when someone is almost finished speaking, who is waiting to speak, or who would like to speak next. Frustration with these conversational pragmatics can lead participants to become less involved in the group discussion or to stop participating altogether, even though they remain physically connected through the medium. In addition to being large enough to be seen, all participants must be visible on the screen during the discussion. Even then, a spatial relationship among participants may be missing, eye contact may be difficult to achieve, and facial expressions can be hard to interpret.

If there are audio delay and visual–spatial relationship difficulties, groups sometimes find the nonverbal communication regulators—such as back-channel utterances ("uh huh," "yeah," "I see"); subtle facial expressions, and other nonverbal cues—difficult to interpret. The utterances may be spoken too softly to transmit through the medium, or, when they do transmit, they may become annoying or interrupt the communication interaction. The result is sometimes awkward turn taking and a lack of spontaneity in the conversation. Group discussion patterns may develop that are different from those occurring in face-to-face meetings. These differences occur in the frequency and duration of participant speaking turns, participant influence, and the power relationships within the group.

Videoconferencing groups sometimes engage in less elaborate discussions, participate in fewer conversational digressions, and experience a reduced amount of synergy in the group's planning activities. In general, videoconferencing groups experience a decrease in the amount of informal, social communication that occurs (Scott, 1999). Face-to-face group meetings allow participants to chat before the meeting begins; to exchange glances, comments, and nonverbal communication during the meeting; and to discuss other topics afterward. These multiple conversations facilitate a social richness in the group and produce a sense of personal involvement that is not easily achieved through either audio- or videoconferencing. Although this loss in the social–emotional content may have a task benefit, as fewer conversational digressions keep the meeting shorter and more focused, over time it can produce an interpersonal relationship cost (Sherblom, 1994).

When we meet face-to-face, we simultaneously perceive nonverbal cues and respond to them while we are speaking. We watch eyes, face, and body posture, listen for back-channel vocal utterances, and attend to nonverbal cues of agreement or disagreement. We may alter what we say and how we say it even as we are uttering words and before we complete a full sentence. Thus, we may end sentences with a different informational content, vocal inflection, affective mood, and meaning than we might originally have intended. In this sense, our small group communication is dynamically co-constructed because there is mutual influence on what we are saying and how we are saying it. In a communication medium other than face-to-face, feedback is not as readily available and is not as immediately influential on communication. Even in audio- and videoconferencing, because of transmission delays and the audio and video characteristics of the medium discussed earlier, we receive less immediate feedback, less diverse types of feedback, and less total feedback in the same amount of time. This reduction in the immediacy, variety, and amount of simultaneous communication and feedback leads to a reduction in how dynamically co-constructed our communication is and results in a loss of social presence.

Influences of the CMC Medium on Communication

Social Presence

Yamada (2009) followed Short, Williams, and Christie (1976) in defining social presence as the sense of immediacy, psychological proximity, intimacy, and familiarity in the communication. It represents the salience of the perceived presence of the other person and of the interpersonal relationship in the interaction. In Chapter 1, we described small group communication as a "transactional process of using symbolic behavior to achieve shared meaning among group members over a period of time." Some degree of dynamically shared feedback and co-constructed communication is necessary to achieve this sense of shared meaning among group members. Social presence is the perception among group members that the communication medium facilitates the development of their social–emotional–relational communication and shared meaning. This sense of social presence affects the amount and diversity of task and social communication that is facilitated by a medium and describes the participant's feeling that other human participants are really involved in the group communication (Short et al., 1976).

An associated concept is described by *media richness* theory, described below, which suggests that one particular medium may not provide as effective a conveyance of complex messages as another (Daft & Lengel, 1986; Walther & Parks, 2002). A rich communication medium through which participants can engage in multiple simultaneous communication with verbal and nonverbal cues, synchronous feedback, a variety of language and inflection, and a personal focus that conveys feelings and emotion along with the informational content produces a greater sense of social presence (Trevino, Daft, & Lengel, 1990). In a face-to-face (FTF) meeting, participants simultaneously exchange more types of information—emotional, attitudinal, relational, and contextual—along with the informational content. A text-based communication medium, however, provides less opportunity for the communication of these simultaneous cues, feedback, subtlety of inflection, and emotional–relational content. Text-based messaging systems, such as e-mail, bulletin board systems, and electronic chat, have a relatively narrow informational bandwidth compared to FTF communication and provide relatively low levels of media richness. This is because text-based CMC consists only of the written message through which both verbal and nonverbal contextual meanings must be communicated (Walther, 1996). It lacks the multiple simultaneous channels of FTF communication that simultaneously carry vocal (pitch, loudness, rhythm, inflection, pauses, and hesitations), facial (eye contact, gaze, apparent interest level, and facial responses), and physical body (attentiveness, posture, gestures, and relaxation) nonverbal cues. The absence of these simultaneous channels means that fewer nonverbal cues are expressed and less social information is communicated in each message. So deciphering the whole of the relational message takes more time (Walther, 1996).

Media Richness.   Perceptions of social presence vary with the communication medium, and communication scholars have arranged communication media along a rough continuum known as the media richness continuum (Daft & Lengel, 1986). Media that do not carry all types of information simultaneously are considered leaner media, since their informational capacities do not facilitate the development of the social–emotional–relational dimensions of communication at as fast a rate.

Face-to-face group meetings provide the greatest opportunity for experiencing rich communication and social presence. Videoconferencing, then audio-conferencing, and finally text-based computer conferencing systems are considered leaner communication media. Given time and continuous communication effort, however, even the text-only CMC groups can share rich personal, social, emotional, and relational information and get to know members as fully human participants, thus experiencing a large degree of social presence. In fact, this characteristic of slower relational development through a leaner medium may even be an asset to the growth of greater depths in personal intimacy, trust, co-orientation, and affection among group members (Walther, 1996).

Synchronous–Asynchronous Communication. Another contributor to the experience of social presence is the extent to which a CMC medium provides *synchronous communication* or *asynchronous communication* among participants. This distinction is a recognition that communication is a process engaged in by participants that involves simultaneous speaking, listening, and interactive feedback rather than a one-way conveying of information.

One can distinguish between the synchronous and asynchronous means of communication provided by each medium. For example, although videoconferencing is synchronous, playing back a videotape of an earlier conference session is an asynchronous form of communication. Audio-conferencing is synchronous, while voice mail is an asynchronous form of audio communication. Computer conferencing systems, instant messaging, and chat rooms provide essentially synchronous communication, while e-mail, list servers, blogs, bulletin boards, and newsgroups provide asynchronous communication.

Even in a "nearly synchronous," text-based CMC medium, such as instant messaging, we complete an utterance and can edit it before we push the enter key and receive a response to any part of that utterance. In a more asynchronous text-based CMC medium, such as blogs, e-mail, and bulletin board messages, we generally complete an entire message containing several utterances or sentences before we receive a response. So, although some forms of communication within each medium are termed synchronous and others are asynchronous, there is really a degree of synchronicity available through the communication in each medium. This varying degree of synchronicity influences a group's communication and experience of social presence.

However, human communication is not technologically determined. Although social presence may be facilitated or constrained by the characteristics of a medium, its richness, and communication synchronicity, it is not determined by them. Human communicators have the ability to enhance or erode feelings of social presence regardless of the medium they use to communicate. For example, if a face-to-face group meeting is poorly attended or poorly facilitated, or if group members are not attentively involved in the group communication, that face-to-face meeting may produce a feeling of little social presence among the group members. Social presence is, however, more easily facilitated and more commonly experienced in FTF group meetings, whereas an effort must be made to achieve it in CMC group meeting contexts.

One type of CMC group that focuses much of its time and attention on the social–emotional–relational dimension of communication is the online support group. Wright (2002) describes one motive for people to participate in an online support group as the ability to transcend geographic distance and time constraints. Participants find it more convenient and flexible to contact other support group members from their home or work computer than to attend a meeting with people at a set time and location. Campbell and Wright (2002) found that once involved in the online support group, however, the group's importance to its members lies in the emotional–relational communication dimensions of receptivity, immediacy, and informality. Participants indicated that a benefit to the online support group, compared to a face-to-face group, is the ability of the group to ignore turn-taking behaviors because of its text-messaging base and to receive numerous simultaneous responses to a question or an issue. Making decisions about a source's credibility and the value of the information received, however, is one of the bigger participant concerns.

Studies of text-based social support groups for people with disabilities consistently report effective use of verbal and nonverbal communication to show social support through the CMC medium, reducing the uncertainty about the situation, oneself, the other, and the relationship, and enhancing the perception of personal control over the situation (Albrecht & Adelman, 1987; Braithwaite, Waldron, & Finn, 1999). The most common form of social support offered in such a group is emotional, with 40% (590) of the 1,472 messages exchanged within the group containing emotional support expressions of empathy and reciprocated emotional expression (Braithwaite et al., 1999). These expressions include positive statements of relationship, affection, confidentiality, encouragement, prayer, sympathy, and understanding. The second most frequently offered form of support is conveyed in messages (33%, 461 messages) of instruction and advice, referrals to experts, situation appraisals, and suggestions for ways to make new life situations more predictable, and help people cope with challenges. The third is expressions of esteem (19%, 275 messages), including compliments, self-concept validations, and statements of positive feelings of importance, competence, and relief from blame. Other forms of support include networking (7%, 71 messages) in the expression of similar interests, situations, and concerns, and supportive offers of tangible assistance (2.7%, 41 messages) that involve performing a task or expressing a willingness to help out. Humor, poetry, nonverbal cues, and signature lines can be used to express support as well. Humor, although frequently sarcastic or ironic in nature, also includes "HAHAHA!" accents in the message. Nonverbal emoticons, such as those for "smile," "blush," "grin," "giggle," smiley faces, and sad faces also play a big role in the messages, as do written expressions for hugs, kisses, shoulder patting, and hand holding (7%, 103 messages). Poetry is used to provide a personal self-expression and emotional support for others in ways that promote self-awareness and self-esteem as well. Finally, signature lines are used to present personally selected axioms and quotations to convey support (Braithwaite et al., 1999). These findings clearly indicate that with a desire, and some communication effort, even a text-based CMC group is capable of providing the communication of social support that develops enduring relationships. A group can communicate in ways that are effective and that support the group's purpose

TABLE 15.2   Social Presence, Media Richness, and Synchronicity

Communication Medium	Communication Verbal and nonverbal	Social Presence Media richness	Synchronous Examples (same time; interactive)	Asynchronous Examples (not at the same time; respond later)
Face-to-Face	**Face-to-face:** Simultaneous verbal content, vocal tone and inflection, facial expression, hand gestures, body posture and angle	Rich medium: All nonverbal modalities available	Face-to-face small group meetings	Nominal group technique
Videoconferencing/ Video recording	**Visual:** Interactive verbal content; nonverbal: vocal tone and inflection, facial expression, hand gestures, posture, and bodily lean	Visual and vocal nonverbal cues available; may be obscured	Videoconferencing	Video recording: viewed later
Audio-Conferencing	**Audio:** Interactive verbal content, nonverbal vocal tone and inflection present	Only vocal nonverbal cues available	Telephone conferencing	Voice mail Voice messaging: listened to later
Text-Based Computer-Mediated Communication (CMC)	**Text-based:** Text, graphics: nonverbal emoticons used	Lean medium: Users create text-based nonverbal expressions	Instant messaging (IMs), text messaging, interactive computer chat	E-mail, blogs, bulletin boards

regardless of the technological medium employed—it just takes communicative effort.

Table 15.2 summarizes the distinctions made for social presence, media richness, and communication synchronicity available in each medium. Face-to-face offers the richest, most synchronous communication. Videoconferencing provides the next richest medium. Audio-conferencing and text-based computer conferencing offer the leanest and least synchronous medium for communication.

Other Influences of the Medium on Social Presence. Several other characteristics of the medium affect the experience of social presence as well. Typing a message is generally more laborious and time-consuming than speaking in conversation. Thus, when using a text-based CMC system, individuals often use abbreviations, shorten their verbal expression, or omit statements that might be assumed—such as utterances indicating attention, understanding, or agreement. Although these shortcuts speed up the transmission of the message, they can also lead to greater uncertainty among participants as to whether others have agreed with them, understood them, or even read what they had to say. Some synchronous text-based systems, such as instant messaging, allow participants to simultaneously type and send messages to each other, without the conversational turn taking present in FTF conversation. This means that participants can generate more messages faster. However, when participants are typing their own messages, they are likely to be less attentive to the messages posted by others. On the positive side, text-based messages are frequently more carefully composed and edited before they are sent than are spoken conversational comments. This can increase the clarity of the overall group discussion. Also, reticent participants are often less apprehensive and thus contribute more through text-based messaging systems, thereby increasing the overall group participation (Graetz et al., 1998). In addition, Bunz and Campbell (2004) found that participants accommodate and respond to the verbal politeness cues embedded in the body of e-mail messages. Messages structured with a greeting or salutation receive more polite responses than messages that lack these formal politeness cues.

Some Effects of CMC on Group Processes

The Interaction of CMC with Group Size, Diversity, and Proximity.   Group characteristics, such as size, diversity, and physical proximity of group members when they meet, interact with the communication technology to further influence a group's decision-making process. Large CMC groups appear to benefit the most from using CMC, as they generate more ideas per member than do smaller CMC groups (McGrath & Hollingshead, 1994). CMC also helps reduce the effort required to exchange information, thus facilitating an increase in the amount of group communication and providing a greater sense of group involvement. More diverse groups experience greater idea generation than homogeneous ones as they bring a greater breadth of knowledge and experience to the discussion. Physical proximity of group members interacts with the communication medium to influence the group's CMC (Valacich, George, Nunamaker, & Vogel, 1994). This suggests that it is not just the technology through which the communication is mediated, but the larger physical contextual cues that influence group communication. Members of groups located in the same room, even though they are using CMC as their only medium for communication, are still more conscious of their personal–social identities, experience greater social pressure, and have a greater tendency to conform to the group's expectations and norms than do members of more widely distributed groups.

Gender Swapping.   Past research has estimated that as many as 40% to 60% of Internet users "gender-swap" in their computer-mediated communication; that is, they identify and portray themselves as a person of the opposite sex in their electronic conversations in chat rooms, instant messages, and e-mail. Although Samp, Wittenberg, and Gillett (2003) found the percentage to be somewhat lower, with only 233 of

TABLE 15.3   The Ten Commandments of Computer Ethics

A set of Ten Commandments was created by the Computer Ethics Institute for distribution among and the guidance of computers users. The Ten Commandments provide a good reference for computer-mediated communication.

1. Thou Shalt Not use a computer to harm other people.
2. Thou Shalt Not interfere with other people's computer work.
3. Thou Shalt Not snoop around in other people's computer files.
4. Thou Shalt Not use a computer to steal.
5. Thou Shalt Not use a computer to bear false witness (or tell lies about someone).
6. Thou Shalt Not copy or use proprietary software for which you have not paid.
7. Thou Shalt Not use other people's computer resources without authorization or proper compensation.
8. Thou Shalt Not appropriate other people's intellectual output.
9. Thou Shalt think about the social consequences of the program or system you are creating or using.
10. Thou Shalt Always use a computer in ways that insure consideration and respect for your fellow humans.

Source: Created by the Computer Ethics Institute at the Brookings Institution, Washington, DC, and viewable online at www.brookings.edu/its/cei/overview/main.htm. The Ten Commandments of Computer Ethics were first presented in Dr. Ramon C. Barquin's paper "In Pursuit of a 'Ten Commandments' for Computer Ethics." To request the Ten Commandments of Computer Ethics in PDF format, e-mail your request with your name, e-mail address, and affiliation to cei@brookings.edu.

their 823 respondents (28%) admitting to having pretended to be a person of the opposite sex online, 370 (45%) of those 823 respondents said that they had suspected and questioned the sex of another online participant.

Computer Ethics.   Underlying successful CMC is our willingness to maintain a high level of ethics. Given the potential for reduced social presence, impersonal actions, and an inability to identify people, it is useful to have a set of ethical guidelines. Table 15.3 provides the Ten Commandments of *computer ethics.*

Choosing a Medium for the Effective Use of CMC

Media richness theory suggests that an important challenge for a group is to think about how to best utilize an understanding of CMC and its influence on group communication patterns and performance to enhance a group's decision-making, problem-solving, and communication processes. The first step is planning for the use of CMC by the group. There are several approaches to thinking about the appropriateness of a medium for small group communication. The first is to choose a medium based on the media richness and complexity of the *communication task.* The second is to think about the language characteristics of the information to be communicated. The third is to consider the *communication functions* to be accomplished.

TABLE 15.4   Choosing a Communication Medium

1. For simple, routine communication, choose a lean medium for efficiency.
2. More difficult and non-routine communication demands a richer communication medium.
3. Use rich media to develop social presence and personal relationships.
4. Use rich media for implementing new plans and strategies.
5. Do not let a lack of media richness restrict the information shared or censor discussion of critical issues.
6. Evaluate the potential use of a new communication technology within the spectrum of available media choices.

Source: Lengel & Daft (1988).

Choosing a Medium for the Communication Task

Effectively facilitating a group's decision-making, problem-solving, and communication processes involves choosing an appropriate medium for the communication task (Lengel & Daft, 1988). For efficient communication, choose a lean medium. More difficult and non-routine communication that requires more discussion among group members to achieve a shared meaning demands a richer medium. The development of new plans and strategies also requires a rich medium for a shared group understanding. Use a rich medium to develop social presence and personal relationships, and do not let a lack of richness in the communication medium restrict the information shared or implicitly censor the discussion of critical issues. Though communicating through a richer medium may require more time and effort, it is better to endure this loss in efficiency than to inadvertently curtail the group's process by choosing a medium that is too lean to effectively accomplish the communication task. Think about the communication purpose and evaluate the potential use of a new communication technology within the spectrum of available media choices. Table 15.4 lists these recommendations for media selection (Lengel & Daft, 1988).

Finding a Language Demand–Technology Fit

If communication media differ in the type and amount of information they carry, then these differences have implications for a group's decision-making and communication processes. A group needs to be aware of the fit between the communication demands of their task and the communication medium they plan to use to meet those demands (Bavelas, Hutchinson, Kenwood, & Matheson, 1997; Farmer & Hyatt, 1994; MacDougall, 1999). Three types of language demands are important to consider in the communication in a group: numeric, verbal, and visual symbolizations (Farmer & Hyatt, 1994). Numeric symbolization depicts the mathematically based aspect of language that requires conveying exact quantities, such as found in numbers and the precise meanings found in mathematical formulas. For business groups, these are represented in the numbers used in budgets, the percentages used to calculate sales commissions or profit sharing, and the formulas used to calculate pay increases or health benefits. Verbal symbolization describes the broad array of concepts, ideas, and meanings present in everyday verbal and nonverbal language that provides the rich, multilayered, and varied interpretation of words. Visual symbolization represents the spatial and geometric information in a picture, chart, graph, or diagram and may show two- or three-dimensional representations of a spatial relationship or of a sequence that occurs through time.

Not every CMC medium carries each of these types of information equally well. Text-based computer conferencing systems, for example, carry numeric information with the precision of written language but have greater difficulty conveying the nuances that distinguish among the multiple meanings of language in the expression of a word or phrase. This can lead to misunderstandings in the interpretation of a message. Without the associated vocal inflection, determining whether a person is being open and honest, critical, sarcastic, or humorous, or even whether he or she is asking a question or making an assertion, can be difficult. The audio channel provided by the telephone and computer audio-conferencing systems carries the verbal and vocal information well but has greater difficulty expressing the precision of complex numeric equations and the spatial relationships present in visual symbolization. Videoconferencing systems that are equipped with document-sharing capabilities can more closely approximate face-to-face (FTF) communication in their ability to fulfill all three types of language demands. To perform effectively, a group must be concerned with the fit between the symbolization system required for its communication task and the communication medium through which it attempts to accomplish that task (Farmer & Hyatt, 1994).

Matching Media Richness to the Communication Function

Considering the communication function can also help a group choose an appropriate medium. Group communication functions can be divided into eight types:

1. Planning functions, such as the development of group agendas, goals, and objectives
2. Functions requiring creativity and the generation of ideas
3. Intellectual functions, such as problem solving
4. Decision-making functions
5. Cognitive-conflict functions, such as resolving conflicting points of view
6. Mixed-motive functions that require group conflict resolution
7. Competitive functions that involve issues of power and status
8. Performance functions when a group implements the project

These types of functions have been shown to differ in their demands on the richness of a communication medium (McGrath & Hollingshead, 1994).

Planning and creativity functions require the least amount of media richness and can effectively be accomplished using text-based computer conferencing systems. Text-based computer conferencing systems may even work better for these functions than face-to-face meetings, as text-based computer conferencing systems have a tendency to reduce participant inhibitions, increase more equal participation, and facilitate group generation of a greater number of ideas. Text-based CMC groups also perform better than FTF groups on idea-generation functions, but FTF groups perform better than CMC groups on intellectual ones. Intellectual problem-solving and decision-making functions require more communication richness and are not generally well accomplished using text-based computer conferencing systems but may be undertaken effectively using audio- or videoconferencing systems. CMC groups perform better than FTF groups on decision-making functions, but FTF groups can perform better on negotiation functions. Mixed-motive conflict-management functions that require negotiation, coordination, and collaboration are also best accomplished through face-to-face communication (McGrath & Hollingshead, 1994). CMC groups take longer to complete problem-solving functions but generate more solutions. CMC groups are also better suited to achieving quality decisions (Turoff & Hiltz, 1982). When used alone, however, CMC is not always a good medium for maintaining group member relationships.

Adopting Effective Group Communication Strategies for CMC

Once a communication medium has been chosen, a group needs to adopt effective strategies for communicating through that medium (Broome & Chen, 1992). The group must first move beyond its habitual group problem-solving techniques to explore and develop methods of communication that will be effective in the medium it is going to use. This may require reframing its problems in new ways or rethinking its group discussion patterns. A group might need to focus its attention on developing shared group meanings, sequentially building on ideas, and promoting double-loop learning within the group to clarify and integrate the group's evolving meaning in a way that is less inhibited by the medium. Group members may need to focus explicitly on the patterns that develop in their shared ideas and the relationships among those ideas, to reduce informational loss induced by the medium. A group may also need to consider balancing their use of technology with the needs of group members and avoid a technological trance of having their decisions driven by the technology instead of the larger context of the group's human relationships. They need to emphasize the group's potential for broadening individual perspectives and promoting the collective ownership of ideas. Finally, they need to integrate their use of CMC within the larger context of the group's planning, decision-making, problem-solving, and communication processes (Broome & Chen, 1992).

Facilitating Effective CMC Group Communication

In addition to these strategies, groups using CMC are most effective when members collaboratively pay attention to and take responsibility for the group's process facilitation. Effective facilitation in CMC groups requires members to competently engage in at least 13 group facilitation roles and 3 additional technology-specific facilitation roles (Clawson, Bostrom, & Anson, 1993). Table 15.5 lists these roles for effective computer-mediated group meeting facilitation.

TABLE 15.5   Effective Computer-Mediated Group Meeting Facilitation

As in face-to-face groups, an effective computer-mediated group meeting facilitator should:

1. Encourage group responsibility and promote member ownership of group process and results
2. Demonstrate a comfortable level of self-awareness and self-expression
3. Listen to, clarify, and integrate information and ideas
4. Ask appropriate, well-timed questions to encourage thought and participation
5. Help keep group focused on and moving toward its goals
6. Create and continually reinforce an open, positive, participatory environment
7. Actively build rapport and relationship
8. Present clear, concise information and well-developed ideas
9. Demonstrate flexibility and willingness to adapt to situation and other group member needs
10. Help achieve a clear meeting process and outcome
11. Constructively manage conflict and expression of negative emotions
12. Encourage and support the expression of multiple and diverse perspectives
13. Manage and adhere to meeting time limits and discussion ground rules

In addition to taking on these face-to-face group roles, computer-mediated group members must also:

14. Have a conceptual understanding of the technology and its capabilities
15. Have an ability to effectively communicate through that technology
16. Be able to create a comfortable understanding and use of the technology among all group members

For more information, see Clawson, Bostrom, & Anson (1993).

Leading a CMC Group Meeting

CMC group meetings also require a strong discussion leader who can prepare a formal presentation and then be willing to lead a relaxed, informal group discussion. This combination of preparation and participation is important to both effective group task and process facilitation. A group leader should prepare participants for a structured, interactive meeting and organize that meeting with an agenda, handouts, and other materials distributed to all participants before the meeting begins. During the meeting, however, the leader should work to reduce the formality of the gathering by using an informal communication style and by encouraging members to participate in the leadership functions. An effective leader must also be aware of participants' nonverbal communication throughout the meeting. Some participants may be nervous and others may be intimidated by the use of technology. These members may need explicit encouragement to participate. A calm, even-tempered, relaxed leadership style becomes particularly critical when the matters under discussion are important to the group and participants become excited. Adequate preparation and a relaxed communication style are important to effective CMC meetings (Sherblom, 1997). Table 15.6 provides a list of these leadership functions.

TABLE 15.6   CMC Meeting Leadership Functions

1. Prior to the meeting:
   a. Schedule the meeting.
   b. Confirm the date and time with all participants.
   c. Schedule the meeting for a maximum of two hours.
   d. Plan an agenda to keep participants focused on the meeting's objectives.
   e. Send the agenda and any resource materials to participants 48 to 72 hours before the meeting.

2. Start the meeting on time and end on time.

3. At the beginning of the meeting:
   a. Identify the purpose of the meeting.
   b. Identify the person who will chair the meeting and facilitate the discussion.
   c. Identify and individually welcome each participant.
   d. Initially take control with a strong, clear leadership role; then relinquish control and encourage participant interaction as the meeting progresses.
   e. Ask participants to identify themselves when they speak the first time to help facilitate participant interaction.

4. After the meeting, prepare and distribute minutes.

Source: O'Rourke (1993).

Summary

Groups increasingly use computer-mediated communication (CMC) in their decision-making, problem-solving, and group discussion processes. Groups can manage the effects of CMC through their choice of a communication medium and through the adoption of effective group communication and leadership skills. The communication medium used should fit the communication task, the language demands of that task, and the communication functions in which the group intends to participate. Effective group communication strategies include paying attention to group problem-solving techniques and discussion patterns, exploring new ways of sharing ideas and building relationships within the group, and balancing the use of the technology with other group member needs. Effective group facilitation promotes a participatory environment for active relational rapport building, a comfortable level of self-expression balanced with active listening, and a constructive management of conflict. CMC requires both a strong discussion leader and group members who will actively take responsibility for the multiple shared leadership functions of maintaining a group focus, a balanced participation, and an even-tempered communication process. With these communication abilities, a small group can successfully engage in computer-mediated communication, accomplishing the groups' tasks while maintaining relationships.

DISCUSSION QUESTIONS

1. What is social presence? What are its important characteristics, and how can a group effectively increase feelings of social presence in its CMC?

2. What are the three types of language demands? Describe each of them and the technology that provides a best fit for communication to meet that demand.

3. What are the characteristics of computer-mediated communication (CMC)?

4. How does CMC differ from FTF communication?

5. Identify the eight communication functions and the media richness characteristics of CMC systems that are best suited to fulfill each function.

6. What are the effects of CMC on groupthink?

7. How do anonymity, group size, and proximity influence participation and communication in CMC groups?

REFERENCES

Albrecht, T. L., & Adelman, M. B. (1987). *Communicating social support*. Newbury Park, CA: Sage.

Bavelas, J. B., Hutchinson, S., Kenwood, C., & Matheson, D. H. (1997). Using face-to-face dialogue as a standard for other communication systems. *Canadian Journal of Communication, 22*, 5–24.

Bordia, P. (1997). Face-to-face versus computer-mediated communication: A synthesis of the experimental literature. *Journal of Business Communication, 34*(1), 99–120.

Braithwaite, D. O., Waldron, V. R., & Finn, J. (1999). Communication of social support in computer-mediated groups for people with disabilities. *Health Communication, 11*(2), 123–151.

Broome, B. J., & Chen, M. (1992). Guidelines for computer-assisted group problem solving: Meeting the challenges of complex issues. *Small Group Research, 23*(2), 216–236.

Bunz, U., & Campbell, S. W. (2004). Politeness accommodation in electronic mail. *Communication Research Reports, 21*(1), 11–25.

Cai, X. (2004). Is the computer a functional alternative to traditional media? *Communication Research Reports, 21*(1), 26–38.

Campbell, K., & Wright, K. B. (2002). On-line support groups: An investigation of relationships among source credibility, dimensions of relational communication, and perceptions of emotional support. *Communication Research Reports, 19*, 183–193.

Clawson, V. K., Bostrom, R. P., & Anson, R. (1993). The role of the facilitator in computer-supported meetings. *Small Group Research, 24*(4), 547–565.

Conrad, C. & Poole, M. S. (2002). Strategic organizational communication in a global economy (5th ed.). Boston: Thompson Wordsworth.

Cummings, T. G., & Worley, C. G. (2005). *Organizational development and change* (8th ed.). Bonston: Thompson South-Western.

Daft, R., & Lengel, R. (1986). Organizational information requirements, media richness, and structural design. *Management Science, 32*, 554–571.

Ellison, N. B., Steinfield, C., & Lampe, C. (2007). The benefits of Facebook "friends": Social capital and college students' use of online social network sites. *Journal of Computer-Mediated Communication, 12*, 1143–1168.

Farmer, S. M., & Hyatt, C. W. (1994). Effects of task language demands and task complexity on computer-mediated work groups. *Small Group Research, 25*(3), 331–366.

Friedman, T. L. (2005). *The world is flat: A brief history of the twenty-first century*. New York: Farrar, Straus, and Giroux.

Gaimster, J. (2007). Reflections on interactions in virtual worlds and their implication for learning art and design. *Art, Design & Communication in Higher Education, 6*(3) 187–199.

Graetz, K. A., Boyle, E. S., Kimble, C. E., Thompson, P., & Garloch, J. L. (1998). Information sharing in face-to-face, teleconferencing, and electronic chat groups. *Small Group Research, 29*(6), 714–743.

Hacker, K. L., & Steiner, R. (2001). Hurdles of access and benefits of usage for Internet communication. *Communication Research Reports, 18*, 399–407.

Hyatt, J. (2006, June 12). The SOUL of a new team. *Fortune*, pp. 134–141.

Lashinsky, A. (2006, June 12). Razr's edge. *Fortune*, pp. 124–132.

Lengel, R. H., & Daft, R. L. (1988). The selection of communication media as an executive skill. *Executive, 2*(3), 225–232.

MacDougall, R. C. (1999). Subject fields, oral emulation and the spontaneous cultural positioning of Mohawk e-mail users. *World Communication, 28*(4), 5–25.

Mazer, J. P., Murphy, R. E., & Simonds, C. J. (2007). I'll see you on "Facebook": The effects of computer-mediated teacher self-disclosure on student motivation, affective learning, and classroom climate. *Communication Education, 56*, 1–17.

McGrath, J. E., & Hollingshead, A. B. (1994). *Groups interacting with technology*. Thousand Oaks, CA: Sage.

Metzger, M. J., & Flanagan, A. J. (2002). Audience orientations toward new media. *Communication Research Reports, 19*, 338–351.

Olaniran, B. A. (1994). Group performance in computer-mediated and face-to-face communication media. *Management Communication Quarterly, 7*(3), 256–281.

O'Rourke, J. S. (1993). *Video teleconferencing*. A paper presented to the 58th annual convention of the association for business communication, Montreal, Quebec, Canada.

Rains, S. (2005). Leveling the playing field virtually. *Communications Research, 33*, 193–234.

Rogers, R. A. (1999). "Is this a great time or what?" Information technology and the erasure of difference. *World Communication, 28*(4), 69–86.

Samp, J. A., Wittenberg, E. M., & Gillett, D. L. (2003). Presenting and monitoring a gender-defined self on the Internet. *Communication Research Reports, 20*, 1–12.

Schrire, S. (2004). Interaction and cognition in asynchronous computer conferencing. *Instructional Science, 32*, 475–502.

Schrire, S. (2006). Knowledge building in asynchronous discussion groups: Going beyond quantitative analysis. *Computers & Education, 46*(1), 4970.

Scott, C. R. (1999). Communication technology and group communication. In L. R. Frey, D. S. Gouran, & M. S. Poole (Eds.), *The handbook of group communication theory & research* (pp. 432–472). Thousand Oaks, CA: Sage.

Shedletsky, L., & Aitken, J. E. (2004). *Human communication on the Internet*. Boston: Allyn & Bacon.

Sherblom, J. C. (1994). Teleconferencing. In A. Williams (Ed.), *Communication and technology: Today and tomorrow* (pp. 155–171). Denton, TX: Association for Business Communication.

Sherblom, J. C. (1997). Teleconferencing. In D. C. Reep (Ed.), *Technical writing: Principles, strategies, and readings* (3rd ed., pp. 556–561). Boston: Allyn & Bacon.

Sherblom, J. C., Withers, L. A., & Leonard, L. G. (2009). Communication challenges and opportunities for educators using Second Life. In J. Kingsley & C. Wankel (Eds.), *Higher education in virtual worlds: Teaching and learning in Second Life*. Bingley, UK: Emerald.

Short, J., Williams, E., & Christie, B. (1976). *The social psychology of telecommunications*. London: John Wiley.

Trevino, L. K., Daft, R. L., & Lengel, R. H. (1990). Understanding manager's [*sic*] media choices: A symbolic interactionist perspective. In J. Fulk & C. Steinfield (Eds.), *Organizations and communication technology* (pp. 71–94), Newbury Park, CA: Sage.

Turoff, M., & Hiltz, S. R. (1982). Computer support: Group versus individual decisions. *IEEE Transactions Communications, 30*(1), 82–90.

Valacich, J. S., Dennis, A. R., & Nunamaker, J. F. (1992). Group size and anonymity effects on computer-mediated idea generation. *Small Group Research, 23*(1), 49–73.

Vess, D. (2005). Asynchronous discussion and communication patterns in online and hybrid history courses. *Communication Education, 54*(4), 355–364.

Walther, J. B. (1996). Computer-mediated communication: Impersonal, interpersonal, and hyperpersonal interaction. *Communication Research, 23*(1), 3–43.

Walther, J. B. & Parks, M. R. (2002). Cues filtered out, cues filtered in: Computer-mediated communication and relationships. In M. L. Knapp & J. A. Daly (Eds.), *Handbook of interpersonal communication* (3rd ed.). Thousand Oaks, CA: Sage.

Warren, R., & Bluma, A. (2002). Parental mediation of children's Internet use: The influence of established media. *Communication Research Reports, 19*, 8–17.

Wood, A. F., Fassett, D. L. (2003). Remote control: Identity, power, and technology in the communication classroom. *Communication Education, 52*(3–4), 286–296.

Wright, K. (2002). Motives for communication within online support groups and antecedents for interpersonal use. *Communication Research Reports, 19*, 89–98.

Yamada, M. (2009). The role of social presence in learner-centered communicative language learning using synchronous computer-mediated communication: Experimental study. *Computers & Education, 52*(4), 820–833.

Photo Credits

Chapter 2   *p. 29* Photo courtesy of Corbis RF

Chapter 3   *p. 49* Photo courtesy of Corbis RF

Chapter 4   *p. 67* Photo courtesy of Stefan Mokrzecki/Photolibrary.com

Chapter 5   *p. 81* Photo courtesy of Mercedes-Benz U.S. International

Chapter 6   *p. 91* Photo courtesy of The Doneger Group

Chapter 7   *p. 118* Photo courtesy of www.comstock.com

Chapter 10   *p. 163* Photo courtesy of Edward G. Leonard
             p. 173 Photo courtesy of The University of Alabama

Chapter 11   *p. 197* Photo courtesy of Maya Design, Inc.

Chapter 12   *p. 209* Photo courtesy of Nucor Steel Tuscaloosa, Inc.

Chapter 13   *p. 231* Photo courtesy of William_Lovelace/Getty Images Inc. - Hulton
             Archive Photos

Chapter 15   *p. 263* Photo courtesy of John Sherblom

Photo Credits

Index